D0083636

*Jeanne Adleman, MA*
*Gloria M. Enguídanos, PhD*
*Editors*

# Racism in the Lives of Women: Testimony, Theory, and Guides to Antiracist Practice

*Pre-publication*
*REVIEWS,*
*COMMENTARIES,*
*EVALUATIONS . . .*

"**T**hese women write with passion and intelligence, and engage our hearts, challenge our assumptions, and move us to a deeper and more complex understanding of the personal, structural, cultural, and historic forces that shape the lives of women. This rich volume is an indispensable addition to the literature that seeks to explore, understand, and embrace the complexity of women's lives."

**Sandra Butler**
Author of *Conspiracy of Silence: The Trauma of Incest* and *Cancer in Two Voices*

*More pre-publication*
*REVIEWS, COMMENTARIES, EVALUATIONS . . .*

"*Racism in the Lives of Women* is honest and complex. Each chapter is a gift to be discovered. Jean Adleman and Gloria Enguídanos have truly fulfilled a vision; they have provided us with a bridge between where feminist work on racism has been and where it can go.

The chorus of contributors may share some similar ideals, yet the individual voices uniquely contrast each other. Together they achieve an inspiring example of how to weave the personal, political, and scholarly. Clearly, each contributor's piece showcases years of personal introspection, dialogue, reading, critical thinking, and synthesis. As a reader I can only begin to imagine the tears, the courage, and the persistence which made the volume a reality.

There is no comparable work."

**Maria P. P. Root, PhD**
Private Practice,
Seattle, Washington;
Clinical Associate Professor
of Psychology,
University of Washington

"In *Racism in the Lives of Women,* Adleman and Enguídanos bring us a varied and stimulating collection of writings about the not-so-easy topic of racism, as well as sexism and anti-Semitism. The collection is as diverse as the authors themselves and has something for everyone who is connected with helping women and men be whole persons. It is as if the editors created multiple conversations among the authors and invited us, the readers, to listen.

Taken as a whole, the book challenges us all to integrate an understanding of racism, and its debilitating forces, into our work. This book is a must read for us all."

**Anne L. Ganley, PhD**
Domestic Violence Program,
Family Therapy Unit,
Seattle Veterans Administration
Medical Center

*More pre-publication*
*REVIEWS, COMMENTARIES, EVALUATIONS . . .*

"**W**hat a wonderful gift Adleman and Enguídanos have given to therapists, theoreticians, and activists! We finally have a comprehensive handbook with concise and challenging analysis, first-voice oral histories, and concrete practice strategies that addresses the complex interaction between race/ethnicity and feminism in psychotherapy.

*Racism in the Lives of Women* stands out because it includes pieces by and for therapists and academicians who are women of color, and whose issues are different but equally important in addressing racism in feminist practice. For any practitioners or theoreticians who want to expand their understanding about working with diverse populations, this text is a must have.

**Valli Kanuha, MSW**
Therapist and Activist,
New York City

"**R**acism in the Lives of Women is an important and vital compilation of psychology on the cross-cultural oppression of women. The women in this volume provide critical and personal examinations of the racism embedded in health care and other structures of power, and in feminism. They challenge us to become not only 'culturally sensitive' but also 'culturally competent.'

This is just the book we in the antiracism movement need–a compelling tool for validation and empowerment."

**Gloria E. Anzaldúa**
Chicana Writer and Cultural Theorist;
Author of *Borderlands (La Frontera)*

The Harrington Park Press
An Imprint of The Haworth Press, Inc.
New York • London

## NOTES FOR PROFESSIONAL LIBRARIANS
## AND LIBRARY USERS

This is an original book title published by Harrington Park Press, an imprint of The Haworth Press, Inc. Unless otherwise noted in specific chapters with attribution, materials in this book have not been previously published elsewhere in any format or language.

## CONSERVATION AND PRESERVATION NOTES

All books published by The Haworth Press, Inc. and its imprints are printed on certified ph neutral, acid free book grade paper. This paper meets the minimum requirements of American National Standard for Information Sciences–Permanence of Paper for Printed Material, ANSI Z39.48-1984.

# Racism in the Lives of Women
## of Women
### *Testimony, Theory, and Guides to Antiracist Practice*

# *HAWORTH* Innovations in Feminist Studies
## Ellen Cole, PhD and Esther Rothblum, PhD
### Senior Co-Editors

New, Recent, and Forthcoming Titles:

*When Husbands Come Out of the Closet* by Jean Schaar Gochros

*Prisoners of Ritual: An Odyssey into Female Genital Circumcision in Africa* by Hanny Lightfoot-Klein

*Foundations for a Feminist Restructuring of the Academic Disciplines* edited by Michele Paludi and Gertrude A. Steuernagel

*Hippocrates' Handmaidens: Women Married to Physicians* by Esther Nitzberg

*Waiting: A Diary of Loss and Hope in Pregnancy* by Ellen Judith Reich

*God's Country: A Case Against Theocracy* by Sandy Rapp

*Women and Aging: Celebrating Ourselves* by Ruth Raymond Thone

*Women's Conflicts About Eating and Sexuality: The Relationship Between Food and Sex* by Rosalyn M. Meadow and Lillie Weiss

*A Woman's Odyssey into Africa: Tracks Across a Life* by Hanny Lightfoot-Klein

*Anorexia Nervosa and Recovery: A Hunger for Meaning* by Karen Way

*Women Murdered by the Men They Loved* by Constance A. Bean

*Reproductive Hazards in the Workplace: Mending Jobs, Managing Pregnancies* by Regina Kenen

*Our Choices: Women's Personal Decisions About Abortion* by Sumi Hoshiko

*Tending Inner Gardens: The Healing Art of Psychotherapy* by Leslie Irene Shore

*Racism in the Lives of Women: Testimony, Theory, and Guides to Antiracist Practice* edited by Jeanne Adleman and Gloria M. Enguídanos

# Racism in the Lives
# of Women
## *Testimony, Theory, and Guides*
## *to Antiracist Practice*

Jeanne Adleman, MA
Gloria M. Enguídanos, PhD
Editors

Harrington Park Press
An Imprint of The Haworth Press, Inc.
New York • London

Published by

Harrington Park Press, an imprint of The Haworth Press, Inc., 10 Alice Street, Binghamton, NY 13904-1580

**Library of Congress Cataloging-in-Publication Data**

Racism in the lives of women : testimony, theory, and guides to antiracist practice / Jeanne Adleman, Gloria M. Enguídanos, editors.
    p.   cm.
    Includes bibliographical references and index.
    ISBN 1-56023-863-1 (pbk.).
    1. Minority women–United States–Social conditions. 2. Racism–United States. I. Adleman, Jeanne. II. Enguídanos, Gloria M.
HQ1421.R33   1944
305.8–dc20
                                      94-20592
                                          CIP

# CONTENTS

# EDITORS

**GLORIA M. ENGUÍDANOS** (1933), born and raised in Puerto Rico, completed her BA at Indiana University and her MA at Ball State, after raising her four children. In 1981 she moved to California with a Minority Fellowship from the American Psychological Association, and earned a doctorate in Psychology at The Wright Institute (Berkeley) where she and Jeanne had first met as classmates. A licensed psychologist presently on the faculty of California State University at Hayward, she coordinates student psychological assessments and referrals, and as head of the Safety Response Team on campus also coordinates responses to psychological emergencies. She particularly enjoys teaching courses in Ethnic Studies and Women's Studies. Gloria is an artist/potter and a grandmother, and considers these important aspects of herself. She and her husband, Bill Clark, are looking forward to living on the five acres of semi-rural land they are purchasing with a view to environmental preservation.

**JEANNE ADLEMAN** (1919) lived through the Depression and World War II years in and around New York City. She went to work young, attended college at night for awhile, finally completed a BA in Education in 1960, and two years later was asked to return to Brooklyn College to teach. By 1969 she had earned an MA in Teacher Education at Columbia University Teachers College, and subsequently taught and supervised teacher training at four different colleges. Jeanne moved to San Francisco in 1972. At age 62 she was accepted into a doctoral program in psychology but withdrew after two years because of rising costs and philosophical differences. A lifelong student of how people learn, grow, develop and change, Jeanne presently maintains a consulting practice in San Francisco where she is also a member of the advisory board of Gay and Lesbian Outreach to Elders. From 1983-90 she served on the Steering Committee of The Feminist Therapy Institute, 1988-90 as Chairperson.

# AUTHORS

LOURDES ARGÜELLES (1943), PhD, is Associate Professor of Gender and Feminist Studies and Chicano/Latino Studies, holding the MacArthur Chair in Women Studies at Pitzer College, Claremont, California. She is a licensed psychotherapist who has published widely in the areas of migration, sexuality and HIV infection. Her book, *A Critical Sociology of Gay and Lesbian Experience*, is due to be published by Routledge in 1994.

MARIA BRAVEHEART-JORDAN (1953), MSSW, LCSW, is a Hunkpapa Lakota/Nez Perce/Choctaw Indian. Maria received her MSSW at Columbia U. School of Social Work in 1976 and is a PhD candidate in clinical social work at Smith College. She is an Assistant Professor at U. Denver Graduate School of Social Work and a Francis Allen Fellow at the Newberry Library. Maria has worked as a mental health therapist on the Standing Rock Sioux Reservation.

LAURA S. BROWN (1952), PhD, practices feminist therapy and forensic psychology in Seattle, Washington. She has written extensively on topics of feminist therapy theory, ethics, and practice, and trains on feminist therapy topics in North America and Europe.

CHRISTINE M. CHAO (1950), PhD, is a clinical psychologist (University of Denver, 1981), currently in part-time private practice because of childrearing responsibilities. A former clinical director of the Asian Pacific Center for Human Development in Denver, she has conducted numerous workshops on Asian mental health and cultural diversity. She is particularly interested in a synthesis of culturally informed psychotherapy and Jungian thought.

DR. CAROLE P. CHRISTENSEN (1939) is a professor at U. British Columbia's School of Social Work and its former director. She has also taught at McGill U. School of Social Work in Montreal, and at the Danish School of Social Work, Copenhagen, specializing in family therapy and human sexuality. Her longstanding interests and current professional activities are in the areas of crosscultural practice, education, model-building and research.

LEMYRA DEBRUYN (1949) is of French Canadian ancestry. She is Chief of the Special Initiatives Team, Indian Health Services; Clinical Adjunct Faculty, U. New Mexico; a founding member of the Takini Network: Lakota and Dakota Survivors Association; a member of the White Buffalo Calf Woman Society; and a founding board member of the Milwaukee Center for Cultural Dance and Awareness. Lemyra holds a doctorate in Medical Anthropology from U. C. Berkeley.

OLIVA M. ESPÍN (1938), born in Cuba, has taught and trained therapists at McGill, Tufts and Boston Universities and is now Professor at the Department of Women's Studies, San Diego State U., and Core Faculty, California School of Professional Psychology, San Diego. Dr. Espín received APA's 1991 Award for Distinguished Professional Contribution to Public Service. She recently co-edited *Refugee Women and Their Mental Health: Shattered societies, shattered lives.*

JAN FAULKNER (1934), LCSW, Assistant Clinical Professor in Psychiatry, U. California, San Francisco, is a Mediation Counselor in the Alameda County Family Court Services, has a private practice in Berkeley, conducts seminars on antiracism and groups for people in interracial relationships. She is the first Z. Lois Bryant Fellow at the U. of Missouri. Faulkner is the owner of the internationally recognized racial stereotype collection, "Ethnic Notions."

YVETTE G. FLORES-ORTIZ (1952), PhD, is assistant professor in Chicana/Chicano Studies at U. California, Davis. She is also a practicing clinical psychologist specializing in family therapy, substance abuse, and family abuse. She has trained and lectured nationally and internationally in the areas of crosscultural psychotherapy, feminist psychology, and treatment of family violence. Biological mother of two and stepmother of two, she is married.

NIKKI GERRARD was born in 1947 in Minnesota, and has her PhD in Community Psychology from the Ontario Institute for Studies in Education, U. Toronto. She brings a community development approach to mental health service delivery. Nikki emigrated to Canada in 1974 to follow her passion of banding bald eagles; her husband shares this avocation. They have two children.

BEVERLY GREENE, PhD, is Associate Clinical Professor of Psychology, St. John's University, and is in private practice in New York City. An APA Fellow, Dr. Greene is author and coeditor of numerous professional publications. She received the 1991 Women of Color Psychologies Publication Award from the Association for Women in Psychology, and the 1992 Award for Distinguished Contributions to Ethnic Minority Issues from APA's Division 44.

TRINA GRILLO (1948) an Associate Professor of Law at the University of San Francisco School of Law, teaches Torts and Mediation. Her Yale Law Journal article, "Mandatory Mediation: Process Dangers for Women," has sparked discussion in the mediation community. She is the mother of two teenagers.

An African-American lesbian anthropologist, originally from Buffalo, N.Y., PATRICIA GUTHRIE (1946) PhD, directs the Women's Studies Program at California State University, Hayward. She is currently completing a book called *Angel of the Poor: The Mother Mary Ann Wright Story.*

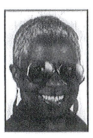

VIRGINIA R. HARRIS (1937) is an African American who works with individuals and groups in transition. She has been a chemist, a human resources manager, and is now an organizational dynamics consultant, facilitator, writer and quilter.

CLARE HOLZMAN (1942) is white, Jewish, middle-class and heterosexual. She is a psychologist in private practice in New York City, specializing in psychotherapy with survivors of sexual assault. She was a member of New York Women Against Rape for seven years, serving as a rape crisis counselor, trainer, and counseling coordinator.

HELEN L. JACKSON (1941), PhD, is clinical assistant professor of psychiatry at U. New Mexico, and is in private practice in Albuquerque. She has chaired the Women of Color Psychologies Award Committee for the Association for Women in Psychology, is an examiner for the New Mexico Board of Psychologist Examiners, and is a psychological consultant to the Albuquerque Public Schools and Children's Medical Services.

NAYYAR S. JAVED (1938) is a feminist therapist in Saskatoon, Canada, born and raised in Pakistan. After receiving an MEd in the USA she taught at the U. of Peshawar (Pakistan) before moving to Canada where she earned a second Masters, in Educational Psychology. Besides her clinical work, Nayyar is an antiracist and feminist activist, organizing racialized immigrant women in Saskatchewan. She is married and has a young adult son.

ELLEN KASCHAK, PhD, has been a feminist academic and activist, therapist and theoretician for some twenty years. She is Professor of Psychology at San Jose State University, where she is Chairperson of the graduate program in Marriage, Family and Child Counseling. She has written and lectured extensively on various topics concerning women, gender and ethnicity, and is the author of *Engendered Lives, a New Psychology of Women's Experience.*

JUDY Y. KAWAMOTO (1943), MSW Simmons College (Boston), Licensed Clinical Social Worker, is a Board Certified Diplomate, a therapist at Counseling and Psychological Services, University of California at Berkeley, and on the faculty of New College of California, Department of Psychology. She is also in private practice in Berkeley.

DORIAN LESLIE (1964) grew up in South Carolina where polite racism and good food were integral to life. Writing and reading anything in print are favorite activities. And, being a black lesbian living in Palo Alto, California, she is in therapy.

LAUREN MACNEILL was born in Cambridge, Massachusetts, in 1963. She is a white lesbian of Irish, Italian and Scottish descent. Her work pursuits include legal and social advocacy on behalf of children and families. When she is not pondering issues of identity, she plays interspeciesly with Maya, the cat.

DONNA K. NAGATA was born in 1953 in Los Angeles, California. She received her bachelor's degree from the University of California, Berkeley, and went on to obtain a PhD in clinical psychology from the University of Illinois, Urbana-Champaign. Currently, she is an associate professor with the Department of Psychology at the University of Michigan, Ann Arbor.

GAIL PHETERSON (1948), born and educated in the United States, moved to the Netherlands in 1975 to help establish a network of Dutch feminist therapists. She was associate professor of psychology and women's studies, U. Utrecht and later became co-director of the International Committee for Prostitutes' Rights. Gail has been a visiting scholar at universities in Europe and North America. She now lives in Paris.

ANNE RIVERO (1943), MSW (UCLA) is a licensed clinical social worker with the Department of Psychiatry at Kaiser Permanente, Montclair, California. She has worked extensively with Latino immigrants and refugees through various community mental health and AIDS prevention programs in California. She has published in the area of Latinas and AIDS.

Born in 1924 in Berlin, Germany, of Lithuanian Jewish parents, RACHEL JOSEFOWITZ SIEGEL, MSW, has spent most of her adult life in Ithaca, New York. She is a feminist psychotherapist in private practice, and a writer and lecturer. Her current professional interests center on Jewish women and on women over sixty.

CARMEN VÁZQUEZ (1949), MEd, was born in Puerto Rico and has over twenty years of experience as an organizer, activist and educator working with diverse communities and movements. She is Coordinator of Lesbian/Gay Health Services for the Department of Public Health in San Francisco (California) and a member of the Board of Directors of the National Gay and Lesbian Task Force.

LENORE E. A. WALKER, EdD, is a licensed psychologist in independent practice with Walker & Associates in Denver, Colorado, and Executive Director of the domestic Violence Institute. An international lecturer who trains at the invitation of governments, private groups, and world health organizations, she has done research, clinical intervention, training and expert witness testimony on the psychological effects of battered women and dynamics of the battering relationship.

NANCY WANG (1943), LCSW, is a psychotherapist in private practice in San Francisco, California, and a professional workshop leader on intercultural understanding. She is also a performing artist, choreographer, writer, and co-director of Eth-Noh-Tec Creations, a nonprofit cultural arts and education organization. Her work in both careers aims always at enhancing ability to love and fulfill life.

EIDELL WASSERMAN (1958) grew up in San Diego and San Jose, California. She earned her Masters and PhD in Clinical Psychology at U. Kansas, Lawrence. After four years in the Southwest working with Indian communities, Eidell has returned to California to work for the National Indian Justice Center, a private nonprofit organization. She lives in Sonoma County with her partner, Lin.

LINDA WEISKOFF (1951) is a Clinical Social Worker who practices psychotherapy in Atlanta, Georgia. She has been a member of a women's counseling collective since 1988. In addition to feminist therapy, Linda finds fulfillment in Tai Chi, singing and baseball. She has a keen interest in acknowledging differences as a key to discovering similarities and wholeness.

STEPHANIE M. WILDMAN (1949), a Professor of Law at the University of San Francisco School of Law, teaches Torts and Feminist Theory and the Law. Her articles on sexism and racism have appeared in various law reviews. She has also written about these issues in the context of classroom dynamics. She is the mother of two children.

# Preface

The initial descriptive title for this book was, *The Significance of Racism in the Psychology of Women: Building Consciously Anti-racist Models of Feminist Therapy.* We called it a working title because we hoped it would change. As a result of the power and direction of the contributions received from its authors, the book took on a life of its own and the present title emerged.

Invitations to submit proposals went to people in our personal networks and to many others. The response was highly encouraging. We received letters of intent, proposals, and occasionally even a first draft to start with. One or two who could not make the commitment suggested others who might, and some who did promise to write for the book also suggested others who could make a unique contribution. At professional conferences we listened to presenters and discussants; those whose thinking seemed to fit with the book were invited to contribute, and several have done so.

In 1991 we signed a contract with The Haworth Press. (By then we had been in planning and negotiating stages for almost a year.) By September 1991 we had a list of 26 proposed themes or topics, all but three of which are presently part of the book in one form or another. By the end of 1992 most, but not all, the contents were on hand in final form.

We are pleased to be including both frequently published writers and others for whom this will be a debut. We are also pleased with the age range of contributors, and as part of an anti-ageism commitment we have asked authors to include their year of birth in their self-descriptions.

As coeditors we followed a method of comparative editing. We read each article separately, then at our regular meetings discussed a few at a time in detail, consolidating our perceptions into feedback for the writers. In this process we discovered that while both of us sometimes had identical reactions to a draft article (or part of one), at other times each of us commented on points the other had not. We found that after our discussions we rarely disagreed. When we did, we would set the manuscript aside till a later date, and usually found that by then our views had become more unified.

We received all kinds of support during this project, and here acknowledge for their diverse help: Joyce Kobayashi, Cherie James, Nikki Gerrard, Bill Clark, Martha Mahoney, and Polly Taylor. We offer special thanks to Jan Faulkner and Natalie Porter for early support and encouragement, and to the coeditors of Haworth's Series on Women, Ellen Cole and Esther Rothblum, for initial enthusiasm and ongoing availability and assistance. We also acknowlege historian Herbert Aptheker for the clarity of his concept that the idea of racism is inseparable from the practice of racism, and that the same holds for antiracism.

*Jeanne Adleman*
*Gloria Enguídanos*

*There is a saying usually attributed to Native American Indians: If you want to understand someone, you must first walk a mile in that person's moccasins. Reading this book may be that kind of experience. If so, it is urgent to remember, always, that a mile is not the same as a lifetime.*

# *PART I.*
# *TESTIMONY*

Invited to contribute to this collection, authors were told that personal as well as academic approaches were welcome. The power of the personal material created the need to open the book with this section.

# Walking on Moonsands

## Carmen Vázquez

*Get back on your boat, Spic! Indian Giver! Chink! Dirty Dago! Cheap Jew! A fight, a fight! A nigger and a white!*

Like an old grainy black and white film where the people move too fast and engage in silent laughing, I recall a childhood reel filled with numerous and often cruel messages about class and race. I spent most of my childhood in a neighborhood called Harlem in New York City. As though it were yesterday, I can still feel the stinging shame of childhood taunts from other children on the playgrounds of Harlem admonishing me to "show a little class" and to "act your age, not your color." I wanted very much to show some class and not act my color. What I understood about class and color, however, was framed by rags and couches. Puertoricans and blacks were poor and we washed the plastic covers on our bargain store couches with rags soaked in vinegar water. White people were rich and lived on Long Island in big beautiful homes with brass door knockers and they sat in their living rooms on fine white leather couches. I wanted to be like them.

From birth, our class and our race are superimposed on us. They celebrate or suffocate the uniqueness of our ethnic heritage and individual identity, demand our loyalty, and give us or deny us privilege. Like gender, class and race are the chisels that shape the contours of how we view the world and how we view ourselves.

The most common myths about class in the United States are the claim to the existence of three classes (lower, middle, and upper class) and the notion that you can pull yourself out of your class if you just work hard enough, meet Mr. or Ms. Right, or invest your savings wisely.

The reality of our lives is a different thing altogether. I was born in Puerto Rico in 1949 to a couple of very poor people who became part of the poverty-driven Puertorican migration to the United States in the fifties. I was five when we arrived at a place I had dreamed would be the moon but was in reality only the city of New York. My dreams of finding streets glittering with silver and gold and of rolling on moonsands were replaced by the harshness of poverty in the lower East Side and Harlem, by welfare and the Projects. Like so many *jibaras*[1] from the hills of Puerto Rico whose parents came to America eager to embrace the dream of prosperity, I spent years getting schooled in the virtues of America where everything is possible if not free so long as you work hard and have faith in the dream.

My growing-up memory, however, is filled with the sorrow of watching Mami and Papi working their butts off and never having enough money to buy their own house or a car or sometimes even a meal for themselves and the seven of us at night. I grew up shielding my mother from the insults of the welfare caseworkers by editing them out of my translation. I grew up to learn that too many teachers can and do give children an "F" for an original essay because "Puertorican children don't write like that." I grew up with a father whose humanity was stripped from him by the poisons of World War II and the indignity of not being able to do the only work he was capable of doing because that war disabled his body and shattered his spirit.

In 1992, thirty-eight years after my parents and I landed on the moonsands of New York, my mom was living on a $300 a month social security allotment and what her children could send her from their paychecks. The spiraling costs of rent and utilities and food in New York City forced her to lose the apartment she called home and move in with my sister, Nancy, and her family. If she needs another place to live and I lose my paycheck, it won't be me she'll be living with because I don't have the resources to shelter her or myself without that paycheck.

My mother and I are not alone. The vast majority of working people in the United States with their little middle-class hope

---

1. Caribbean Spanish for poor girls from the mountains.

floating in their dreams are, in fact, one or two paychecks away from poverty. The great wringing of hands and moaning we hear from the economists and the policy makers over the increasing gap between the haves and the have-nots is cast as a worrisome development in a society that has otherwise only had the smallest of gaps between its lower, middle, and upper classes. This is a lie. We have always been a society of haves and have-nots.

Given that we have the technological capacity to give every single person in our society everything they can possibly need to lead whole, healthy, and productive lives, the continuing unbridged "gap" between the haves and the have-nots becomes increasingly difficult to justify. In the United States, racism and the stratification of the working class along income levels have been the mechanisms most successful in insuring the perpetuation of a system where control of the country's material surplus remains in the hands of the few and not the many.

The fifteenth-century European ideology of superior and inferior races, cast in the Americas as the difference between "savages" and Christians, permitted invading Europeans to annihilate or enslave people considered "racially or morally inferior" to themselves. It was not difficult for European immigrants who became small landowners in the American West and urban trade and craft workers to accept the notion that indigenous people, former slaves, or any non-white person deserved less than they did. Evidence of their entitlement came in the form of higher wages and greater access to education, borrowing power, and all the amenities of life in a democratic industrial society. The middle class became entrenched in American lore very early as a haven for white workers, not all workers. It was not and still is not a color blind economic phenomenon.

It is by no means a bad system if you're sitting in the control room. By blurring the distinctions between oppression and exploitation, and their intersection, those who control the material surplus in our society are assured of a divided working class.

Oppression is a function of social power that denies or minimizes an individual's right to human or civil democratic rights such as the right to free speech, the right to due process, the right to vote, or the right to equal protection under the law. Limitations on democratic and civil rights translate into the limitation of an individual's capacity to secure work, shelter, food, education, and health care. Exploitation, on the other hand, is the difference between what an individual's work produces for an owner and what they are paid in wages for their work.

Technological advances and a higher standard of living make the day-to-day existence of the working class in the United States one that is no longer easily distilled into clear depictions of exploited workers and cruel owners. The middle-class camouflage of the essentially exploitive relationship between wage earners and owners makes it difficult for U.S. workers to recognize themselves as a class of people who can cohere politically in defense of their own interests. Attempts to organize and unite U.S. workers are continually fractured by divisions along lines of sex, race, sexual orientation, and income levels. The golden aura and allure of the middle class soften the edges of oppression for women, people of color, lesbians and gay men, or anyone experiencing oppression in our working class while obscuring the exploitation of American wage earners, top to bottom.

The 1990 census once again confirms that women of color are the poorest people in our working class. Consider the Filipina or African-American woman who works for the minimum wage flipping hamburgers for somebody making millions on those burgers. She sleeps with her children in a single room and the only health care she knows is when she thinks she's dying—or she is dying—and her health care is in an emergency room. She will never be in line for that promotion to manage Chez Mac because she don't talk good English or her skin is too dark and her kids will most likely repeat the cycle. When that is your experience, you know both exploitation and oppression.

In that same working class there coexist with the hamburger flipper the teacher, nurse, and bus driver whose earning potential rarely exceeds $40,000 and whose efforts to maintain a middle-class standard of living ultimately lead them into debt far beyond their earning potential. A few rungs up the ladder toward the top of our working class is the woman who earns $80,000-100,000 a year working for a major pharmaceutical firm. She works her eyeballs raw trying to improve on that new treatment for AIDS while major stockholders rake in billions in profits.

I do not pretend that there is no material difference between these women or men and our hamburger flipper. When the chemist, teacher, nurse, and bus driver lose their paychecks, however, our hamburger flipper will be waiting for them with knowing nods because they will all be a lot closer to inhabiting the same rung on the class ladder that she has been on all her life.

For the people sitting in the control room, this highly stratified and leveraged buyout of the working class works like a charm. Our poor hamburger flipper and our chemist might even be the same color, but it's not likely they are going to sit down and have a drink to hash out their class identities and common ground anytime soon. The middle class is a cultural reality in the United States. It has terrific marketing and lots of sex appeal as the prerequisite stepping stone into the glossy ad world of the most exclusive club of all–the owning class. I mean, progressive politics is nice and all that, but if there is a choice between a leather love seat and plastic "early Puertorican," what am I to choose?

The romance of poverty is highly overrated. If you are a poor person who has never had the opportunity to make that choice, you will choose the leather couch or that which will make it possible for you to get the couch. The bottom line, as I envision a progressive reality, is not that we should all be poor but that the benefits bestowed on the upper echelons of the American working class, otherwise known as the middle class, can easily be made available to the rest of the class including the extension of the U.S. labor force working for U.S. employers in Asia and south of the border.

Throw the ideology and economic expression of racism into my old grainy black and white film, however, and the vision disintegrates. We claw at each other, insult each other, murder each other. We fight each other for the largest share in a diminishing social-benefits pie rather than uniting in demanding a broader and fairer distribution of the wealth that is rightfully ours because we create it.

I focus on class because it is impossible for me to extricate my personal experience and my political understanding of racism from my class identity, not when I know what the reality of my mother's life is. I focus on class because my reading of American history tells me that race has been a terribly effective tool for obscuring what class divisions really mean in our society. I focus on class because indentured servants of European descent had more privilege than an indigenous person or an African slave in colonial America. I focus on class because immigrants from Asia, the Pacific Islands, Central and South America, and the Caribbean have been added to the list of peoples whom today's debt-strapped and pension-bound "indentured servants" of European descent can still feel superior to. I focus on class because many of us who espouse a feminist or progressive agenda keep acting as though racism, sexism, and heterosexism, or any form of oppression, are simply bad ideas. Increasingly, we deal with the "isms" as nasty prejudices we learned when we were young which we can undo by taking a workshop where we get to name our own social pain, hug and cry a little, and then move on to the safety of our individual and separate communities.

I know this is not true. I know racism is anguish and death. I know racism is the continuing genocide of America's First Nations. I know racism is the enslavement of Africans, Jim Crow laws, and all the inhumanity of "white only" life. I know racism is all the Chinese people who worked and lived and died without ever knowing citizenship in this country they helped build. I know racism is concentration camps for Japanese-Americans during World War II. I know racism is all the Mexicans and Central Americans who die crossing the river to "freedom" or are condemned to hunger and poverty on the other side of that river. Racism is not incidental to American society. It is fundamental to it. It is what fuels the middle-class limbo dream that so entices us.

Like racism, the political reality of sexism won't be wished away. Sexism uses women's bodies to sell cars, booze, and the American way. Sexism tells women that we haven't any say in when and how we choose to reproduce or enjoy the sexual pleasure of our bodies. Sexism is every prosecutor who ever humiliated a woman with questions about her "enticement" of the man who raped her. Sexism is 14 white male members of the United States Senate Judiciary Committee making a mockery of Anita Hill's testimony in the Clarence Thomas confirmation hearings. Sexism is not incidental to American society. It is fundamental to it. It too must be understood within the context of a class society as a division even older than racism.

There is another "ism" fundamental to class society as it exists in the United States: heterosexism. This is not to be confused with heterosexuality, a sexual orientation to what is culturally accepted as the "opposite sex." Heterosexism is the presumption of heterosexuality that renders lesbian/gay and bisexual people, our lives and our needs, invisible. Heterosexism results when homophobia (the fear and hatred of people whose sexual orientation is toward their own sex) becomes a political force. As a lesbian, I cannot accept the often brutal reality of heterosexism and homophobia as mere prejudicial whim. Heterosexism is a distinct form of oppression buttressed by laws and religious dogma that sanction discrimination against us, prohibit the free expression of our sexuality, and fan the flames of bigotry and hatred that fuel homophobic violence. Heterosexism assaults us daily with its images and its laws and its denial of our love, our children, our homes, our jobs, and our humanity. Homophobia kills us: in mental wards, on the streets, and in the terror and paralysis of our own fear. Heterosexism and sexual repression are not incidental to American society. They are fundamental to it.

The political implications of extending repression to one of the deepest areas of personal communication and meaning in our lives are profoundly class-bound. Both sexism and heterosexism and their day-to-day manifestation as sexual repression have played a much overlooked role in the development of class society.

In Marcy Rein's (1991) powerful words:

> Sex has been a tool for power and control since Columbus got lost and hit the shores of the [new world]. Sexual exploitation has accompanied colonialism, the genocide of indigenous peoples, slavery, wage slavery, discrimination against immigrants, Jim Crow laws, imperialist wars, and the ongoing differential integration of women into the workplace. Sexual myths have been among the most poisonous underpinnings of racism; e.g., the myth of the black male rapist that provided the ubiquitous rationale for lynching. Women's subordination in society is continually reinforced by the myths surrounding our sexuality.

Today, the most reactionary forces in U.S. society are waging full scale war against everything but hetero sex in the bedroom with the man on top and the shades drawn down.

Before proclaiming our allegiance to multicultural anything or to the struggle against racism, we must understand the role of economic injustice and class privilege in the perpetuation of racism or any oppression. We must do so because it exists. We must do so because if you have to stay in the closet in order to keep the paycheck that pays your rent, you are a victim of economic injustice. We must do so because women who work for a living are still earning $0.65 to every dollar a man makes. We must do so because health-care funding gets cut while billions of U.S. dollars are spent on bombing the Iraqi people back into the stone age. We must do so because the real life conditions and day-to-day struggle for survival of an African-American woman who is a single mother and addicted to drugs cannot be understood or addressed without understanding and addressing–in a concrete way–the role that both economic injustice and racism play in that woman's life.

I've had enough of dying and violence and hiding and being made to feel individually responsible for my own life's pain and oppression or my mother's exploitation. Naming the pain and the willingness to hear someone else's pain begins the process of healing and consciousness, but it doesn't end the pain. Consciousness without action means nothing. You can't take consciousness to the bank.

Class is a calling for me, a calling to work for a political agenda that prioritizes health and jobs and homes and education above the madness of bombs and the disgrace of human degradation and exploitation for profit. I see no other way. There are still Puertorican children dreaming of walking on moonsands who will know only poverty in their lives. There are still African-American children and children from Asia and the Pacific islands who serve as fodder for the War on Drugs. There are still indigenous children dying of hunger and alcohol poisoning and tuberculosis on the few tracts of land left to America's First Nations. There are still women and men living the last days of their lives on corrugated cardboard beds in the streets.

I want the children I know and all children to walk on "real" moonsands because they can. I want them to never, ever be hungry because they don't have to be. I understand that I must act together with those who share the limitations and breadth of my experience, if we are ever to realize the possibility of a society where each and every individual lives with dignity.

Those of us who do not control the material surplus in our society must learn to recognize and defend each other. We need to nurture and support those among us who through song, dance, film, or the written word and the spoken word give voice and form to an ideology and culture that mirrors the true life experiences of the many who experience oppression and exploitation and not the few who experience privilege. We must defend affirmative action and abortion clinics and the civil and human rights of all people of color, all women, all lesbians and gay men, and all workers no matter how unconscious some white queers and straight hamburger flippers are.

When we have done that, and even as we are doing it, it will be infinitely easier to see the differences among us in this sprawling American working class not as barriers to protect us from each other, not as differences that we have to rank and catalogue as better or worse than our cultural framework or our experience of oppression, but as precious threads in the exquisite fabric of what we call our humanity.

## REFERENCE

Rein, Marcy (1991, Fall). *Crossroads: Queer Relations: The Lesbian/Gay Movement and the U.S. Left*. Berkeley, CA: Institute for Social and Economic Studies.

# Salience of Loss and Marginality: Life Themes of "Immigrant Women of Color" in Canada

## Nayyar S. Javed

Emotional distress in the lives of "non-white" immigrants has in the past been attributed to their cultural traits and racial background (Furnham & Bochner, 1986). More recent literature examines the role of context and the effect of uprootedness on their mental well-being (Siddique & Wakil, 1991). The literature suggests that immigrants do not readily avail themselves of mental health services (Sue & Zane, 1987). Explanations usually center around culturally based beliefs, and/or irrelevance of therapeutic approaches.

Although the assumptions underlying these explanations are appropriate, they ignore the salience of racism within mental health settings. In exploring the hesitancy in accessing mental health services by non-white immigrants, the meanings of inequalities in their lives must be considered as critical. I feel my life experiences as a racialized immigrant, including my work as a therapist and an activist, will provide better understanding of the issue.

In the process of sharing experiences with other "immigrant women" in Canada, I realized the sense of oppression our social definition as "immigrant women" engenders for us. Consequently, I decided to liberate us from the label and name our lived reality by calling us "racialized women."

Racialization is experienced in different ways by men and women. This chapter is based on the experiences of racialized immigrant women who entered Canada as "dependents" of their husbands. The struggles of other racialized women, though important, are beyond the scope of this chapter.

### *RE-ROOTING*

In my struggle to re-root myself in Canadian society, I have encountered numerous obstacles. Many times I felt defeated, lost, and hopeless. Each attempt I made to knock down the walls separating me from the society took a huge emotional toll. I was painfully reminded of my "otherness." Otherness is a social construction for the representation of those of us who are seen as "undesirable." It keeps us at the margin of society. It is an identity I never knew before; coming to grips with its meanings was a humiliating realization. The feelings of loneliness made me homesick. I missed belonging to my surroundings and that sense of self-assuredness with which I had walked through the journey of my life. I thought my spirit was breaking up and I became self-conscious in a way which was totally strange to me. Strangeness permeated my life.

Then I met other women who had similar feelings, who spoke many languages and came from diverse cultures yet we all shared the same feelings of alienation and hurt. We had all come to Canada with a vision of a better life. Our dreams got shattered and our hopes for a better life died. We met each other in varied settings, in their homes and mine, and in my office at the Saskatoon Mental Health Clinic, as we struggled and organized to lobby at province and national levels. The more we talked and listened to each other, the more aware we became of our losses and our marginality. We all felt the weight of racism and sexism.

Some of us also talked about experiences with mental health therapists and other health professionals. They too treated us as strangers. Mental health professionals do not seem to ask us the right questions. We feel their discomfort with our "strangeness." They seem not to understand that our status as strangers is extremely painful and can cause depression, anxiety, insomnia, and more. Though temporarily numbed by pills that physicians and psychiatrists prescribe, these pains never go away because we still remain "strangers." The permanence of being strangers is rooted in the social structures erected to keep us away from the center of the society. We are pushed to the margin.

Canada defines us as "Immigrant Women of Color," a social construction. In earlier cross-cultural discourse, marginality was viewed as a "syndrome." According to Furnham and Bochner (1986), the notion of "marginal syndrome" was introduced to the literature by Park in 1928 and Stonequist in 1937. Their descriptions of "marginal syndrome" are summarized by Furnham as follows:

> It refers to individuals who are members, or aspire to membership of two racial or cultural groups which have mutually incompatible norms, values, or entrance qualifications . . . the term marginal refers to the location of such individuals . . . they are on the margin of each. (p. 30)

In light of more recent literature (Appiah, 1990; Djao & Ng, 1987; Siddique & Wakil, 1991), I find it difficult to accept the notion of marginal syndrome. My own experience of immigrating to Canada and interacting and working with women and men of different cultures makes me doubt the idea of "incompatible cultural norms." Despite differences, there are many universals binding all cultures. As well, human beings have enormous capacity for adaptation to new cultural settings if their lives are not complicated by exclusionary practices in public policy and in social interactions.

I argue that we are pushed to the margin for the purpose of maintaining the social structures that restrict our access to the privileges available to the dominant groups. We are the "minority," they are the "majority." This very minority/majority polarization reflects a power relation of domination and subordination. Our physical characteristics, our cultural, linguistic, and religious backgrounds are used to maintain our subordination and to protect the interest of the dominant groups and their sense of entitlement. Keeping us in the margin defends their location at the center. The walls between margin and center cause us to feel defeated, devalued, and homeless–defeated because our struggles to move to the center are crushed; devalued because who we are and what we believe are rejected; and homeless because we are treated as outsiders.

Despite our diversity, and often our citizenship, we are indiscriminately labeled "immigrant women." Immigrant women have been an integral part of Canadian history but the phrase "immigrant women" seems to be associated with the shift in Canadian immigrant policies, which are not too different from those of the United States. Canada loosened its immigrant policies to meet a demand for cheap labour. In the sixties, Canada relaxed bars to immigration from more impoverished countries. At the same time, dominant groups in Canada started to feel scared of losing white supremacy. Governments were very careful in keeping the balance between maintaining a status quo and fulfilling the labour market needs. In achieving these goals, language played a central role. In earlier history, hyphenations such as "Ukrainian-Canadian" were used to differentiate the "ethnics" from those perceived as "Canadians." With the changes in the demographic composition resulting from the shift in immigration policies, phrases such as "visible minority," "immigrant women," and "women of color" started to emerge in the Canadian daily discourse. Obviously, it was an attempt to differentiate the newcomers from Asia, and from Central and South America, from the rest of Canadians. The newcomers replaced those assigned to the bottom of the power hierarchy.

The phrase "immigrant women" reveals location in the margin but obscures the reason for it. Its racist bias (Djao & Ng, 1987) remains hidden by the word "immigrant," which suggests that once we settle down here and learn Canadian ways, we will be treated differently. We would believe it except that our immigrant sisters from European countries and the U.S.A. are not viewed as "immigrant women." My friends who have immigrated from those countries laugh when I ask how come I am an immigrant and they are not.

Moreover, many of us who come from South and Central America, the Middle East, Afghanistan, and Pakistan are quite "white." Despite the supposed desirability of white skin, we are referred to as immigrants. I therefore assert that this label itself is racist and I will not use it in this chapter. Instead, as noted above, I refer to us as *racialized women*.

Entry to Canada confronted us with a systematic process of devaluation—of who we are and what we have brought along. Our cultural, religious, and linguistic backgrounds are subliminally associated with our race. Cultural differences are seen as cultural "deficits," our languages are assessed as "restricting the development of 'higher cognitive capacities,'" and our religions are presented as "barbaric." Our experiences are discounted, our educational credentials are discredited, and doors of opportunities are slammed in our faces. With rare exceptions, we are pushed into the job ghettos which are unacceptable to everyone else.

The discomfort invoked by our presence in social encounters is displayed to us, sometimes by a staring gaze and other times by avoidance of eye contact and other ways of distancing. We are reminded by these behaviours of the eternity of our otherness. The yearning to belong gets stifled at each juncture of our new life. Feeling ignored, undesirable, and unwanted we walk through the "land of opportunities" and wonder where are those opportunities everyone tells us about. We have heard about equality and freedom in Canada but have never experienced it. We ask, "Is there something wrong with us?" And when we start to believe that the reason we have not achieved equality and freedom is that there is something wrong with us, we start to kick ourselves and then may begin to participate in our own marginality.

Our devaluation by the society remains invisible when our men talk about racism. So-called multicultural policies do not take racism into account, and racialized men ignore the gender issues. Male critics have brought racism out of obscurity, but make no mention of sexism in their analysis.

Similarly, feminist analysis of oppression has not included our realities. Our feminist sisters tend not to challenge many social assumptions about us. They find us "smelly" and "submissive" and see our cultures as male-dominated and "barbaric." We do not deny the presence of male dominance in our cultures, but we are also aware of the extent of patriarchy in Canada. We experience it every moment of our lives. Racialized and alone, most of us endure our oppression silently. In the countries we left behind, we were at least equal to other women, and we had access to mechanisms compensating for our subordination to men. Yet many well-meaning individuals tell us to be thankful for "the freedom and equality in Canada." What equality are they talking about? Their own?

Since our experiences are rendered invisible in the analyses of oppression, we start to feel invisible. We hide parts of our lives from our own sight because, if we allow our vision to encompass the totality, we will fall apart. The fear of falling apart keeps us numb and we try to endure humiliations with dignity. We do not want anybody to put the label of denial on us because what we refuse to see is so horrible that the only way to survive it is to ignore its existence. However, we miss the freedom to acknowledge our pains. A deep sense of loss permeates our lives.

## *LOSS: OUR COMPANION IN OUR LIFE JOURNEY*

Trapped in a web of contradictions within the Canadian society and within our consciousness, we confuse reality with its presentation. We hear about equality in the Canadian Charter of Rights, yet our lived reality contradicts it. We know the political origin of our representation and its consequences yet we become the image constructed for our representation. "Image," according to Bhabha (1991) is an illusion of "presence, a sign of identity's absence." The absence of the identity we were familiar with generates a deep sense of loss, that is an ever-present companion in our life journey.

Rejection of who we are is a pressure we feel in all encounters. We react to it in many ways. Some of us try to change our appearance. We bleach our hair and our skin. Others adopt the "Canadian lifestyle" and resent our origin. Nothing changes except that we lose who we are and who we used to be. The new woman feels as strange as her surroundings. "Otherness" becomes ingrained and we become self-conscious. Despite trying, we find it hard to see ourselves as Canadian. Almost no one calls us Canadians, and if it does happen we feel awkward. Our sense of being "other" goes through many stages: denial, resistance, and eventually, in most cases, acceptance. We may start to believe that we deserve this social treatment.

Many of us, however, do succeed in resisting the pressures to change our identity. An activist sister in the racialized women's movement commented on her resistance:

> What I believed was viewed as stupid and who I was, was not acceptable to them. I told myself I don't have to be like them to be good.

Cultural uprootedness and dislocation engender loss for all those who go through the experience (Furnham & Bochner, 1986). In recent literature loss entailed in the dislocation has emerged as a significant life stressor (Canadian Task Force on Mental Health Issues Affecting Immigrants and Refugees; 1988). Leaving behind one's support network and familiar settings, and severing significant attachments, take an enormous emotional toll. Gradually, however, the sense of loss can dissipate *provided* the individuals are accepted into the new culture. New attachment bonds can be built to replace the ones left behind. Individuals do learn the new culture and develop skills to function within its social structures.

Racialized individuals in Canada, however, are faced with racism and other barriers that prevent them from doing so. The struggles of racialized women are defeated because of both gender and racial background. Consequently an eternal sense of homelessness permeates our consciousness. We work hard to buy or build houses in Canada but the home we search for exists nowhere. Some of us start to feel like impostors, which generates further awkwardness and anxiety. I have been living in Canada for the past 16 years and have worked very hard to regain the sense of feeling at home. Still, like many other racialized sisters, I have lost the sense of self-efficacy I had developed in the culture of my origin.

## OUR RESTRICTIVE ROLE

Regaining a sense of self-efficacy depends less on the individual's capabilities than on his or her access to power and social privileges. As racialized women, we are at the bottom of the social hierarchy. As a racialized minority, we get excluded from formal and informal society networks which play an important part in the cultural learning. Many of us are encouraged by our families to avoid acculturation. Seeing us adapting to the Canadian lifestyle threatens our men. As women, we are expected to preserve our culture and transmit it to our children. Preserving our culture and learning the new culture are not mutually exclusive. Both can and must be done to enrich our lives, but we need support and opportunities and we seldom have either.

Our role as women and emotional service providers restricts us to the bounds of our homes, or ethnic communities. Therefore, our interactions with the rest of society are limited. Isolation from the society deprives us of the informal mechanisms of language learning, and lack of English language skills sets us apart from the society, which adds to our isolation. It is a vicious cycle and breaking it requires support from our husbands, fathers, and sons. The silence imposed on us reminds us of the time when we did speak and what we said was understood. We felt competent because we had the tools for functioning in life. We expressed our joys and sorrows, asked for help if we needed it, and offered help if others around us needed it. Silence now reminds us of our oppression. We feel powerless and trapped on a racist terrain.

## MENTAL HEALTH SETTINGS

The emotional impact of loss is obvious but it takes diverse forms. Questions related to loss experiences of individuals are therefore vital to the effectiveness of therapy. Yet, our losses are seldom taken into account by therapists, who think we should be grateful to be here. Instead, we are labeled by therapists with pathologizing DSM III categories and we feel cheated because painful themes of our lives are totally ignored.

Racist ideology has rendered too many therapists "cognitively incapacitated" (Appiah, 1990) and therefore they do not see us as who we are but as our color, race, accent, and our culture–our differentness from them. To them, we appear to be those images constructed for portraying us. Appiah (1990) uses the construction of "cognitive incapacity" in describing people who possess superior mental abilities but fail to make distinction between reality and their assumptions in the treatment of racialized individuals.

In examining the cognitive incapacity of therapists we need to look into the political origin of their biases. We cannot ignore the fact that the very notion of race was legitimized by "science" (Miles, 1989). Our educational institutions systematically practice racism. A therapist trained in these institutions is almost inevitably embedded in their institutional cultures. Liberation from assumptions fostered by these cultures is a step toward overcoming cognitive incapacity, but this becomes possible only when the therapist reviews and questions her world view, informs herself of the reality of racialized women, and recognizes the many faces of racism.

In the past, racialized groups were presented as unfit to live in the civilized cultures of the "West." Such overt racism is probably decreasing in most academic settings but the fact that our issues remain obscured reveals another form of racism. Countless incidents of put-downs of those who have the courage to research this illustrate the racism within the establishment.

Keeping racism invisible in the construction of knowledge and failing to challenge racist assumptions encourage systemic discrimination. A concerted effort is needed to eliminate systemic racism. Token representation of racialized groups on the faculty and an occasional lecture on racism by "an ethnic guest" are practices which make little change. Rather, they tend to create an illusion of change which adds to perpetuating racism.

In conclusion, we, the racialized women, need to keep talking about our experiences and how they impact on us. We must organize to regain our voice and insist on including it in mainstream feminism. We must remind the institutions training therapists to include our reality in their teaching, and we must insist that mental health service providers stop racist practices. When we reach out for help, we have to overcome many more barriers than others. That in itself is a challenge and we need to be commended for taking it up.

Similarly, feminist therapists must become aware of our struggles for surviving in isolation. They must support us in eliminating racism and take up the challenging task of seeing us as who we are despite social labels ("minorities," "immigrants," etc.). We urge them to view these labels as pathologizing us in a way similar to how DSM III diagnoses pathologize women who seek therapy. Discarding the labels, our therapists can enter our inner landscape and will be able to understand our losses and see how imposed marginality has become internalized, ingraining a sense of inferiority in our consciousness. Then, maybe, real help can be available and clinicians will no longer wonder why their services are underutilized by "this population."

We need to talk with each other in an open and honest way.

# REFERENCES

Appiah, Kwane Anthony (1990). Racism. In David Theo Goldberg (Ed.), *Anatomy of racism*. Minneapolis, MN: University of Minnesota Press.

Bhabha, Homi K. (1990). Interrogating identity: The postcolonial prerogative. In David Theo Goldberg (Ed.), *Anatomy of racism*. Minneapolis, MN: University of Minnesota Press.

Canadian Task Force on Mental Health Issues Affecting Immigrants and Refugees (1988). *Review of the Literature on Migrant Mental Health, Health and Welfare*. Ottawa.

Djao, W., & Ng, Roxanne (1987). Structured isolation: Immigrant women in Saskatchewan. In Kathleen Storric (Ed.), *Women: Isolation*. Toronto: Methuen Publications.

Furnham, Adrian, & Bochner, Stephen (1986). *Culture shock: Psychological reaction to unfamiliar environments*. London, New York: Methuen Publications.

Miles, Robert (1989). *Racism*. London and New York: Routledge.

Siddique, C.M., & Wakil, S.P. (1991). Theories of immigrants' mental health and well-being: A preliminary examination in the context of South East Asian immigrants' experiences in Canada. Unpublished report.

Sue, S., & Zane, N. (1987). The role of culture and cultural techniques in psychotherapy: A critique and reformulation. *American Psychologist,42*(1), 37-45.

# Personal Reflections
# of an Anglo Therapist
# in Indian Country

Eidell B. Wasserman

*It must be understood that at best, we are offering generaliza-
tions about both the anglo society and the traditional Native
America culture.*[1]

## INTRODUCTION

As a non-Indian mental health professional working in Indian
Country I have faced many unique challenges, including a need to
redefine my concept of psychotherapy. The intensely personal nature of the psychotherapeutic process demands that the mental
health professional be especially sensitive to avoiding interventions
and approaches based on beliefs absorbed while growing up in an
anti-Indian society; such beliefs are unlikely to respect the clients'
cultural and spiritual values. Most often, the therapist becomes
aware of her false beliefs by experience. In this paper I explore my
experiences living and working with several Indian communities in
the Southwest, focusing on life and work in a geographically isolated Reservation community.

In 1988, in response to the disclosure that a multiple victim
molestation had occurred on the Reservation, I was hired by an
Arizona Tribe to develop a child sexual abuse treatment program
there. While Tribal people often identify the Tribal Nations they are
writing about, such behavior by a non-Tribal member may be considered exploitative. Therefore, I will protect the Tribal members'
privacy by not specifically identifying them. My four years of

working with Tribal mental health and social service programs has included three different Tribes throughout the state of Arizona, representing different cultures and lifestyles. My work has focused on child welfare issues, providing direct therapeutic services, administrative functions, and training.

Providing training to community members who can continue the therapeutic efforts after the professional is no longer working on the Reservation is essential. How is it possible for a city-raised, white, Jewish, lesbian psychologist to live and work effectively in a rural, Reservation environment in a manner which respects the indigenous values of the community and spiritual/cultural integrity of her clients?

## BEGINNINGS

As a non-Indian I have found working on a Reservation a tremendous challenge. Each Anglo person is seen as a representative of the United States governmental system which has so profoundly oppressed Indian people.

One issue confronting the non-Indian therapist working with Indian clients is that of boundaries. I was trained in a conventional university program in which I learned that "professional distance" from clients is essential to maintain the objectivity necessary in a therapeutic relationship. However, community members made it clear that I was insulting them by refusing their offered hospitality. I found professional distance a liability. In order to gain acceptance within a community it may be necessary to be as much a part of that community as possible, rather than being perceived as a distant outsider.

In addition to the majority society's racist oppression, there may be internalized oppression. For example, there is a "joke" in Indian Country about two fishermen. The two have been fishing all day and the Anglo's bucket is empty while the Indian's bucket is full. The Anglo asks the Indian, "How is it that we have been fishing for the same amount of time, have caught the same number of fish, but my bucket is empty while yours is full?" "That's easy," the Indian replies, "every time you catch a fish and put it in the bucket, it jumps out. Every time I catch a fish, as it tries to jump out, the others reach up and pull it back down."

While many Indians identify a need for trained members *from their community* to provide therapeutic services, others are apprehensive that their own people will not maintain confidentiality, and therefore prefer a non-Indian therapist. I have often received clients' requests for a non-Indian therapist saying they believed that an Indian therapist would discuss their problems "at the dinner table." Sometimes, too, a community member's past reputation is used to discount their present accomplishments. I once had a person call me and irately ask why I had sent "that drunk" to her house. The man she was referring to had been sober for six years and was a trained member of our program's staff, but in her mind he may always be "that drunk." Such unwillingness to support members of their own community in the changes they make in their lives is an example of internalized oppression.

The therapeutic process is encumbered when there is any internalized belief that Indians are not as good as Anglos. There would almost certainly be a psychological conflict for clients between seeing their therapist as a representative of the society which oppresses them and seeing that person as someone who can help them empower themselves. The conflict may be equally strong for the therapist.

True empowerment comes from, among other sources, recognizing one's own oppression and acting to overcome it. One of the reasons therapy may be successful is clients' believing that the therapist has the ability to help them with their difficulties. Faith plays an equally important role in *all* types of healing.

An Anglo therapist may be given a certain amount of credibility because she or he is non-Indian and, therefore, automatically perceived to be competent. The therapist then must deal with the delicate balance of using the clients' faith in her to help the clients recognize their own abilities. A client who equates competence and value with "non-Indian" may lose faith in the Anglo therapist who attempts to help her or him understand that Anglos and Indians are neither inherently competent nor incompetent simply due to race. Such an attempt may undermine a client's faith in the therapist without increasing self-confidence. The therapeutic challenge is to foster the client's personal growth, despite inherent difficulties.

To accomplish this goal, the therapist must work with the entire community to foster community-wide feelings of value and self-worth, and one of the difficulties in such work is the anti-white attitudes which the Anglo therapist may face. There is a constant awareness among Indian people that trained, non-Indian professionals have skills and expertise that can be helpful to the Indian community and a concurrent feeling of resentment at the Anglo people and their institutional and political systems which prevent Indian people from gaining those skills. These feelings may be denied and introjected as internalized racism, or form the basis for anti-white attitudes, or both. Among virtually all the people I have worked with, both Indian and non-Indian, it is accepted that, as a Tribal employee, if there is a conflict between you as a non-Tribal member and another person who is a Tribal member, the Tribal member will win.

In the face of such covert and overt anti-white attitudes, it becomes increasingly difficult for an Anglo therapist to monitor her own racist attitudes to keep from indulging in them as a defensive reaction. I have been told directly by some Tribal Council members that they were not concerned with how I was treated as an employee, since I was just going to "write a book about your experience and get rich."

## GAINING ACCEPTANCE–CONDITIONALLY

These experiences reflect only half the picture. There were many supportive people within the community who made my stay worthwhile. It was possible for me to see significant change in individual clients and families. I am deeply grateful for the many good friends I made during my time on the Reservation and for their continued friendship. Despite the many difficulties and the disillusionment I experienced on the Reservation, I have great respect for the people who continue to struggle against unimaginable odds to improve their own lives and their communities.

As a therapist and a human being, I experience a variety of feelings toward my clients. Some of these feelings are detrimental to the therapeutic relationship and I must engage in self-monitoring to ensure that these feelings do not enter into the therapy session. However, living and working in what I often perceived as a "hostile" environment, I experienced those negative feelings hovering in the periphery of my awareness on a constant basis. Racist feelings would surface whenever I experienced frustration or anger with a client, whereas in other settings, I would have experienced other defensive reactions.

A non-Indian therapist must constantly monitor her own feelings as she works with her clients and interacts in the community, and constantly be aware of the potential to alienate clients by her attitudes or beliefs, or by violating Tribal customs without even being aware of doing so. There is no one correct way of behaving in all Indian communities. Nor do all members of a given Tribe share the same interpretation of Tribal mores and values. Thus a non-Indian therapist runs a great risk of unconsciously alienating people by naive behaviors in addition to any existing racism.

A therapist must accept being the object of public scrutiny, the subject of gossip, and having her actions and motivations questioned publicly. The therapist's off-duty life can influence her therapeutic efficacy as much as her clinical skills. The communication "grapevine" in any small community is very effective and provides speedy, although not necessarily accurate, information to many residents. A therapist must attempt to stay out of the grapevine gossip whenever possible, while living in the community.

In many Indian communities, direct confrontation is not acceptable. Rather than informing the therapist that she has in some way been offensive, the client may simply assume that the offense was intentional, possibly just another example of a non-Indian lacking respect for the client's culture and beliefs. The client may never bring up the specific concern directly with the therapist. Even if the therapist initiates a discussion regarding the possibility that she has in some way offended the client, cultural factors mitigating direct confrontation may prevent the issue from being satisfactorily resolved. This is especially likely if the therapist's infraction touches on traditional religious beliefs which cannot be discussed with a noncommunity member.

## A NEW PERSPECTIVE:
## THE COMMUNITY AS THERAPIST

The communal nature of an Indian community challenges the efficacy of individual therapy. There can be a great deal of stigma for individuals seeking therapy. The extended family and friends may be threatened by the potential of systemic influence resulting from individual change, and may actively work against such change. Due to the strong family connections and extended family influence, it is important to develop intervention strategies which address these considerations.

In order to establish an effective therapeutic strategy, the entire community must be seen as the client. Since "talking psycho-therapy" was not related to traditional means of healing in the communities I worked in, part of the therapeutic process was the development of support systems for change and the education of community members concerning the function and goals of psycho-therapy for those who chose to utilize it. It is part of the therapist's education to understand the traditional familial, cultural, and spiritual forms of healing and to integrate these approaches with therapeutic techniques.

As a therapist, I attempted to keep the awareness that I always had many things to learn. Indian co-workers constantly imparted knowledge, and I tried to be ready to receive it whenever and however it was shared. Their knowledge was rarely imparted in clearly didactic fashion. It came to me in many forms, often through stories or other indirect modes that I learned to interpret and incorporate.

Not only is the entire community a "client," but the community becomes the healer as well. Community involvement in the therapeutic process is the best method for ensuring lasting change. Unless the non-Tribal therapist marries into the Tribe, or forms some other significant attachment, most are going to leave the Reservation some day, often within two or three years of arriving. As mentioned above, providing training to community members who can continue the therapeutic efforts after the professional is no longer working on the Reservation is essential.

This approach means that community members are active and

visible members of treatment teams, community education, and prevention efforts, and become practitioners functioning independently. The key to successful intervention is community investment.

Large groupings of people, such as villages or communities, experience loss, grief, anger, and other emotions just as individuals do. A community-wide healing ceremony or celebration can have therapeutic impact in creating a positive environment for change. The village itself can give the feeling of positive acceptance for its members, if this is the collective feeling of the members. Similarly, feelings of distrust and shame can be experienced as permeating forces, limiting the personal growth possible for members, and compelling the community as a whole to deal with the resultant distress.

## COMMUNITY-BASED INTERVENTIONS AS A THERAPEUTIC MODEL

As a prelude to individual, group, or family therapy, activities must be initiated which allow adults and children to become familiar with the nature of the therapeutic process. These activities may include recreational programs for children, support groups, and activities groups for teenagers.

These types of group activities assist children, for example, in learning how an Anglo therapy group operates. Many had not participated in group activities which have rather strict rules, as a conventional therapy group does. It may be a new experience for them to be in a group setting where people are expected to sit quietly while one person talks about something personal. Verbal discussions about feelings, and sharing personal information with others outside the family, may be foreign concepts to the child. A recreational group for children can be a first step toward organizing children into a group with a specific, shared purpose and introducing the ideas of structure, limits, mutual respect, and trust-building with other children.

Similarly, many adults may never have discussed family problems outside of the family. They may expect a therapy relationship to be the same as going to a relative for advice. It is important that the client and therapist discuss their individual expectations of the

therapeutic relationship and process to avoid future misunderstand-
ings. A client, for example, may expect that the therapist will provide direct assistance in daily living (e.g., providing transportation)
if she sees these activities as the source of her problem. The therapist may view her role as helping the client to become self-sufficient
through verbal, insight-oriented therapy, especially if the therapist
is unaware of alternative ways of learning.

Many Indian clients I have worked with are oriented more toward doing rather than toward talking as a means of handling problems. The client who expects the therapist to "do something," and
the therapist who expects to help the client gain insight which will
lead to change are both likely to leave their interactions disappointed and frustrated. Such differences in expectations of psychotherapy are of course also found in other settings. It is always
important for the clinician to be aware of the potential existence of
differing expectations and to ensure that these expectations are
clarified early in the treatment process.

One of the most familiar metaphors for therapy is seeking help
from a relative. This conceptualization of therapy may lead to actions such as a client coming to your house at midnight seeking
advice because she has a problem. Traditional healers are often
available 24 hours a day. It may not be inappropriate to go to a
traditional healer at 3:00 a.m., so it may be difficult for clients to
understand that they cannot call on their therapist at any time, in a
similar manner. Clients may feel that boundaries do not exist in
terms of where, how, or when they interact with the therapist. The
therapist must learn to adapt to these differences.

Educational activities can include community cookouts, co-spon-
sorship of conferences, and networking with local resources to
bring educational opportunities to the Reservation. A broad-based
activity, such as a cookout, allows people to come together in a
positive way and the therapist to become known within the community or to give an educational talk. Similarly, by participating in
community events, the therapist gains a sense of the community: its
values and traditions.

While a barbecue or recreational group may not fit mainstream
psychology's definition of a psychotherapeutic intervention, such
activities can be extremely productive tools to begin the process of

empowerment. Community members become a part of the treatment team and service providers, planning and implementing activities which are needed within that community.

As a therapist, community activism became my most potent tool. Through the facilitation of community support groups, potential leaders emerged and I could support their development. Clients developed into co-workers. Therapy developed into a partnership.

However, the therapist's support of a person who desires to change her life is not sufficient by itself. An Indian woman who decides that she wants to improve her life will not automatically be supported and accepted by her family or community. The more likely scenario is that the men in her life will be threatened, she will be criticized for seeking individual recognition, and her family will be harassed. While the criticism for self-promotion may reflect a cultural value, there may also be elements of internalized oppression, sexism, and racism at work. It is frustrating for the non-Indian therapist to recognize the internal barriers which may be blocking a client's or co-worker's progress. No less is the frustration for the client or co-worker who recognizes that her personal growth is not progressing at the pace or to the depth she desires.

Non-Indian therapists may not only view the process of change from a different frame of reference than their Indian clients do; they may also have a time frame which is inappropriate. The most frequent mistake is attempting to rush the treatment process. Similarly, a therapist who does not invest the time necessary to get to know the community's needs, and does not attempt to address those needs, is rushing the process.

## A FEW FINAL THOUGHTS

Keeping in mind that I was employed first in response to a multiple victim child molestation, my attempts had to be toward facilitating change within the community. This creates two enormous dilemmas for a therapist/administrator. One, are the changes somehow a product of her own cultural conditioning and unconscious, unwanted, racist beliefs–or are they genuinely necessary? Two, and even more difficult, how to respect the community's values while introducing elements of change. If my experiences are any guide, there are no easy solutions. Satisfactions must be found in the imperfect processes themselves.

## NOTE

1. Charles Horejsi, Magel Bird, Wayne Bruno, Opal Cajune, Lois McClure, Linda Warden, Delma Redneck, Kathy Ross, Joe Pablo, Steve Snell. Traditional Native American Cultures and Contemporary U.S. Society: A Comparison. Unpublished and updated manuscript received by this author about 1988.

# A Bridge over Troubled Waters: Being Eurasian in the U.S. of A.

Christine M. Chao

*In order to win the certainty of oneself . . . recognition is essential.*

–Frantz Fanon (1967)

This chapter will entwine two aspects of my experience: the personal and the professional. It is an untangling and a sorting out of the meaning of my racial and ethnic identities. It is how, in part, I have come to understand what it means to be Eurasian and grow up and live in the United States. In the field of clinical psychology, who you are, how you have struggled with your own issues, and how you continue to deal with them may be the most salient factors influencing your work with clients.

This chapter then, contains personal observations discussed and shared with friends and loved ones, with clients, with supervisees, with students. I am fortunate to have been able to work with Asian American, Asian immigrant, Asian refugee, African American, and Chicano clients as well as clients of European ancestry. What they have taught me has also "gone into the pot." What I have learned about myself through formal and informal therapy sessions is also distilled and offered to you.[1]

I am a second generation Eurasian. I had an Irish grandmother born in the town of Athai in the county of Kildare and a Chinese grandfather born in the city of Toisan, in the province of Guandong, in what is now the People's Republic of China. The remaining grandparents, born in the United States, were of Polish and English ancestry.

It is important to realize the wide range of ethnic and racial blendings that can occur with one parent being of Asian descent. In itself "Asian" actually contains very little information. To what ancestry does the "Asian" part refer: Korean? Chinese? Thai? Indian? Vietnamese? Cambodian? Japanese? Taiwanese? Laotian? Each Asian culture is different from the others and will leave its unique stamp on the person's psyche. In the United States one seldom hears "Eurasian" anymore, although it was used for me and other same-age cohorts of similar backgrounds. New wars have been fought and politics have created new nomenclature. Since the wars in Southeast Asia, children with one American parent and one Southeast Asian parent are referred to as Amerasian. Again, does that adequately capture who the person is? The offspring of a Cambodian mother and a third-generation Irish-American soldier is different from the offspring of a Vietnamese mother and an African American father. And different from these two will be the child of a Laotian father and a Chicana mother. Into this equation now throw issues of social class and educational background. The permutations and combinations abound in dizzying numbers. Each culture experiences and recognizes pain differently, each understands happiness differently; each culture defines work and play differently, each has its own tempo and rhythm.

It is the responsibility of the therapist to help the client examine culture the way the therapist would encourage the exploration of any other facet of their client's life, giving it the same respect and import. Within a person's culture can be found much pain and confusion as well as much that is strengthening and healing. To neglect that aspect of a person's psychological makeup is to overlook what can be a plumb line to the deepest levels of a person's being. Bringing cultural unconsciousness into individual awareness can be extremely energizing and life-promoting.


### WHAT'S IN A NAME?

*What you have received as an inheritance from your fathers you must possess again in order to make it your own.*

—Goethe

In line with our patriarchal culture I carry the Chinese surname of my father and decided to keep it when I married. Why? In definite part, out of a reaction to the racism I experienced. In addition to the pride I find within my name, it has also been the occasion of pain. What you have struggled with to accept or attain you do not give away lightly. Traditionally, most Asian women do not change their names when they marry. However, this part-Asian woman also acknowledges the women's movement in making easier the option of retaining my original surname.

As an adult I asked my father for a Chinese name. I wrote to him, "Your Eurasian daughter, 3/4's European-Caucasian, 1/4 Chinese-Asian wants her Chinese name. Logic posits that 3/4 is greater than 1/4, therefore the "I" should equal the 3/4 European-Caucasian. However, in my heart it never worked that way. It was always 3/4 + 1/4, and the +1/4 changed many things and made all the difference." I did not want my American English name transliterated into Chinese sounds. I wanted a Chinese name written in characters. Characters that, when I try to write them, look awkward and elementary. But it does not matter. Names signify and though I may rarely refer to my Chinese name in public, it points me to a place inside myself.[2]

For any person, that "place inside the self" is multi-leveled, richly textured, and goes deep. It partakes of the family and one's personal history. It partakes of one's culture: the immediate American one, still pregnant with so much possibility yet standing accused of so much wrong and evil, as well as cultures from many lands, from many ancestors. It is important for a person to know the names and stories of those *Abuelos* and *Abuelas*, to know one's *Babcia*, one's *Obachan*. It grounds you. It connects you at first to a network of family members, then to extended members, then to the ancestors, those who have gone before you. And if you can go deeper still, to your core, to your "soul" in Jewish and Christian language, to your "Buddha nature," then there is the possibility to connect with others outside your personal sphere in their truest humanity.

I offer the above not so much as a personal discourse on my background but because we all carry names and those names are important. The names this society subtly encourages and discourages, the names that were and are erased upon entering this country, the names people feel they have to shorten or change are not based on happenstance but on underlying premises that merit examination. A corollary is to examine the underlying reason that certain names are continually mispronounced and/or misspelled. What unconscious wish do we harbor to make everyone the same?

Adolescent sons and daughters of recently arrived Southeast Asian refugees frequently change their names to more American ones. Are these young Laotian, H'Mong, Cambodian, and Vietnamese reacting to a pervasive fear in this country, a fear that goes back even before the founding of this country; a fear of that which is different? The response to that fear, historically, has not been to understand or examine it but to distance oneself from the feared object and (perhaps) obliterate it, consciously and unconsciously seeking to continue a hierarchy based on race (Caucasian) and ethnic group membership (usually Northern and Western European).

What explanation do you give to a Laotian child whose teacher will not use her surname except for the first initial followed by a period, because it is too long, has too many vowels, too many syllables? She and her family have lost their country; their motherland. They are in effect cultural orphans. What does it mean, psychologically, for us and for them to take away that name?

In some instances refugees and immigrants have deliberately and with great thought changed their names, signifying that they are starting over and want to put behind a traumatic past. Whether or not that trauma has been understood, worked through, and grieved is another issue. For some people a change of name can symbolize a transformation of the person; for others, the change reflects suppression of pain too great to face.

When working with recently arrived Southeast Asian refugees a topic that must inevitably be addressed is that of racism in the United States. Oftentimes they will have been the recipient of discrimination based on class status, educational background, or membership in a particular ethnic group within a race (e.g., Chinese-Vietnamese), but not discrimination based on racial features. So I begin to explain that just as coming to a new country makes you particularly vulnerable to catching the diseases of that country, they may easily find themselves victims of racist attitudes and practices.

In addition, they themselves must guard against becoming infected with racist attitudes which they in turn inflict on others or pass on to their children.

Racism is perhaps the "original sin" of this country. The Constitution and the Bill of Rights did not include African Americans or women or the indigenous people who preceded Europeans. The Bill of Rights did not prevent the passage of the Chinese Exclusion Act or the building of World War II internment camps, filled with American citizens of Japanese descent. The consequences of those acts have been visited upon all of us, whatever our racial or ethnic background.

## A MINORITY OF MINORITIES

*You can't pretend you're white. You can't pretend you're Japanese. You're half. You're going to have to accept the fact that you're the minority of minorities. There is no other minority beyond you. . . . You're part of all, but all of none.*

–Kitahara Kich (1982)

The attainment of an interracial identity, such as Eurasian, is an ongoing, developmental journey, at times painful, at times confusing. Even within one family some offspring may actively embrace the racial part considered by American society as the "minority" aspect of their background, while others deny that aspect any significance or downplay its role. While it might be psychologically ideal to assert one's unique identity, there are many barriers that will be encountered, leaving one with a reactive or defensive stance towards issues of race and culture.

Like other racially mixed children, racially mixed children of Asian heritage often have to deal relatively early in life with existential-type questions such as "Who?" and "What are you?" That these fairly personal and intrusive questions can be asked with no hesitation is an indication of how deep our fear is that the other will contaminate us.

The social norms and etiquette of what constitutes "polite

topics" of conversation are often blithely ignored when dealing with racially mixed persons. People of all racial groups often feel at liberty to dissect your appearance. This often serves to announce that you are not really one of them, thus unconsciously or not so unconsciously preserving the "purity" of their group. I have had white people say to me, "Yes you really are Chinese; I can see it in your hair, in your eyes." And then, I have had Asian people say, "Oh you do not look Chinese at all; look at your hair, look at your eyes." So you stand disqualified by each group, orphaned by each group, grappling with questions such as, "What makes one really Asian or really white, or really African American?" What's the role of skin color, shape of eyes, color and texture of hair, language(s) spoken, name given, food eaten?

In Spike Lee's movie, "School Daze," he deftly satirizes in tragicomic song and dance routines the "Wannabees," those African-Americans who want-to-be, want-to-pass for white, hoping for a larger piece of the American pie reserved for those who are light-skinned.[3] For many children and adolescents of mixed Asian heritage, Wannabee takes on an ironic twist; they wish at times and "want-to-be" at times either all one race or all the other race.

Another phenomenon that children, adolescents, and persons of mixed Asian heritage face is that the mislabeling that occurs makes them recipients for racist remarks which can leave them in a quandary about how to deal with the other person. For example, someone complains about reparation monies being paid to Japanese-American survivors of the internment camps, "I can't believe we're paying those Japs all that money. We should have kept them in those camps and shipped them all back to Japan." Does the part-Japanese person speak up and reveal that part of herself? Does she remain silent and then later feel terribly ashamed that she let the remark go uncontested? Either way there can occur an assault on the soul.

In part, this is about "passing." Some persons with Asian heritage can do it, others cannot. The fact that "passing" occurs illustrates the strength of racism's grip on this culture, because "passing" in the United States virtually means passing for white. It can be done actively or passively. Within some families, some of the offspring will actively declare that they are white, while others in the family will actively claim their Asian background as the part they show the world.

There is also the strange sensation, not unaccompanied by a certain measure of guilt, of the world "passing" you (passive passing). For example, if most people did not know my last name, did not see my father or pictures of my Chinese relatives, then I would be "passed over" as white and accorded all the privileges thereof. That certainly occurred and I undoubtedly benefited from it. However, deep within myself I know that, but for a sorting of the genes in a slightly different way, but for a tad more melanin, I would not be "passed" over and the indignities and worse that Chinese and others have suffered in this country would also be mine. As people of color in the United States have to deal with "post-traumatic stress" because of racism, those who are racially mixed have, at times, to grapple with survivor's guilt, for having escaped some of racism's more lethal effects.

I am reminded that the power that racism wields is formidable when I realize the effects it had on myself and my siblings even though we did not look particularly Asian. A classmate, the daughter of a prominent figure in our town, told me with great pity in her voice as we walked home from our third grade class that I would never get anyplace in life because my father was Chinese. As my blue-eyed mother walked home from the grocery with a woman in the neighborhood, this woman shared the latest gossip: "A family of chinks are living in the corner house."

At home we were told we had descended from a line of emperors, but still one sibling would hope that my father would not come to pick her up from school because for at least a week she would have to deal with being called chink. Years later, that same sister and I were visiting San Francisco's Chinatown for the first time. We had been walking for only about ten minutes when she stopped in the middle of the street and declared we had to leave. She could not stand one more minute being among tourists gawking at Chinese and "Chinese things," saying how everything was so "quaint and fascinating." I understood, though I made her stop for lunch. (My stomach rules when my feet should be moving.) The paradox is that my sister and I were also tourists in Chinatown. We were both part of the crowd and not part of the crowd.

At times I would like to indulge in some righteous indignation and some pure hate with regard to what has gone on towards members of my immediate family, as well as on behalf of all Chinese who have come to this country, but there is a limit to where I can go with these feelings. My anger cannot totally cut white people off because part of who they are I am also. Remember the 3/4 + 1/4 equation? Where does the 3/4's leave me? This is my paradox, and the paradox shared by many who are racially mixed. I know what makes my blood boil and yet I am also privy to the other side. No easy answers; I literally live in the tension of the opposites.


## CAN YOU BE CHINESE AND STILL HAVE FRECKLES?

*All the time I was growing up I was laughed at and called "long nose.'*

> —65-year-old Eurasian professional
> from the People's Republic of China.[4]


When things get rough, it would be nice if the person with mixed Asian ancestry could find some comfort within the Asian community. This is not always the case. Many times, because of the insistence on the purity of one's line, racial mixing through marriage is considered a heinous act that can only bring shame; the blot is seen as being carried by one's immediate family and extended family as well as by the ancestors. In Vietnam, these Amerasian children have been called "children of the dust."

Often an Asian grandparent will display subtle signs, perhaps all the more damaging psychologically for the pretense that they don't exist, that the racially mixed grandchild is not quite as legitimate as the grandchildren who are not mixed. A Korean-American grandmother was more strict with her grandchild who was full Korean than with her other grandchild who was mixed, explaining that this latter child could not help but be wild as he had barbarian (white) blood in him.

Persons of mixed Asian ancestry who have made a deliberate choice to learn their Asian language often report the discomfiting and even painful experience of speaking the language to someone who ignores them but speaks to someone else, in their native tongue, about how odd this person is who does not look Asian but can speak their language. This is the "flip side" of the much-touted Asian politeness and good manners.

I remember a friend of mine looking at a photograph of my Chinese grandfather and commenting, "He does not look very Chinese." (Remember this was the grandfather from whom I traced my line to emperors!) At first I was dumbfounded. Then I raged inside and bit my tongue before I could say, "What exactly did you want him to look like? Charlie Chan? Is that your idea of a 'real' Chinese person?" Only much later did I realize how much my anger stemmed from my own feelings of self-doubt. Did I look Chinese enough? Could I be Chinese and still have freckles?

An interesting interchange occurred between some Asian-born refugee adolescents and some fifth generation Asian American adolescents during a retreat designed to train Asian peer counselors in high schools. Asked to define what it meant to be Asian, the students who were born in Asia laughed at the simple-mindedness of the question. It was easy; you spoke Cambodian, or Vietnamese, or H'Mong, or Lao and you were born in Cambodia, or Vietnam, or Laos. After a while a silence was noticed. Finally an American-born young woman asked, "What about me? What am I?" She had been born in Colorado, spoke only English, yet all her life experienced herself as different from the majority of her classmates and on numerous occasions she had been harshly reminded of her differentness. Was she also Asian?

## A BRIDGE OVER TROUBLED WATERS

*Rest. In peace*
*in me*
*the meaning*
*of our lives*
*is still*
*unfolding.* [5]

—Alice Walker (1985, p. viii)

In the end it comes to this. You are what you are. You juggle the disparate parts of yourself. You negotiate between your ancestors. You live with the knowledge that some of your forebears could easily have built the internment camps to which others of your forebears were sentenced; that maybe some of your distinguished ancestors occupied the stately halls of Congress when the Chinese Exclusion laws were passed.

In closing I can only share with you what I have experienced. In my dreams Polish ancestors come to me in brilliant robes and golden hair. A wild Gaelic witch has visited me. An Asian shaman hands me objects to be my talismans. These are all my ancestors.

You build bridges over which you walk. Sometimes you linger on one side, sometimes the other. Hopefully, at times that bridge can take you to those deepest places within yourself. Sometimes that place is a place of tears or rage. At other times you can enjoy the great cosmic humor with which God . . . Nature . . . the Buddha . . . the Fates . . . blessed you.


## REFERENCE NOTES

1. It is my strong bias that you cannot work effectively with other people in psychotherapy unless you have worked in therapy yourself. You cannot take someone beyond the point you occupy. Thus, work on yourself, which may take many guises, becomes an ongoing commitment. It keeps one honest. It keeps one humble. The dual issues of how a therapist "of color" deals with her ethnic identity within the context of a therapeutic relationship either with her own therapist or with her client, where the therapist or client may or may not be of a similar background, is another complex issue that cannot be addressed here.

2. Written in Pinyin, which is the current system of romanization for Chinese characters, my Chinese name is Zhao Mei Ying. The family name comes first followed by the generational name "Mei" which all my sisters carry and which mark us as being of a common generation. Mei means beautiful. Ying means clever.

3. In "Jungle Fever," Spike Lee's 1991 film, he shows the painful "flip side" for a light-skinned African American woman who, in a dramatic, achingly poignant scene, enumerates all the names she has been called because of her skin color. The scene presents an example of color being used as a litmus test to gauge loyalty and commitment to a group.

4. Personal communication from a woman from the People's Republic, whose name and profession should not be revealed for reasons of personal security.

5. In this poem, which is also the dedication of the book, Walker writes that it is "for two who/slipped away/almost/entirely:/my "part" Cherokee/great-grand-mother/ . . . and my white (Anglo-Irish?)/great-great-grandfather." One raped the other and the poem is about building a bridge, holding the pain and the rage, and out of that forging meaning that is actively and in the present discovering itself. As is said, "It is deep."

# REFERENCES

Fanon, Frantz (1967). *Black skins, white masks*. New York: Grove Press.

Kich, Kitahara (1982). Eurasians: Ethnic/racial identity development of biracial Japanese/white adults. Unpublished doctoral dissertation, Wright Institute Graduate School of Psychology.

Walker, Alice (1984). *Horses make a landscape more beautiful*. New York: Harcourt Brace Jovanovich.

# Racism in Academia:
# A Case Study

Patricia Guthrie

*As a politically and socially aware African-American, one of my realities is the recognition, as well as the expectation, that when white people are present, something racist is going to happen.*

–"Carol"

When I was invited to contribute to this volume, the editors told me that the book so far contained little about women of color and racism in any part of the academic world. Since I have an old friend who had sometimes briefly told me of instances of racism she experienced where she teaches, I decided to interview her for this book. This paper is based on the interviews I conducted in 1992 with my friend, an African-American academic. She has given me permission to quote her and to tell her story. Names and places have been fictionalized. I call the central character "Carol."

## RACISM:
## EARLIEST RECOLLECTION

Carol was six years old. She and her family had been in their new house almost a year. The five-year-old white girl next door, Shelly, and Carol had become fast friends. Except for Wednesdays, when Carol attended the Young Men's Christian Association for swimming lessons, Shelly came over to Carol's house every day after school. Carol learned that most people attending the "Y" are Christians. Since Shelly and her family were practicing Jews, she never went with Carol to the neighborhood "Y." So most afternoons, except Wednesdays, Carol and Shelly would hook their arms around one another's waists and wildly kick their skinny legs high into the air. Somewhere, on television or at the movies, the pair had seen images of French Can-Can dancers, and that's what they wanted to be when they grew up.

Shelly's birthday was rapidly approaching. Virtually all that the two friends talked about was the party, which this year was to be held in the park. But as the day of the party approached, Carol still had not received an invitation. Finally she asked Shelly about it. Carol vividly recalls Shelly's sad face as she stood with her head down, unable to answer. Instead, she rubbed her right thumb on the skin of her left forearm just below the elbow. Carol understood. *Her skin was black and because of that she could not attend the party.* Carol has not thought about this in a very long time. It happened 40 years ago, and yes, Carol still feels the pain.

Writing this study, I have kept in mind the connection that Rothenberg (1988) makes between racism and power:

> *Racism involves the subordination of people of color by white people.* While an individual person may discriminate against white people or even hate them, his or her behavior or attitude cannot be called "racist." He or she may be considered *prejudiced* against whites and we may all agree that the person acts unfairly and unjustly, but racism requires something more than anger, hatred, or prejudice; at the very least, it requires *prejudice plus power.* The history of the world provides us with a long record of white people holding power and using it to maintain that power and privilege over people of color, not the reverse [Rothenberg's emphasis]. (p. 6)

Rothenberg's definition is useful because it calls attention to the most significant component of racism–*power.* It serves as a guidepost in helping me to analyze and discuss the on-the-job racism that Carol recounts as she is interviewed.

In the context of this paper I discuss white university women, primarily but not exclusively those who exercise some degree of power within academia. This is by no means to say that such women hold the same kind of authority, control, and domination as their white male counterparts. However, many of these white women, some of whom have gained their power as a direct result of the feminist movement, are so positioned as to wield considerable influence over others.

## RACISM IN THE WORKPLACE: PERSONAL TESTIMONY

Carol is in the department office, where the white secretary calls her "Sue." Carol corrects her, reminding her that her name is Carol. Carol wonders, "Why does she think I'm Sue?" Moments later when Sue walks through the door, Carol knows the answer. The embarrassed secretary offers a lame excuse about the mix-up in names. "You two are dressed alike," she tells Carol. They are not, however, dressed alike nor do they look like one another. What they have in common is their blackness.

An administrator asks Carol to participate in graduation. Carol thinks it is important that faculty of color be present on such occasions. The faculty are together in the dressing room, putting on the various caps, gowns, and hoods of the institutions where each earned their highest degree. Carol truly enjoys a graduation with all the academic regalia, the happy and relieved graduates, and their proud supportive family members. She likes to march around in her bright gold gown from the University of Rochester. She is the only one in a gown that color. She says she feels like Big Bird, and loves it. She is really into the spirit of the graduation, when Rosa, a Latina colleague, approaches. They are glad to see one another and throw their arms around each other. Then Rosa tells Carol that everyone in her department has received a lay-off notice except herself, and that one white colleague had looked Rosa in the face and called her "a half nigger." Graduation does not feel pleasurable to Carol after that.

A white woman, who had served on a search committee through which Carol was subsequently hired, asks Carol to write a letter of reference for her. The white woman says to Carol, "Tell them how I picked you up off the streets of Harlem and gave you a job."

## *A VERY PUBLIC INCIDENT*

The issue of racism forcefully involved Carol when she agreed to participate in a conference on multiculturalism in colleges and universities, and to coordinate and facilitate a session titled "Colleges and Universities and the Issues of Race and Class in the Feminist Movement."

Carol put together an extremely interesting panel, and invited a white woman department chair to serve as discussant. Every seat was filled. One of the papers highlighted specific examples of white university women's racism and abuse of power on a different campus.

Following the presentations Carol, as facilitator of the session, introduced the white discussant, giving her name, the department she chaired, and the university where Carol and the discussant were both teaching. The discussant told the audience that in addition to the department she currently chaired she had in the past chaired the Department of Women's Studies. To Carol's surprise, she then announced with apparent pride, that she had "given" that Chair to Carol.

Her statement was challenged during the discussion period by the presenter mentioned above, who told the audience that this example, of a white woman believing that a Women's Studies Department somehow belonged to her to do with as she saw fit, particularly vis-à-vis a woman of African descent, was exactly what her own presentation had identified as racism and abuse of power.

For Carol this was welcome support, but it was also less than half the story:

> That woman and I first met when she was Chair of Women's Studies at Osborn University in New England, where there is a reputation for liberalism. A recent catalog describes Osborn as a campus concerned with diversity and multiculturalism. Students of color make up nearly 25% of the student body; 30% of the staff employees are minority. Thirty-four percent of the faculty are female and 19% minority. I was originally hired as a part-time lecturer teaching lower division introductory Women's Studies courses. After three years I was offered and

accepted a tenure-track joint appointment in Women's Studies and Sociology.

Carol now serves as chair of the Department of Women's Studies and her teaching responsibilities are divided between the Women's Studies and Sociology departments. She reports, however, that on the day of the conference:

> My insides churned and turned, but I continued to facilitate the session, acting as if what the discussant had said and the presenter's rebuttal had nothing to do with me. On the outside I was cool.

Like most African-American women operating in white milieus, Carol has learned to continue with the business at hand—at least on the surface—even though she is in great pain and turmoil. This is not a skill that we are proud of; it is something we have unfortunately had to learn in order to survive in hostile environments.

As Chrisman (1992) says:

> Blacks have always been forced to play roles in this society, both to accommodate and to thwart white America's obsession with racist stereotypes. The existential circumstances of black life itself require constant improvisation and manipulation, simply to survive. (p. xxi)

Carol continues the previously untold story of her encounters with female department chairs at Osborn:

> Shortly after my acceptance of the tenure-track position, this same Chair of Women's Studies asked me if I was "at all interested" in chairing that department. I replied that I would really enjoy the opportunity to make use of the education and experience that had more than prepared me to do the job. But when it seemed she would not be getting the chair of another department, a position she wanted, she withdrew her "gift."
>
> Only when she was assured of another department to chair did she call me back in to tell me finally I could serve as Women's

Studies chair. Neither my abilities nor what might be best for Women's Studies–let alone my feelings!–played any part in this. She really did see Women's Studies as her personal and private domain to do with as she wished.

Hooks (1990) refers to this phenomenon as follows: "As more and more women acquired prestige, fame, or money from feminist writings or from gains from [the] feminist movement for equality in the workforce, individual opportunities undermined appeals for collective struggle" (p. 36). As for the other part of the untold story, here is Carol again:

> After I had accepted the Sociology position, the Sociology chair invited me in to discuss the courses I would teach during my first year as a department member. Without any of the usual niceties of academic discourse, she told me point-blank that she wanted me to teach lower division courses–for two reasons. One, she wanted me to "get used to" the department, and two, she wanted me "to attract students to the department." I was stunned. This was 1991 and this white woman was telling me to my face that she wanted me to be window-dressing for the department!

Carol adds:

> I could only conclude that it was racism that kept me from teaching upper division courses. The last department hire before me, a white man, taught upper division classes his first semester of employment. I had no more need to get used to the department than he had had. Furthermore I have had my PhD since the early 1970s and have taught at the college level ever since, including at one of the Seven Sisters colleges[1] and at a prestigious east coast state university. I had taught upper division courses at both–all this prior to Osborn.

Carol is an experienced professor and she is tired:

> tired of remaining silent in the face of their racism, tired of giving up bits of my soul, tired of looking them in the eye and

masking my pain and acting as if their conduct is normal and acceptable. Tired of them telling me how to deal with racism "appropriately." Tired of worrying about the possible repercussions connected with confronting their racist behaviors. I want to put my talents and energies to better use.

## RACISM IN THE WORKPLACE: FURTHER PERSONAL TESTIMONY

Carol mentions to Barbara, a white faculty member, that she has asked a Latina colleague to consider teaching in the Department of Women's Studies. Barbara asks, "What about her accent?"

A vintage picture postcard of singer Sarah Vaughn hangs on a bulletin board in Carol's university office. It is the only photo on her side of the office. Carol's white office mate wants to know, "Is that your sister?" Carol tells me, "They really do think we all look alike." And I know just what she means.

The department hires an African-American temporary part-time secretary to assist the full-time one. Carol is thrilled to have the extra help. As the part-timer prepares to leave at the end of the semester, she thanks Carol for her professionalism. "You're the only faculty member who acted like I was here. You're the only one who ever gave me work."

Neither Carol's reporting nor my discussion can do more than hint at the full range of racist actions and statements experienced by women of African descent, and by many other women of color, in all areas of university life. We can give only an *idea* of the breadth and depth of academic racism. All too often it is just the usual order of business. Presenting Carol's experiences simply means identifying some of the wrongs that have been done to one African-American professor.

By writing Carol's story I hope to add to the growing dialogue between African-American women and those of our white sisters who show an interest in confronting their racism, classism, ageism, and homophobia. A part of that dialogue centers on white university women, many of them holding some degree of power in their roles as presidents, deans, directors, and chairpersons. Some number of them also masquerade as feminists. I say *masquerade* because a consciousness of racism, classism, ageism, and homophobia, and a commitment to seriously confronting these issues, are utterly essential to any individuals calling themselves "feminists."

Lorde (1993) considers the issues inseparable, and says, "The absence of these considerations weakens any feminist discussion of the personal and the political" (p. 10). Unfortunately, many white women who have attained or have been granted relative power tend to deal with these issues in much the same way as do their traditional or establishment white university brothers and fathers. The problem with this approach, according to Lorde (1991), is:

> *[T]he master's tools will never dismantle the master's house.* They may allow us temporarily to beat him at his own game, but they will never enable us to bring about genuine change. And this fact is only threatening to those women who still define the master's house as their *only* source of support [Lorde's emphasis]. (p. 11)

It is my hope that this paper will in some way help in the struggle to end racism in higher education. I have specifically, in this testimony, called to task the racism perpetuated by white university women in positions of power. I have kept the focus on the women, partly because women are the focus of this book, and also in order to show that even when sexism is presumably irrelevant, racism is so entrenched that its perpetrators may not even know they are perpetuating it. Though I have not dealt with the racism of white *males* in academia, I am all too aware of its existence and power. But that reality does not excuse or ameliorate white women's racism.

> On two separate occasions Carol has gone to the university's cashier window to purchase her faculty parking sticker, only to be asked, before she can state her purpose, "You've come to pay the fee for the remedial English class?"

There is not yet any end to the examples that could be given. We who have fought for our advanced education, and are presently charged with educating people called students, now find only too frequently that the most difficult aspects of our profession are educating our colleagues and also sustaining our courage in the teeth of both unconscious and deliberate racism.

## NOTE

1. "The Seven Sisters" is the collective name given to some of the most prestigious women's colleges in the eastern United States: Barnard, Bryn Mawr, Mount Holyoke, Radcliffe, Smith, Vassar, and Wellesley. Some now admit male students but they all remain predominantly women's colleges.

## REFERENCES

Chrisman, Robert (1992). Introduction. In Robert Chrisman and Robert L. Allen (Eds.), *Court of appeal: The black community speaks out on the racial and sexual politics of Clarence Thomas vs. Anita Hill*. New York: Ballantine Books.

hooks, bell (1990). Black women: Shaping feminist theory. In Sheila Ruth (Ed.), *Issues in feminism: An introduction to women's studies*. Mountain View, CA: Mayfield Publishing Company.

Lorde, Audre (1993). The master's tools will never dismantle the master's house. In Laurel Richardson & Verta Taylor (Eds.), *Feminist frontiers III*. New York: McGraw-Hill.

Rothenberg, Paula (1988). *Racism and sexism: An integrated study*. New York: St. Martin's Press.

# Some Painful Experiences of a White Feminist Therapist Doing Research with Women of Colour

## Nikki Gerrard

For weeks I avoided writing this chapter about the upsetting parts of my experience when I, a white woman, began to do research with women of colour. As I sat contemplating what to say, I saw the faces of many women: the women at the conference of feminist therapists in 1989 who were angry and hurt because of what white women had said or not said that was racist. I can still see the faces of the white women who were bewildered and hurt by these accusations. I see the faces of the many women of colour I know and have talked with over the past seven years, some of them angry and bitter, others hurt and embattled. Some of these women of colour have given up the struggle to address the racism of white women and do not see us as their sisters; others are still fighting it but the struggle seems to go on and on. Whatever I say in this chapter, some people will hate it, some people will like it.

In talking about my experiences in the research I did with women of colour, I feel I am breaking rules because I am telling a side of the story that I have never seen in print in feminist literature. I believe it's a side that needs to be told because others have had similar experiences and similar feelings and we need to recognize, embrace, and use them in order to get beyond them. We need to understand the dialectical nature of what I experienced.

Articles about racism within feminism have been evident in every feminist journal I have read in the past few years. In every

My warm thanks to Dr. Paula J. Caplan for her great assistance in helping me complete this chapter.

feminist activity I have been involved in during the same time, the critique of racism there has been heard at one time or another. I believe it is a critique white women have needed to hear and address. If racism is not eradicated from the women's movement, it will divide and conquer us as nothing before ever has.

Part of addressing racism is to hear the stories of women who have been the targets of it. The research in which I was involved was an endeavour to render visible the stories of women of colour who had been clients in mental health systems. In pursuit of that goal I had a variety of experiences, some of them very warm and positive, some of them painful and negative. It is the latter of which I write in this chapter. I write about them because it is my hope that my story will provide understanding and support for all women who are either the direct targets of racism or are involved in the eradication of it, through activism, research, education, etc. I expect some will say that what happened to me, my impressions and feelings, and the meaning I have made of those experiences are due entirely to my own racism, lack of sophistication, and lack of awareness; that I "just don't get it."

I entered the research as a white, feminist therapist graduate student with extensive knowledge about sexism in mental health systems. I expanded my work to include women of colour as a result of participating in and observing both racism and anti-racism work in Toronto's women's community. I say "participating in racism" because I believe that all white people, consciously or not, are agents of racism. When I came to consciousness about my own racism I began anti-racism work, but I do not believe that any of us is ever free from the effects of racist socialization. Anti-racism work is always work-in-progress.

As a white feminist therapist I was situated in a mental health system in which some of the clients are women of colour, but in which women of colour are hardly ever consulted about policies and practices that affect them, and they are rarely put in positions of leadership or decision making. Furthermore, many authors (e.g., hooks, 1981, 1984; Davis, 1981; Currer, 1984; Mercer, 1984; Spelman, 1982; Smith & Stewart, 1983) who were writing about women of colour's experiences of racism had called for documentation of more experiences. These factors led me to want to explore, with women of colour, their experiences as clients in mental health systems.

The research was qualitative: my method was to listen to the women talk about their experiences. The discussions were open-ended, and the women were encouraged to say whatever they wanted. After a year of seeking and interviewing participants, I had interviewed ten women of colour. Two were Native women; the other eight were all immigrants–four from the Caribbean, one from India, one from Africa, one from England, and one from the United States.[1] A thorough discussion of why this happened, and how things might have been different if the eight women had been born in Canada, is beyond the scope of this chapter.

Early on I contacted a black feminist therapist who, on the telephone, sounded enthusiastic about my study. She said she thought four of her clients would be interested in being interviewed and she was willing to be interviewed herself. When we met four days later at a pub, within ten minutes she said to me, "I talked to my clients, and they said to tell you, and I agree, that you should fuck off." She said that "all of this" had been done and written about before, but nothing had happened as a result of it, and it was like vomiting over and over again. All anyone ever did, she added, was look at it and say, "Yuck." Despite my protestations that no one had studied women of colour's experiences of racism and sexism in the mental health system before, she adamantly refused to participate in the research. However, she and I continued to talk for the next six hours about many different things, including her practice, her experiences of racism as a professional in other agencies, her family, and so on. By the end of the evening I was aware that I liked her, she said that she liked me, and we had connected on many personal levels, but we would not be working together on the research.

By the next day, I was feeling angry, hurt, and frustrated. I could accept her not wanting to participate in the research, but I needed to comprehend why her response had been so strongly negative, especially considering the six hours of talking that took place afterward. I got the sense that her response was related to the fact that she felt we were separated by too huge a chasm, the chasm of racism–and chasms created by systems of oppression tend to be seen with especially painful acuity by the targets of that oppression. So, yes, we could come together and engage in a rich and satisfying way, but there is a chasm she felt we could not bridge, and the chasm exists despite our feminist politics and our lives as women.

As I examined my own feelings I realized that I had reacted to her as I do to anyone who leaves me feeling dismissed and power-less. I realized that this probably was part of how it would feel to be black: to have whites reject, dismiss, and disempower me without any knowledge of who I am as a person. This possibility didn't ease my feelings, but it gave me a window on what being a target of racism might be like. I felt like a victim, without agency.

As I thought further about her response, I considered the pain and vulnerability felt by someone who has been a target of mistreat-ment, when she is talking to someone who has *not* been targeted in that way and who therefore might not truly or fully understand the stories of that lifelong, inescapable abuse. Indeed, she had ex-pressed outrage at the prospect of black women speaking (reliving) that pain for whites to "study" without necessarily helping the black women. (I call being hurt by research "research abuse" and discuss it later in this chapter.) But when *she* could choose the topics, she felt secure and safe enough to talk with me for hours. Part of the complexity of this dilemma was that I could understand her concern but also felt hurt because she seemed to assume that I would not be sensitive to the black women's feelings and would not ensure that the work would be used to help them.

What this woman provoked in me was a more deeply critical look at racism: How is it played out in the lives of some women of colour? How does it feel? What happens to those of us who are white when we are rejected, dismissed, and cut out from the dis-course? In order to honour her resistance I had to accommodate my own feelings of anger and hurt. I use the word "accommodate" because I don't think one can overcome these feelings. By accom-modating, I mean that I saw her resistance in the context of her reaction to racism in our society. I accepted that I am part of that society and I am white, so I am an agent of racism. Her refusal of me was, perhaps, part of her resistance to racism.

I want to relate another incident, one that occurred at a large conference on women's mental health. A Native woman had said, before meeting me, that she wanted to be interviewed for this research. After talking to me for a few minutes, she described a previous time she had been interviewed for a research study. The incident had raised many unresolved issues for her, she had been left holding the emotional bag, and the researcher had never gotten in touch with her again. I consider such behaviour research abuse.

By research abuse I mean the practice of researchers parachuting into people's lives, interfering, raising painful old feelings, and then vanishing–leaving the participants to deal with the unresolved feelings alone and isolated. There is often a sense of "us" and "them" perpetrated by researchers so that the subjects feel "examined," sometimes exposed and judged. In contrast to this, I wanted to follow Oakley's (1981) plea for researchers to be sensitive to the feelings and needs of those on whom our research is based. I wanted us all to be participants. Above all, I wanted the ultimate goal of my research to be social change (Kirby & McKenna, 1989), so that those who participated in it–and others–could directly benefit from it. Even so, I was still the researcher, and therein existed a power imbalance for which I knew no answers; I only knew the struggle.

I told this Native woman that I understood her concerns and indicated that only if she felt comfortable being interviewed would I want to do so. I gave her my interview guide, and she looked it over. The next day she returned it to me and said she decided not to be interviewed, that she had a personal problem and didn't want to deal with that *and* the interview right then. Although I was disappointed, I could understand her decision. It was what followed that hurt me.

I invited her to my workshop, and she attended the last ten of the 90 minutes. The last ten minutes was discussion; the substance of my work had been presented in the first hour. But on the basis of the interview guide and those ten minutes, she said that my work was "just another study of us."

Woven into this and the first woman's story in this chapter are two issues which amplify the issue of research abuse. Bishop, Manicom, and Morissey (1991) discuss the hostility from the community toward researchers because of differences in race, class, etc., between the researcher and those being researched. Given this predisposition to hostility based on previous experiences, part of the challenge and frustration of trying to do this work is genuinely wanting to be of service to such groups but knowing that as a non-member of the group I will necessarily be limited in how much I can foresee and understand about their experience, no matter how willing I am to listen and learn. This, coupled with Briskin's (1991) observations about what she calls "identity politics," in which we tend to get isolated in our "identity" experiences (e.g., race, class, sexual orientation, etc.) and don't focus on the commonalities among us, left me, as a white woman, automatically excluded from the possibility that I might use the research responsibly. I not only felt personally hurt by this, but I also saw it as a tragedy for all women who are committed to eradicating racism.

Finally, the last incident I will relate involved a black woman who had been asked by an acquaintance of mine if she would be interested in participating in the research. The woman had never met me or heard of me before. The acquaintance told me the woman had called me a "blood clot," a term associated with menstrual blood and meant to be grossly insulting. When I asked my acquaintance what she had said about me to this woman to warrant such a reaction, she said that she had mentioned only the research and that I was white. My acquaintance postulated, however, that the virulence of the woman's reaction could have been triggered by something as awful as the suspicion that I was really working for the immigration department, seeking slyly to pick up evidence to keep certain women from gaining landed immigrant status in Canada.

I could well imagine that immigrant women's reactions to me would understandably reflect their real powerlessness in the face of such institutions as the Department of Immigration, and their resulting fears. It seemed that perhaps I, personally, was not so much at issue here as was my socially constructed dominance *vs.* her non-dominance and the meaning my dominance had for her. Once again, though, understanding this did not prevent me from feeling anger, frustration, hurt, powerlessness, and even fear. Given this kind of reaction, what other ideas, rumours, or fantasies about me might I encounter? Was there *anything* I could do about it? To what extent might someone go to stop me? What was happening, that my inquiring into women of colour's experiences as clients in mental health systems provoked such strong reactions?

In the good moments, when I don't get hooked emotionally by these experiences and become enraged and stuck in that anger, I am able to see the power and complexity of racism which harms people, overpowers people, white people and people of colour, and makes us do things we otherwise wouldn't do, say things we otherwise wouldn't say, deny our reality, and prohibit personal connections that, but for racism, are there and alive. In the good moments, I have clarity, understanding, and grief.

I have gone from being well-meaning and both intellectually and morally curious about my own and others' racism to being variously enraged, sympathetic, hostile, and back to something in the middle. I have become sensitized about my reactions to people of colour in all places, at all times.

I have learned more about my own racism than I had ever thought I cared to know. I am not neutral in this discourse. My experiences have stripped me of my imagined neutrality. It feels, at one and the same time, as if none of these experiences are good and none of them are bad, and yet they all are good and all bad. The dialectical nature of this work means that one does not enter such research and come out unaffected.

For those women who are contemplating racism research, I want to emphasize something that is difficult to convey because of its dialectical nature. Although it may appear that I have "damned" the women who resisted participating in the research, this is absolutely incorrect. Yes, they did what they did, and it hurt, but as a researcher and a feminist, it was the feelings they engendered *in me* that are so important to me and my learning. Those experiences, and the resultant feelings, have brought me to a level of understanding that I simply could not have gained without that pain and struggle. Be prepared for that pain and struggle. It is not something you can say is good or bad, but it is *necessary*. It *has* to be personal before it can be political.

The challenge to convey meaning, make interpretations, form theory in this area, and practice anti-racist work is enormous. I do not believe we have the language or the conceptual paradigms to communicate fully what happens due to racism, to racism and sexism together, and to racism within feminism. Oftentimes what happens or what is said is positive and negative at the same time. I am reminded of Pat Parker's poem entitled, "For the white person who wants to know how to be my friend" (1978):

> The first thing you do is forget that i'm Black.
> Second, you must never forget that i'm Black.

I have made an effort at addressing these challenges and I feel I have fallen far short. I made many mistakes. But I do believe that the work is important and vital and for me the work goes on.

The experiences I have related in this chapter have been mostly negative, but I also had many wonderful and positive ones. I learned from the women of colour who did support me in this research that this is not totally a woman of colour/white woman issue, as of course it can't be. To assume homogeneity within any group of women is erroneous, but I think we forget that in this struggle. The women of colour who did support me in this research are adamantly opposed to black/white separatism, opposed to excluding white women from research about racism. I learned from them that there are many different perceptions of what is racist and what is not. They taught me as a white woman, as a therapist, never to render invisible the differences between myself and others but never to assume that I know what the differences are. Even the woman who told me to "fuck off" also taught me, in word and in deed, about resistance. When I asked her about the resistance of women of colour to racism she said, "To survive is to resist."

## NOTE

1. There was a shared feeling among the women I talked to who said that they were glad they hadn't been born in Canada as they felt they would have had lower self-esteem if they had been exposed to racism when they were children. These women were also more inclined to see racism as political, not personal. Since these were the women who did talk to me, these are the factors which may have been significant.

## REFERENCES

Bishop, Anne, Manicom, Ann, & Morissey, Mary (1991). Feminist academics and community activists working together. In Jeri Wine & Janice Ristock (Eds.), *Women and social change: Feminist activism in Canada*. Toronto: J. Lormier.

Briskin, Linda (1991). Feminist practice: A new approach to evaluating feminist strategy. In Jeri Wine & Janice Ristock (Eds.), *Women and social change: Feminist activism in Canada.* Toronto: J. Lormier.

Currer, Caroline (1984). Pathan women in Bradford: Factors affecting mental health with particular reference to the effects of racism. *International Journal of Social Psychiatry 30*, 72-76.

Davis, Angela (1981). *Women, race and class.* New York: Random House.

hooks, bell (1981). *Ain't I a woman: black women and feminism.* Boston: South End Press.

_____ (1984). *Feminist theory from margin to center.* Boston: South End Press.

Kirby, Sandra, & McKenna, Kate (1989). *Experience, research, social change: Methods from the margins.* Toronto: Garamond Press.

Mercer, Kobena (1984). black communities; experience of psychiatric services. *International Journal of Social Psychiatry 30*, 22-27.

Oakley, Anne (1981). Interviewing women: A contradiction in terms. In Helen Roberts (Ed.), *Doing Feminist Research.* London: Routledge and Kegan Paul.

Parker, Pat (1978). *Womanslaughter.* Oakland: Diana Press.

Smith, Althea, & Stewart, Abigail (1983). Approaches to studying racism and sexism in black women's lives. *Journal of Social Issues 39*(3), 1-15.

Spelman, Elizabeth (1982). Theories of race and gender: The erasure of black women. *Quest 5*(4), 36-62.

# A Japanese American Therapist Discovers Feminist Therapy

Judy Y. Kawamoto

Ever since becoming a psychotherapist over 16 years ago, I have been wondering what the clinical implications are for doing therapy from a cultural perspective that is not entirely Western in orientation because the therapist is not entirely Western in orientation.

I have taken a long and winding path to find some answers to this question and have only recently found how feminist therapy relates to this question.

I am a *Sansei* or third-generation Japanese American. That means my grandparents came from Japan, and I was raised in a fairly traditional Japanese family even though most of those years were spent in a predominantly white environment.

When I reflect upon this fact, I find it rather saddening to realize how isolating this was for me and my family in terms of our not being able to benefit from the experience of being surrounded by or even merely involved with a community that was culturally and ethnically more like ourselves. This isolation from an intact Japanese American community, or Asian American community of any sort, began with World War II and Japan's attack on Pearl Harbor, followed by the evacuation and internment of thousands of Japanese Americans on the West Coast into American concentration camps. It is with much relief that I can skip over detailing the history of this event because it has been a subject frequently talked about in recent years and therefore is presently in the consciousness of many Americans.

My parents and three-year-old sister were living in Seattle, Washington at the time, and within months of Pearl Harbor were evacuated from there to return to Wyoming to live with my father's parents in the town where he had spent his adolescent years. They were spared the humiliation and hardship of the camps because Wyoming is in the "interior of the country," a phrase used by the government when locating campsites which fit their standards of national security. People could either go to a camp, or go to "the interior" if there was someone there who could provide them a home and/or a job. In fact, there was a camp located not too far from my grandparents' town.

My family gathered up what they could carry with them, and overnight changed their lives from being city dwellers in Seattle's Japan Town, to being farm dwellers in a small town in Wyoming with few Asian faces of any kind.

My father, who had been attending the University of Washington at night and working by day, had to give up his chance for a university education, something he strongly valued and to this day regrets not having had. My mother gave up her community of friends, most of them other Japanese American women like herself, and her independence as a mother and housewife, to join her husband's family in Wyoming. There she assumed the more traditional role of daughter-in-law, a position without much status, freedom, or independence. The community in which they lived suddenly found reason for rescinding my grandfather's membership in the local Rotary Club, and my father experienced rejection from businesses and people he had known growing up when he tried to find work outside the small farm. My family thus experienced the painful racism of silent exclusion and unjust victimization.

This was the beginning of my nuclear family's isolation from their ethnic community and this was where and when I was born.

Farm families by definition live rather long distances from their nearest neighbor, and communication becomes rather formalized or stylized as opposed to spontaneous. This was true for my family's communication with their closest Japanese American farm neighbors. We seldom saw them and when we socialized, it was usually for a purpose or event.

We eventually left farming and moved to what was for me a large urban metropolis–Denver, Colorado. In Denver, we lived in an all white, middle to upper-middle class neighborhood, and the schools I attended reflected this fact. I later went on to attend a predominately white university and graduate school.

The clinical question posed at the beginning of this article parallels a similar question I have often asked about my life in general: how much of how I think and what I do is because of my Japanese self, how much is because of my mainstream American self, and how much is just plain personality? Or where is the line between heritage and acculturation?

I have always felt slightly envious of the Japanese American friends I have met over the years who were raised in intact Japanese American communities because, with a little thought, the answer to these questions seemed easier to sort out. The homogeneity of their immediate community allowed them to grow up in a cultural majority. When they entered the white mainstream culture, they were able to see more clearly just what was different from their most intimate of experiences. There existed specific details of their lives that could be compared to and contrasted with mainstream culture.

Not so for me. Until I left home as an adult and had the opportunity to mingle with other Asian Americans and people of my color, my personal experience of growing up Japanese American was primarily shameful and negative. The very fact that I could speak to no one about what was clearly different about me and my life enhanced my negative thoughts and perceptions about myself and kept my shame secret and subterranean. My attempts to understand myself became an internal and secretive sorting-out process. As a result, my overriding self-perception was to see any difference between myself and others as myself being wrong and the other being right. Surely I needed to change myself to fit in. The white American mainstream was not only right, it was also better.

The Civil Rights Movement of the 1960s and 1970s, my own politicization over civil rights, the war in Viet Nam, and the opportunities I had to live in cities with large, intact, ethnic communities were the factors which broke through my isolation and allowed me to talk about these heretofore negative and shameful self-concepts. I slowly began to identify myself as positively bicultural and to strive to understand the nuances of that identity.

Today the issue of the bicultural person who is also an ethnic/racial minority is being eloquently and creatively addressed by such contemporary novelists as Julia Alvarez, Salman Rushdie, and Bharati Mukherjee, to name a few. It is with pleasure, joy, relief, and sometimes pride that I read their work and know others are reading them too.[1]

I first read Dr. Takeo Doi's book *The Anatomy of Dependence* (1973) sometime shortly after it was published here in the United States, while I was still a beginning therapist. At the time, I thought his discussion of the complicated and peculiarly Japanese concept of *amae* was interesting and shed some light on the conundrum of biculturalism. However, at that time, I really did not relate this concept much to myself or my own behavior. It was not until I read Carla Bradshaw's article, *A Japanese View of Dependency: What Can Amae Psychology Contribute to Feminist Theory and Therapy?* (1990), that that same concept suddenly took on new life and meaning, not only illuminating some aspects of my personality, but also giving me a new perspective on and a different understanding of my work with clients.

The word *amae* is the name for a very complex interpersonal interaction in the Japanese culture. There is no word in English for this concept. Literally, amae means sweet, or sweetness; figuratively, and psychologically, one could say it has to do with one person presuming upon someone else and being confident that he/she will be indulged, much as a child exhibits childish behavior with a parent (Doi, 1973, p. 18), taking advantage of the parent's love for him/her. This is a non-hostile interaction automatically understood by those engaged in it. Among the Japanese, the ability to *amaeru* is also understood as a universal interaction, found among animals and therefore taken for granted. It is interesting how the literal translation of sweet or sweetness implies that a person is being sweet or has a certain kind of sweet behavior which elucidates a reciprocal kind of behavior from the person being "sweet-talked" or presumed upon.

For me personally, as a third-generation Japanese American woman and a therapist, perhaps the most interesting and useful aspect of *amae* psychology is that of vulnerability and helplessness. Doi talks about how surprised he was, during a stay as a visiting scientist to the National Institute of Mental Health at Bethesda, Maryland, to observe, behind one-way mirrors, that American psychiatrists appeared to be "extraordinarily insensitive to the feelings of helplessness of their patients. In other words, they were slow to detect the concealed amae of their patients" (Doi, 1973, pp. 21-22). Doi goes on to explain that because western psychoanalytic psychotherapy assumes the goal of patient self-reliance and independence (a reflection of western culture as a whole), the therapist's inability to acknowledge the client's childlike desire to be momentarily indulged tends to "abandon the patient to his helplessness" (Doi, 1973, p. 22).

In reflecting upon my own work with clients, I have come to believe that there remains in my unconscious behavior a residue of *amae,* and that I unconsciously have allowed my clients to *amaeru* and, without thinking, have indulged them.

One memorable clue to this insight came from a statement made to me by a friend and colleague. She once told me, "You give me what I need [emotionally] before I even know what that is." Along similar lines another friend and colleague told me several times in a complimentary but somewhat puzzled tone how unusual it was that I seemed to get along fine with even the most difficult personalities (staff members) in our clinic. She finally explained it by saying, "You seem to bring out the best in people."

These comments were made in the spirit of compliments, and at the time I received them as such. Each time, however, I was left with both their feelings of goodwill and my own negative suspicions about what these comments really meant about my personality. I harbored a lurking fear that perhaps they were an indication of some deep, underlying pathology, some borderline qualities such as merging and/or an unclear sense of my own identity. Perhaps I was just a chameleon who could blend in so well with the environment that it never made a statement about its own individuality. Can anyone whom everyone seems to like be an emotionally honest person who can also be respected? I felt haunted by self-doubt and the fear of somehow being "found out" to be a fraud.

Now I can see these previously puzzling and troubling statements as observations that may have indicated the speakers' puzzlement as well for not being able to find a word for what they were trying to tell me about myself. Thanks to Bradshaw's article, I can understand this "something" to be my unconscious and automatic ability to allow a person *amaeru* to–in this case meaning to seek indulgence–and mostly to be gratified and satisfied.

In a more humorous vein, perhaps this ability to *amaeru* explains why, over time, I have accumulated as gifts an inordinate number of container-type objects, mainly vases and decorative boxes. One could surmise that these container-objects were given to me by people who unconsciously have experienced me as a safe holding place or repository for their feelings!

But how is it that this ability to allow one to *amaeru* and to satisfy it remains operable for me, three generations removed from my cultural roots? It is somewhat ironic, but I believe the answer lies in my personal experience of racism.

One of the central themes of specific and generalized racism is that the victimized individual is left feeling worthless, unimportant, unheard, and powerless, feelings that become one's identification on some very deep level. Sometimes the level is so deep that one is not even aware that she or he is operating out of that negative identification. It just becomes a way of life, the damaging aspects manifesting themselves in subtle forms.

My own way of manifesting this sense of voicelessness was indeed to keep silent and to listen to people and to respond in such a way as to try to make them feel better. Furthermore, it didn't occur to me to expect this treatment to be reciprocated. As was to be expected from this attitude, I became a listener to a lot of people in all kinds of interactions. I must add that over the years I have found any number of people who were caring, humane, and interested enough in me, that lasting, loving friendships have developed between us. But as a style and way of presenting myself in the world, I mostly have been the interested listener (not phony on my part), who indulges the other person's desire and need to be heard, understood, and perhaps helped, but does not expect the same in return.

In addition, my parents' experience of racism has not been without impact in my life. The treatment of Japanese Americans at the outbreak of World War II is an increasingly recognized example of blatant and outrageous racism victimizing over 100,000 innocent people and leaving them devoid of access to or recourse for fair and equal treatment. Similar to how survivors of the Holocaust have helped us recognize and explore the reality of survivor guilt, I believe my parents' experience of racism imbued in me early on an unconscious identification with victimization and helplessness.

Also, within the Japanese culture, there is an expression, *"shikata ga nai,"* which means "it cannot be helped." While racist attitudes may tell us this is a passive resignation which inhibits action and self-determination on the part of Japanese people, another way of viewing it is to say that it is an expression of acceptance of what appears to be the sometimes unpalatable truth of a situation. This acceptance is one factor which helped the Japanese people to survive oppression, including harsh feudal systems in Japan and racism in this country. However, it is true that there is a paradoxical twist to this in that this ability to accept hardship can enhance a person's acceptance of negative, racist attitudes and situations which can only be changed by forceful voices speaking out against them.

Finally, these elements of culture and racism in our society, in combination with *amae,* provide strong positive elements for making a good therapist: one who can allow the client's feelings of helplessness and/or victimization, can identify with them, empathize, and not expect an emotional return from the client.

I am not sure that I can quite convey the profound sense of relief I experienced after reading Bradshaw's article. This different perspective on understanding myself as well as my work has not only been enlightening, but best of all, has been self-affirming. Deeply painful self-doubts have diminished and have been overtaken by an even deeper self-acceptance. Furthermore, in her article, Bradshaw presents a detailed, eloquent, and scholarly rebuttal of James Masterson's racist analysis of Japanese culture (Masterson, 1985). His ethnocentric, western interpretation disparages and trivializes an ancient cohesive culture and, in the name of psychology, further damages the self-esteem of those of us whose identities have already suffered from the negative blows of racism in our personal lives.

Finally, the connection Bradshaw makes between *amae* psychology and feminist theory and therapy addresses some of my recent thoughts about traditional psychological ideas and attitudes toward the issue of separation. Just as I found my initial encounter with Doi and *amae* psychology interesting but difficult to apply to myself, so was my initial encounter, years ago, with feminist therapy. Because of this, my pursuit of feminist theory and therapy was inconsistent and usually made me feel that I was neglecting putting time and energy into understanding and developing therapy and theory as it pertained to ethnic/racial minority clients. Now, however, as I review some of the writings of the Stone Center women and reread their thoughts and ideas about the self-in-relation and "women's growth in connection" with one another, I have a new way of relating to their discussions on the issue of separation.[2] In fact, some of their language and theory sound to me very much like another language for *amae* psychology! Their feminist psychology is challenging the value of separation as we understand it in the context of mainstream, white-male, western psychological theory. These feminists are even going beyond the challenge and are reinterpreting some basic female behavior in a positive and theoretically sound way, just as *amae,* when named and understood in context, is not pathological behavior.

In my attempt over the years to develop understanding about cross-cultural/multicultural psychology, I have been learning about the group as the important component of many ethnic minority cultures. In some cultures, one's primary allegiance is to a larger group, whether family, extended family, or community, and primary aspects of one's identity are drawn from this relationship to the group.[3] In other words, members of the group do not find it unusual to see themselves as being interdependent beings within the group. They come to rely on their interdependency for healthy functioning. This also gives them a sense of safety and support. This reliance on interdependency among group members is quite different from, if not opposed to, the western idea that one's goal, above all else, is to become an individual who is independent and self-reliant in the world at large.

For me, this is one crucial juncture where some theories of feminist psychology and some theories of multicultural psychology join together, as both are essentially challenging traditional psychology's view of separation and individuation.

In conclusion, I can say that it is with renewed interest and a feeling of pleasure that I can now see ways of approaching feminist psychology that are not inimical to multicultural and cross-cultural psychology. That the two have much in common is no longer just an abstract idea. It is a personal experience of both which expands my truth and gives me some concrete ways of considering an integrated theoretical framework.

## NOTES

1. Perhaps the authors would not care to have their creative works reduced to the subject of biculturalism, yet this was a personally rewarding, if not all-inclusive, perspective for me to take as I read *How The García Girls Lost Their Accents*, by Julia Alvarez, *The Satanic Verses*, by Salman Rushdie, and *Jasmine*, by Bharati Mukherjee.

2. Jordan, Kaplan, Miller, Stiver, and Surrey (all at the Stone Center at Wellesley College) have recently published *Women's Growth in Connection*, a book covering ten years of evolving ideas and writings about the psychology of women. It speaks clearly of the evolution of ideas about separation and individuation from a female perspective as initially introduced by Jean Baker Miller in 1976.

3. The literature on cross-cultural, multicultural counseling is growing rapidly. Three books I have found helpful, about the importance of the group and interdependency among group members, are McGoldrick, Pearce, and Giordano (1982); Sue and Sue (1990); and Manuel Ramírez III (1991).

## REFERENCES

Alvarez, Julia (1991). *How the García girls lost their accents*. New York: Penguin (Plume).

Bradshaw, Carla (1990). A Japanese view of dependency: What can amae psychology contribute to feminist theory and therapy? In Laura S. Brown & Maria P. P. Root (Eds.), *Diversity and Complexity in Feminist Therapy*. New York: Harrington Park Press. Also in *Women and Therapy, 9* (1/2) and 9 (3).

Doi, Takeo (1973). *The anatomy of dependence*. Tokyo, New York and San Francisco: Kodansha International, Ltd.

Jordan, Judith et al. (1991). *Women's growth in connection*. New York: Guilford.

Masterson, James F. (1985). *The real self: A developmental, self, and object relations approach*. New York: Brunner/Mazel.

McGoldrick, Monica, Pearce, J. K., and Giordano, J. (Eds.) (1982). *Ethnicity and family therapy*. New York: Guilford.

Miller, Jean Baker (1976). *Toward a new psychology of women*. Boston: Beacon.

Mukherjee, Bharati (1989). *Jasmine*. New York: Random House (Ballantine).

Ramírez, Manuel, III (1991). *Psychotherapy and counseling with minorities*. New York: Pergamon.

Rushdie, Salman (1988). *The satanic verses*. New York: Viking.

Sue, Derald, & Sue, D. (1990 ). *Counseling the culturally different* (2nd edition). New York: John Wiley & Sons.

# Prison of Color

Virginia R. Harris

Colorism is the prejudicial or preferential treatment of same-race people based solely on their color.[1] I would add: colorism is to ascribe value and privilege to a same-race person based on lightness of color.

Clarence Thomas' stated preference for light-skinned women is colorism. A 1989 lawsuit brought against a dark-skinned supervisor because of alleged color discrimination by a light-skinned woman was colorism.[2] When my 80-year-old aunt, who dyes her hair, tells me I am too dark to wear my hair its natural gray, that is colorism (as well as ageism). Underdeveloping the pictures of dark-skinned people in my college year book so no one looked too dark was colorism.[3]

The phenomenon of ascribing worth based on color is generally attributed to African Americans, but colorism is active among all groups. In every group there are variations in color, with "value"[4] rated on the lightness of hue. Blonde and blue-eyed Aryan[5] is "preferable" to "swarthy" southern European. Traveling in China, I observed that the light Chinese were the Party members and functionaries, the dark Chinese were laborers and farmers. The Chinese assigned our group of eight American women rooms based on color. (Two dark-skinned African American women in one room, one light-skinned African American woman and a Chinese American in another, two blonde white women in a room, two brown-haired white women together, and two white women with almost black hair in the last room.) In New Mexico, the Hispanics[6] I met were adamant about not being Mexican and touted their Spanish (read white) heritage. A Filipino American friend, whose parents are Filipino, who was born in the Philippines, was told by darker Filipinos that she was "too light to be Filipino."[7] Light skin is prized. The belief that dark is evil, inherently less intelligent, and immoral is internalized.[8] People of color don't seem to recognize this as another racist divide-and-conquer tactic. By engaging in colorist behavior we collude in keeping white supremacy in place.

I have done considerable work to be aware of and rid myself of internalized racism. I am conscious of the many overt/covert/subtle ways internalized racism determined how I navigated a world bent on my destruction. I was therefore surprised at the extent and depth of the pain and hurt triggered by writing this paper. As much as racism from whites or cross-racial hostility[9] from other people of color hurts, my deepest hurt came at the hands of those who are like me—colored—Negro—Black—African American.

One night during the summer of 1991, watching television, I heard the following: "black is the glue that holds this country together."[10] My immediate reaction was, yes! A further thought: hatred of blackness will tear this country (the world?) apart. We live in and by a racial hierarchy with black at the bottom. No matter how bad things get, all non-blacks can unify around that fact, can hold still another truth to be self-evident—they ain't black. Richard Pryor, in the 1970s, did a monologue on how the Vietnamese immigrants were taught English. The first word learned? Nigger. The audience howled. I laughed, too. The truth of his statement still stares us all in the face.

My father used to say, "You can't throw mud on someone without getting your hands dirty." So, if I am glue, you are either glue or stuck to me. The best glue is invisible, flexible, does not deteriorate, has no odor, is non-toxic, and dries clear and fast. That definition aptly describes the image I tried to portray for many years, while at the same time fighting with every ounce of strength not to be held in my "place"–invisible, cohesive, and unshaken by racism (or any other form of oppression, for that matter). Racism and its legacy, colorism, made me struggle to be something I am not–white and male. I straightened my hair and tried to lighten my skin, while denying it: "I use Nadinola[11] because it's the only thing that controls these blackheads." No pun intended. It didn't work. I was still female. I was still dark.

When I was growing up, calling someone black was worse than calling them nigger. We sat on the porch steps and compared our colors. Who was the darkest? Who was "it" in a terrible game of degradation? I was "it" more times than not. I fought my sister and brother because they called me black. I generally got beaten up in those fights and then beaten again by my light-skinned mother for my loud, violent, attention-getting behavior. No matter the provocation, I had acted BLACK. The insidious irony is I am not darker than my brother and sister, I was made to THINK I was. Not only was racism outside waiting to rip me apart, the legacy of racism was active in our house. How did this come about? Why was it so important to make distinctions that don't exist?

My eyes itch from unshed tears. My parents' venom, born in their issues with color, spewed out–hidden, unspoken, violent–inside our house. I learned not to cry when I was hurt or in pain. My mother was the beat-you-until-you-cry type. I "showed" her. I could take the worst she could dish out–without crying. A victory, I thought.

A little history: My mother's father, one son of a slave and her master, blamed his mother for the circumstance of his birth. (None of his children could tell me her name.) He hated white people and dark-skinned people. He could have "passed," but never did–to my knowledge. Even though he married a dark-skinned woman, he told his children not to marry dark because black was evil and no good. All his sons complied. One daughter complied; another daughter married a dark-skinned man, divorced him, and was mistress to a white-skinned black man for over 40 years. My mother didn't comply, but when angry with my dark-skinned father, said, "I should've listened to my father."

From the time I can remember everyone was described by color, down to a half or quarter shade darker than someone else.[12] If the person was dark, the description was negative, especially if the person was female. If for some reason the woman deserved a compliment, it was followed by " . . . but, she's so dark." "Marry light and improve the race," was the unequivocal message. All the men, on both sides of the family, in my parent's generation married light-skinned women. My father's "other women" were even lighter than my mother. All my male first cousins married white women. What a difference a generation made! To this day all my mother's sisters say color was not an issue in their family!

I got the message: no good, dark, ugly, not worth black men's attention, unattractive, and not wife material. I believed it. "I'll show them" became my watch phrase. I might be dark . . . but, just you wait and see. I excelled in school. The man I married, to whom I was "superior" by virtue of class and more education, was lighter than me, had all the necessary credentials (degreed professional), and paid me minimal attention. When my sister met him she asked, "How did you ever get a man like that?" She, on the other hand, married two very dark-skinned men. "The blacker the berry . . . ," she used to say. But was she trying to be the lighter one and therefore "superior" to those men based on her color? I wonder.

Black has been the glue that kept me stuck in a prison and in being victim. I am a dark-skinned woman who internalized the negativity society teaches about darkness. My internalized racism, colorism, and sexism have shaped an existence which I can only call a prison of color. I wanted to be impenetrable, not feel the pain. So, I built walls to protect myself. They have gotten thick over the years and I am tightly bound inside a hated cell, my skin color. A posture created to "protect" myself from the excruciating pain of being black in a world where "biases . . . subscribe . . . Blackness as non-good 'Otherness.'"[13] The walls were my armor against the world where I did battle against everything, with everybody. The walls held me in place, restricted me like a girdle. Self-hatred is the tightest girdle anyone wears. I've been walled off, boxed in by my color, restricted in ways that are becoming clearer.

My prison—both protector and enslaver. Each wall familiar, like a face I remember, but can't recall the name. I pace this enclosure until I recall the names. ANGER. That's easy—smooth as glass, cold to the touch. I turn a corner. INVISIBILITY. A contradiction learned early—a wall of distorted mirrors. Another corner. INADEQUACY. A well-paved, smooth wall requiring constant maintenance to keep the image of inadequacy at bay. Another corner, another contradiction. OVER/UNDER ACHIEVING. A wall of different sizes and kinds of broken rocks set in the cement of control. The plight of a smart little black girl, simultaneously applauded and slapped. ANGER and INADEQUACY confront each other as do INVISIBILITY and OVER/UNDER ACHIEVING.

I search for solace in this place that "protected" me in the past.

But it feels so different! I thought the jagged edges, the hot acid rage were covered, hidden forever by the layers of control plastered over them. The internalized value system that states I am less than human because I am a descendant of Africa oozes out like pus from an infected cut. I've lived with the pain of being a woman, being black, being a victim, being hated, being angry, being invisible. I have survived in a world bent on my destruction. But, if I am to be free, I must know these walls and for what they stand.

ANGER–a friend–the only emotion allowed in my family. Righteous anger covering a pool of helpless, hopeless rage so close to the surface but rarely expressed. All the hurt and pain I've suppressed about how I was/am perceived and treated because of my color came screaming to the surface as I engaged with another dark-skinned woman to write this paper about colorism. I felt such rage (at her) I was unable to breathe. Rage burst to the surface because a dark-skinned woman had had a different experience with colorism than I had. I was catapulted back to my childhood where fist fights and worse were common fare.

My reaction in the present recalled an incident. Seven African American women talked about how color had affected our lives. We varied from beige to black-brown (the color we used to call "African" when we were ignorant of Africans' color variety). All seven of us had experienced the pain of being the "darkest" at one time or another. Two had experienced being the lightest, also. The black-brown woman was enraged. None of us could know and understand the kind of pain she had experienced. It was clear to me, at the time, that she needed to be the victim. I thought her rigid and closed-minded. All of us had painful experiences with colorism but she was unable to allow any of us our pain because her pain was so intense.

Six years later, I found myself acting out the same rigidity and closed-mindedness. My friend's different experience with being dark-skinned did not "validate" my pain. My pain felt even more intense in the comparison. The more we talked about our very different experiences with being dark-skinned black women, the more enraged I became. I held on to my old and new pain tenaciously, placed blame for all that pain on my friend. Not only was my hurt very deep, my need to hold on to that hurt was as deep. I needed to be the victim and I needed my friend to be responsible for my victimization. My parents and the community that hurt me when I was a child were gone, the system was too big and unyielding. If I allowed a different experience with colorism, somehow I would be erased. Not just my experience invalidated, but an erasure of SELF. Erasure slams me into the wall INVISIBILITY.

We African Americans are all colors. While racism distinguishes between us from dark to light, we still somehow become all the same. We are interchangeable in some instances, and in others not. It depends on the use the dominant culture has for us in the particular moment. Hollywood cast Sidney Poitier as Thurgood Marshall in a made-for-TV movie, erasing the white-skin privilege Marshall had traveling throughout the South in the 1940s and 1950s. "60 Minutes" did an expose about a New York employment agency's discrimination against blacks. The two African Americans who brought the suit were dark. The agency, to prove the charges false, gave a light-skinned black woman the "privilege" of recanting the charge. The abject pain on her face as she tried to rationalize a corporate memo that clearly implied, "discriminate, just don't get caught" was heartbreaking. How did she deal with that pain? Did she beat herself up, search for all the ways she failed? Did she make other black people responsible and render them invisible in order to feel she had some power? Was she able to hold it together so her bosses wouldn't know what she felt?

It is devastating when your illusionary world comes crashing down. The worst images reflected in those distorted mirrors haunt you. Feelings of INADEQUACY jump up like ghoulish Jacks-in-the-box, unexpected and terrifying. This wall's smooth surface is an illusion. INADEQUACY is wet tar that gets all over your best dress and you weren't even conscious of being near the wall. As I struggled to erase the belief that I was inadequate, I simultaneously erased pieces of mySELF. If I couldn't be a white male–the only thing that would make me adequate–I would best them at their own game–be more efficient, faster, take on more projects. I stood up to the power structure at work (all white men)–ignored my pain and hurt. I felt most adequate (powerful) when I proved white men (and later white women) wrong, using their own data and the statistical methods I'd learned in their universities, only to get stuck once again in the tar of INADEQUACY when the racism and sexism were dismissed and I was ignored. What had I done wrong? How could I make them see? Civil rights bills and Executive Orders provided some recourse for unfair treatment in the workplace. But what was the recourse in my life? I stood, feet sealed in cement, dodging feelings of inadequacy, but getting pummeled over and over again.

I built an elaborate system of musts and shoulds, none of which left me room to breathe, to BE. I stood rigidly on the "American" principles I had been taught even if white people didn't. I became the champion for causes of race and gender while denying how I was used by those in power to keep people of color and women under control. My option? Prove that the together, competent, get-things-done image was the real me.

The jagged rocks in the wall of OVER/UNDER ACHIEVING are splattered with the tar of INADEQUACY. We were taught in childhood that we had to prove we were twice as good to get ahead. Education was the key, so the more education one had . . . By the time I left graduate school, unable to find a job, I said "twice as good to get half as much." It was clear to me that getting a PhD had more to do with endurance than with ability. When I finally got a job in my field, my abilities were measured by the kind of research I did. But the kind of research I was assigned came through a white man's race/gender filter. If I completed a project quickly it was scrutinized for mistakes, accuracy double-checked. After 12 years of "research" it dawned: Just because I majored in chemistry, I didn't have to work in it for the rest of my life. "How can you give up the prestige of chemistry for personnel?" I was asked. Easy. I never felt the "prestige" chemistry was supposed to afford me. All I felt was rage at being a glorified dishwasher. They told me I couldn't switch from science to administration, so I showed them. In personnel I saw the records documenting a history of extensive racism and heard my boss argue to pay a person of color (or woman) less money. My boss asked me, "Who do you think you are? What makes you think you have the credibility to make these kinds of charges?"

Twenty years later racism is alive and well. "This is a country where racism has been the longest standing national neurosis."[14]

Without racism, colorism would not exist. I obscured my pain about colorism by fighting hard against racism. I thought if I fought hard enough, the pain would go away. It didn't. Writing this paper brought all the feelings to the surface with an intensity I never experienced in the past. The armor I'd worn against the pain no longer worked. I had no scapegoat or no object for the feelings. They were real. They were intense. They were mine.

I maintained two stances in the world. The outward one conquered obstacles, projected an "in charge" IMAGE. The inward one, a battered, dark-skinned child who believed she could do nothing to be acceptable, whose identity was her victimization. I wanted to be warm, protected, loved, and nurtured. I wanted a womb. I built a prison. I can continue to internalize the hatred I've learned from my family and the society. I can continue to turn it on myself and those like me. I can continue to envy those lighter than me, feel superior to those darker than me. I can continue to be an instrument of my destruction.

Yes, I could. But I choose to live a conscious life, making conscious choices to BE a whole person. Rejecting the value system where self-esteem and self-worth are based on being "better than," and where as an African American woman I am defined as "less than," would seem easy. But the power of the glue of hatred is greater than I ever imagined. It is a full-time, lifetime job undoing my socialization. I am learning to embrace all facets of who I am, to embrace a SELF rooted in BEing equitable in my soul, learning to nourish well-being and differentness in SELF and others.[15]

## NOTES

1. Alice Walker (1983). If the present looks like the past, what does the future look like? *In Search of Our Mother's Gardens*. New York: Harcourt Brace Jovanovich, p. 209.

2. The *New York Times*, May 23, 1989, p. 1.

3. This reality hit home 33 years after the fact when showing a friend how much color determined women's popularity and recognition in the 1950s when I was in college. All (women's and men's) our colors were washed out to a medium gray. If light-skinned, the contrast in the photograph is sharper than if dark, where there is almost no contrast.

4. I use quotations marks here and throughout the manuscript to show irony, sometimes sarcastically and, finally, to show how language has been misused to further racism and other oppression.

5. Aryan has no validity as a racial term, it designates a family of languages. Hitler and the Nazis used the word to designate the "super race." Even though Hitler and many of the leading Nazis didn't fit the model superman, it was the standard to be achieved as evidenced by the breeding experiments conducted to produce as many blond blue-eyed members of the "master race" as possible. Through my eyes, this is still the standard to be met. I use Aryan here in its Nazi context.

6. The progressive Latino community in San Francisco no longer uses Hispanic, but uses Latino instead. The State continues to use Hispanic.

7. Conversation with Noemi Sohn, 1992.

8. Merlin Stone (1981). *3000 years of racism.* New Sibylline Books. Describes racism as a process that takes place in distinct and definable stages.

9. I use the term cross-racial hostility to differentiate the behavior of people of color toward each other from the racist behavior of whites toward people of color. See, Virginia R. Harris and Trinity A. Ordona (1990). Developing Unity Among Women of Color: Crossing the Barriers of Internalized Racism and Cross-Racial Hostility. In Gloria Anzaldúa (Ed.), *Making face, making soul haciendo caras.* Aunt Lute Foundation Books, San Francisco, p. 304.

10. I spent weeks trying to track down the exact quote. I got the transcript and a video tape of the program; neither one has the statement on it. Since I am one of five people I know who watched the program and afterwards with whom I had discussions about the statement, I am sure it was not my imagination. What happened to the statement? One more in the series of distortions, misrepresentations, and censorship.

11. A bleaching cream, popular in the 1950s and still advertised in *Ebony* magazine.

12. Often, even now, when another African American woman, who is the same color as I am, describes another African American woman to me she generally says "darker than you," or "lighter than me," never the other way around.

13. Joyce Elaine King and Thomasyne Lightfoote Wilson (1990). Being the soul-freeing substance: A legacy of hope in Afro humanity. *Journal of Education,* *172*(2), p. 11.

14. Eleanor Holmes Norton (1992, January/February). . . . And the Language Is Race. *Ms.*, *II*(4), p. 43.

15. King and Wilson, ibid., p. 9.

# Raising White Children
# in a Racist Society

Jeanne Adleman
with contributions from Donald, Martha, and Joan Mahoney,
and Judith Mahoney Pasternak

Any perception that racism hurts only people of color is false. People of color are most dangerously impacted, and white people accrue both known and unrecognized benefits from the system of racism. But we who are white are also damaged by being led to believe we are better than others when we are not; by being kept ignorant of all but the white histories sanitized, distorted, and taught in our schools; by being encouraged to live in fear of those oppressed in a system of white dominance; even by our being set up as targets of the fury of the dispossessed, or of those who react to whites as for centuries whites have to them. And we who are white women are damaged because all such factors keep us apart from women with whom powerful alliances might otherwise be built and prevail to our mutual benefit. Division and estrangement between whites and Americans of color support a system that oppresses the majority of both, for the benefit of relatively few.

An important element in American life, especially from about 1934-39, was the major struggle to unionize American industrial workers. Racial issues arose in force, however, when large numbers of underpaid southern black workers were recruited and imported to northern states without knowing they were being hired as strike-

---

This essay is dedicated to the women of the National Negro Congress (especially, but not exclusively, Thelma Dale and Ruth Jett) who propelled the organization forward during World War II and who, as I worked under their leadership in those years, educated me about racism in ways that have stayed with me for almost 50 years.

breakers, "scabs." Unions were slow to learn the need for racial equality, instead confusing scab hatred and racial hatred.[1]

As an adult, I saw myself as part of a movement for a better world. In the shifting alliances during and after World War II, it seemed clear to me that Nazism had been Germany's and later Europe's evil, and that racism was ours in the United States.

In 1947 I married, and became stepmother to Judith, then seven years old, and Joan, then four. I gave birth to Martha in 1948, Donald in 1950.

## WHAT WERE WE TRYING TO DO, AND WHY, AND HOW?

As one of two parents of my biological children, and one of four parents of Joan and Judith, I shared with the three other adults an intention to encourage in the children strong values of social justice, of the worth and equality of all people. We were all four, for a time and to varying degrees, part of what is currently known as the Old Left. We wanted the children to have good lives, lived not at the expense of others. I was an idealist despite a rather strong practical core.[2] Gradually relinquishing the hope of seeing a better world in my lifetime, I continued to hope the children would grow up to help bring it about in theirs. I believed that a combination of education and collective organizing would eventually bring it about.

We wanted the children to feel loved; to respect themselves, each other, and other people; to abhor violence and war. I particularly wanted them to be able to transcend traditional girl/boy role limitations and to question authority; to have opportunities to experience differences among people and to know that we, at least, valued the differences. I also wanted them to know there were many ways to earn one's living that are equally deserving of respect.[3]

When Donald was six months and Martha two years old, I landed a part-time job that required finding in-home childcare to cover the hours between my leaving for work and my husband's return from his. A pleasant young black woman answered my advertisement. Having been well-schooled during my years at the National Negro Congress about the politics of domestic work, I struggled to find an ethical resolution of my discomfort at being a white employer of a black woman. When she mentioned that her son was the same age as my daughter and that her mother would take care of him, I made plain he was welcome to come with her if she wished, and she did. I dealt with the wage inequality by setting her hourly rate at exactly half of mine, so that we ended up with the same income per hour.

Martha was about three years old when my friend Edward E. Strong died.[4] The great Paul Robeson would be singing as part of the funeral service and I took her with me. People at the service overflowed the church and onto the street. Many of my old friends were there, of course, and I felt very much at home in the shared sadness. When Robeson came out of the church to sing again for those of us in the street, I was glad that Martha was with me and could hear, in this special context, one of the great voices of the century.

In somewhat later years the children listened endlessly to a record of Robeson singing *The Ballad for Americans*. Among the lines sung by Robeson on that record were some excerpted from Lincoln's speeches; "Man in a white skin can never be free while his black brother is in slavery, and we hereby highly resolve that these dead shall not have died in vain, that government of the people, by the people and for the people shall not perish from the earth!"[5]

In September, 1954, Donald was officially two weeks too young to enter public kindergarten. By now I was working full time. I called every private kindergarten in the yellow pages until I found one with transportation service available. It was not far from where we lived, but it was another world: it was all black.

These were the years when we might watch, on television, young Negro children who, to get to school, had to walk a gauntlet of white people filled with hate who spat on and threw stones at the children. The children's heroism was inspiring, and also terrifying to me as a mother. I knew very well that a white child would have greater protection, but how would he feel as an "only"?

I visited the kindergarten and talked with its proprietor. I asked what her reservations might be. Never before had white parents applied to her, but talking with her reassured me. Nevertheless I watched Donald for signs of difficulty, or reluctance to go to school. If that had happened I would have felt obligated to leave my job. (I did not have a *career*, I had a relatively good job as a secretary.) But he spent the school year at that kindergarten with fewer incidents or problems than he had had at his previous (all-white) nursery school.

Some summers we were all six together on short family vacations. Other times Judith and Joan spent summers with their mother and stepfather or at camps of their choosing. In 1958 Martha and Donald had their first summer at Apple Hill Camp in New Hampshire, a private camp with a truly integrated counselor staff and a great racial mix of children. They returned there each summer for several years.

Interacting with the children's minds as they grew, I was excited by the ways they learned and by my own potential for teaching them critical thinking and doing it creatively. Since I had not become a heroine of any revolution, I would settle instead for being an unsung everyday kind of worker in the field of knowledge for social betterment. In 1956, I returned to college to become an elementary-school teacher.

## *WHAT HAS EVOLVED?*

At this writing Judith, a long-time activist and journalist in the lesbian-feminist movement, is primarily active in the tenants' movement and the broad Left. Donald, who does not like working under or over anyone else, is the owner-worker of Studio Woodworks. Joan and Martha are both professors at different Law Schools.

In preparation for this essay I wrote to each of them asking what they remembered, what had mattered to them in childhood, how racial issues are or are not present in their lives today, and what about their children now? Their responses follow.

### *Donald Mahoney (born 1950)*

I don't remember specific incidents. I knew we were always taught the equality of all people, that different colors and cultures were neither inferior nor superior, that all had beauty of their own, and that the differences were definitely all right. What I most remember about living in Brooklyn is from when I was seven to about twelve, and it is the difference between the Jewish and the Italian kids. I had friends among both, and with my Irish last name I trod the line between. I never felt I fit in anywhere.

Apple Hill Camp is my first real memory of being among numerous kids of several different racial groups. I remember them as being different in customs or cultures but not different as kids. I think my first crush was probably on Satya Singh.

When we moved to Manhattan the school zoning put me in Booker T. Washington Junior High. It was just about three blocks from our apartment, but when I walked in there it seemed to be an ocean of black and brown faces, and I could tell that we white kids would be in the minority. I figured it would be a tough school, but Brooklyn had been tough in its own ways too. I had watched people get beaten up in Brooklyn at times, and it would happen in Manhattan as well.

The kids I made friends with were black and Puertorican. I used to hang around school after hours playing handball. Kids who played handball were pretty mixed; basketball was mostly but not only black kids.

When my mother and father separated and I went away to Stockbridge to finish high school, the kids I first made friends with were the black and Puertorican kids there, but it didn't take long before I developed white friends too. I was one of the most generally social people at Stockbridge. I had no color lines so had more friends than many other students, because I never kept anyone out. My very first real relationship, around 1965-67, was with Cheryl who is black.

As an adult looking back, I can say that race has not guided conscious decisions of mine. I never lived or didn't live anywhere because of it. I have also *not* excluded from my life people who are racist provided I saw other values in them, even though I have never approved of racism. I also think that if nonracist people associate only with other nonracist people, we would live in isolated pools of thought, and where would people learn different behaviors and attitudes? However if someone were racist and avaricious and generally hateful, that would be different.

Today I am living in a small city, mostly white. There are not many places to work here. The college and the Job Corps may be the major employers, and when I worked for the Job Corps there were more black people on that staff than anywhere else in town.

How do I help my children deal with racial issues? Basically, I don't. I try to facilitate their education. I'm not trying to teach them to believe what I believe; I encourage them to draw their own conclusions. Samantha's early years with her mother, before I came into their lives, were spent on the South Side of Syracuse, in a black neighborhood. If anything she knew more black than white people. Rudie is still pretty young. Where she goes to day care there have been black people working occasionally but not many black children.

[I had "interviewed" Donald by phone after he had read my request letter, taking notes in the shorthand I learned as a secretary and have never forgotten. In the course of his responses, I asked him about his year in the otherwise all-black kindergarten. "I don't remember that," he answered. Even prompted by my reminder, he does not remember it. I find this very surprising. I would have expected him to remember it. Did it seem to him at the time so unexceptional, or natural, that it was not worth remembering? Quite possibly.]

### Martha Mahoney (born 1948)

What I remember and consider that you modeled for us children was your emphatic insistence on the dignity of people. You told me that we called the housekeeper "Mrs." because it was a sign of respect, and that part of the oppression of domestic workers was being called by their first names. I think you felt closer to your black women friends than you would have appeared to us–yet somehow, in your discussions of important people in your life, they appeared as such powerful, interesting, intelligent, attractive figures that there was a cumulative positive effect.

My summers at Apple Hill Camp combine into a kind of golden experience. It was racially integrated and culturally mixed, with some counselors and campers from other countries.

The books I read influenced me a lot. Besides the books bought specifically for us kids and those I would find in the public library, I was never forbidden to read any of the adult books we had in the house. I remember several on black history. I was twelve when I

read *The Passion of Sacco and Vanzetti*, by Howard Fast. I was sure
that at the end they would be fine but they were killed, and I
couldn't stop crying. My father said, "What happened was horrible!" *My reactions were validated.* I also read Fischer's biography
of Gandhi. These and other books helped shape my life.

For me it was all connected: working for civil rights, for human
rights, and against the Viet Nam war when that began.

I wanted to go to Mississippi in 1964 for Freedom Summer but
you said I was too young. I remember turning on the news during
my sixteenth birthday party to see if Andy Goodman had been
found yet, because some of my friends knew him.[6] I was glad my
life was not in danger but I felt as if I was missing something
important, vital. Later, when Martin Luther King, Jr. was killed in
1968, I remember the feeling of being unable to change things as
the war and assassinations and riots went on.

When Amanda was an infant, my husband was on strike and I
was the only one working. Amanda was in the only child care I
could afford, one of eight children (the only white child) with a
babysitter. Later, I didn't want to have my children in all-white
schools, but it wasn't always easy. After my marriage ended and I
was at Tulane University, both Amanda and Jeffrey were at Tulane's Child Care Center, which was somewhat integrated at first
but became whiter over time. They went to a public magnet school
in New Orleans created and maintained to include equal numbers of
black and white students. We lived for eight years in student family
housing at Tulane and Stanford with graduate student families from
around the world–an environment of lots of privilege, little cash,
and lots of cultural diversity.

Since starting graduate school I've written, taught, and published
on race and class, on white privilege and feminist theory.

In Miami, Jeff's elementary school mixed wealthier white kids
and less-wealthy black kids, resegregated through gifted and advanced placement classes. Once, on the same day, a white kid called
him a Jew and a black kid called him a white motherfucker.

Their middle school is almost equally black, Hispanic, and white.
Amanda's closest friends are a Jewish girl, a Bahaman girl, and a
Cuban boy. She feels confident that she "doesn't make decisions
about people based on race." She seems comfortable when (as on a

recent field trip) she is the only white in an environment. But I often feel it is hard to help my children with racial issues. Amanda wouldn't see the movie, *Malcolm X* because she had been hurt and was angry at having been called "white devil" by kids in school when it came out, but now she says she will see it when it comes out on videotape. Black anger seems difficult or impossible for white kids to confront.

For myself, I'm never remotely sure I'm doing anything right with Amanda and Jeff–about race, education, love, anything else. I'm probably teaching them lots of things I have no idea of. And I wonder what they will make of it all themselves. I realize as I write that I'm reflecting my own strongly held belief that many points of formative interaction, occurring at different developmental moments in life, shape our concepts of race.

### Joan Mahoney (born 1943)

I remember very few incidents or experiences from my childhood in which race was particularly important. One of the advantages of being white is being able to not think about race. I remember books, even for young children, with pictures of children of different races. I remember books about black history being around the house and I remember social events in which African American adults were part of the group. I don't remember having black friends myself.

As an adolescent I became active in the civil rights movement, an involvement that has continued into adulthood. When I was 16, a group of my school friends and I went to Washington on a Youth March for Integration. We also formed a Student SANE chapter at school, marching against bomb testing and for nuclear disarmament. To me it was all connected; the Cold War, and spending on the military, was part of the political/economic system that discriminated against blacks.

In college I had a mixed group of friends, all of us very political. I remember long discussions about black separatism, integration, etc. After college, I was part of a group who went to Montgomery, Alabama, for the final day of the march to Selma. I am convinced that my political activity in those years was very much related to my childhood, and to the various influences of my parents' politics, having to do with race but also a great deal more.

The most important choice involving race that I have made in my life was the decision made a while after Monte and I married, to adopt Rachel. I understand the opposition of many people of color to transracial adoption but I also think the most important thing a baby needs is a permanent home. Also, Monte has spent most of his adult life so far working in a largely black environment, and one of his former African American colleagues is Rachel's godmother.

Having an African American child has changed us. My sons, now young adults, feel the difference as well, even though no longer living at home. We are not a white family anymore. We are a mixed family, and we have to be aware of race in every decision we make about where to live, where Rachel will go to school, even where to travel. I'd like to take a trip sometime soon to a country like Jamaica, so Rachel can experience what it is like to be in the majority, in a place where blacks direct traffic, teach school, and generally run things. We are also planning a trip to Africa when Rachel is 10 or 11 years old.

Last year Monte and I discovered a group in Kansas City called The Multiracial Family Circle, which consists of mixed families, most mixed through marriage but others through adoptions. Discussions in the group about how to be a multiracial family in a racist world have been very helpful.

My social relationships with blacks have changed too. There are several black women students at my school who have children. We spend a lot of time talking about the best places to live in the area, about schools, and we spend a *lot* of time talking about hair and skin care.

Strangers react differently to us. African Americans are more likely to smile or chat when we are with Rachel. With some whites, the reaction depends on whether my husband is along or I am alone with Rachel. If the former, their look takes in the three of us and they presume she is adopted. If we are alone together, she and I, then we receive what I think of as "The Look"–a glance at me, a glance at her, then back to me with a hostility that seems to say, "You've been with a black man."

I have recently written a paper that discusses legal and other implications of transracial adoption, and elaborates on the many meanings of not being a white family any more.[7]

### Judith Mahoney Pasternak (born 1939)

Growing up in all-white communities, I didn't have much contact with African Americans in my childhood except as domestic workers and, occasionally, friends of my parents. I do remember Brownie McGhee playing guitar at my father's fortieth birthday party. I have a sense that I knew, early on, that racism existed, though I don't think I used that word for it, and that it was wrong. By the 1960s I was marching for civil rights, and I especially remember being in the March on Washington in 1963.

When my husband and I decided in 1970 that we wanted to live with the kids in a house, not an apartment, we bought a house in Laurelton, Queens, one of the few neighborhoods in all of New York City that was specifically integrated. But by 1976 there were no more white families on the block. My older son, years later, referred back to his seventh-grade class as having been 90% black. I suggested that we take out his yearbook and count. The class had been 50% black. It was that conversation that taught me the importance of actually counting how many in any group are people of color, or women, or lesbians (instead of relying on an intuitive perception, which all too often exaggerates–as my son's did).

In my early years in the women's movement, racism was on my mind though perhaps not uppermost. But in my current political activity I am often the one at any meeting who says something like, "That panel is all white–shouldn't we rethink who should be speaking?"

How I deal with my own kids on this issue now that they are adults is, I hit them over the head with it every thirty seconds. They roll their eyes and say, "Don't you ever see anything that doesn't have race in it?" But I remember how, when they were small, I dragged them every summer to Shakespeare plays in Central Park, and they would ask, "When is it going to be over?" Now they go on their own. My goal essentially is consciousness of racism as an issue. My kids are definitely conscious, though none is actively political. What helps is that we *talk* about everything.

My own consciousness evolved through growing up in a left-wing family, where what we now call racism was bad and socialism was good.

## CONCLUDING THOUGHTS

I am filled with appreciation for who these four people are today, who they have become, alike and different as they are. I am grateful that so much of what has been important to me is important to them, each in her or his own way.

When Judith mentions that she doesn't think we used the word *racism* in our family during her growing years, I suspect she is right, but I am unable to remember at what point it entered our shared vocabulary. I think there would have been levels of terms: from prejudice (reflecting ignorance), to bias (reflecting ill-will), to discrimination (ill-will in action), to *race hatred*, responsible for the very worst actions by whites such as hounding children on their way to school, or persecutions under law, or lynching, or the casual murders of blacks by whites, on the streets—especially but not exclusively in the South, and even more often then than now, by police officers.

I am concerned that the necessary compression of so many years has resulted in my being less than completely honest, or in my obscuring the complexities of an attempt to live a worthy life. There is no simple input-outgrowth process. It is surely possible that each of these growing individuals might have paved their own roads and arrived at who they are today even if their parents had been reactionary and bigoted; other people have.

Agreeing with Martha's comments in her final paragraph, I too conclude that it is less the details of what is taught by parents that children hold in memory or that influence them, than it is the matrix in which the teaching is embedded. What we teach and what we communicate may not be the same but teaching what we value is still important. What one teaches and another learns may well be different but are not necessarily opposite.

Ultimately this essay is a review of the attempt by four people to rear offspring according to our values while yet encouraging their independence, and of my attempts to keep racism, by whatever name, in the foreground of their awareness. Whether because of or independent of our/my efforts, things have come out rather well. Even unsuccessful struggles against injustice are better than no efforts at all. Though no one success does the whole job, every success is nevertheless important.

## NOTES

1. Fifty years later these economics are being repeated as impoverished and exploited countries compete with each other enticing U.S. manufacturers to open factories where poverty forces people to work for pennies, and under terrible conditions.

2. That is, I went about the daily business of my life–school, or work, or mothering, or any two or three of those–while still entertaining fantasies of becoming a revolutionary heroine like Elizabeth Gurley Flynn or Dolores Ibarruri ("La Pasionaria" of Spain's fight for its popular front government).

3. With hindsight I can see that I failed to include, explicitly or implicitly, *un*paid housework or child care as deserving of respect–unless their father was the one, from time to time, performing those tasks. Not to worry: he was the one whose authority was never questioned, the one whose role had built-in respect.

4. Ed Strong had been the Executive Secretary of the National Negro Congress prior to enlisting in the Army in 1944 even though he had been exempted from the draft because of a physical problem. He was the person who had hired me as office manager; after he left, Thelma Dale became Acting Executive Director, and I was the person who put out the organization's monthly newsletter.

5. Music by black artists (among others) was a significant part of our home life; sometimes we didn't have television, but we always had a record player.

6. Andrew Goodman was one of the three Civil Rights workers–James Chaney and Michael Schwerner were the other two–who were killed in Mississippi in the summer of 1964.

7. Joan Mahoney, The Black Baby Doll: Transracial adoption and cultural preservation, *U. Missouri Kansas City Law Review*, Spring 1991 *59*, 3, pp. 487-501.

# Born Chinese and a Woman
# in America

Nancy Wang

Western dragons slay their terrified victims with fire and sharpened claws. Eastern dragons symbolize wisdom, good luck, and fortune. What looks the same is not necessarily the same.

This chapter is addressed to all Americans. It is about the conflict and confusion that can dwell within the Chinese American woman and that can surround her in her Anglo-American environment. It is about the subtle and not-so-subtle racism that faces her because she is sometimes assumed to be a foreigner and at other times assumed to be "more American than my white friends." It is about the racism that seems to be inherent in a country that assumes itself to be monocultural, demands that it be monocultural, when in truth it has always been multicultural. The demand in turn is made unequivocally that every person of color be of that monoculture, be "white," yet it is shadowed with the statement that they can never be "white."

The results of this unresolvable dilemma have devastated many Chinese American women. Self-denial and self-hate become a way to solve the problem, placing a heavy toll upon our ability to live our lives with our own cultural integrity, that of being both Chinese and American. We are not only misunderstood by others but, worse, we often misunderstand ourselves. I call this *double bind racism*, an agreement between others and the self to commit racist attitudes and behaviors against ourselves, binding us in our own cycle of self-hatred. In an attempt to alleviate our pain, we look to Anglo-American paradigms to understand and resolve our turmoil, only to perpetuate this pain of double bind racism. In this state, our own well-being and the society to which we are contributing are both cheated. It is essential that both our Chinese culture and our American culture are understood in our particular upbringings. Each of us has a weave of cultural traits peculiar to our own experience and it is from that weave that we will be better equipped to heal the pain of racism's impact.

## CHINESE CULTURAL VALUES

Chinese culture is very distinct. Its Confucian influence, Taoist, and Buddhist philosophies have made our way of life a very particular intertwining. In some ways, it is easy to live within Chinese culture because of its clear rules and expectations, but this clear structure also binds each individual tightly within a very narrow path.

The collective is the one value that dictates the rest. It says that the group is more important than the individual. First comes the family, then the clan, then the village, and then the country. The individual does not have any importance except as a contributing member of each collective. If she excels, it is not for herself, but for her group. She must maintain self-reliance, but not independence, and an interdependency within her group, if not a dependency. Business is never a private enterprise, but a family endeavor. This is very different from America's *independent rugged individualism, competition*, and *do your own thing*. Let's look at how this one culture value, "collective," impacts the individual now residing outside the original culture, and within one that does not recognize this first culture as valid or comprehensible. I will be speaking in the extreme in order to make clear the psychological conflict experienced within.

## THE COLLECTIVE AND NON-DIRECT ACKNOWLEDGMENT

In working with Chinese Americans in therapy, one common denominator seems to be an overriding sense of "not being good enough" and "therefore, I am not loved," because approval is usually the Chinese culture's expression of love. While many Anglo-American neighbors praise their children, and TV children are praised by their parents, verbal reinforcement for, or acknowledgment of, something positive is not usually a part of Chinese culture. One neither compliments nor acknowledges a positive trait, deed, or accomplishment. This would disrupt the collective by singling out the individual. From another point of view, it is said that the ancestral spirits wish to whisk away all good children to themselves; thus, parents must deny their goodness out loud in order to keep their good children with them here on Earth. Whatever the original source, today's Chinese American children experience the lack of acknowledgment and the out-loud denial of their goodness as real criticism and rejection. Even as adults at age 35, we are compared unfavorably to cousins, neighbors, etc. If a desired behavior or task is realized, there is no direct acknowledgment of a job well-done; it has now become the expected behavior. We are unable to understand such ritualized communication, because our point of reference is not Chinese, but Anglo-American: teachers and parents praise children, whereas "at home, I'm not praised." The interpretation becomes "I am not good enough no matter how hard I try." This apparent lack of approval becomes "I am not loved." If, however, Chinese Americans were in touch with this cultural mandate, the parents' non-direct expression of sacrificing for their children, and their approval and bragging to a third party just out of earshot, would be understood as love and appreciation. Loving facial expressions, though not as magnified as those of Anglo-Americans, and physical affection, even if not as demonstrative as those of Anglo-Americans, do communicate love. But that love may go unrecognized if we seek only an idealized Anglo-American mode of expression as *the* expression for love and approval.

Now imagine entering the Anglo-American world with this "not good enough" belief, and with the underlying need for approval that Chinese Americans bring to the workplace, to social circles. What do Anglo-American bosses and co-workers, the Anglo-American friends, do with our need for approval, with our unending attempts to try harder, do better? What does this do to us?

## *INCLUSIVENESS AND PLEASING AS COMPONENTS OF COLLECTIVE*

Growing pains are difficult for anyone. Coming of age, moving from youthful naivete into a womanly wisdom, is a process that almost all women eventually go through. However, growth in self-realization and self-determination becomes complicated for Chinese American women. With our strong Chinese cultural mandate to "belong," to be "inclusive," and to "please," finding our maturation becomes difficult with the dominant society providing us only marginal acceptance. Instead of experiencing the satisfaction of inclusiveness, our genuine desire to please may become a distorted and desperate need to please in order to belong. Will we make personal choices for ourselves or will we remain the child whose behavior is caught up in seeking inclusiveness? Or will we simply withdraw?

If we do fight to belong, the realities of racism will take a toll on our sense of womanhood as we struggle to do what we think is required of us by others, with the unspoken hope that we will be accepted. We strive constantly to please: *do more, do bigger, do better* than what our white sisters need to do to be included. As we consistently bump up against non-acceptance in this racist atmosphere, we will blame our failures on ourselves. Neither black nor white, we think in our invisibility that perhaps we can and must become more white. In our failure to be acknowledged as white, our shame and our need for inclusiveness will push us to try even harder to be a white woman. But if we are acknowledged as "white," it also serves to invalidate our Chinese cultural heritage. It invalidates who we also are.

Chinese American women often grow up not feeling as if they've really grown up. Our seeming inability to please and be included makes us feel like a reprimanded little girl. The average Chinese American woman's short physical stature does not help, either: we cannot fit into "women's" clothing, our legs hang from our chair never touching the floor, we must look up to everyone as we speak to them. We are the only ethnic group to be legally "excluded" by America's immigration laws from 1882 to as recently as 1965, with those already in the country not allowed to become naturalized citizens.[1] There seems to be an inherent attitude by both the Chinese American community and the dominant culture, that Chinese Americans are "outsiders." Within the psyche, this is a struggle that we deal with ongoingly.

## THE COLLECTIVE AND SHAME, DISAPPROVAL, AND ENDURANCE

Shame and disapproval are instituted, intrapsychic mechanisms used in the Chinese culture. When living solely in the Chinese culture, shame, as a shared community value, is held in perspective as a means of socialization. Maintaining the rules of respecting each other publicly, of protecting each other's face, of clarifying acceptable and expected behavior, becomes a task in partnership. If we behave well, we and our family are accepted. We are an important thread in the fabric of the village or the clan, to the collective. We will be a contributor rather than a disrupter. We will be allowed to take care of the family in peace and dignity, and be assisted if assistance is needed. Shame intends to limit our behavioral choices. In that sense, it assists the individual in her life circumstances. But, if we have been shamed and are unable to resolve the problematic behavior, public shaming, as well as self-judgment and self-condemnation, make living with oneself and the community a difficult process indeed.

With shame as a background for discipline, it is almost a matter of life and death what other people think of us. We must at all times live our lives as if someone were watching and judging us on the merits of our behavior. We are trained to be hypersensitive to the verbal and non-verbal viewpoints of others; continuously hypervigilant, we watch for cues to determine our actions. Not only is the collective more important than the individual, but what we exemplify reflects upon the entire family and line of Ancestors. If we do not behave according to Chinese rules of behavior, there will be disapproving talk and the entire family will suffer. The individual's shame is the family's shame; in America, it becomes the community's shame, the entire culture's shame. In a sense there is no "individual" shame, although it is experienced very personally. Rather, each individual carries the shame for the entire line of Ancestors, family, and community and we carry the added burden of having the entire community victimized by our shameful behavior; at the same time, that very community holds judgment against that behavior.

To the average Anglo-American, the Chinese American woman's hypervigilance and hypersensitivity to others may seem passive, indecisive, and lacking in fortitude. Our attitude is "wait and see" rather than a swift and firm approach. In a western environment, our seemingly weakened position of hesitation may be easily manipulated and taken advantage of, leaving us confused, feeling stupid and ashamed. Yet, we endure, for endurance has made possible the survival of the family for thousands of years through famine, depression, and other life-threatening circumstances. Thus, we attempt to read the external cues more correctly each time. Unfortunately, doing so prevents us from seeing the interactive mechanism of our Chinese value within the Anglo-American context, leaving us ignorant, as there is no need to be ashamed. We do not know that there are other ways to correct the situation in which we find ourselves. Self-denial and self-hate become a rooted reality in our experience of self, causing negative impact upon issues of success in every area of our lives.

The pressure to perform is great. Living in Anglo-America, we may in fact experience shame just for being not good enough, for not being white. The infamous "glass ceiling" in the work world keeps us striving and perfecting our performance, yet without the successful results of our white peers. Still, we must endure and continue to perform to win our place and our family's place in the community, and in our world of expectations.


## OBEDIENCE TO THE COLLECTIVE

Chinese culture stresses obedience to authority. One is expected to obey authority, even if one disagrees with the issue or the person in authority, because to do otherwise is to bring shame not only upon the persons involved, but to the extended families as well. To disagree, at least publicly, is not acceptable behavior. It is losing face both for the authority figure and for the persons disagreeing.

Wrath descends, as we saw in China's Tianamen Square tragedy in 1989.

The authority figure in Chinese culture is anyone older than oneself, such as elders and even ancestors. Authority is also assigned to an entity seen as larger and more powerful than one's own, such as America's dominant Anglo culture, which holds great authority not only in America, but the world over. So to give America's dominant culture this respect and obedience is also to accept the way in which the dominant culture perceives my value or lack of it. As a woman, too, I cannot be more than a second-class citizen, and in traditional Chinese families, daughters are considered far less valuable than sons. To act in accordance with Chinese tradition's expectations regarding obedience, I am to accept, to yield to the treatment rendered me. As a less-worthy family member, a less worthy citizen, it means yielding to an onslaught of behaviors and attitudes that attack my self-esteem, my assertiveness, my ability to act positively on my own behalf. If I can know consciously that I am acting, it is crippling enough. But I might still find the fortitude to quietly build a successful life going through the back door. However, if I accept these points of view as truth, not being good enough burns deeply, affecting everything I do and feel. I am left diminished in spirit.

Thus to be less valued by my family, my country, and even less valued than the white woman, who is already a second-class citizen herself, the message becomes loud and clear that not only are we not good enough, but we can never be good enough. It is written everywhere. Where do I look for equality, for validation? If I receive it, would I recognize or believe it? This, then, is what we carry with us as we fight to build a life for ourselves.

## FATALISM AND THE COLLECTIVE MANDATE

Chinese are taught to avoid public conflict whenever possible. The wait-and-see attitude is demanded in response to difficulty. One is to work out problems quietly, accept consequences quietly as well, and continue to persist in one's life despite trouble or pain. This is obviously different from, and contrary to, what is seen as a "Western" mode: assertion, aggressiveness, intervention, any of which would disobey the collective mandate, bringing attention to the individual, shame to the other party, and mean not enduring the difficulty. The result for many Chinese Americans is that we are seen as both passively accepting and highly tolerant of high-stress situations. In the workplace, this translates to overworking or over-extending oneself and one's responsibilities. It becomes an expected behavior of Chinese Americans by most employers. Working overtime without taking lunch breaks for months is common. Couple this with women's childrearing responsibilities, and it is a time of tremendous, unrelenting stress. Chinese children are usually made to take on responsibilities unequaled by their white American peers. But there seems no alternative. Everyone must work for the whole, and all of us must endure; that is noble and that is just the way it is. Being high-task in approach to life, and obedient to the mandates of our roles, we persevere fatalistically, as daughters, as mothers, as wives, as workers.

It is not surprising that suicide among middle-aged and elderly Chinese women is the highest in this country. (See Table 1.)

From 1971-1980, suicide for Chinese Americans between ages 15-24 tripled.[2] We can only speculate on the possible motivations behind such high suicides for Chinese females. Perhaps suicide may seem the only viable alternative to a troubling predicament for some women whose developing identities in their youth have clashed with the values of their family and yet cannot meet the demands of the majority culture; or whose roles in their older years have now diminished, and who are caught between traditional Chinese cultural values and the contrasting American sociological styles that their children have adopted. Such a woman has nothing yet, or she has nothing or no one left to whom she is accountable or loyal to keep her at task, keep her alive. She fatalistically appraises her life. This is it. There is nothing that can be done.

## THERAPY:
### AN ALTERNATIVE TO SUICIDE

When might a Chinese American woman enter therapy? When the pain is past her remarkably high tolerance level, when at the edge of sanity, and/or when the crisis is well into traumatic shock;

TABLE 1. Female suicides per 100,000 population.

|  | Chinese | White |
| --- | --- | --- |
| Ages 43-54 | 13.89 | 11.18 |
| Ages 55-64 | 15.52 | 9.59 |
| Ages 65-74 | 22.61 | 7.45 |
| Ages 75-84 | 44.32 | 6.03 |
| Ages 85+ | 49.93 | 4.92 |

even then, she is likely to take this step only at the request of someone in authority, someone outside her family and community.

Her Asian culture, sometimes unbeknownst to her "Americanized" self-portrait, has caused her to value stoicism, not to make waves, to persist no matter what, and to value "saving face," shaming no one, particularly self and family. With the need to be acceptable in the eyes of both her own community and the Anglo-American community, she demands even more perfection from herself and must not reveal the depth of her emotional problem or feelings of loss of control. This demands a kind of self-perpetuating isolation in regard to her pain, a need to minimize and deny it. She overcompensates in every area of her life, until she can no longer hold it together. Often the severity of her emotional pain is neither consciously known nor identifiable to her. Therapy is the final expression of failure. She takes this step only when she sees life falling apart.

Under these conditions, Crisis Therapy is the initial phase. The therapist needs to immediately deal with the very concrete issues, helping her to mend and pick up the pieces, and to minimize the shame by validating her courageous decision to enter therapy. If the stoic mechanism is not respected, if the therapist feels a premature wish to peel away the layers to induce affect that is seen in other cultures, she should resist that wish or much harm may be done, and may even cause the client to terminate therapy. A display of affect is considered improper, if not shameful. It is seen as an imposition on another as well as calling attention to oneself. It is not being stoic.

When trust is in place, the affect comes; sometimes quietly, sometimes like waters through an open floodgate.

If she remains in therapy, in time her personal ordeal of being Asian in America comes to light. She may speak of emotional, sexual, and physical abuse by a frustrated parent or a husband. Perhaps the pain and shame of her "promiscuity" is revealed, discovering that it is really about seeking acceptance, affection, and attention as a confirmation of her worth; and then only to be sexualized as a curio piece and left on the shelf. She may complain about accommodating her colleagues in the workplace who, not being Asian, take advantage of it instead of reciprocating the accommodating behavior, or being the object of sexual jokes by white men who not only need to prove their manhood by debasing a woman, but also find a racist freedom in using the Asian female as the object of a joke. Once again, the myth of the "sexual mystique," the "exotic," the "sexy promiscuous" Asian female leads him to her. Why? Perhaps because, historically, all Chinese women were assumed to be prostitutes during the gold mining years of the mid-1800s; even in 1870 legislation was passed in California preventing the immigration of any Asian woman who could not present "satisfactory evidence" that she was a person of "correct habits and good character."[3]

## *WHAT IS BEING CHINESE AMERICAN?*

When the Chinese first came to America in the 1850s, the dominant Anglo-Americans considered us "inferior to any race God ever made."[4] A law passed in 1854 branded us as "incapable of progress or intellectual development" and therefore not allowed to testify in court. In 1863, a law was passed to prohibit us, along with Indians, from giving "evidence in favor of, or against, any white man."[5] Racist attitudes have prevailed for 150 years now. There is a legacy of hostility and discrimination against Chinese Americans, both institutionally and personally. Six generations later, Chinese Americans are still not simply "Americans." We are the "Invisible American," the "Model Minority." Translation: we keep our place, don't speak out. We go about our business without making waves. We tolerate abusive discrimination. It appears to be permissible to commit racist crimes against us.

Textbooks, the media, the arts, and our lack of representation in government, teach American children anti-Chinese racism, and support racist violence against us. As recognizable stereotypes, we can be made familiar entities by the dominant culture and therefore easier and safer to deal with. Their expectations of us are clear: we are to tolerate acts of racism. The message is clear: we do not belong. It keeps us at the edge of our country, of our home, of acceptance. We are still marginal citizens after 150 years of history and of planting our roots in America; we are marginal due to the color of our skin, the texture of our hair, the shape of our eyes, the sounds of our names.

Only white Americans are seen as real Americans. Americans are viewed as white not only in America, but all over the world. Wherever I go, I am asked where I come from because in their perception I am not "American." When I answer "I am American," or "I was born in New Orleans," the next question is "No, where do you *really* come from?" And I think, "I'm fifth-generation American (on my mother's side). Am I not American by now?" But as a young girl, I would think, "Am I not white by now?"

Chinese women, in Anglo-America, have a lifelong *struggle* to identify ourselves with pride, self-love, and as beautiful. We *struggle* for our right to healthy self-esteem. First we are painfully bound in childhood by schools and the media telling us what we are and what we can ever hope to be. Later, in the larger world, we discover the whole of society telling us by the ways in which they do or don't intermingle with us, how unimportant we are to them. Socially, politically, in the workplace, in the fashion world, the arts, and even in government, it is the Anglo-American who tells us who we are and determines what we are worth. We clearly witness the continuing dismemberment of the African American family and culture, and the ongoing genocide of the Native American. Who are we then drawn to emulate? The oppressed or the oppressor? I recall how as a child in New Orleans, I had the difficult task of choosing in which section of the bus to sit, from which drinking fountain to drink, and whether to use the White or "Colored" public restrooms. Even as a girl of seven, I knew it was better to be white in America, but I felt guilt toward the African American, so I chose to sit in the last row of the white section. Yes, I learned very early that it was better to be white in America, but I hadn't learned that I could never be white in America. So I, and thousands of other Chinese American women, tried real hard to convince ourselves that we were white: we tried to paint our eyes big and round; we learned to be embarrassed by our parents, hoping they would speak English in public and wear Western clothes. I remember hating to bring the Chinese birthday presents my mother bought for my white friends. I even kept my Chinese American friends separate from my white friends. From about age seven to eleven, when playing house with my white friends, the Sears catalog models were who we pretended to be and what our children and husbands looked like. Of course, there were no Asian, African, Mexican, or Native American models from which to choose. People of color have always been in America. In the 1950s, too. But where were our reflections?

As teenagers, how many of us would cringe at the school textbooks that printed only one kind of picture of Chinese: political cartoons that made us look like rat-faced, buck-toothed cowards running away from butcher knives with our queues waving behind? Later, as young women, we would be nicknamed "Susie Wong" from a movie about a Chinese prostitute and a big white man. How many times would a man ask us whether our vaginas were slanted? Is this what it is to be a Chinese American woman? We did not make up those words, those pictures, those images, those characters. We did not print magazines or make movies that showed America as only white. We have, however, paid the bitter price: psychological and emotional pain, denial, and self-hate.

## BUT WE ALL LOOK ALIKE, RIGHT?

Not only is there a vast difference between Japanese and Chinese cultures and physical characteristics, Korean and Cambodian, Filipino and Thai, but there is also a vast difference between being a Chinese immigrant living in America and being an American of Chinese descent living in America. Yet we are all lumped together by white Americans who think of us as Chinese or Japanese. This kind of homogenizing by Anglo-Americans is not necessarily an individual's fault, but it increases the non-recognition and continues the devaluation of our already struggling identity.

Immigrant Chinese and Chinese Americans may look alike to most other Americans. We do not look alike to each other and we do not necessarily have the same behavioral traits. Yet we are not completely different from each other either. Immigrants may consciously draw from their native cultural source, though often unbeknownst to Chinese Americans, they, too, draw from that same source. The Chinese culture cannot be completely eliminated from Chinese Americans even after 150 years.

Immigrants often have a deep and abiding connection to their native culture. This gives them a structure by which to hold onto their sense of self: cultural rules and expectations, language, a clear, uninterrupted understanding of each other's non-verbal communications. They know they are Chinese. But by the second, third, fourth, fifth, and sixth generation, we know ourselves as Americans who happen to be of Chinese descent, who just happen to look Chinese. With each successive generation, the Chinese culture is gradually diluted. Educated and media-seduced in the Anglo-American system, Chinese Americans no longer know clearly which are Chinese cultural values and which are the values inherited from Anglo-America. If there has not been a conscious effort on the part of our parents to instill Chinese pride and knowledge of the culture, we interpret who we are and how we behave from a solely Westernized American point of view. This is a drastic and painful mistake, for it affects, in the deepest way, our ability to know ourselves. With this misinformation and misunderstanding, how can I know the source of my behavior and therefore make appropriate and intelligent choices for my life? There is little power in traveling a circular road filled with misinformation. The integrity of my identity, that is, being *both* Chinese and American, suffers.

An Asian American woman possesses complexity, a richness that lies between the East and the West, and within both. We are the embodiment of many cultures, not one, and herein lies the understanding of who we are and how we live our lives. To ignore any one is to deny a part of ourselves. To deny a part of ourselves is to miss the whole of who we are.

Each of us must find an integration, a working partnership

among all the American cultures that have influenced us. A conscious understanding of both the Eastern and the Western societies is essential to healthy self-esteem. We must begin to be sensitive to the nuances of being multicultural: which parts are Chinese and which parts are Westernized; which parts are an integration of the many. Each part must be valued.

To be a whole human being with self-dignity is the goal. It is attainable. It is our right.

## NOTES

1. Wu, Cheng-Tsu. *Chink!* (New York: The World Publishing Co., 1972), Chapter 1.

2. Division of Vital Statistics, National Center for Health and Statistics, unpublished data calculated by Elena S. H. Yu, PhD and William T. Liu, PhD. Copy of data obtained from The Asian American Health Forum in San Francisco.

3. Wu, Cheng-Tsu. *Chink!* (New York: The World Publishing Co., 1972), p. 12.

4. Ibid., p. 3.

5. Ibid., p. 13.

# *PART II.*
# *THEORY*

The personal does not automatically become political, and women's shared experiences do not become feminist theory without analysis, comparisons, and attention to both history and possibilities. Theory-building is the work of integrating these processes.

# Institutional Racism
# in the Mental Health Professions

Beverly Greene

The dominant culture's disparaging views of African Americans are pervasive and institutionalized. Guthrie (1976) writes that psychology as a discipline emerged during a historical period when Western culture was permeated by overt racism and social Darwinism. Consequently, research questions and paradigms within psychology and other mental health disciplines emerged out of this context rather than apart from it. Kamin (1974), Karier (1972, 1986), Kirsch and Winter (1983), and Kramer (1973) suggest that personal, social and religious beliefs influenced psychologists in the assumptions they held about human behavior. Influenced by the racism within the social climate of the time, a body of literature emerged which clearly accepted the view of the inferiority of African Americans and the natural superiority of white Americans. This work was used to reinforce rather than challenge or objectively explore the credibility of such assumptions. However racism within mental health disciplines by no means began nor did it end here.

Institutional racism expands the parameters of racist behavior beyond the person-to-person realm of deliberate, individual acts. Pinderhughes (1973) describes the essence of institutional racism as a relatively constant pattern of prejudice and discrimination between one party who is idealized, favored, and given privileges based on their favored status, and another who is devalued, exploited, and deprived of privileges chiefly because they are members of devalued groups. The privileges accorded or denied to devalued people are not simply superfluous frills but are often basic necessities of life, or opportunities to develop their skills or talents as fully as possible.

American institutions were designed and organized by many persons who believed in the superiority of white persons. Such attitudes became a part of the mechanisms of our institutions, which by design operated in ways that would perpetuate what their creators believed to be true. One result was the creation of institutional barriers to the full and equal participation of African Americans in American institutions and in the opportunities that they often provide. America's institutions became the instruments for perpetuating the devalued status of African Americans as well as the myths of superiority of white Americans (Butts, 1969; Greene, 1986; Pinderhughes, 1973; Poussaint, 1990). Research in mental health was and continues to be used by American institutions to support the continuation of its system of racial privilege, hence the racism which has been an integral part of mental health institutions continues to have a negative impact on the delivery of psychological services to African Americans and members of other devalued groups as well.

A criticism of traditional mental health disciplines is their failure to appropriately label the dysfunctional aspects of behaviors of dominant and powerful groups and their members (Brown, 1992). There continues to be a similar reluctance to acknowledge the detrimental effects of those behaviors on dominant group members. Instead, non-dominant group members find themselves blamed for their disadvantaged status and admonished for failing to work hard enough in a system which they are told rewards people for their hard work. They frequently find their appropriate challenges or negative reactions to unfair treatment pathologized as well. A review of pertinent examples of racism in mental health literature will serve as the focus of this chapter.

Prior to the legal abolition of slavery, the 1840 census included individuals in mental hospitals categorized by race. Census data indicated that fewer African Americans in the South were confined to mental hospitals than in the North where greater numbers of African Americans were free. These statistics were used to suggest that African Americans were "uncivilized" and could not manage life outside of some "protected" status in which white persons were in control (Thomas & Sillen, 1972). This questionable interpretation of census data was used to support arguments that slavery served a beneficial purpose for African slaves and that it should be continued for their own good. The need to believe that slavery was actually beneficial for African Americans was so strong that other assumptions followed which by today's standards seem ludicrous.

The term "drapetomania" was introduced by a Louisiana surgeon and psychologist who was charged, in 1851, with the task of explaining why slaves attempted to run away from plantations or escape from bondage whenever they had the opportunity (Poussaint, 1990; Thomas & Sillen, 1972). Drapetomania became the diagnostic label applied to describe a mental disorder afflicting slaves who wished or attempted to escape from their master's domain. This may be highlighted as an illustration of how white Americans comfortably accepted a practice which was unquestionably destructive to African Americans. The acceptance of racist practices as the healthy norm was so complete that its appropriate rejection could be depicted as pathological. Such explanations served the political purpose of obscuring and distorting the exploitive nature of a practice which many persons criticized at the time and which could not continue in a society which purports to be based on Christian and democratic ideals without some rationalization. Similarly, African Americans in contemporary environments may find their appropriate rejection of racist behaviors and practices, or their heightened sensitivity to the potential for exploitation incorrectly interpreted as if it were pathological (Greene, 1994; Homma-True, et al. 1993; Mays, 1985; Poussaint, 1990).

Other "scholarly" work followed which purported to scientifically and objectively validate the popular assumption of the inferiority of African Americans. This came to be known as the deficit literature, as its most salient feature was to label African Americans deficient along many dimensions when compared to idealized, not realistic, depictions of white persons. Much of the deficit-oriented research generated about African Americans appears to have been designed to simply reaffirm and perpetuate popularly held beliefs and stereotypes about them. This served not only to justify the maltreatment of African Americans, but to maintain the levels of social privilege accorded white Americans which derived from presumptions of white supremacy. It did not however constitute a valid scientific or psychological inquiry which would have objectively examined pertinent information about the adaptive skills, resilience, and valid cultural differences which still exist between many Americans of different ethnic backgrounds.

Mays (1985) and Karier (1972) suggest that it was no accident, but rather by design, that individuals who were central to the development of the intellectual assessment movement in the United States were also some of the strongest advocates for eugenics control. It is suggested that there was a functional relationship between the psychological testing movement and corporate industry. Corporate industry financed many areas of scientific and psychological research. It is not surprising that the results of this research were often key ingredients in the development of public policies, the creation of legislation, the enactment of laws, and the disbursement of public funds in ways which were favorable to corporate interests and philosophies (Mays, 1985; Karier, 1972).

A significant body of literature emerged at the end of World War I amidst great concern about the numbers of immigrants entering the United States, competing for scarce resources, and a perceived need to limit their immigration on "scientific and objective" grounds. During this period up through the early 1940s unprecedented numbers of African Americans migrated from the South to northern cities competing with white Americans for declining numbers of jobs in a slower post-war economy (Hale, 1983; Homma-True et al., 1993; Ruiz, 1990). The beginnings of the intellectual assessment movement were emerging at that time and its early, primitive instruments became tools of institutional racism. They would be used to limit the immigration of specific nationalities, contribute to the development of legislation which made it possible to legally sterilize those who were considered "undesirables, or feeble-minded," and to create the illusion of objective scientific instruments which could be trusted to determine who would be granted educational and occupational privileges and opportunities and who would be denied them (Hale, 1983; Kamin, 1974; Karier, 1972). The negative consequences of traditional patterns of privilege, on non-dominant group members, would be used to reinforce racist beliefs as well as to justify the discriminatory practices which evolved from those beliefs. Test scores and other forms of "objective" measures could be used to convince disenfranchised and exploited persons that their unfortunate lot was based on their own natural limitations. This predisposed many members of non-dominant groups to blame themselves for their exploitation, diminishing the likelihood that they would press for changes in social arrangements which control the distribution of wealth and opportunity (Greene, 1994).

The first test of intelligence was designed by Alfred Binet, in France, in 1905 (Hale, 1983; Kamin, 1974; Karier, 1972; Kirsch & Winter, 1983). Binet was commissioned to design a test for the purpose of identifying children who required special educational programs and to design remedial courses for them (Hale, 1983). Binet never considered his test to be a fixed measure of intelligence and protested its use as a means of rank ordering and then denying educational opportunities to children (Kamin, 1974; Kirsch & Winter, 1983). Nonetheless, American psychologists who imported the test promptly used the instrument to support the contention that certain races were endowed with less intellectual ability than others, that those abilities were inherited, and that they could be accurately measured by these instruments. American psychologists took these assumptions one step further when they asserted that "low intelligence" as measured on these instruments was directly linked to the potential to become a criminal, and to low social and low moral capacity (Hale, 1983; Kamin, 1974; Karier, 1972). Once a lack of individual and social worth was connected to the concept of low intelligence it became easy to argue that the state had the right and responsibility to control the freedom and reproductive capacity of many individuals, without their consent, and could do so in ways that would be considered unacceptable otherwise (Kamin, 1974; Karier, 1972; Thomas & Sillen, 1972). The realistic effects of a legacy of discrimination and exclusion on many oppressed persons were either minimized or not acknowledged at all in explanations of test performance.

Lewis Terman, Maud Merrill, and Henry Goddard were prominent figures in the validation and revision of Binet's scales into the Stanford-Binet intelligence test and were all major proponents of the view that intelligence was a quantity fixed for life, primarily determined by heredity (Hale, 1983; Kamin, 1974; Karier, 1972;

Kirsch & Winter, 1983; Thomas & Sillen, 1972). Terman (1916) wrote:

> Their [a pair of Indian and Mexican children] dullness seems to be racial, or at least inherent in the family stocks from which they come. . . . They cannot master abstractions, but they can often be made efficient workers. . . . They constitute a grave problem because of their unusually prolific breeding.

Terman was also a leading member of the Human Betterment Foundation, a pro-eugenics organization (Kamin, 1974). Based in California, the group was instrumental in the proliferation of sterilization laws based on concepts that argued for the need to maintain "racial purity" and control the propagation of "potential criminals" (Kamin, 1974; Karier, 1972). Poor performance on these burgeoning intellectual assessment instruments became synonymous with mental defect, which in turn was used to imply the presence of social defects. With this foundation, the United States pioneered in the sterilization of persons labeled mentally defective, without their consent, twenty years before other nations would follow suit with similar practices (Kamin, 1974; Karier, 1972; Thomas & Sillen, 1972). Many of the leaders and founding theoreticians of psychology made significant contributions to the development of these policies (Hale, 1983; Karier, 1972, 1986).

According to Robert Yerkes (1921), "IQ tests brought into clear relief . . . the intellectual inferiority of the Negro. . . . Education alone will not place the Negro on par with its [sic] Caucasian competitors." William McDougall in the same year wrote, "In the great strength of his instinct of submission we have the key to the history of the Negro race" (Thomas & Sillen, 1972). These views were shared by Edward L. Thorndike who wrote in 1920, "To him that hath a superior intellect is given also on the average a superior character" (in Thomas & Sillen, 1972).

A Committee on Scientific Problems on Human Migration was established by the National Research Council in the period post World War I. It later published *A Study of American Intelligence* (1923) authored by Carl Brigham (1930), then Assistant Professor of Psychology at Princeton University. In this dubious study, Brigham touted the superiority of the "Nordic" draftees of the war and expressed his concern about the "inferior germ plasm of the Alpine, Mediterranean, and Negro races." He wrote:

> We face a possibility of racial admixture here [in the United States] that is infinitely worse than that faced by any European country today, for we are incorporating the Negro into our racial stock, while all of Europe is relatively free of this taint. . . . The decline of American intelligence will be more rapid than the decline of the intelligence of European national groups, owing to the presence here of the Negro.

Brigham later became secretary of the American Psychological Association. He went on to become secretary of the College Entrance Examination Board where he was instrumental in the development and the design of the Scholastic Aptitude Test, the primary screening instrument of American colleges and universities (Kamin, 1974).

Henry Garrett (1961), a past president of the American Psychological Association, member of the National Research Council, and chairman of the department of psychology at Columbia University was a strong proponent of racial segregation and eugenics. He wrote that intermarriage and desegregation would "destroy the genetic lead of the white man" and that "the state can and should prohibit miscegenation just as they ban marriage of the feeble minded, the insane, and various undesirables, just as they outlaw incest." Garrett went on to distribute half a million pamphlets to American teachers, summarizing what he believed to be the implications of desegregation as evidenced by 60 years of intelligence testing (Mays, 1985). They were: *How Classroom Desegregation Will Work*; *Children, Black and White*; and *Breeding Down* (Garrett, 1961; Karier, 1972; Mays, 1985; Thomas & Sillen, 1972).

In 1969, the *Harvard Educational Review* published Jensen's (1969) contention that approximately 70 percent of human intellectual capacity was predetermined by hereditary factors which were more or less immutable to environmental enrichment. Jensen postulated the presence of two genetically different types of intellectual processes (Thomas & Sillen, 1972). Level I ability was deemed associative in nature and considered to be most useful in rote learning and simple memory tasks. Level II ability was deemed conceptual in nature and required for abstract concept formation and complex problem solving (Jensen, 1969). It is no surprise that Jensen found Level I ability more characteristic of African Americans and Level II ability more characteristic of white Americans.

The data used to establish Jensen's contentions were drawn in part from the studies of twins by Sir Cyril Burt. These studies were later criticized for methodological and statistical errors. There were additional questions about the origins of Burt's data with some critics suggesting that portions appeared to have been fabricated; however, Burt's death and the destruction of his data precluded any complete resolution of those questions (Kamin, 1974). Despite legitimate scientific objections to many of the assumptions inherent in this work, Jensen's assumptions were fairly widely accepted and were used in making educational policy decisions (Kamin, 1974; Karier, 1972; Mays, 1985).

Hernstein (1971) then at Harvard University wrote, "as technology advances, the tendency to be unemployed may run in the genes of a family about as certainly as bad teeth do now" (Kamin, 1974; Karier, 1972; Mays, 1985). While African Americans were not the only ethnic group maligned by this fallacious research, they may be among the more negatively affected by it. Both the high physical visibility of African Americans, because of their skin color, and the personal fears now legitimized by this research, provided many persons with a justification for discrimination against and scapegoating of African Americans as a group. The core of these beliefs in the intellectual assessment arena remains a subject of debate which persists to this day.

Cordes (1987) reviews Gottfredson's research, which attributes the average differences between African Americans and white Americans, in IQ scores, to real differences between the races in mental ability which is associated with negative outcomes. Gottfredson asserts that a "higher proportion of all African Americans would perform poorly in mentally demanding jobs than the proportion of whites, even if there were no differences in education, training, and experience between the two groups." She further contends that more complex jobs require skills of judgment and decision making that go beyond the knowledge that can be acquired through education and training.

Sociologist Robert Gordon (Cordes, 1987) carries Gottfredson's assertion one step further. He maintains that differences between African Americans and white Americans on group IQ scores explain differences between the two groups in rates of crime and delinquency. In his analysis, racial differences in group IQ scores were touted as "more successful" in explaining racial differences in rates of crime and delinquency than income, education, or occupational status, and that intelligence tests are not biased against African Americans. He warns that if these are inherited factors and if "lots of low IQ people are having lots of children out of wedlock, neglect of sex education may lead to higher crime rates" (Cordes, 1987). Both Gottfredson and Gordon presented their findings at the national conference of the American Psychological Association in August of 1986, over 80 years after the "revision" of Binet's original instrument.

Williams (1974) writes that the fundamental issue in the "great black-white IQ controversy" has little to do with cultural test bias, the nature of intelligence, or the heritability of IQ, but of hindering and obstructing the equal admission of African Americans to America's mainstream and denying them access to the opportunities within that realm. He refers to the way that IQ and achievement tests are used as examples of scientific racism and suggests that they are merely updated versions of the old "Whites only" signs in the segregated South. The pervasive misuse of intelligence tests has often served as one of the underpinnings of institutional racism. Williams (1974) warns that the users of these instruments may often serve as the "hired guns" who operate as a part of a silent racial war. Test results may be used to disguise the effects of centuries of racist practices as a problem or deficit in the victims of those practices.

These forms of institutional racism were not limited to the arena of intellectual assessment; rather, they were pervasive in other mental health literature as well. The work of Sigmund Freud does not tend to infuse racial bias directly into its formulations although it is riddled with gender bias. Nonetheless, America's obsession with racial differences and their meaning is reflected in psychoanalytic writings beginning with the *Psychoanalytic Review* and the

*American Journal of Psychiatry* which were both permeated with blatant examples of racial bias (Thomas & Sillen, 1972).

In 1887, G. Stanley Hall, first president of the American Psychological Association, referred to African Americans as a "primitive race in a state of immature development" (Thomas and Sillen, 1972). In the *Psychoanalytic Review*, the first psychoanalytic periodical in English, founded in 1913 by William Alanson White, African Americans were depicted as a race at "a relatively low cultural level . . . who during its years of savagery has learned no lessons in emotional control" (Thomas & Sillen 1972). Carl Jung, in an address to the Second Psychoanalytic Congress in 1910 and a later work in 1930 commented that "living together with lower, barbaric races, especially with Negroes exerts a suggestive effect on the laboriously tamed instinct of the white race and tends to pull it down" (Jung, 1930; Thomas & Sillen, 1972).

Lauretta Bender, regarded as a pioneer in American child psychiatry, wrote in 1939:

> There has appeared to be a special pattern in behavior disorders of Negro children that displays itself in several ways. This is related to the question of motility and impulse. Two features which almost anyone will concede as characteristic of the race are 1. the capacity for so called laziness and 2. the special ability to dance. The capacity for laziness is the ability to go to sleep or to do nothing for long periods, when it fits the needs of the situation. The dancing represents special motility patterns and tendencies. These two features present themselves in the behavior problems that come to us and may be an expression of specific brain impulse tendencies.

Kardiner & Ovesey (1962) suggest that the personality traits of African Americans are so inextricably linked to their oppressed status that they cannot overcome an inevitable absence of self-esteem and presence of self-hate. Based on interviews with only 25 subjects, their conclusions fail to acknowledge the undeniable presence of adaptive coping mechanisms throughout the history of African Americans as well as their capacity to develop appropriate subjective understandings of the institutional barriers that confront them (Greene, 1994). Similarly such findings presumed a homogeneity among African Americans as a group by suggesting that they have a response to racism which is uniform in its constituents and its intensity. This line of thinking can and no doubt did serve to reinforce a dangerous, self-fulfilling prophecy in psychotherapy. If African Americans are inevitably overwhelmed by racism, clinicians who treat them might assume that therapy cannot be helpful since it does not eliminate racism directly.

African Americans have been reported to be more resentful and suspicious (Gardner, 1971), difficult to establish rapport with, incapable of insight, non-verbal, and concrete (Jones & Seagull, 1977). The adaptive value of suspiciousness in African American clients as a reasonable and even adaptive response to their traditional treatment from mental health institutions must not be minimized.

## SUMMARY

Thomas & Sillen (1972) warn contemporary mental health clinicians against feeling superior to their predecessors. While this chapter focused on the legacy of racism in mental health for African Americans, it does not mean that other cultural groups escape unscathed. An examination of racial, ethnic, gender, heterosexist, and other forms of bias in mental health reveals the ease with which "objective science" can be distorted when it serves the interest of dominant and powerful groups. In a most disturbing manner it reveals how easily those distortions can be accepted despite the oppressive practices they may support.

Because racism and other oppressive attitudes are deeply rooted in the cultural fabric and mechanisms of American institutions, racist practices may be routinely acted out by people who do not consciously accept racist views, unless they carefully scrutinize the agendas of those institutions and the often subtle consequences of their actions (Greene, 1986). Material reviewed here may seem so absurd that one is tempted not to take it seriously. However, its influence on the thinking of contemporary mental health clinicians should not be underestimated. Many of the old arguments supporting discrimination against members of non-dominant groups, presumably because they are inferior, are still with us.

# REFERENCES

Bender, Lauretta (1939). The behavior problems of Negro children. *Psychiatry, 2,* 213-228.

Brigham, Carl C. (1923). *A study of American intelligence.* Princeton, NJ: Princeton University Press.

_____ (1930). Intelligence tests of immigrant groups. *Psychological Review, 37,* 158-165.

Brown, Laura S. (1992). A feminist critique of the personality disorders. In Laura S. Brown & Mary Ballou (Eds.), *Personality and psychopathology: Feminist reappraisals* (pp. 206-228). New York: Guilford.

Butts, Hugh F. (1969). White racism: Its origins, institutions and the implications for professional practice in mental health. *International Journal of Psychiatry, 8,* 914-944.

Cordes, Colleen (1987, February). "IQ" gap linked to job lags, crime. *The APA Monitor, 18*(2), 20-21.

Gardner, LaMaurice (1971). The therapeutic relationship under varying conditions of race. *Psychotherapy, Theory, Research & Practice, 8,* 76-86.

Garrett, Henry E. (1961). The equalitarian dogma. *Mankind Quarterly, 1,* 253-257.

Greene, Beverly (1986). When the therapist is white and the patient is black: Considerations for psychotherapy in the feminist heterosexual and lesbian communities. *Women & Therapy, 5,* 41-65.

_____ (1994). African American women: Derivatives of racism and sexism in psychotherapy. In B. Rossof & E. Toback (Eds.), *Challenging racism and sexism: Alternatives to genetic determinism.* New York: Feminist Press.

Guthrie, Robert V. (1976). *Even the rat was white: A historical view of psychology.* New York: Harper Row.

Hale, Robert L. (1983). Intellectual assessment. In M. Hersen, A. E. Kazdin & A. S. Bellack (Eds.), *The clinical psychology handbook* (pp. 345-376). New York: Pergamon Press.

Hernstein, Richard (1971). IQ. *The Atlantic,* 43-58; 63-64.

Homma-True, Reiko, Greene, Beverly, Lopez, Steven, & Trimble, Joseph (1993). Ethnocultural diversity in clinical psychology. *The Clinical Psychologist 46*(2), 50-63.

Jensen, Arthur (1969). How much can we boost IQ and scholastic achievement? *Harvard Educational Review, 39,* 1-123.

Jones, Alison, & Seagull, Arthur (1977). Dimensions of the relationship between the black client and the white therapist. *American Psychologist, 32,* 850-855.

Jung, C. (1930). Your Negroid and Indian behavior. *Forum, 83,* 193-199.

Kamin, Leon J. (1974). *The science and politics of IQ.* New York: John Wiley & Sons.

Kardiner, Abraham, & Ovesey, Lionel (1962). *The mark of oppression: A psychological study of the American Negro.* New York: World Publications.

Karier, Clarence (1972). Testing for order and control in the corporate state. *Educational Theory, 22,* 154-180.

_____ (1986). *Scientists of the mind: Intellectual founders of modern psychology.* Urbana, IL: University of Illinois Press.

Kirsch, Irving, & Winter, Christine (1983). A history of clinical psychology. In C. E. Walker (Ed.), *The handbook of clinical psychology, 1* (pp. 3-30). Homewood, IL: Dow Jones-Irwin.

Kramer, Bertram (1973). Racism and mental health as a field of thought and action. In C. Willie, B. Kramer, & B. Brown (Eds.), *Racism and mental health* (pp. 3-23). Pittsburgh, PA: University of Pittsburgh Press.

Mays, Vickie M. (1985). The Black American and psychotherapy: The dilemma. *Psychotherapy, 22* (2S) 379-388.

Pinderhughes, Charles A. (1973). Racism and psychotherapy. In C. Willie, B. Kramer, & B. Brown (Eds.), *Racism and mental health* (pp. 61-121). Pittsburgh, PA: University of Pittsburgh Press.

Poussaint, Alvin (1990). The mental health status of Black Americans, 1983. In D. S. Ruiz (Ed.), *Handbook of mental health and mental disorder among Black Americans* (pp. 17-52). New York: Greenwood Press.

Ruiz, Dolores S. (1990). Social and economic profile of Black Americans, 1989. In D. S. Ruiz (Ed.), *Handbook of mental health and mental disorder among Black Americans* (pp. 3-15). New York: Greenwood Press.

Terman, Lewis (1916). *The measurement of intelligence.* Boston: Houghton Mifflin.

Thomas, Alexander, & Sillen, Samuel (1972). *Racism and psychiatry.* New York: Brunner/Mazel.

Williams, Robert L. (1974, May). Scientific racism and IQ: The silent mugging of the Black community. *Psychology Today,* 32-33; 37-38; 41; 101.

Yerkes, Robert M. (Ed.) (1921). Psychological examining in the U.S. Army. *Memoirs of the National Academy of Sciences, 15.*

# On Knowing You Are the Unknown: Women of Color Constructing Psychology

## Oliva M. Espín

I recently found a quote from Paulo Freire in one of bell hooks' recent books that I think applies to what all liberation movements, including feminism, are about: "We cannot enter the struggle as objects in order to later become subjects" (1990, p. 15). I find this thought particularly relevant when we are reflecting on the impact of racism on theories of the psychology of women.

I believe the feminist movement has functioned to provide opportunities for many women to develop and maintain a sense of self-worth. In its present historical reality, however, the women for whom the movement most fully provides such validation are white and middle class. Women of color, feminist or not, are seldom idealized, respected, valued, or presented as role models in whose footsteps other women would want to follow.

It is certainly true that women of color validate and respect each other. It is also true, however, that in a context of cultural imperialism those women of color who are developing feminist theoretical perspectives frequently do not feel fully validated by either white feminists or people of both genders in their own ethnic group. For the most part they are simply unknown to most white feminists and considered irrelevant by people in their own ethnic group. Most definitions of the concepts of "feminist" or "woman" assume either that all women are included in one version of feminism or that women of color "do not fully understand" what sexism really is and what feminism is supposed to mean. Women of color do not fully "belong" unless they are willing to learn from white women what feminism "really is." The term "feminist" is frequently attributed only to white women by women of color and white women alike.

When statements are made about the "need to include" women of color in theories or organizations, in the very statement of the need for their inclusion the assumption is being made that some other group (meaning, of course, *white* women) "owns" and defines the movement in which the women of color are to be included. Including women of color is seen as either a duty performed out of guilt or a generous act towards those less fortunate than the "owners" of the movement. However, guilt is for the most part useless and generosity tends to be humiliating for those who are the object of it. The thought that a true feminist movement, and feminist psychology in particular, are really non-existent as long as only some women are being mirrored and idealized by the movement, does not occur to those who, consciously or unconsciously, see themselves as the guilty and generous "owners" of the feminist movement.

I would like to say very strongly that there will never be a true feminist movement, and more important for us as psychologists, there will not be valid theories of the psychology of women as long as this movement and these theories are based on a very limited sector of the population (Espín, 1991). Ironically, this is the same criticism that we as feminists have of a male-oriented psychology.

Indeed, this whole issue of inclusion is not about "affirmative action" but, rather, about *the nature of knowledge*, both in the psychology of women and in the discipline of psychology as a whole. The theories and the research we now have are, for the most part, incomplete and faulty pieces of knowledge, no matter how elegant they may seem. As I have written elsewhere:

> Post-modern understandings of the multiplicity of realities that constitute the reality of the world, leave no room for naive descriptions of women, the world, or human life that incorporate only one perspective on that reality. No matter how privileged that reality may have been in the past, it is as partial as all others. (Espín, 1991, p. 5)

White feminists, for all their good intentions, are no more immune to blindness created by privilege than their male counterparts are (McIntosh, 1988). As Simone Weil put it many years ago (cited in Young, 1990, p. 39), "someone who does not see a pane of glass, does not know that she does not see it." This is precisely the curse of the privileged: that they do not see anything that does not have to do with themselves, and on top of that, believe that what they see is universal truth. Thus there is an inhibition of the real capacity to know.

Those who do not partake of that privilege, however, know very well the existence of that pane of glass; they know it is impossible for them to go through this barrier–the more effective precisely because it is unseen. In fact, the non-privileged can be better "knowers" and more knowledgeable. Their vision tends to be clearer; they see themselves, they see the glass pane, and they know who is on the other side of that glass. That is why women and other oppressed people have a clearer vision of reality than white males and other oppressors.

Bell hooks' (1990) comments about the Freire citation I opened with expand on this point:

> This statement compels reflection on how the dominated, the oppressed, the exploited make ourselves subject. How do we create [a] world view, a consciousness, an identity, a standpoint that . . . not only . . . opposes dehumanization but [a] movement which enables creative, expansive self-actualization? Opposition is not enough. . . . [The] process [of becoming subjects] emerges as one comes to understand how structures of domination work in one's own life, as one develops critical thinking and critical consciousness, as one invents new, alternative habits of being, and resists from that marginal space of difference inwardly defined (p. 15).

What I interpret from the standpoint of a theory of feminist psychology as I read this statement is that women of color need to take a central position in the creation of feminist theory *as creators* of the theory, not as people who are generously or guiltily included by others. I also read in this statement that from the new consciousness and critical thinking born of our own experiences and our own "difference[s] inwardly defined" a new "creative, expansive self-actualization" will develop. But I don't think this is something women of color can, will, or should do in our own little corners or in small spaces on programs. I believe it is a contribution women of color will have to make as feminist psychologists for the benefit of *all* psychology, or in whatever profession or way of life we might be.

The success of this task presupposes both willingness and effort on the part of women of color to develop our own "critical consciousness" and "critical thinking" in order "to understand how structures of domination" have affected our psychology and in order to invent "new, alternative habits of being." Clearly, this is not a minor task, either personally or theoretically, considering that it is to be undertaken in a context of oppression and cultural imperialism where one is, indeed, the "unknown."

Up to now, the feminist movement and feminist psychology theory, as part of that movement, have suffered from the limitations created by the cultural imperialism prevalent in all of psychology. Iris Young (1990) writes:

> Cultural imperialism involves the paradox of experiencing oneself as invisible at the same time that one is marked out as different. The invisibility comes about when dominant groups fail to recognize the perspective embodied in their cultural experience as *a* perspective. These dominant cultural expressions often simply have little place for the experience of other groups, at most mentioning or referring to them in stereotyped and marginalized ways. This, then, is the injustice of cultural imperialism: that the oppressed group's own experience and interpretation of social life finds little expression that touches the dominant culture, while that same culture imposes on the oppressed group its experiences and interpretation of social life. (p. 60)

This is, indeed, the experience of "knowing you are the unknown." It is the experience of knowing that the dominant cultural paradigm, including the relatively new paradigm of feminist psychology, sees you only as the different one, as the one who has only a partial view of reality, while it gives to itself the right to see its perspectives as universal rather than culturally determined, and, therefore, also different from the perspectives of others in its own way.

To assume that race and class should only come into feminist psychology theory when we are referring to women of color misses the most important insight of feminism, i.e., that the psychology of each individual woman is influenced by her social context: that the personal is political and the political impinges upon the personal. In so doing, it limits the development of true feminist psychology in very serious ways because when the psychology of white women is assumed to be influenced only by her gender and not her race, a very important understanding is missing. Just as we can understand the sexism a woman of color experiences only when we understand its connection to the racism she does experience, to understand fully how the particular forms of sexism she experiences influence a white woman, we must understand its connection to the racism she does not experience. In fact, "attempts to isolate gender from race and class, typically operate to obscure the race and class identity of white middle class women" (Spelman, 1988, p. 209) and thus limit the understanding of both white women's psychology and the psychology of women of color.

Some efforts by feminist therapy theorists, for example those of the Feminist Therapy Institute (Brown & Root, 1990) and the recent Women of Color Institute of the Association for Women in Psychology, raise my hopes about a new understanding and opening among white feminists. Other contexts, however, continue to leave me very discouraged. Even though it has become somewhat common practice to add a few women of color to the lists of feminist foremothers or theoreticians, they, or their names, may be included in a token fashion, without real knowledge of their points of view or deep consideration of the meaning of those points of view for white feminists. Few white feminists would recognize names of feminist theorists of color such as Patricia Hill Collins, Audre Lorde, bell hooks, Gloria Anzaldúa, Maria Lugones, Aida Hurtado, Maria Root, or Trinh Minh-ha, compared to the numbers who easily recognize white women theorists such as Gilligan, Miller, or Chodorow. For the most part, women of color continue to be mentioned in small asides, footnotes, or digressions from the main topic and almost always as the *object* of theorizing, rather than as the *subject* who theorizes and whose theories are part of the common knowledge. As bell hooks (1984) says:

In more recent years, racism has become an accepted topic in feminist discussion not as a result of [women of color calling

attention to it] . . . but as a result of white female input validating such discussions, a process which indicates how racism
works. (p. 51)

A feminist theory that is derived from the experiences of those
theorizing requires the presence of women of color as generators of
theory as *subjects* rather than *objects*. The focus on "difference" in
psychology has walked into feminist theory unanalyzed; therefore,
difference can be seen as natural and unchangeable and/or as signifying deficiency. Difference will continue to imply the existence of
a norm and thus abnormality on the part of those who are different
from that norm, rather than variability in human experience.

A few examples of how a focus on human variability–a perspective that makes the experience of women of color as central to
psychology as that of any other human group–could enrich both the
psychology of women and psychology in general might help to
illustrate my point. Since I cannot possibly cover in a few pages
every aspect of what a feminist exploration of psychology could
and should entail, I focus on a few illustrations based on my own
interests within psychology.

Most feminist psychology theory (e.g., Chodorow, 1978; Gilligan, 1982; Miller, 1986) takes the psychological characteristics
prevalent among contemporary middle-class women in Western
societies to be the essential component of the psychology of
women, without stopping to consider that most of these characteristics are, rather, defense mechanisms developed by women to deal
with conditions of oppression. If women are so proficient at human
relations, it is probably because that ability has been their survival
tool in a male-dominated world, not because ability for human
interaction is intrinsically connected with female chromosomes.
Only if the oppressive social conditions that have determined most
women's behavior can be removed will we be able to assess
whether some of the values that society has abandoned to women
are indeed part of "women's nature" (Espín & Gawelek, 1992).

I believe that a social constructionist paradigm that sees psychological characteristics as a result of social and historical processes,
not as natural, essential characteristics of one or another group of
people is the more productive approach in the study of human

diversity than some of the other traditional paradigms accepted in psychology. Theories of the psychology of oppression and resistance to oppression help us understand the impact of the socio-cultural context in the development of personality and in the psychotherapeutic context. For example, Freire (1970) has described the impact of internalized oppression in determining behaviors and aspirations that otherwise seem completely individually determined.

Language is also an important and neglected variable in studies of personality development and identity formation. I agree with the post-structuralist concept that the structure of reality is modified by the language used to describe it. Language is not transparent and does not merely reflect and describe human experience. Rather, it is an active creator of that experience.

For women who speak more than one language, there is yet another component in the development of personality and the expression of psychopathology. What I have learned from doing therapy with bilingual individuals is that self-expression in areas such as sexuality is highly influenced by the use of one or the other language (Espín, 1987). Expressions of pathological affect, or of strong emotional states, and the experience of the self are affected by the language used to describe them. An important aspect of language usage for women of color is its connection with self-esteem and identity development. Language and speech do not occur in a vacuum. In the United States, the dominant society ascribes inferior social status to Black English and to bilingualism. The differential valuing of languages and accents has a profound impact on the development of self-concept and identity. When bilingual skills are devalued, also devalued are those parts of the self that have developed in the context of another language (Espín, 1987).

We need to look seriously at other societies and cultures searching for models of development that, precisely because the Western/Anglo-Saxon model is different from them, may teach us about other possibilities for being human. Psychodynamic theories place great emphasis on the existence of an internal individual world that is shaped by interactions with the mother during infancy. Deep-seated beliefs about the influence of mothers, especially in object relations theory, presuppose a certain form of family organization that is not only sexist, but also culturally and class biased. How are we to understand psychological development based on relations with an other (the object) if the role of this other and the relationship between the developing child and this other are significantly different in different cultures? (Espín & Gawelek, 1992).

According to Watson-Franke (1988), matrilineal societies provide us with an alternative perspective. In her view, matrilining creates a different valuing of mothers (and women) and different father and husband roles for men from those to which we in patrilineal cultures are accustomed. "In congruence with the centrality of women, matriliny creates strong female role models, with the mother playing the essentially significant part" (p. 4). While in patriarchal societies matrifocal families are seen as less valid than male-headed households, in matrilineal societies, matrifocus represents the legitimate philosophy. Western theoreticians, raised within a patriarchal context, find it difficult to conceptualize as healthy a family context in which women are central. "The centrality of women in female-headed families has no publicly acknowledged and supported structural force" (p. 4).

The female-headed family of all races is still seen as deviant in most of the Western world. Because the model of healthy family derives from a patriarchal society that resists and rejects a central position for women, it describes many Black and Latino families as well as all lesbian families as "dysfunctional." But what would happen if we looked at them from a different paradigm? What implications would this have for object relations theories? Belief that an idealized nuclear family structure is essential to healthy personality development can be questioned when one observes or studies other societies where children develop and become healthy adults in different family structures.

Even feminist critiques of object relations theories in terms of their emphasis on mother and their potential for mother-hating seldom question the socio-cultural context in which the mother is immersed. Much less do they question aspects of that context that might be as influential as the mother in the psychological development of the child (Espín & Gawelek, 1992).

It is extremely important to take a critical look today at the ritual of therapy, a ritual that has changed perhaps too little since Freud's time. Feminist therapy has challenged many of the traditional models, but how do models of feminist therapy apply across cultures, classes, etc. (Espín, in press)?

Women of color lead lives immersed in unique experiences which uniquely qualify them to transform the personal in their lives into the political or theoretical perspectives necessary to create a true psychology of all women. Women of color are therefore essential partners in the development of feminist psychology and feminist therapy.

Paraphrasing Gloria Anzaldúa (1987) and Maria Lugones (1990), women of color who are feminist live on "the borderlands." We know more than one world and "travel" between different "worlds." In doing so, we develop new experiences, new territories and new languages not known by those who inhabit only one world or speak in only one language. We know possibilities unknown by others. We can develop those possibilities to the enrichment of everyone, but only if we are *subjects*, known and respected as equals in the task of building a new world for all women. If we continue to be treated as *objects* when acknowledged at all, we will never be known by others and perhaps not even fully by ourselves. The richness and knowledge we could offer the feminist movement in general and feminist psychology in particular will forever be lost. I believe that all of us in this book, as well as its readers, can play a role in steering the feminist movement in this most enriching direction. We are all, together, the *subjects* and the *owners* of this movement.

## REFERENCES

Anzaldúa, Gloria (1987). *Borderlands/La Frontera*. San Francisco: Spinsters/ Aunt Lute.

Brown, Laura S., & Root, Maria P. P. (Eds.) (1990). *Diversity and complexity in feminist therapy*. New York: Harrington Park Press.

Chodorow, Nancy (1978). *The reproduction of mothering*. Berkeley: University of California Press.

Espín, O. M. (1987). Psychological impact of migration on Latinas: Implications for psychotherapeutic practice. *Psychology of Women Quarterly, 11*(4), 489-503.

_____ (1991, August). *Ethnicity, race and class, and the future of feminist psychology*. Invited address presented at the 99th Convention of the American Psychological Association, San Francisco, CA.

_____ (in press). Feminist approaches to therapy with women of color. In L. Comas-Díaz & B. Greene (Eds.), *Women of Color and mental health: The healing tapestry*. New York: Guilford Press.

Espín, O. M., & Gawelek, M. A. (1992). Women's diversity: Ethnicity, race, class and gender in theories of feminist psychology. In Laura S. Brown & Mary Ballou (Eds.), *Personality and psychopathology: Feminist reappraisals* (pp. 88-107). New York: Guilford Press.

Freire, P. (1970). *Pedagogy of the oppressed*. New York: Seabury Press.

Gilligan, Carol (1982). *In a different voice*. Cambridge, MA: Harvard University Press.

hooks, bell (1984). *Feminist theory from margin to center*. Boston: South End Press.

_____ (1990). *Yearning: Essays on race, gender and cultural politics*. Boston: South End Press.

Lugones, Maria (1990). Playfulness, "world"-traveling, and loving perception. In G. Anzaldúa (Ed.), *Making face, making soul/Haciendo caras*. San Francisco: Aunt Lute.

McIntosh, Peggy (1988). Understanding correspondence between white privilege and male privilege through Women's Studies work. (Working Paper #189). Center for Research on Women, Wellesley College, Wellesley, MA.

Miller, Jean B. (1986). *Toward a new psychology of women*, 2nd ed., Boston: Beacon Press.

Spelman, Elizabeth (1988). *The inessential woman: Problems of exclusion in feminist thought*. Boston: Beacon Press.

Watson-Franke, M. Barbara (1988, July). *Siblings vs. spouses: Men and women in matrilineal societies (South America and North America)*. Paper presented at the International Congress of Americanists, Amsterdam, Holland.

Young, Iris M. (1990). *Justice and the politics of difference*. Princeton, NJ: Princeton University Press.

# Anti-Racism as an Ethical Norm in Feminist Therapy Practice

Laura S. Brown

## INTRODUCTION

The ethics of practice, as broadly construed, have always been a core concern for feminist therapists. Ethics in feminist therapy are not simply a set of rules or principles that either proscribe or prescribe. Instead, the political philosophy underlying feminist therapy, in which the achievement of revolutionary social change is a goal, has made the value-ladenness and morality of our practice a central and lively concern. Ethics thus provides a point of unity for feminist therapists with otherwise fairly diverse styles of practice and other underlying theoretical orientations (Rave & Larsen, 1990).

Inattention to racism by white feminist therapists stands in direct contradiction to basic tenets of feminist therapy ethics which call for an anti-oppressive stance (Kanuha, 1990). I believe that white feminist therapists can more thoroughly understand anti-racism as

This chapter is an ongoing process stemming from earlier work. These include parts of a workshop presented at the 1990 Conference of the Association for Women in Psychology. My thanks go to the women who participated in that workshop and who contributed to my ongoing thought process on this topic. An earlier revision of some of that work appeared as an article titled "Antiracism as an ethical imperative: An example from feminist therapy" in *Ethics and Behavior, 1*, 1991. My special thanks go to my colleague and friend Anne Ganley who has been a model, support, and necessary irritant for my professional and personal development on this issue, to Maria Root, colleague, friend, and sister-creator of the feminist therapy snorkeling symposium for our ongoing discussions on many of the points raised here, and to Gloria Enguídanos and Jeanne Adleman for their astute editing of this chapter.

an ethical norm if we see racism as leading to failures of mutuality, lack of respect, violations of boundaries, and imbalances of power in psychotherapy, terms that are inherent to discussions of feminist therapy ethics in other realms such as money, sexuality, and role overlap.

## FAILURES OF MUTUALITY AND LACK OF RESPECT

White feminists have been criticized by women of color (Davis, 1983; hooks, 1981; Moraga & Anzaldúa, 1981; Lorde, 1980; Walker, 1983) for writing and speaking of "women's experiences" as if we refer to all women when our data bases are primarily or exclusively white (Brown, 1990; Kanuha, 1990). White feminist therapists developing theory have relied more upon the work of white males than on concepts and models derived from the theorizing of people of color. We communicate, by this choice of where to cast our gaze, a lack of respect for the intellectual contributions of thinkers whose work reflects cultures outside of white dominant societies. White feminist therapists have tended to trivialize women of color in our words and actions; we have made their lives invisible, their voices inaudible. We have communicated the meta-message that women of color are unimportant to feminist therapy theory and practice.

Such unthinking relegation of women of color's insights to a category of lesser value is inherently destructive to mutuality, to the process of empathy and connection. Such evidence of institutionalized racism may be especially painful to women of color when it comes from white feminist therapists because we have declared ourselves to be attentive to and concerned with oppression (Kanuha, 1990). We are, by default, telling women from North American ethnic minorities, both our colleagues and the recipients of our services, that the only important oppression is gender-based, and that their experiences as targets of racism, or the combination of racism and sexism, are of lesser or no importance.

White women cannot be respectful of women of color if we in any way deny the presence of racism as a dynamic in our relationships with one another. We cannot feel with, or for, each other if one of us, a white woman, is denying her behaviors and their impact on the other of us; with such denial there is no mutuality in connection, no acknowledgement of the unique life which each brings to our encounter.

Additionally, as Jeanne Adleman has pointed out (1988), our failures to acknowledge racism become barriers to mutuality and respect between white women as well. When we do not talk between ourselves as white women about the violence we do to ourselves, our integrity, and our personal sense of morality by our participation, witting or not, in racism and the privilege of our white skin, we have a silence between us. This silence becomes a loss of connection with unconscious process which may lead to a failure of therapy as the therapist's inner voice becomes inaudible to her. Racism unacknowledged constitutes a lie of omission and a disownership of self.

## RACISM AS BOUNDARY VIOLATION

Typically in feminist therapy ethics boundaries have been defined in terms of sexuality and physical contact. Yet personal boundaries are more than sexual. A woman's identity, her sense of herself in her race and ethnicity, her pride or shame in her roots, and her awareness of her culture are all aspects of the boundary phenomenon that are insufficiently attended to by most white therapists.

In this frame, we can conceptualize racist behaviors and attitudes, both covert and overt, as violations of boundaries. Such violations can take many forms. Ignorance of women of colors' realities and experiences is chief among them (Yamada, 1981; Moschkovich, 1981; Lorde, 1981). Internalized domination (Pheterson, 1986), the oppressor-within of white women, often leads us to believe that we really know and understand the experiences of women of color, either because of our powerful socialization in a white racist society to experience our whiteness as evidence of wisdom or expertise, or because we assume that what we know of one woman of color generalizes to all such women. We fail to learn about the immense variability of experiences among women who are lumped together by racist notions. Consequently, white women, who by virtue of our skin belong to the dominant group which defines the social discourse, frequently violate the identities of those women who do not fit our stereotypes of what a woman from a particular group "should" be. When and if white people utilize as sources those studies of people of color conducted by white people, rather than defining as most expert the voices of people of color themselves in all their variations, this constitutes a form of objectification, similar in its impact to sexual objectification, a quality which I would suggest is one of the defining qualities of a boundary violation.

A second common violation of boundaries by white women, this one arising from indifference or lack of information, is the use of our clients who are women of color to educate us. This is different from attending to and valuing the client's experience in that the white therapist has the expectation that she will learn something of a special nature from this client above and beyond what is learned in all therapeutic exchanges. Making of clients of color into our unpaid (and usually paying) teachers constitutes the same sort of role reversal and abuse of therapist power as the use of clients to explicitly care for our emotional emptiness (Hill, 1990). Similarly, we may use our client of color to fill an intellectual void. The message sent to the client of color is that she must care for the therapist's ignorance in order to reduce her risk of being uncared for in therapy. The double-bind is that often the client of color feels that in order to get what she needs emotionally from therapy, which may not even be directly concerned with questions of her racial identity, she must tolerate her white therapist's ignorance and not challenge the latter's errors too strongly or with too much anger for fear of being pathologized as "paranoid" or "defensive" (Boyd, 1990).

White women also violate boundaries through racism when we impose the assumption of similarity of experiences upon women of color, both clients and colleagues. Oppressions are *not* equivalent, and we cannot rank them hierarchically (Kanuha, 1990; Siegel, 1990), yet when white women attempt to use our experiences of sexist or heterosexist oppression as our sole referent for understanding race or cultural oppression, our white privilege often operates so as to subsume and thus reduce even *those* experiences of women of color. In effect, we engage in a blurring of boundaries so as to reassure ourselves of connection with a woman of color. The violation of boundaries caused by engulfment, by the unwillingness on the part of white feminist therapists to acknowledge and delineate differences as well as similarities between ourselves and women of color, persists in part because such acknowledgements can be disconcerting. They remind us of differences, of how we are not all "sisters" together, of how white women benefit every day from racism unless and sometimes even if and when we act against it.

## POWER DYNAMICS

Feminist therapists have a shared ethical commitment toward the development of egalitarian relationships, wishing to practice in ways that reduce unnecessary asymmetries between the power of client and therapist, that empower the client to self-knowledge and self-value, and that lead to increasing mutuality in the therapist-client relationship while preserving those aspects of the frame of therapy that help prevent exploitation or abuses of power.

Inattention to racism serves to perpetuate unspoken power imbalances, and may heighten the power of the therapist if she is white and her client is a woman of color. For if the therapist/white woman does not at some point take the responsibility to open the discussion of racism as a dynamic between them, and take leadership in making the issue important in both the real and symbolic relationships of therapy, the power dynamics of both therapy and racism will probably operate so as to silence the woman of color to at least some degree, leading to a permanent and problematic power imbalance between them if not an outright end to therapy. The silence of the white feminist therapist communicates that the experiences of being the target of racism in the life of her client of color, and in the therapy room, are unimportant. The white woman will have, without speaking, imposed her unexamined values on her client of color. The effects of racism are such that unless white women take the initiative to acknowledge racism as an issue for ourselves, women of color will be excluded or will choose to absent themselves from the precincts of feminist therapy because white people will have taken the power to define the "legitimate" terms of discourse. White women's behaviors can determine to a large degree whether an intellectual or physical space will even be safe, much less inviting, for women of color to enter and inhabit as anything approaching equal co-creators, either as clients or colleagues.

This is clearly not to say that feminist therapists of color as a group are so weak and needy as to lack power or need special protections; they do not. Rather, it is to point to the ethical problem for white feminist therapists that results when we fail to acknowledge the privilege given us by our skin color and the impact that our whiteness has on colleagues who are women of color. As Marie Root and I noted, writing together as a racially mixed woman and a white Jewish woman for whom these issues are a very alive part of our personal relationship, it is insufficient for white feminist therapists to deplore the absence of feminist therapists of color in our midst and hope that they will join us. If white feminist therapists do not actively solicit the participation of feminist therapists of color, do not make the room for a large enough group of women of color to be constituted so as to have impact on the system, and do not take seriously what we are told about the barriers to equal participation that we erect via our covert racism, we will have been exclusionary (Brown & Root, 1990), and will have perpetuated a power imbalance that is inherently racist. If this is the case between white feminist therapists and our colleagues of color, how much more is our racism a source of gross power imbalance between ourselves and the women of color who are our clients.

## *MAKING CHANGES*

In undertaking a process to change the status quo, we must acknowledge that we are embarking on a lifelong and often difficult endeavor of integrating anti-racism into our ethical frameworks. White North Americans are encouraged in our racism, both conscious and unconscious, by almost every element in our culture. The lifelong ethical challenge will be to look in the mirror and see the subtle ways in which racism infiltrates itself; at times, this self-confrontation will be painful because of how we will see ourselves. We are at risk of overlooking our covert participation in oppressive processes, including racism, because such internalized domination is so ego-dystonic.

In first writing this chapter, for instance, I was struck with the realization of how infrequently I and other white feminist therapists refer to theories of personality and psychopathology that have been developed by people of color. This awareness was stimulated by the fact that I had recently been reading a great deal of material written by people of color as I reviewed book chapters for some friends (Comas-Díaz & Greene, 1994), and perused a series of lectures on human diversity published by the American Psychological Association (Jones, 1991; Sue, 1991).

This most recent self-confrontation underscores for me how important it is to get the kind of education that will raise our consciousnesses and empower us to better understand and change our participation in racism. It is essential that this be both cognitive and experiential; the one learning experience in the absence of the other will be a less powerful corrective because it will not address the multi-faceted nature of our learning of racism. Racism is both thought and felt; to unlearn it, to learn how to work against it, requires education of both heart and mind.

Almost all of the work done in the helping professions to create this sort of education against racism has been done by therapists of color. In feminist therapy, for example, the work of Boyd (1990), Bradshaw (1990), Bradshaw and Root (1994), Comas-Díaz (1987), Comas-Díaz and Greene (1994), Espín (1984, 1987, 1994), Espín and Gawelek (1992), Greene (1986, 1990), Ho (1990), Kanuha (1990), Mays and Comas-Díaz (1988), Protacio-Marcellino (1990), Root (1985, 1990, 1992), Sears (1990), and Vásquez (in press), among others, has created a foundation upon which a vision of a multicultural feminist therapy can begin to be built. White feminist therapists cannot continue to rely on our colleagues of color for this education, which often means asking that they encounter yet again our covertly racist attitudes and behaviors. Instead, an ever larger percentage of this work must be, and is beginning to be, the product of anti-racist white women.

A next step in the ethics process involves the development and clarification of standards for anti-racist practice. This is bound to be a complex process because there are few general principles to elucidate. We cannot, for example, require that a white feminist therapist see "X" number of women of color in her practice, since this choice belongs to clients. This also smacks loudly of tokenism as a problem-solving device, not one which will accomplish our ethical goals. We may, however, be able to develop standards that suggest that anyone who calls herself a feminist therapist will have had, and will continue to pursue, the kind of emotional and didactic education in cultural literacy and anti-racism described above.

At a minimum, an ethical practitioner of feminist therapy should be able to adhere to the guidelines for practice with clients of color published recently by the Board of Ethnic Minority Affairs of the American Psychological Association, developed by a group which included several feminist therapists of color. Documents such as this define a minimal standard of multicultural competency which, while being acquired, serves as a challenge to racism in the white therapist. The development of an anti-racist perspective may come to be seen as one of several criteria for competency in feminist therapy, without which one might not ethically call herself a feminist therapist. This standard would assume that being anti-racist is important for a feminist therapist regardless of the racial composition of her client population.

Finally, there is the process of self-criticism and mutual confrontation. This is not the final step in real life, where confrontation has usually come first, and has been necessary for many white women to begin making education and consciousness-raising on our racism a priority. In the real world, people of color are continually confronted with the racism of white people and culture. An ethic of anti-racism in feminist therapy asks that white women share in that experience of confrontation. Some of us, both white and women of color alike, have avoided confrontation; others have met confrontation with silence, or have fled. Because racism has been a source of rage and pain for women of color, their confrontations of white women are not and cannot always be easy to deliver or hear. Nor are women of color the only ones confronting racism among white women. White women are increasingly taking the responsibility to do this and we, too, are discovering that our confrontations of each other will sometimes be hard to express and to hear.

Thus, perhaps most essentially, we must build an ethical imperative of self-confrontation about racism as a first step. It is a simple yet powerful thing to acknowledge that, by virtue of being raised white in a white-dominant culture, it is nearly impossible for anyone to be free of white racism. This first step cannot be skipped because it allows us to begin to push aside shame and guilt which stop us from action to change. It creates the possibility of leaving denial behind, of owning the racism within ourselves, which we wish to disown, so that we can transform it.

## REACHING AGREEMENT ON CHANGES

We can and must also agree to confront one another, and white women must not rely upon the rage and courage of women of color to confront us. But I stress the word *agreement*; just as feminist therapists have a covenant among ourselves to confront sexual abuses in therapy, so must we join in wanting to know about our racism. A problem that I have observed in past experiences of confrontation of racism among white feminist therapists has been that we have often not agreed to accept these confrontations from anyone, and have been angry and resentful when they happened. An agreement to engage in (and, in consequence, be the recipient of) mutual constructive confrontation will not make this process comfortable, but it will take the necessary step of legitimating anti-racism as a spur to ethical confrontations among feminist therapists. Just as we want to hear about our other ethically problematic attitudes and behaviors early in the process so that we can change more easily and with the least ongoing harm to all concerned, so we, feminist therapists, white and of color together, must want to hear about our racism, which is another ethically problematic way of thinking, feeling, and being. The agreement to hear, see, and know about racism in ourselves is the core of making anti-racism a norm for ethical feminist therapy practice.

## REFERENCES

Adleman, Jeanne (1988, May). *Dealing with racism during therapy when client and therapist are both white women.* Paper presented at the Seventh Advanced Feminist Therapy Institute, Seattle, WA.

Boyd, Julia A. (1990). Ethnic and cultural diversity in feminist therapy: Keys to power. In Evelyn White (Ed.), *The Black women's health book: Speaking for ourselves* (pp. 226-243). Seattle: Seal Press.

Bradshaw, Carla K. (1990). A Japanese view of dependency: What can Amae psychology contribute to feminist theory and therapy? In Laura S. Brown & Maria P. P. Root (Eds.), *Diversity and complexity in feminist therapy.* New York: The Haworth Press.

Bradshaw, Carla K., & Root, Maria P. P. (1994). Asian American women. In Lillian Comas-Díaz & Beverly Greene (Eds.), *Women of color and mental health.* New York: Guilford Press.

Brown, Laura S. (1990). The meaning of a multicultural perspective for theory-building in feminist therapy. In Laura S. Brown & Maria P. P. Root (Eds.), *Diversity and complexity in feminist therapy* (pp. 1-22). New York: The Haworth Press.

Brown, Laura S., & Root, Maria P. P. (1990). Editorial introduction. In Laura S. Brown & Maria P. P. Root (Eds.), *Diversity and complexity in feminist therapy* (pp. ix-xiii). New York: The Haworth Press.

Comas-Díaz, Lillian (1987). Feminist therapy with mainland Puerto Rican women. *Psychology of Women Quarterly, 11,* 461-474.

Comas-Díaz, Lillian, & Greene, Beverly (Eds.) (1994). *Women of color and mental health.* New York: Guilford Press.

Davis, Angela Y. (1983). *Women, race and class.* New York: Vintage Books.

Espín, Oliva M. (1984). Cultural and historical influences on sexuality in Hispanic/Latin women: Implications for psychotherapy. In Carole Vance (Ed.), *Pleasure and danger: Exploring female sexuality.* London: Routledge and Kegan Paul.

_____ (1987). Issues of identity in the psychology of Latina lesbians. In Boston Lesbian Psychologies Collective (Eds.). *Lesbian psychologies: Explorations and challenges* (pp. 35-54). Urbana: University of Illinois Press.

_____ (1994). Feminist approaches. In Lillian Comas-Díaz & Beverly Greene (Eds.), *Women of color and mental health.* New York: Guilford.

Espín, Oliva M., & Gawelek, Mary Ann (1992). Women's diversity: Ethnicity, race, class and gender in theories of feminist psychology. In Laura S. Brown & Mary Ballou (Eds.), *Personality and psychopathology: Feminist reappraisals.* New York: Guilford.

Greene, Beverly (1986). When the therapist is white and the patient is Black: Some considerations for psychotherapy in the feminist heterosexual and lesbian communities. *Women and Therapy, 5,* 41-66.

_____ (1990). What has gone before: The legacy of racism and sexism in the lives of Black mothers and daughters. In Laura S. Brown & Maria P. P. Root (Eds.), *Diversity and complexity in feminist therapy* (pp. 207-230). New York: The Haworth Press.

Hill, Marcia (1990). On creating a theory of feminist therapy. In Laura S. Brown & Maria P. P. Root (Eds.), *Diversity and complexity in feminist therapy* (pp. 53-66). New York: The Haworth Press.

Ho, Christine Kan (1990). An analysis of domestic violence in Asian American communities: A multicultural approach to counseling. In Laura S. Brown &

Maria P. P. Root (Eds.), *Diversity and complexity in feminist therapy* (pp. 129-150). New York: The Haworth Press.

hooks, bell (1981). *Ain't I a woman: Black women and feminism*. Boston: South End Press.

Jones, James (1991). Psychological models of race: What have they been and what should they be? In Jacqueline D. Goodchilds (Ed.), *Psychological perspectives on human diversity in America* (pp. 3-46). Washington, DC: American Psychological Association.

Kanuha, Valli (1990). The need for an integrated analysis of oppression in feminist therapy ethics. In Hannah Lerman & Natalie Porter (Eds.), *Feminist ethics in psychotherapy* (pp. 24-36). New York: Springer.

Lorde, Audre (1980, April). *Age, race, class, and sex: Women redefining difference*. Copeland Colloquium, Amherst College, Amherst, MA.

————— (1981). An open letter to Mary Daly. In Cherrie Moraga & Gloria Anzaldua (Eds.), *This bridge called my back: Writings by radical women of color*, (pp. 94-97). Watertown, MA: Persephone Press.

Mays, Vickie M., & Comas-Díaz, Lillian (1988). Feminist therapy with ethnic minority populations. In Mary Ann Dutton-Douglas & Lenore E. A. Walker (Eds.), *Feminist psychotherapies: Integration of feminist and therapeutic systems* (pp. 228-251). Norwood, NJ: Ablex.

Moraga, Cherrie, & Anzaldúa, Gloria (Eds.) (1981). *This bridge called my back: Writings by radical women of color*. Watertown, MA: Persephone Press.

Moschkovich, Judit (1981). But I know you, American woman. In Cherrie Moraga & Gloria Anzaldúa (Eds.), *This bridge called my back: Writings by radical women of color*, (pp. 79-84). Watertown, MA: Persephone Press.

Pheterson, Gail (1986). Alliances between women: Overcoming internalized oppression and internalized domination. *Signs: Journal of Women in Culture and Society, 12*, 146-160.

Protacio-Marcellino, Elizabeth (1990). Towards understanding the psychology of the Filipino. In Laura S. Brown & Maria P. P. Root (Eds.), *Diversity and complexity in feminist therapy* (pp. 105-128). New York: The Haworth Press.

Rave, Elizabeth J., & Larsen, Carolyn C. (1990). Development of the code: The feminist process. In Hannah Lerman & Natalie Porter (Eds.), *Feminist ethics in psychotherapy* (pp. 14-23). New York: Springer.

Root, M. P. P. (1985). Guidelines for facilitating therapy with Asian-American clients. *Psychotherapy: Theory, Research Practice, Training, 22* (2S), 342-348.

Root, Maria P. P. (1990). Resolving "other" status: Identity development of biracial individuals. In Laura S. Brown & Maria P. P. Root (Eds.), *Diversity and complexity in feminist therapy* (pp. 185-206). New York: Haworth Press.

————— (Ed.) (1992). *Racially mixed people in America: Within, between, and beyond race*. Newbury Park, CA: Sage.

Sears, Vickie L. (1990). On being an "only one." In Hannah Lerman & Natalie Porter (Eds.), *Feminist ethics in psychotherapy* (pp. 102-105). New York: Springer.

Siegel, Rachel Josefowitz (1990). Turning the things that divide us into strengths that unite us. In Laura S. Brown & Maria P. P. Root (Eds.), *Diversity and complexity in feminist therapy* (pp. 327-336). New York: The Haworth Press.

Sue, Stanley (1991). Ethnicity and culture in psychological research and practice. In Jacqueline D. Goodchilds (Ed.), *Psychological perspectives on human diversity in America* (pp. 47-86). Washington, DC: American Psychological Association.

Vásquez, Melba J. T. (In press). Latinas. In Lillian Comas-Díaz & Beverly Greene (Eds.), *Women of color and mental health*. New York: Guilford.

Walker, Alice (1983). *In search of our mothers' gardens: Womanist prose*. New York: Harcourt, Brace, Jovanovich.

Yamada, Mitsui (1981). Asian Pacific American women and feminism. In Cherrie Moraga & Gloria Anzaldúa (Eds.), *This bridge called my back: Writings by radical women of color* (pp. 71-75). Watertown, MA: Persephone Press.

# Violence, Migration, and Compassionate Practice: Conversations with Some Latinas We Think We Know

Lourdes Argüelles
Anne Rivero

Several years ago the first author was teaching a course on immigrant and refugee women at a graduate school of social welfare in Southern California. The class of approximately 20 students, some of whom were of Latino ancestry, had recently begun working as interns in public agencies and had a number of recent Latina immigrant and refugee women in their caseloads. In the early part of the course it became apparent that in spite of their work experience, academic backgrounds in ethnic studies, and, in some cases, relevant family history, the majority of the students had fully partaken of the common misbeliefs and generalizations which have evolved about transnational migration dynamics of Third World women.

Though the students admitted to not having explored in depth the migration experiences of their female clients or family members, they had a ready set of assumptions about why those women had been motivated to undergo the hardship of migration. They presented beliefs commonly understood about rather narrowly defined political and economic forces, and seemed to assume that this was the end of the story. Absent from their speculations about these women's histories and possible contributing factors to their migration were issues of gender violence, enforced sex and gender roles, sexual orientation, sexual abuse and assault, or coerced motherhood. No one suggested the possibility that for some women transnational migration may have been one more strategy for managing or escaping from gender and sexual abuse and victimization. Few envisioned the women as being involved in an ongoing struggle to reconstruct the rigid and confining gender roles received in their countries and cultures of origin. No student ventured into speculating about whether or not issues of same-sex erotic attraction or orientation might have been a contributing influence in women's decision making in their migration odysseys. These classroom observations seem to have been reflective of the fact that ethnic and women's studies curricula and immigration research do not, for the most part, include in-depth exploration of gender role issues, erotic orientation, and sexual exploitation dynamics as key elements in migration motivations, resettlement processes, and return migration patterns (Argüelles, in press). The acknowledgement of the sex selectivity factor in migration, of the demand for female immigrant labor in certain U.S. industrial sectors, of sex-role changes in transplanted households and in new workplaces, and the occasional reference to oppression and exploitation of women in the domestic and public spheres of both the sending and receiving countries does not exhaust the study of migration dynamics among women.

In consideration of frequently overlooked influencing factors this paper seeks not only to include the voices of immigrant and refugee women, but to listen for those parts of their messages that are usually unheard or omitted. It is based on conversations with over 100 Latina women who themselves had experienced a transnational migration journey with a final destination of the United States. We have listened to them and believe the content of their stories to be crucial for understanding women's migration processes and for the development and implementation of effective and compassionate helping strategies in immigrant and refugee communities. Their words are often about gender and sexual violence factors, sexual orientation and erotic desire, ethno-gender abuse, and heterosexist oppression. Their words also recount their experiences of resistance, survival, and transformation.

We met these women in the course of doing clinical mental health work, AIDS prevention education, and immigration and human rights advocacy in Southern California and in Tijuana and Mexicali, Mexico in the late 1980s and early 1990s. Notes were made on dialogues with the women, after which the material was re-verified with them for accuracy whenever possible. Any mistakes or misinterpretations were corrected so that the final version could be a reasoned account agreed upon by the authors and the persons described or quoted.[1]

Some of the initial conversations took place during informal moments of sharing at the end of health education *platicas* or talks given in safe houses in the San Diego area. On one such occasion there were seven women present, all of whom were recent immigrants or refugees from Mexico, Guatemala, and El Salvador. Sara Hernandez, a woman from Ciudad Guatemala who was seeking work as a seamstress, came to express thanks for the information just received. She revealed that for the first time she had some understanding of "the parts of me below the waist." She said that she felt stupid for having been married for 12 years and not having better understood her body. She added that she wished she had known more before about prevention of AIDS and other sexually transmitted diseases, but stated that even if she had possessed such knowledge she would not have been able to do anything about it. She went on to say, "Back home I couldn't say anything. My husband would force me to have sex whenever and in whichever way he wanted. I was sick of him. That is why I came here. Things aren't so great here, but at least I got away from him and his abuse." When asked about her hopes for the future she replied, "I hope to go back one day, but not if I have to depend on him. In my country it is not possible for a woman to make it on her own just as a seamstress. I need to stay here long enough to save some money and learn English. I want to be able to go back and start a little business and do work for the gringos living in my country."

The other women listened in silence. Then, one by one, as if having received permission to reveal long-suppressed secrets, they began to give testimony to various combinations of violences that contributed to their decisions to leave their homelands. Dolores was one such woman. She was an adolescent from Sonora who quietly stated, "My uncle had been using me sexually since I was about three years old. My mother knew but could do nothing about it because she depended on him. We all did. My father left when I was born, and we depended upon my uncle even for food. Since I was old enough to understand my mother told me to go North. It was her only way to protect me. But even if she had not said it, I would have come.''

The words of Chini, a woman from San Salvador, quickly followed. "I know my parents knew I was different because I was always falling in love with some woman they knew. So when I was 17 they told me to come to the United States and to send money back to them. My sisters were not permitted to come, but then they were not beaten up as often as I was. We all were beaten though. I was also scared of the war and of the soldiers. I don't like men too much. They make me scared. One almost forced himself on me but I was able to make him stop. I am glad that I don't have to think that I may be infected with AIDS. I don't take drugs either.''

Mila, a 24-year-old woman from Tijuana, spoke next. "When I was 14 they found me kissing my best girlfriend. It was a pretty deep kiss. So they beat me up, and then they took me to this priest. He fondled me and wanted to go all the way. My father wanted me to get married immediately and have a baby so I could get cured. I ran away and crossed the border. I was 15. I wanted to come here anyway because of the jobs and because the place is cleaner. We are poor back home.''

Marta, a 19-year-old woman from a town near San Salvador, then spoke. "I was raped by the son of the mayor when I was 12. My father is a policeman and he wanted no trouble. So I was sent to find my brother here. I was glad at first to come. Now I'm not sure, and I am very lonely. I am glad I know about this AIDS and what to do including getting tested. I also hope I can avoid ever being raped again.''

The words of Esmeralda, a woman from Ensenada, concluded the testimonies. She reported, "I could have put up with the poverty and with all the other problems like the bad health of my oldest boy, but I could not take all the beatings that my husband gave me. He wanted me to continue to have babies, but I would tell him that three was more than enough. I only wanted two babies in the first place. He beat me up when he found out I went to the clinic and asked for an abortion. He almost killed me. I left one night. I went to Tijuana and then crossed over. I had to leave my kids behind with my mother.''

There were no dry eyes in the room, but there was a sense of relief in having given testimony that was met with the compassion that often comes from having shared similar experiences. We talked a while longer, and then the women were asked individually if the notes made of their stories reflected what they had said and what they really meant. A few details were added and two women offered some minor corrections. Sara Hernandez asked that her full name be used whenever her words were presented to someone else.

Several months later we engaged in lengthy conversations with several women in the offices of an immigration advocacy center in Los Angeles County. These conversations dealt more specifically with perceptions of differences in the nature of violence perpetrated against immigrant and refugee women in border cities and in the United States compared to similar types of violence experienced in their places of origin. We made notes of conversations with six women. All agreed that upon arriving in the border towns unaccompanied by men, the violence and abuse that they had to endure was of a more public nature than that which they had experienced earlier in their lives.

Consuelo, a woman from Guerrero, explained it this way. "When I was six my father took me and then again when I was eight and he had just come back from the North. Then a boyfriend raped me when I was 13. But they did it quietly so I could keep it a secret. They did not talk when they were doing it, so I closed my eyes and tried to sleep. I just told my sister. I was very ashamed, but nobody knew but her. In Tijuana the boss in the *maquila* raped me, but he did not do it quietly. He did it in front of his son to prove he could still do it. He kept saying that I should be grateful because I am getting old. I could not return to work. Everyone knew, so I crossed the border two days later. If I had not left, the other men would have tried to make it with me. I was so ashamed."

Another change articulated by the women was the degree to which their color, ethnicities, and nationalities were implicated in the abuse and violence they suffered upon arrival in the United States. Maria Rosa, a woman from El Salvador, shared her experience and emphasized its seemingly culturally sanctioned nature. She put it this way. "Officer X raped me at X. He kept calling me 'Wetback' and 'Indian' as he did it. He also said that he was an officer, and so he could do this. The other officer was watching and smoking. I guess they figure they have the right to do this. Who would challenge them?" After a long pause Maria Rosa added, "To be seen as a bad woman is bad enough. But to be Salvadoran here is a curse. You can't do anything to avoid that."

Conversations such as these have continued in the context of our clinical work with more time, privacy, and opportunity to explore in depth the impacts of these violences as Latina immigrant and refugee women attempt to cope with the physical, emotional, and spiritual impacts of ethno-gender and sexual abuse and the stresses of migration and resettlement. As with abused women of all ethno-national groups the scars of abuse have left these women with impaired emotional resources with which to cope with the stresses of everyday life (Schechter & Gary, 1990). Depression, anxiety, fear, mood swings, rage, suicidal ideation, and dissociative states are daily experiences in their lives and the presenting symptomatology in our offices. However, unlike women of some other ethno-national origins and of higher social locations, these women have few material resources with which to cope with the sequelae of gender, sexual, and ethno-racial violence. The combination of resettlement stresses and the aftermath or simultaneous endurance of abuse was explained by Estela, a woman from Ciudad Guatemala. She related, "I knew it was going to be hard making it here without much of an education, but I thought that my strength and my faith in God would get me through. But I cannot do it. I cannot work 12 hours a day and then go home and be yelled at, hit, and spit at. It is too much."

Some women who bravely endured the migration journey in a successful attempt to escape violence and abuse find their efforts to build a new life through the resettlement process destroyed by current violence. In some cases the damage may manifest in the form of incapacitating disorders such as Post Traumatic Stress Syndrome. The words of Margarita, a Salvadoran woman in her early thirties tell one such story. "I was used sexually as a child, and my husband knew this when he married me, so he considered me someone worthless, someone he could do anything with. When I didn't want to be intimate with him he would beat me and say horrible things to me, and would say I was no good as a wife. I had forgotten most of what happened to me when I was little, and when I left my husband to come to this country I thought I could be free of all that stuff for good. I did well until one night when a man broke into my room and tried to rape me. Now I am terrified all the time. I can't sleep, and I remember a lot of things I never wanted to know. I am afraid at night, and afraid to go out of the house." Margarita was so terrified of men that she was unable to walk on the street or go to work, and was so depressed and anxious that she needed medication before she could begin to work on her trauma resolution. She asked her therapist how you can heal from something that keeps happening.

Though the majority of the abusers of the women were males, in a small proportion of cases other women including their mothers, sisters, lesbian lovers, or the spouses of male perpetrators have been implicated in the abuse. This more unusual type of history was recounted by Georgina, a 27-year-old woman from Mexico, at a time when she was so alone, desolate, and suicidal that she had to be hospitalized. She revealed, "My mother hated me. She beat me physically and verbally. She would beat me with rosebushes so that the thorns would be left sticking in my skin. She was very close to my older brother. When I was older he would have sex with me and then he would beat me too. When I was 15 I tried to kill myself three times. I tried again when I was 16." At 18 Georgina managed to escape from her home to begin her journey to the United States where she wandered from place to place in constant fear that her mother would one day find her. On the day she was seen in psychiatric emergency she had been abandoned by her male partner. She had no traditional female support system that she could turn to, as she had such a fear and mistrust of women.

In recent times some instances of violence and abuse against immigrant women, including some in which other women were co-perpetrators, have been reaching public attention through the media. In one such case a conviction was brought against the abuser, Paul Garcia. He was found to have kept one Guatemalan woman and one Salvadoran woman as sex slaves after having engaged them as seamstresses and then keeping them imprisoned in his home. The women were beaten, raped, and tortured repeatedly. They were also forced to clean and cook by Garcia's wife, and to care for the family ("Man Guilty of Kidnapping," 1992). The impact of these few instances of women abusing women serves to further isolate the victims by the invalidation of traditional sources of support. As explained by Estela, "You are brought up to see other women as your competitors [for men]. Then as time goes by you make women friends, and you know that that is not always true. But then some woman abuses you and that's it. Women become your worst enemies."

In the process of coping with the impacts and actualities of gender and sexual abuse and ethno-national and heterosexist oppression these women we came to know have engaged in a variety of resistance, survival, and transformational strategies. Unlike some abuse victims, of other ethnic backgrounds or legal status, the majority of the women to whom we spoke were undocumented or in the process of trying to legalize their status, and were fearful of reporting their assailants to the police. In addition to the traditional reasons given by other crime victims for not calling the police such as "nothing can be done" and "the police would not want to be bothered" (Zawitz, 1983), these women reported being truly afraid that police officers would deport them and/or rape them. Instead of turning to law enforcement, a number of alternative strategies were adopted in the attempt to escape or manage the violences that beset the women in their resettlement contexts.

The first strategy, more popular among women involved erotically with other women than among heterosexuals, was to resort to what is perceived as masculine attire and mannerisms. This practice has a long history in societies as different as the United States, Mexico, England, and France (Faderman, 1981; Garber, 1992; Wheelwright, 1989). In our conversations the women have reported considerable success with this technique. Chini has found that dressing like a male seems to make her more intimidating even for those people who know that she is a woman. In her words, "Some think I am a man and so they don't bother me. They are looking for girls. Others who know I am a woman think that maybe I can defend myself like a man so they are less likely to try something. When they try I'll be ready for them. Besides I like it."

A second strategy involved forceful intimidation or forceful self-defense. Encarnacion, a woman from Michoacan, reported that since she owns a gun she feels more confident when she goes out. She added, "My daughter says that I even walk like a man now."

She also reported that she has used the gun to intimidate her brother-in-law, who has been making passes at her since they were both living in Mexico ten years ago.

A third strategy has involved a kind of geographical and time bounding coupled with anonymity and disengagement from traditional networks of support. The women reported that they were careful to live in places where their old acquaintances and families had less chance of finding them. They also would avoid certain streets and particular times to be out. Though this strategy, according to several women we spoke to, has helped them in avoiding extreme forms of violence, the costs in terms of isolation and constraint have been quite high. Conny, also from Michoacan, reported that she has seldom ventured out of the confines of her neighborhood after having endured a gang rape more than three years before. She works at home doing piecework which a *comadre* delivers and picks up for her. She also avoids going out at night. Conny, to whom we talked in an AIDS prevention session held in a laundromat close to her home in San Diego, spoke at length about wanting to go back home to Mexico just to feel more free to come and go and be around people to talk to.

Another strategy is one that we can label religious or spiritual and has entailed involvement with mainstream and non-mainstream institutional religious structures. The women have found a considerable amount of support in these settings, though a few have reported some attempts at exploitation of a sexual and/or economic nature by priests, pastors, or healers. We asked what had been most helpful in their spiritual strategy of resistance. Some of the women articulated that in some such settings, particularly those in which other women like themselves participated or where a woman acted as a spiritual advisor, no false hopes were encouraged. In these instances the realities of their lives were taken as given, and the extreme difficulty of changing those realities was acknowledged. There was less of the fatalism or of the shallow spirituality of hope that had once disappointed them.

A handful of the women we talked to mentioned that they had seen a counselor or therapist of one sort or another, and the reviews about those experiences were mixed. One persistent negative comment, however, was that some of the counselors felt that individual change was necessary before the women could engage in strategies to redress wrongs.

As with migration and resettlement, return migration may also be mediated by the combined experience of gender and sexual violence and ethno-national discrimination. Where once migration to border cities or onward to the United States was seen as escape from intolerably violent conditions at home, with the passage of years the past may have become recreated or reinterpreted in the context of a difficult present. The familiarity of the homeland may have come to be fantasized as more comfortable or safer than the present situation. For others return migration is the dream they dreamt before they left home and has remained their continued fantasy throughout their migratory experience (Grinberg & Grinberg, 1989). Idalia, a woman from Ciudad Mexico commented, "I never thought I would go back, though I always dreamt about it. Of course the city I imagined in my dreams was not the actual one I left. But things got so bad for me in the United States. I was fired because I was a Mexican and a lesbian, and I was without a job for months. Then my brother came to the U.S. and looked me up. He had molested me as a child and wanted to continue with that. I was homeless for a few weeks, and Mexico seemed my salvation. I went back and I stayed for about a year, but it didn't work. It was the same old stuff back there: my father drunk and abusive with my mother and trying to make it with me. Then one day the police came to the bar where I liked to go and rounded up most of the women. So I came back here. I am not really happy here, but I have a job now, and in Los Angeles I don't think my brother can find me. In Mexico City they manage somehow to find me, and what I want is not to be found."

Our conversations with these immigrant and refugee women whose migration motivations and outcomes as well as their gender definitions, ethno-racial identities, and sexualities have been greatly impacted by intimate and public violence have convinced us of the need to reexamine our understandings of transnational migration. We see the necessity of expanding empirico-theoretic frameworks to incorporate a detailed consideration of the reinforcing patterns and dynamics of abuse and coercive control to which women are subjected at the interpersonal and macro-structural levels of everyday life in both their countries of origin and in their resettlement settings. In addition, more work is needed to elucidate the costs and benefits of specific strategies with which these women may resist these forces, survive their impacts, and transform their received gender roles and messages about sexuality and sexual orientation as well as about other perceived attributes of self. Such understandings are urgently needed for the development of effective helping modalities for progressive work in immigrant and refugee communities.

On a more personal level these conversations are rich in important implications for both of us. They have led us to the realization that in our previous work on migration we had not fully recognized the import of abuse and violence in the creation and reinforcement of psychological and structural borders in the everyday lives of women. We have learned to listen more carefully to women's histories and to make our range of inquiries broader and deeper.

We have also been able to learn of the influence of context and setting in facilitating such trusting conversations. It is now clear that settings in which sexually related content, such as STD prevention or family planning, is already being discussed can best facilitate the disclosure of coercive sex experiences and other types of abuse. We have realized the importance of safe spaces for the revealing of such sensitive and personal material, spaces which become intimate by the very nature of the experiences shared therein.

We have also been reminded of the need for appropriately prepared internal space for the reception of both the experiences and the trust of women such as those mentioned above. We have learned that to listen and hear we must quiet the mind of its internal chatter and preconceived notions and allow the space necessary for the words of these women, in whatever form their stories may emerge.

Most importantly, we have witnessed the power of compassion in the interactions and sharings among the women. In the giving of their stories and their trust they have taught us again and again of the healing nature of a non-judgmental and compassionate openness to one another's experience and of the transformative potential of bonding through shared womanhood that blurs the boundaries of self and other.

Finally, the women have refreshed us with balance and spirit by reminding us that there is much more to their lives than tragedy and victimization. This was expressed by Sara Hernandez as a follow-up to her personal revelations when she added, "But don't look so sad! There is more to my life than ugly things (*cosas feas*). I'm going to give a big party when I get my own place. I have dreams."

## NOTE

1. Though the use of terms such as "abuse," "violence," and "assault" used in varying ways by different persons and groups can lead to some misunderstanding, we have chosen to make the sharing less demanding for the women by refraining from asking them to precisely define their terms. We saw our primary task in this work as one of documenting conversations with the explicit purpose of assisting these women and others like them in their struggles, in line with feminist perspectives on violence/abuse research and treatment. Therefore our focus was on encouraging and facilitating the exploration by these women of the experiences of force used against them.

## REFERENCES

Argüelles, Lourdes (in press). Tata's teachings and moral alibis in feminist scholarship and pedagogy. *The California Sociologist, 14,* 1-2, 71-79.

Faderman, Lillian (1981). *Surpassing the love of men: Romantic friendship and love between women from the renaissance to the present.* New York: William Morrow.

Garber, Marjorie (1992). *Vested interests: Cross-dressing and cultural anxiety.* New York: Routledge.

Grinberg, Leon, & Grinberg, Rebecca (1989). *Psychoanalytic perspectives on migration and exile.* New Haven: Yale University Press.

Man guilty of kidnapping, raping two women could get 200 years. (1992, November). *Inland Valley Daily Bulletin,* p. B7.

Schechter, S., & Gary, L. (1988). A framework for understanding and empowering battered women. In Murray B. Straus (Ed.) *Abuse and victimization across the life span* (pp. 240-253). Baltimore: The Johns Hopkins University Press.

Wheelwright, Julie (1989). *Amazons and military maids: Women who dressed as men in pursuit of life, liberty, and happiness.* London: Pandora.

Zawitz, M. (Ed.) (1983). *Report to the nation of crime and justice: The data.* Washington, DC: U.S. Department of Justice.

# Double Positive:
# Lesbians and Race

Dorian Leslie
Lauren Mac Neill[1]

Racism affects all people, and the impact of racism on lesbians merits special attention. In the climate of our racist, sexist, and heterosexist culture, living with one oppressed identity is complex; living with plural oppressed identities can seem overwhelming. Challenges manifest on three principal levels: identity, community, and intimate relationships.

For lesbians of color, conflicts can abound: how do they integrate identities of lesbian, woman, person of color? White lesbians are not accepted by their white cultural community, because they are lesbians; still, they have access to power because they are white. Power is increased or decreased by other kinds of identities, such as socio-economic class, gender, age, and physical ability, among others. White lesbians who wish to work toward anti-racism must confront their own racism and position of white privilege, and challenge themselves to work consciously and without condescension toward ending all oppressions. Understanding the nexus of racism and heterosexism demands vigorous exploration and analysis.

## ISSUES OF COMMUNITY

"Community" connotes membership, inclusiveness, a sense of shared characteristics and values. We learn our early sense of identity from communities such as family, neighborhood, gender, and religious affiliation. All people are members of several communities. A feeling of belonging can be nurturing and empowering. At the same time, some communities can be exclusive, intolerant of difference, and can require strict adherence to values and norms.

Many lesbians of color describe a sense of displacement, of not feeling truly accepted or at home in either the majority lesbian community or in their ethnic community. This sense of displacement is fostered and sometimes even encouraged by racism in the lesbian communities and by homophobia in ethnic minority communities. White lesbians, particularly those who are politically active, can experience frustration and confusion when dealing with racial issues. Without fully understanding the issues involved, their efforts can be misguided, and thus frequently ineffective or potentially harmful.

## RACISM IN THE LESBIAN COMMUNITY

The majority of the most visible lesbian community is composed of white, middle-class and upper-class lesbians. Because of this, lesbians of color, as well as working-class lesbians of all racial groups, often feel misunderstood, marginalized, or unrepresented by the better-known community and organizations. Many communities, wishing to amend this problem, actively solicit the participation of women of color. While many argue that the lesbian community, having endured its own oppression, is more understanding of the struggles of other minority groups and as such is less racist than society at large, racism does exist in the lesbian community, and it hurts lesbians of color *and* white lesbians.

Racism in the lesbian community is manifest in several ways. Ethnic minority lesbians often experience a sense of not belonging or of tokenism in the majority lesbian community. The women's newspaper in Dorian's community campaigned heavily to recruit "women of color." Dorian joined, her appropriate suspicion allowing her to think she was getting an "easy invitation." She wondered, "Do they think I'm black enough?" Was her presence as a dark-skinned black woman enough at the monthly contributors' meetings? As a black lesbian, was she "woman of color" enough to include Latinas, Asians, Native Americans?

Exclusion is racism. Overt exclusion exists when the leadership and/or membership of gay rights organizations is composed largely of white people. Paradoxically, the unchecked, and frequently erroneous, perception of inclusion is likewise racist. Covert or unconscious racism exists when predominantly white lesbian communities make assumptions about shared values and goals. For years, Lauren spoke on panels about issues of sexual orientation and said, "lesbians feel" or "lesbians want" not realizing that what she meant was "*white* lesbians feel" or "*white* lesbians want."

Unconscious racism occurs when white lesbian communities acknowledge racism but distance themselves from any personal responsibility, believing that lesbians have transcended racism. Racism is alive in the lesbian community when white lesbians fail to analyze and discuss their experience *as* white lesbians, to acknowledge how they have internalized and do not question white cultural values. However well-intentioned, organizations often fail to critically examine their possibly racist goals or structures. Lauren was part of a rape crisis collective that wanted to recruit more women of color as volunteer advocates. They never considered the politics of rape regarding race, they never looked at how, even with their collective structure, they might be unconsciously exclusive.

## HOMOPHOBIA IN COMMUNITIES OF COLOR

Homophobia exists in ethnic minority communities for several reasons. In the context of a dominant culture in which the values and traditions of white culture(s) are pervasive, maintaining and continuing an ethnic minority culture is threatened. People of color can feel resentful of white gay people's ability to "pass" as members of the dominant heterosexual community. Further, many people of color are confounded by a person's desire to take on yet another oppressed identity. While the cause of homosexuality remains a controversial subject even among members of the lesbian, gay, and bisexual community, the belief that homosexuality is a choice, as opposed to being innate, can exacerbate this confusion and frustration.

One form homophobia takes is a kind of racial stereotyping by the ethnic communities: the contention that lesbianism is "a white thing." Ethnic minority communities in the United States often believe that homosexuality is a defect of the dominant culture, and that if members of their community are acting as homosexuals, they are only doing so to be more like white people, and could and should stop. Ethnic communities can promote the idea of lesbianism being "a white thing" to discourage women of color from living lesbian lives. They contend that white women, having a higher level of privilege, can more easily abandon their lives with men. Lesbianism by any woman of color can be seen as destructive to the cause of racial civil rights, partly because she may choose to focus her social and political energies on her other oppressed identity, and partly because she may draw unwelcome negative attention to the community.

Homophobia also manifests in the language used by ethnic communities to refer to lesbians. It is not only in American English that many of the words that refer to lesbianism are pejorative.

One defense against the encroaching white culture and the obliteration of the minority culture is to bear children, to educate members in values, traditions, languages of the culture, and to further bond and strengthen connections with other group members. As such, some ethnic minority women feel pressured to bear children and perpetuate the race. For example, some African-American women, having internalized images of the "strong, black woman" responsible for creating more members of the black race, feel that if they admit to loving women they are betraying their people.

The face of homophobia has changed over time, and this change is attributable to greater economic and social mobility. A generation ago, economic necessity and more overt white racism meant that black gays lived within the black community; there they were tolerated, if not altogether accepted, although many lived fairly closeted lives. More recently, their movement away has led to less tolerance and made more permissible overt homophobia from the black community.

To counteract racism in the lesbian community and homophobia in communities of color, oppressed groups also recognize the differences in politics, class, culture, and race, and don't fight for priority status. Ethnic communities and lesbian communities must realize that it is not they who have created the system of oppression, but rather straight patriarchal white culture that has created and has the power to enforce it. The tendency to cross-blame other persecuted communities is easier on the community's psyche because it is less daunting than acknowledging the power of white oppression. It is imperative that all oppressed groups seek to understand, and define, oppression for themselves.

White lesbian communities must take responsibility for educating themselves about anti-racism. They need better networking in communities of color, not simply among their few friends. White lesbian communities can challenge the notion of "community" as necessarily singular, and critically examine their goals and values. Ethnic minority lesbians must recognize the importance of spending time with others of their sub-group for affirmation and inspiration. These efforts are not without pain, but all communities can learn through the process.

## ISSUES OF IDENTITY

"Coming out" is the phrase used to describe the process through which one recognizes her homosexuality, and acknowledges it first to herself and then, usually, to others. A similar process exists for coming to an awareness of one's racial identity and its meaning in the world. For both white lesbians and lesbians of color, these processes inform and affect each other in many ways.

Several studies describe certain key stages in identity development, both for homosexuality and ethnic identity.[2] Although the processes differ somewhat, there are three key stages common to both. The earliest stage involves a complete internalization of dominant cultural values; a middle stage is characterized by an embracing of the minority identity and a complete immersion in that culture; the final stage involves identity synthesis, a more personal understanding of the identity within the culture, with an ability to selectively accept or reject parts of the cultures. These stages are not, however, universal. Moreover, some lesbians of color reject entirely the possibility of "coming out ethnically."

For a lesbian of color, coming to terms with her racial identity and coming to terms with her sexual orientation often occur separately. For some ethnic minority lesbians, discovering and accepting racial identity impairs the exploration of their sexual orientation.

For other lesbians of color, coming to terms with lesbianism may inhibit examining issues of racial identity. For still other lesbians of color, the process of coming out–either as an ethnic or a sexual minority–can strengthen and encourage the other coming out. For some white lesbians, the coming-out experience is a process through which they can begin to empathize with the experiences of oppression of people of color.

Because race and sexual orientation are two identities that are given a great deal of meaning and weight by the dominant culture, fragmentation–and not integration–is fostered. Many lesbians of color feel rejected from their own cultural and ethnic communities. They frequently describe this as more painful than rejection from dominant or mainstream society. The need to assert an ethnic identity becomes more pronounced within the context of a racist dominant culture when the ethnic identity is readily visible. The rejection that ethnic minority lesbians feel from their own communities can be especially painful because they are then shut off from the place in which they can receive refuge from the racism outside, as well as sustenance, support, and affirmation of one's racial identity.

White lesbians are also rejected from their own culture; yet the experience is markedly different from that of lesbians of color. Many white people have a very loose sense of connection to "white culture(s)," so that the isolation does not seem as complete, or the loss as great. In fact, many white lesbians are not likely to even describe their rejection as being from "white culture"; rather, they will describe being rejected by their family of origin, or a particular town or region, or some other characterization that may in fact describe white culture, yet not consciously. White lesbians who feel a cultural attachment to a particular ethnic identity may feel the pain of rejection more acutely than white lesbians not similarly attached. Lauren had been wanting to attend a festival of Irish culture in Northern California. Then she read an article about these festivals being fruitful recruiting grounds for neo-conservative hate groups, and felt too afraid to go to one. She felt hurt and saddened, cut off from a piece of who she is.

There is a diversity of opinion about which, if any, identity takes precedence for any particular group. Such experiences are highly personal, and do not seem to follow any prescribed pattern or rules.

Still, the ways in which identities co-exist appear to be influenced by factors such as the timing and possible overlap of the processes of identity formation, the degree to which one is readily visibly identifiable as a minority group member, and the context or situation. Dorian came out at college, and hung around mostly white gay people. She felt more like a lesbian than a woman of color; "lesbian" was her social and political identity.

Since the earlier stages of minority identity formation are characterized by much internalized racism and homophobia, recognizing and dealing with cultural and sexual identity requires acknowledging that one's ethnic culture is most likely homophobic and that the dominant culture is racist, sexist, and heterosexist. The need for empowerment within the minority community often manifests itself along gender lines. Images of male dominance prevent women from being accepted in independent or powerful roles. The lesbian, with no male as a part of her identity, becomes invisible.

Internalized racism and internalized homophobia involve a person taking in and believing the myths of the dominant culture about a minority identity. Since these myths are usually negative, internalized racism and internalized homophobia frequently result in negative self-image, conscious or unconscious dislike of the group's members and characteristics, disassociation from same-group members, and a desire to distinguish oneself from the group. For white lesbians, racism and internalized homophobia can manifest in a desire to distance from other white women, and to prove themselves as more enlightened or aware of racial issues.

Therapy can be helpful with identity formation and exploration of internalized oppression, and can assist in healthy integration and balance of identities. Conversely, therapy can also be seen as being a white, middle-upper class indulgence. Having a therapist of a similar cultural background or sexual orientation, or both, can help. The therapist needs to be acutely aware of potential issues, given the therapist's own racial identity and sexual orientation vis-à-vis that of the client. One technique that can be useful is to deal with identities separately and with that understanding begin to integrate them.

## RELATIONSHIP ISSUES
## AND INTERRACIAL LESBIAN COUPLES

Interracial relationships present challenges and opportunities to explore the experiences of racism, white privilege, and cultural homophobia. While racism in society affects all lesbians, lesbians in interracial relationships face particular challenges. How does the white lesbian deal with racism and cultural homophobia directed at her partner? How does the lesbian of color deal with being lover to a member of the oppressive class, and the homophobia of her own community? Together, how do they examine and deal with the different perceptions, experiences, and values of each partner?

Lesbians in interracial relationships challenge and confront racism in themselves and in the other, in perhaps more active, overt ways than those in same-race relationships. Within the development of her interracial relationship Dorian has said, "I want to know that you love me, that you know that my experience is different from your own. That you recognize that you cannot suffer for me, that some of my oppression cannot be your own."

Both women can experience pressure to choose lovers from within the race, or risk being accused of betrayal of their communities or of internalized racism. Lesbians of color in interracial relationships may respond to this by not acknowledging other lesbians of color when with their partners, or they may be ignored by other lesbians of color. They can experience pressure to be a representative of the race, to know everything pertaining to the race, and to teach all of these lessons to their partners.

Lesbians in interracial relationships confront differences in culture and values in areas such as the role of family, the role of the individual, money and economic issues, food, religion, childrearing behavior, and homosexuality. Recognition of the differences is essential. Sometimes the couple will find that the differences are destructive or divisive; other times, the partners will find them strengthening and enriching.

White lesbians usually have not had to evolve armor to deal with racism; thus they may be less prepared than their partners to deal with racial incidents or comments. They may be less likely to interpret a situation as racist. Further, the white partner in an interracial relationship may not fully appreciate the risks involved or the differences in their coming-out experiences.

Interracial couples can benefit by developing a plan for dealing with racial situations. With such a plan, interracial couples can avoid blaming each other, and each partner can take time to examine her own responses independent of the other's. For the white lesbian in an interracial relationship, strategies for survival include acknowledging her privilege, and recognizing that it is her partner who is the target of racism.

The interracial lesbian couple can benefit by viewing racism on a societal level as well as on the personal, by recognizing that racism is a set part of the culture and society, and by recognizing that the perceptions of the couple include racial and lesbian stereotypes and that some of these exist for each partner.

Issues that arise in interracial lesbian relationships cannot always be isolated and resolved by the couple alone. Therapy (individual, group, and couple), experiential workshops, and support–either formal or informal–can be helpful. Connecting with other interracial lesbian couples can also be beneficial. Being a partner in an interracial relationship and working through these issues can teach a process for examining other interpersonal relationships with different racial and cultural issues.

The challenges presented by looking at the nexus of homophobia and racism can be frustrating but exciting. The connections and insights can lead to a critical examination of all power structures. The process is a valuable learning experience and can be a springboard to the eradication of all oppression.

## NOTES

1. We are two lesbians, one black and one white. We drew here on our own experiences and on formal and informal interviews with women we know.

2. See, e.g., Oliva Espín (1987). Issues of identity in the psychology of Latina lesbians. In Boston Lesbian Psychologies Collective (Eds.), *Lesbian psychologies: Explorations and challenges* (pp. 35 ff.) Urbana and Chicago: University of Illinois Press.

# Sexism, Racism, and the Analogy Problem in Feminist Thought

Trina Grillo
Stephanie M. Wildman

Progressive white feminists, with anti-racist politics, seeking to educate and explain the experience of sexism, often compare sexism to racism. The use of this analogy suggests that the "analogizer" believes her situation is the same as that of a person of color. Nothing in the comparison process challenges this belief, and the analogizer may think that she understands the other's situation in its fullness. The analogy makes the analogizer forget any difference and allows her to stay focused on her own situation without grappling with the person of color's reality.[1]

Several identifiable phenomena occur in any predominantly white group whenever sex discrimination is analogized, implicitly or explicitly, to race discrimination. Although the analogy may be made for the purpose of illumination, to explain sexism and sex discrimination, an unintended result ensues–the perpetuation of racism/white supremacy.[2]

When a speaker makes a comparison between sexism and racism, the significance of race becomes marginalized and obscured, and the different role that race plays in the lives of people of color and of whites is overlooked. The concerns of whites become the focus of discussion, even when the conversation has been one supposedly centering on race discrimination.[3] People with little experience in thinking about racism/white supremacy, but who have a hard-won understanding of sexism, might assume that they comprehend the experience of people of color and therefore are able to speak about the pain of racism from that point of view.[4]

These phenomena have much to do with dangers inherent in what might otherwise be a creative and solidarity-producing process–

analogizing sex discrimination to race discrimination. Analogies implicitly promise that discussing and comparing oppression could lead to coalition and understanding. On an individual psychological level, the way we empathize with and understand others is by comparing their situations with some aspects of our own. As Lynne Henderson (1987) explains:

> Analogizing, or drawing upon one's own experience to understand another's feelings or experiences, is a part of relating to another, if for no other reason than that no one has exactly the same experiences as anyone else. . . . [I]t is possible to draw on one's own similar experiences to understand another.

Roberto Unger (1975) describes the importance of analogy in the human thought process: "We compare the issues about which we have the greatest certainty with those that baffle us more." So while we need analogies to deepen our consciousness and to make progress in our thinking, analogies must be used with care to avoid perpetuating racial domination.

## HOW THE SEX/RACE ANALOGY PERPETUATES PATTERNS OF RACIAL DOMINATION

Comparing sexism to racism perpetuates patterns of racial domination by marginalizing and obscuring the role of race, making it one of a laundry list of isms or oppressions that society suffers. This marginalization and obfuscation is evident in two distinctly recognizable patterns: (a) taking back the center from people of color so that white issues remain or become central in the dialogue; and (b) the appropriation of pain, or the denial of its existence, which results when whites who have compared other oppressions to race discrimination believe that they understand the experience of racism.

### Taking Back the Center

White supremacy creates in members of the dominant group the expectation that issues of concern to them will be central in any discourse. Analogies serve to perpetuate this expectation of centrality. This problem is worsened where those involved, because of the way they have been treated by society, are accustomed to being the center of the stage; it feels natural, comfortable, in the order of things.

The harms of discrimination include not only the easily identified disadvantages to the victims, such as exclusion from housing and jobs, or stigma imposed by the dominant culture, but also the advantages given to those who are not its victims. The white, male, heterosexual societal norm is privileged in such a way that its privilege is rendered invisible. As Kimberlé Crenshaw (1989) has explained:

> According to the dominant view, a discriminator treats all people within a race or sex category similarly. Any significant experiential or statistical variation within this group suggests . . . that the group is not being discriminated against . . . Race and sex, moreover, become significant only when they operate to explicitly *disadvantage* the victims; because the *privileging* of whiteness or maleness is implicit, it is generally not perceived at all. [Emphasis in original.]

Because whiteness is the norm, it is easy for whites to forget that a white perspective is not the only one. Thus, members of dominant groups may assume that their perceptions are the pertinent perceptions, that their problems are the central problems which need to be addressed, and that in discourse they should be the speaker rather than the listener.[5] Part of being a member of a privileged group is being the center, the *subject* of all inquiry in which people of color or other non-privileged groups are the objects.

So strong is this expectation of holding center stage that even when a time and place are specifically designated for members of a non-privileged group to be central, members of the dominant group frequently attempt to take back the pivotal focus. We call this stealing the center.[6] Members of dominant groups will frequently steal the center with a complete lack of self-awareness, even using guerrilla tactics where necessary.

This phenomenon occurred at an annual meeting of Law and Society, where three scholars, all people of color, were assigned to speak to the plenary session about how universities might become truly multicultural. Even before the dialogue began, the views of many members of the organization were apparent by their presence or absence. While the audience included nearly every person of color who was attending the meeting, many whites did not attend.

During the talks, one of which was devoted specifically to the topic of integrating multicultural materials into the core curriculum, a white man got up from the front row and walked noisily to the rear. He then paced the room in a distracting fashion, finally returning to his seat. During the question period he was the first to rise, asking how multicultural materials could be added to university curricula without disturbing the "canon"–the exact subject of the talk he had just, apparently, not listened to.

The speaker answered politely, giving an example of how he had assigned a Navajo creation myth to accompany St. Augustine, highlighting Augustine's paganism and resulting in each reading enriching the other. He refrained from calling attention to the speaker's rude behavior during the meeting, or to his questioner's presumption that the material the speaker saw as most relevant to his own life was central and "canonized," while all other reading was peripheral, and, hence, dispensable.

When people who have not been considered entitled to the center move into it, however briefly, they are viewed as usurpers. One way the group temporarily deprived of the center reacts is to make sure that nothing remains for the perceived usurpers to be in the center of. Some whites who did not attend the plenary session, but might have done so had there been more traditional, i.e., white, speakers, may have stayed away because they were exercising their privilege not to think in terms of race or because they resented the "out groups" having the center. Absence is a tactic that deprives out groups of even that minimal time in the center allocated to them.

Stealing back the center is another such tactic. The man who stomped through the room and then asked the already-answered question was using this guerrilla technique quite effectively.

The problem of stealing the center exists apart from the issue of analogies; it will continue as long as any group expects, and is led to expect, to be the center of the universe. But the use of analogies makes this problem more critical, for once an analogy is taken to heart, it seems to the center-stealer that she is NOT stealing the center, but continuing the discussion on the same topic, and one that she knows well.[7]

### Appropriation of Pain

Part of the privilege of whiteness is the ability not to think about race. Whites need to reject this privilege and to recognize and to speak about their role in the racial hierarchy. Yet whites cannot validly speak for people of color, but only about whites' own experience.

When whites speak about race they need to avoid appropriating the pain of subordination. Comparing sexism to racism gives some whites a false sense that they understand the experience of people of color. White people grasping an analogy between an oppression they have suffered and race discrimination may think that they understand the phenomenon of racism/white supremacy in all its aspects, and believe that their opinions and judgments about race are as cogent as that of victims of racism. But they are not. They cannot feel the same pain. Whenever we employ analogies to teach, trying to show the oppression in a particular situation, we should be careful. In borrowing the acknowledged and clear oppression, we should not neutralize it or make it appear interchangeable with the oppression under discussion.

## LISTENING ACROSS PRIVILEGE

Whites who wish to end discrimination want people of color to teach them about race and are often unwilling to use their personal resources to explore this dangerous subject. As bell hooks (1989) has written:

> In talking about race and gender recently, the question most often asked by white women has to do with white women's response to black women or women of color insisting that they are not willing to teach them about their racism–to show the way. They want to know: What should a white person do who

is attempting to resist racism? It is problematic to assert that black people and other people of color who are sincerely committed to struggling against white supremacy should be unwilling to help or teach white people. (p. 117)

She says that many people of color have responded with unwillingness to teach whites about combating racism/white supremacy since it often seems that white people are asking people of color to do all the work. She concludes: "It is our collective responsibility as people of color and as white people who are committed to ending white supremacy to help one another." Hooks is encouraging people of color to continue to struggle with whites about racism. To some whites the need for such encouragement may seem surprising, since many whites might ask, "How can we work on racism by ourselves, without people of color?" Listening to the reality of people of color is very important to learning about the oppression of racism/white supremacy. But whites need to examine their (our) own role in benefiting from that social construct. When we as white women analogize sexism to racism to emphasize the disadvantaging imposed by the culture upon us as women, we must also remember the privileging imposed by that same society upon us as whites.

Trying to educate whites about race is dangerous for people of color, who risk not only that whites will not care and will prefer to perpetuate the status quo, but also that even caring whites will not hear or understand the pain of racism. Talking about racism/white supremacy is painful for whites in a different way. Whites have to confront their privileged role in a race-based hierarchy.

We share a primal, and not unreasonable, fear that if we open ourselves enough to be really comprehending of another's pain, we will lose our sense of the legitimacy of our own pain. And yet, as long as we are human, the first filter through which we look will be the one constructed by the events of our individual lives. The use of analogy exacerbates this natural desire in each of us to have our own struggles receive recognition. For if we can permit ourselves to be convinced that another's experience is "just like" ours, we are then exempted from having to fully comprehend that experience.[8]

## CONCLUSION:
## RECOGNITION TIME

Given these problems which analogies create and perpetuate, should we ever use them? We do need analogies, which are an essential part of everyday conversation and human connection. Starting with ourselves is important, and analogies may enable us to understand the oppression of another in a way we could not without making the comparison.

But it is also important for whites to talk about white supremacy, not leaving all the work for people of color. Questions remain concerning how analogies to race can be used without reinforcing racism/white supremacy. Although there are no simple answers, we offer one preliminary suggestion to guide the use of comparison in daily discourse: *distinct recognition time*.

The problem of analogies to race marginalizing and obscuring racism/white supremacy may be mitigated by the concept of distinct recognition time, recognizing both the need to honor the pain of those oppressed by other forms of subordination and the need not to steal the center away from the oppression that is the focus.

An African-American woman law professor teaching a seminar on women of color and the law, reports that she finds it very hard to focus the students on gender issues; they want to stay with race. Why might this happen? If the first filter through which one looks at the world is not acknowledged, one may not be able to move on to other, perhaps even equally important, filters. By combining a series of socially subordinated groups in one list, or class, and not identifying distinct recognition time allowed for one specific oppression or another, other than to use them as reference points for an analogy, we create an inability to focus on any of them. This does not mean that the oppressions are unrelated, but rather that they must be studied separately as well as together. To allow these separate, distinct recognition times might relax people. Talking about an oppression in its fullness would include examining the relationship of that oppression to others. In other words, within the context of the discussion of racial oppression one could talk about the effects of, for example, class and gender.[9]

Distinct recognition time is critically important to enable groups to work together. In a racism class at one law school, Stephanie was asked to team-teach a class on Jewish Racism and African-American Anti-Semitism. The Jewish students felt that anti-Semitic remarks had been made throughout the semester and that nowhere in the law school were issues of anti-Semitism addressed. The students of color felt that during the one class in the curriculum to address their issues, once again white students had taken the airwaves from the students of color for their own purpose. Both groups were right. Each needed recognition time.[10]

Analogies are necessary tools to teach and to explain, so that we can better understand each others' experiences and realities. We may have no way to understand each others' lives except by making analogies to events in our own experience. Nevertheless, a fundamental tension exists whenever analogies compare other oppressions to racism. The use of analogies provides both the key to greater comprehension and the danger of false understanding. The comparison perpetuates white supremacy/racism, but is also a necessary tool to teach about the oppression being compared. Any analogy to race must be used ethically and with care. We must always be sure at the conclusion of any analogy discussion that we are deconstructing rather than perpetuating societal racism.

## NOTES

1. A different, more expansive treatment of these issues appears in Trina Grillo and Stephanie M. Wildman (1991). "Obscuring the Importance of Race: The Implication of Making Comparisons Between Racism and Sexism (or Other-Isms)," *Duke Law Journal* 1991,397.

2. bell hooks describes her realization of this connection between racism and white supremacy: "the word racism ceased to be the term which best expressed for me exploitation of black people and other people of color in this society and . . . I began to understand that the most useful term was white supremacy" (1989 p. 112). She recounts how liberal whites do not see themselves as prejudiced or interested in domination by coercive control, yet "they cannot recognize the ways their actions support and affirm the very structure of racist domination and oppression that they profess to wish to see eradicated" (113). For these reasons white supremacy is an important term, descriptive of American social reality. In this article the authors have chosen to link the term racism to it as a reminder that the perpetuation of white supremacy is racist.

3. In such a discussion essentialist presumptions may be implicit; it will be assumed, for example, that all women are white and all African-Americans are

men. For discussions of essentialism see Gloria T. Hull, Patricia Bell Scott, & Barbara Smith (1982); Elizabeth Spelman (1988); Angela Harris (1990); Kimberlé Crenshaw (1989); and some of the authors in this book.

4. Although this article discusses analogies between sexism and racism, the phenomena we describe apply to analogies between other forms of oppression, for example, heterosexism and anti-Semitism.

5. See Stephanie M. Wildman (1988). "The Question of Silence: Techniques to Ensure Full Class Participation," *Journal of Legal Education, 38,* pp. 149-150.

6. Parents of young children who try to have a telephone conversation will easily recognize this phenomenon. At the sound of the parent's voice on the phone, the child materializes from the far reaches of the house to demand attention. Of course, children do not dominate parents in the same way that stealers of the center dominate excluded groups. However, the felt urgency to be in the center is comparable.

7. In one sex discrimination class, the assigned reading consisted of three articles by black women. In the discussion, many white women focused on sexism and how they understood the women of color by seeing the sexism in their own lives. The use of analogy allowed the white women to avoid the implications of white privilege and made women of color feel that their distinct experience had been rendered invisible.

Additionally, many members of the class had evidently not done the reading. Although the end of the semester was near, could this have been a guerrilla tactic to retake the center?

When a group of socially subordinated categories are lumped together, oppression begins to look like a uniform problem and one may neglect the varying and complex contexts of the different groups being addressed. If oppression is all the same, then we are all equally able to discuss each oppression, and there is no felt need for us to listen and to learn from other socially subordinated groups.

8. And for the listener, when understanding is presumed to exist, but doesn't, the emotion generated is rage. For a discussion of women of color and anger in the context of mediation, see Trina Grillo (1991). "The Mediation Alternative: Process Dangers for Women," *Yale Law Journal, 100,* p. 1545 ff.

9. What happens, for example, when middle-class blacks succeed in the white academic world, and then are relied on to speak for all blacks? Such topics are foreclosed when race and gender are talked about as wholly separate but nonetheless interchangeable, analogous problems.

10. Bernice Johnson Reagon (1983) emphasizes both the difficulty of building coalitions and their critical importance.

# REFERENCES

Crenshaw, Kimberlé (1989). Demarginalizing the intersection of race and sex: A Black feminist critique of antidiscrimination doctrine, feminist theory and antiracist politics. *Univ. Chicago Legal Forum,* 1989, 139 ff.

Grillo, Trina (1991). The mediation alternative: Process dangers for women. *Yale Law Journal, 100*, 1545 ff.

Grillo, Trina, & Wildman, Stephanie M. (1991). Obscuring the importance of race: The implication of making comparisons between racism and sexism (or other -isms). *Duke Law Journal,* 1991, 397 ff.

Harris, Angela (1990). Race and essentialism in feminist legal theory. *Stanford Law Review, 42,* 581 ff.

Henderson, Lynne (1987). Legality and empathy. *Michigan Law Review, 85,* 1581, footnote 37.

hooks, bell (1989). overcoming white supremacy: a comment. In *Talking back: thinking feminist, thinking black* (pp. 112-119). Boston: South End Press.

Hull, Gloria T., Scott, Patricia Bell, & Smith, Barbara (Eds.) (1982). *All the women are white, all the men are black, but some of us are brave.* New York: Feminist Press.

Reagon, Bernice Johnson (1983). Coalition politics: Turning the century. In Barbara Smith (Ed.), *Home girls: A Black feminist anthology.* New York: Kitchen Table: Women of Color Press.

Spelman, Elizabeth (1988). *Inessential woman: Problems of exclusion in feminist thought.* Boston: Beacon Press. New York: The Free Press, A Division of MacMillan.

Unger, Roberto (1975). *Knowledge and politics.* 258. Boston: Beacon Press. New York: The Free Press, A Division of MacMillan.

Wildman, Stephanie M. (1988). The question of silence: Techniques to ensure full class participation. *Journal of Legal Education, 38,* 149-150.

# Historical and Material Determinants of Psychodynamic Development

## Gail Pheterson

### In memory of Ricky Sherover-Marcuse

*If we should start telling the truth . . . it would mean that we
expose ourselves to the fate of human beings who, unprotected
by any specific law or political convention, are nothing but
human beings. I can hardly imagine an attitude more dangerous, since we actually live in a world in which human
beings as such have ceased to exist for quite a while.*

–Hannah Arendt (1943)

Historically repetitive relations of domination and material
conditions of daily life interweave with personal experiences in the
process of psychodynamic development. This essay is an initial
attempt to demonstrate the persistent ahistorical and amaterial bias
of even innovative psychological theory and to sketch parameters
for a more politically conscious understanding of psychic life. I will
begin by elaborating definitions for my purposes of "historical,"
"material," and "psychodynamic."

## DEFINITIONS

*Historical* relations of domination are defined by continuous or
cyclic systematic subordination of certain groups by other groups
through means of violence, labor exploitation, constraint, isolation,
humiliation, denial of resources, and denial of rights. The dominant
group justifies its behavior by claiming and attributing superiority

to a real (physical, biological, genetic, cultural) or invented (mythical) distinguishing characteristic, such as white skin, pure blood, upper class or male sex, and by disassociating from and attributing inferiority to a supposedly distinct–real or invented–characteristic, such as black skin, impure blood, working class, or female sex. Forms of domination vary widely across political, historical, and cultural contexts and differentiate from one another in content so that, for example, one oppressed group may be accused of stupidity and another of cunning intelligence, one of brute force and another of frailty. Persons are assigned to multiple, sometimes ambiguous or even contradictory, social categories and then placed on a power hierarchy, their position being determined not by biological fact and not by any other inherent quality (though it may be rationalized as such) but by historical precedent and sociological relation. The lives and liberties of persons in oppressed groups are far more menaced than the lives and liberties of persons in dominant groups; nonetheless, given the dynamic social construction of power hierarchies, dominant persons risk revolt, revenge, and abandonment by subordinates or reclassification into an inferior social category.

Early experiences of submission and domination in intra-familial and extra-familial context foster reality-distorting psychic defenses for persons in both oppressed and dominant positions. Those defenses, whose function is to avoid anxiety, resist change despite the dangers and inhumanities of the status quo. Insofar as patterns of submission and domination are repetitive and insofar as they are linked to survival, freedom, and integrity, collective history touches at the core of psychodynamic development.

*Material* conditions include everything from food, shelter, education, medical care, rest, and transport, to physical and mental labor. Labor must be measured by duration, danger, tedium, and burden, such as the weight carried on one's back or the care of dependents. Material reality includes parameters of choice/force, equity/exploitation, self-development/service-to-others, mobility/restraint, and all resources required for survival, health, comfort, autonomy, self-defense, and escape.

Psychodynamic development is always staged in a concrete material situation which can be the source of early security or anxiety and of early assumptions of entitlement or subservience. It is not only the material conditions under which one lives that are significant but also the conditions one apprehends. The witnessing of humiliation, exploitation, or violation of people with particular social characteristics (be they family or strangers), the identification or disidentification with those people, and the realization of the historical continuity of such abuse are psychodynamically significant experiences for persons in all positions. For example, if children see black women, be they family or strangers, working long hours cleaning the homes of white people and receiving less money and less respect than the white employers who are seen to work fewer, more flexible hours for which they receive more money and more respect, those children will draw psychodynamically significant conclusions according to their identifications and disidentifications. Thus, Audre Lorde (1984) tells us:

> I wheel my two-year-old daughter in a shopping cart through a supermarket in Eastchester in 1967, and a little white girl riding past in her mother's cart calls out excitedly, "Oh look, Mommy, a baby maid!" And your mother shushes you, but she doesn't correct you. And so fifteen years later, at a conference on racism, you can still find that story humorous. But I hear your laughter is full of terror and dis-ease. (p. 126)

*Psychodynamics* refer to the:

> pattern of motivational forces, conscious or unconscious, that gives rise to a particular psychological event or state, such as an attitude, action, symptom, or mental disorder. Those forces include drives, wishes, emotions, and defense mechanisms. (Goldenson, 1984, p. 601)

It is the presence of psychic conflict that makes the pattern of forces necessarily dynamic (Laplanche & Pontalis, 1988). Psychological theorists most often interpret psychic conflict in the context of familial relationships. It is my conviction, and the thesis of this essay, that psychodynamic analyses require interpretation also of historical and material context. The family, whatever its cultural form, is not the only influence on personality. And familial relations are not insulated from past and present world events. Mothers, fathers, and other primary caretakers are critical not least of all for the interpretations they provide of the historically repetitive and materially decisive factors within and outside the family that determine a child's satisfactions, frustrations, safeties, and dangers. Barbara Cameron (1981), a Lakota Indian, vividly describes this interplay between familial interpretation and extra-familial (racist) danger:

> One of the very first words I learned in my Lakota language was *wasicu* which designates white people. At that early age, my comprehension of wasicu was gained from observing and listening to my family discussing the wasicu. My grandmother always referred to white people as the *wasicu sica* with emphasis on *sica*, our word for terrible or bad. By the age of five I had seen one Indian man gunned down in the back by the police and was a silent witness to a gang of white teenage boys beating up an elderly Indian man. I'd heard stories of Indian ranch hands being "accidentally" shot by white ranchers. I quickly began to understand the wasicu menace my family spoke of. (p. 46)

Referring to her present life, Barbara Cameron writes:

> I sometimes panic when I'm the only non-white in a roomful of whites, even if they are my closest friends; I wonder if I'll leave the room alive. (p. 47)

It would be a ridiculous and grave distortion to imagine any psychodynamic treatment of Barbara Cameron's fears and mistrusts without appreciating the *realities* of her early experience in which the world was divided into us Indians and them bad cruel violent white people. It would, however, be wrong–and racist–to believe that all Indians (even all Lakota Indians) have the same childhood experiences or that familial dynamics are not as diverse and significant among Indians as among any other people. It is appropriate to assume that the historically repetitive domination of diverse Indians in North America through humiliation, exclusion, and murder has affected the psychic development of everyone–not only of the politically conscious–whose historical position identifies them with either the targets or the agents of this oppression.

Lillian Smith (1978) describes the racism childhood trauma she experienced from the dominant position:

> Neither the Negro nor sex was often discussed at length in our home . . . but by the time I had learned that God is love, that Jesus is His Son and came to give us more abundant life, that all men are brothers with a common Father, I also knew that I was better than a Negro, that all black folks have their place and must be kept in it, that sex has its place and must be kept in it, that a terrifying disaster would befall the South if ever I treated a Negro as my social equal and as terrifying a disaster would befall my family if ever I were to have a baby outside of marriage. (pp. 27-28)

Lillian Smith's account illustrates the interwoven mechanisms by which positions of dominance (as a white person) are glued with guilt and shame to positions of subservience (as a woman); psychological intimidation of children by adults can thus function to shape girls into racist white-identified woman who, along with "their" men, perceive female obedience to sexual norms as a condition for the preservation of the family and the nation.

Racist violence and ideology undoubtedly scar psychic development. Barbara Cameron and Lillian Smith's descriptions testify to that painful process. Especially during the last two decades an immense and rich literature has been produced which reveals the psychologically traumatic transmission of diverse domination imperatives. The present essay has been inspired by years of immersion in such emotionally charged accounts expressed in literature, oral testimony, social science research, and consciousness-raising groups. The implications of those accounts for psychological theory and practice are enormous and of general importance. Historical and material realities are not supplementary pieces of information relevant to only certain categories of people but, rather, fundamental parameters of everyone's development. Biographers often explore the interaction of family background and historical context in the lives of their protagonists. I suggest that every person's life requires such multi-faceted analysis and that the task is both psychodynamic and political in nature. I also suggest that psychological disciplines are not yet well-equipped for this undertaking.

## *NORMAL PSYCHIC DISTURBANCES*

Beginning with early critics of Freud's biological and familial interpretations of neurosis, there have been clinicians and researchers who have attempted to contextualize theories of development. Although those innovators have contributed in various ways to psychological theory, they have failed to give psychodynamic coherence to relations of domination, nor has that been their aim. Even those motivated by a critique of ethnocentric or androcentric biases in psychology and even those focused directly upon specific violent forms of domination–such as the rape of women, the lynching of blacks, or the genocide of Jews–have rarely included patterns of oppression as general determinants of personality development.[1] I believe the reason for this failure is an (unconscious) refusal to call normative relations of domination into question on a psychological level or even to recognize domination as normative.

### *Non-Deviant*

Historically, the first theorists to question Freud's disregard for extra-familial context became known as the culturalists, most notably represented by Karen Horney, Erich Fromm, Abram Kardiner, Clara Thompson, and Harry Stack Sullivan. Those theorists, influenced by their contemporaries in anthropology, demonstrated the cultural construction of psychic normality. They argued that what is normal in one culture may not be normal in another and that cultural context must be understood if one is to diagnose and treat psychic disturbance. The culturalists were theoretically radical in their day; however they somehow managed to validate "culture" while ignoring the material relations that define it. In *The Neurotic Personality of Our Time* (1937), Karen Horney raises one material question in a footnote when she asks, "What are the differences in the life conditions of men and women in our culture that account for a difference in the development of jealousy?" (p. 17). Never does she address that interesting question nor any other of its kind. Whatever is normal within the culture, such as men's and women's different life conditions, is for Horney outside the scope of psychological study. She writes that:

> A neurosis is a psychic disturbance brought upon by fears and defenses against these fears. . . . For practical reasons it is advisable to call this disturbance a neurosis only if it deviates from the pattern common to the particular culture. (p. 29)

One specific characteristic of neurosis is rigidity in reactions or "a lack of that flexibility which enables us to react differently to different situations" (p. 22). But again:

> Rigidity is indicative of a neurosis only when it deviates from the cultural patterns. A rigid suspicion of anything new or strange is a normal pattern [in certain cultures]. (p. 23)

Horney does not specify the practical reasons for excluding non-deviant psychic disturbances from her definition of neurotic nor does she elaborate the contours of such normalcies. Might those contours help us to understand psychodynamic development? Might they be basic determinants of relational disturbances in private and public life?

Karen Horney wrote *The Neurotic Personality of Our Time* in 1937. The ethnocentrism she criticized within psychology is still with us today although it is no longer socially acceptable in raw form. The usual challenge to ethnocentrism remains a culturalist validation of any behavior that is normal within a given culture. There are certain theorists, such as the transcultural psychiatrists, who do reject both ethnocentrism and the cultural relativistic response. Suman Fernando (1989) and Roland Littlewood and Maurice Lipsedge (1989), for example, have demonstrated that oppressed persons in one culture manifest similar mental health problems to oppressed persons in another culture, thereby indicating that neurosis is tied more to relations of subordination than to deviation from cultural patterns. Those researchers are acutely aware of racism as a mental health problem. However, they seem to view those who enact racist behavior as a *sociological* phenomenon–given their normalcy–and those who suffer from racist abuse as a *psychological* phenomenon–given their conspicuousness as objects of attack and their distress, both of which portray them as deviants in need of psychological treatment. Recognition of the stress caused by systematic mistreatment and analysis of specific stress syndromes related to different oppressions undoubtedly facilitates coping and recovery from abuse among the oppressed. But attention to individuals in subordinate positions fails to problematize either the normalized psychic disturbance of persons in dominant positions or the domination relation itself.

### Non-Extreme: From Fascists and Rapists to Survivors

I assume that Horney and other culturalists focused upon deviance in order to help people adjust to their actual life conditions, normal disturbances included. However, during the same years that those theorists were developing their adjustment model of psychological health, fascism was rising in Europe and certain social philosophers, notably of the Frankfurt School in Germany, were beginning to examine psychic rigidities that might underlie fascist potential in normal, culturally well-adjusted persons. Confrontation with horrific human behavior as a majority dominant pattern during the Second World War affirmed the need to study prejudice and hate as non-deviant dimensions of personality. The extensive post-war research investigation in the United States of *The Authoritarian Personality* conducted by T. W. Adorno, originally of the Frankfurt School, together with Else Frenkel-Brunswik, Daniel Levinson, and R. Nevitt Sanford and sponsored by the American Jewish Committee (1950) elaborated characteristics of the anti-democratic, ethnocentric, and prejudiced personality. Individual fascist potential was measured by the famous Fascism (F) Scale. Correlatives of fascist potential were sought in character structure, early familial patterns, cognitions, and attitudes. The authors conclude that "the majority of the population are not extreme . . . but middle" [on the F-scale]. They further conclude that middle-scorers or normal prejudiced people are better rewarded in society than low-scoring tolerant people and less guilty since they do not go against the prevailing social standards (p. 976). Extreme fascist potential is thus declared psychologically pathological whereas non-extreme fascist potential or normal prejudice is declared psychologically benign and maybe even socially advantageous. Horney might have said that prejudice is a "normal rigid suspicion of anything [or anybody??] new or strange."

Interestingly, by the 1960s psychologists had largely turned their attention away from potential fascists to actual survivors of fascist persecution, specifically Jewish survivors of the Shoah.[2] At present there exists an extensive clinical literature about those survivors and their children (e.g., Bergmann & Jucovy, 1982; Epstein, 1979; Wardi, 1992). Might this literature, a rare source of psychodynamic analysis grounded in historical and material reality, be useful for the present inquiry? Might analyses of psychic responses to genocidal persecution, the most unimaginable extreme, help us understand psychic responses to oppression within democratic societies? Before considering this question I must make a few obvious but slippery distinctions.[3] Violence can be a means of extermination and/or a means social control. The term "survivor" in the context of the Shoah signifies living beyond others in one's group whose death was the result of a fascist design of extermination. For a victim of violent social control, the term "survivor" is a misnomer. Violence as social control–including random, regular murders–is a warning against insubordination rather than a strategy of annihilation; survival of subordinate groups as such is required because those groups are needed, be it for labor exploitation–as in the case of women, workers, and people of color–or be it for use as scapegoats on whom to blame social ills–as in the case of Jews, gypsies, homosexuals, and prostitutes. On a political level using fascist metaphors for subjugation within states ideologically committed to democracy undermines our defense against actual fascism and colludes with the illusion that modern democracies are free of enduring patterns of domination. On a psychodynamic level, lack of sociological precision risks gross misinterpretation of psychic reality.

With the above distinctions firmly in mind, I do believe that details of material survival and historically located abuse are subject matters of general relevance to psychodynamic theory and that the extreme can enlighten the normative. There is no valid reason for contextualizing psychic responses to catastrophic circumstances and not contextualizing psychic responses to ordinary circumstances. Here are two examples of possibly fruitful extrapolation from the psychodynamics of genocidal persecution to the psychodynamics of normative abuse within modern democracies.

In a book comprising numerous psychoanalytic studies of Shoah survivors and their children, Bergmann and Jucovy (1982) report that concentration camp survivors often transmit to their children impossible expectations to provide meaning to their empty-feeling lives and often transmit a suspicious attitude toward the external world, which is perceived as hostile (p. 20). The significance of "empty-feeling," "suspicion," and "hostile world" are linked here to particular extreme circumstances. It is not unusual, however, to find rigid expectations, attitudes, and perceptions among those who have suffered normative dangers and violations such as exclusion, discrimination, battering, and sexual abuse. Identification with those experiences–from the most catastrophic to the most banal–are likely to elicit some degree of psychically contagious anxiety and defense, the intensity and form of which will depend upon an interaction of external and internal reality. Genocidal persecution is not required to elicit psychic defense; daily mundane humiliation will do.

As a second example from the same book, psychoanalysts report that children of survivors are preoccupied with how their parents survived, whether they were betrayers or heroes (p. 44). Those children face the task of understanding their parents' past experiences without degrading or idealizing them (p. 61). What is the developmental task for children whose parents have endured–or perpetuated–normative violations? Perhaps it is not to evaluate their parents as betrayers or heroes, war images drawn from extreme circumstances, but might it not include evaluation of their parents' integrity in the face of humiliation, constraint, or economic pressure? Imagine, as a most non-extreme example, girls and boys who observe the strength versus weakness of their mother's resistance to sexist social demands, and–from the dominant position–of their father's collusion with such demands. Don't children need to understand their parent's responses–in social context–without degrading or idealizing them, without shame or defensive loyalty? Information about parental experiences of social subordination or domination is critically relevant to psychodynamic theory whether the assault be considered severe, medium, or mild by diverse criteria.

Depending upon interpretations and consequences in early life, even mild parental experiences as abused or abuser can shape children's self-concepts and defense systems.

\*   \*   \*

Psychological research on the domination of women by men has followed a course somewhat parallel to psychological research on fascism. Although there has not been a study of sexist potential analogous to the Adorno study of fascist potential, feminist researchers began to illustrate in the 1970s and early 1980s that male violence against women is normative rather than exceptional, whether the woman be wife or maid or total stranger to the male aggressor. The early studies were sociological in orientation. Susan Brownmiller's treatise (1975) and Diana Russell's extensive epidemiological surveys (1973; 1982; 1984) demonstrated that men's rape of women, for example, is a means of intimidation and control within a relation of systematic domination; Angela Davis's critical essay (1981) demonstrated that white men's manipulation of the rape charge is a means of justifying the exploitation and abuse of black women and the scapegoating, incarceration, and murder of black men. In the late 1980s sociological research continued, although a profusion of feminist research and practice in psychological disciplines shifted public attention from the relation of domination to women's processes of psychological recovery from abuse. One is reminded of the prior shift in attention from fascist potential (as a normative psychology) to survival syndromes (as an extreme psychology of certain oppressed persons). In regard to sexism, the initial demonstration of sociologically normative male violence against women implied a sociologically normative female experience of aggression (or threat of aggression). However, psychological theorists and practitioners, including feminists working in the intrapsychic framework of their disciplines, tended to psychologically particularize the violated party, the woman, and to universalize the violating party, the man, as a sociological fact with which women must reckon. Only the most extremely violent men, such as mass murderers, were viewed psychologically, and then as carriers of distinct pathologies unrelated to normalized patterns of male aggression.[4] In reality, the woman is as sociological a phenomenon as the man, although in a subordinate rather than dominant position; and the man is as psychological a being as the woman, although his normal psychic disturbances are socially defined as legitimate expressions of authority.[5]

Analysis and treatment of women and girls who have been violated by men has become one of the most-publicized, and perhaps best-funded, specialties of feminist psychology. Separate individual diagnostic labels and separate therapeutic recovery groups now exist for women defined as survivors of incest, survivors of battering, survivors of rape, survivors of alcoholic fathers, survivors of abuse in the sex industry, and so forth. The recovery process includes the disclosure of having been violated and often the taking on of a survivor identity. "The [rape] victim," according to Colao and Hunt (1983), "has to mourn the identity she feels she has lost in the assault" (p. 208). O'Hare and Taylor (1983), specialized therapists of incest survivors, suggest that groups have "two facilitators: a survivor to provide safety and trust and a non-survivor to break the secrecy" (p. 227).

Those groups have undoubtedly provided enormous support to many thousands of women. The theoretical foundation upon which they are based, however, poses some problems. First of all, misapplication of the term "survivor" (or "non-survivor") risks undermining the significance, as I discussed earlier, of genocide and of violence against women, the latter being a strategy not of annihilation but of social control. I offer this linguistic reservation tentatively because I do understand that feminists have embraced the term "survivor" in rejection of the passive helpless connotations of the term "victim." Inventing language appropriate to our situation is no easy task. But the problem here is not only linguistic. There is also an underlying mystification in the division of women into those who have been abused and those who have not been abused. That division obscures the violent preservation of male domination over women in general. Abuse is an *experience*, one with psychic as well as social consequences, but it is not an *identity*. Indeed, women have historically been identified–and divided and controlled and punished–on the basis of men's protective versus abusive treatment of them. We risk collusion with that historical precedent when we distinguish different kinds of women, be it with sexist language of the damaged and the pure or be it with feminist language of the survivor and the non-survivor. Those labels attach abuse to the interior psyches of women as if it was a personality trait of certain female persons rather than a manifestation of oppression defined by a social relation.[6]

It is important in this context to examine what constitutes abuse on a psychological level. Freud wrote:

> We ask ourselves what it is that is actually dangerous and actually feared in a situation of danger. . . . It is plainly not the injury to the subject as judged objectively, for this need be of no significance psychologically. (1974, p. 93)

Survivor theorists Bergmann and Jucovy (1982) report that responses to natural disasters or to arbitrary war attacks do not cause the same psychic damage as "continuous, systematic, and organized assault [on] a people . . . singled out as a group that is less than human" (p. 52). It is not abuse per se that cuts into the gut of psychic integrity but the assumption that a certain people warrant such treatment on the basis of their supposed inferior or unworthy natures. Whereas not all women suffer the same degree or quality of actual abuse, all women are endangered by sexist normative attitudes and practices. As French sociologist Colette Guillaumin (1991) describes:

> What woman does not fear for her physical safety, her bodily integrity, even for her life? And if she had no fear, wouldn't men constantly remind her that she is in danger, that she shouldn't go there, shouldn't do so and so, and that it would be wiser to be with a man when going about or just living. . . . The killing of women is not new. . . . A social deed can be both old and new . . . an historic landmark. . . . Yes, it is a shock, but it is not a shock of the unknown; it is a shock of pain, of anger. In fact, it is a shock of the known, the "I can't believe it" of the known that is not acknowledged . . . of *unbearable* reality. (pp. 10-12)

What a woman loses when she is assaulted by a man is not her identity but her defense against recognition of an unbearable reality.

That reality, the threat of danger to women as a group regardless of their individual behavior, is the crucial gender secret. The less secret the danger, the more the woman is blamed and stigmatized for violences committed against her. Many women live in multiply vulnerable positions of sex, race, age, and class oppression. Each of those vulnerabilities functions to enforce material exploitation.[7] So black women, migrant women, prostitutes, working-class and poor women, for example, are known to be endangered, are considered already violated, and are thereby marked as women available for further service and abuse. Women assumed to be unviolated know the consequences of being identified as abused, consequences so threatening that they often prefer to hide and sometimes deny even to themselves their oppression.

Evidence that male violence is a normal social pattern is typically used not to denounce individual and institutionalized subordination of women but rather to promote greater so-called protection of women who are considered pure or innocent. That protection takes the form of ritualized and/or legalized controls over women's private and public lives, such as specialized prohibitions for women against working night shifts. Laws and customs are thus rationalized as necessary to protect women from abuse at all costs (the cost of liberty, economic and sexual autonomy, freedom to circulate or travel, access to resources, right to participate in public life, etc.) because once abused, women are supposedly damaged forever.

Significantly, while men are implicated as women's protectors, they are immunized as women's violators. French linguist Claire Michard (1988) demonstrates how men disappear from the scene of the crime in speech. Here are some of her examples: "One of the women *was put to death*," "she was immediately *arrested and beaten*." Those erasures of men as agents of violence contrast sharply with the following examples of women's linguistically proven guilt: "the murder of the new born *by his mother*" or "the crime *committed by this woman*" (p. 46). It is exactly such asymmetrical conventions, in this case linguistic, which reinforce psychic disturbances rooted in normative patterns of domination.

Specific psychic responses to identification with a threatened, disparaged, and accused group depend upon the interpretations and enactments of domination in familial context. Given individual differences, all girls react to the general menace of male violence with more or less rigid psychic strategies of self-defense.[8] Those defenses may take the form of denial, guilt, shame, or disassociation from female persons who are public targets such as (other) girls and women of color, (other) working-class women, (other) migrants, or (other) lesbians. Specific psychic responses to identification with a dominant group likewise depend upon early interpretations and enactments of domination in familial context and likewise reflect more or less rigid strategies of defense, in this case against recognizing the full humanity of subordinate persons. It is impossible to understand an individual's psychological reaction to experiences of abuse without examining her already deeply implanted system of defense. And it is impossible to understand the reactions of female and male witnesses, friends, lovers, therapists, and judges to an incident of abuse without examining those people's own deeply implanted systems of defense against the "unbearable reality."

### Non-Different

I have so far illustrated the inadequacy of theories which isolate profiles of deviant, extreme, and violated persons as a methodology for psychological analysis and intervention. Those theories fail to examine psychic disturbances bred in normative social patterns of domination. Imagine society in graphic form as a square. Individuals and groups which are considered maladjusted to the square are extracted by psychological professionals, placed outside or on the margins of The Square and labeled neurotic, pathological, or damaged, thereby leaving The Square intact. I have been arguing precisely for an investigation of the normal psychic disturbances within rather than outside or on the margins of The Square. I turn now, as a last example, to a school of theorists who do indeed regard The Square critically but whose analyses serve to reinforce rather than to challenge normal disturbances of domination and submission. The particular style of ahistoricism and amaterialism represented by these "difference theorists," as I will name them, merits careful examination due to its mystified defense of the status quo and due to its international influence on feminist theory.

Difference theorists claim that what I call the normal square is male-biased in that women are either absent or present in degraded form. To correct this bias they would not change The Square but would construct a complementary *different* square for women. In conceptual language, their answer to the male norm is a female norm. So we now have a male normal square which is characterized by qualities of power, independence, action, and justice and a female different normal square which is characterized by qualities of dependence, human connection, and caring. In the words of Carol Gilligan (1982):

> By positing . . . two different modes, we arrive at a more complex rendition of human experience which sees the truth of separation [his mode] and attachment [her mode] in the lives of men and women and recognizes how these truths are carried by different modes of language and thought. (pp. 173-174)

Many women whose particular oppression requires qualities other than dependence and caring know that these "truths" do not apply to them. They also know that they have the credentials to be expelled from the female square by the guardians of normality. As resistance to the economic, social, and physical violences of expulsion, they may respond—as normal women responded to normal men—with their own *different* square. So we could have additional female squares, all normal and all characterized by stereotypic positive qualities: perhaps a black women's square characterized by strength, a Jewish women's square characterized by intelligence, a lesbian square characterized by independence, and a working-class women's square characterized by resourcefulness.

Dominant society is not threatened by different persons as long as those persons fill the normative functions assigned to their social category; for example, as long as white women care for their men and black women carry the burden of heavy labor, celebration of white = normal women's connectedness and black = different women's strength is quite acceptable. Colette Guillaumin (1981b) elaborates:

> The dominant group, as the great Standard, could not ask for anything better than that we should be different. What the dominant group can't stand, on the contrary, is similarity, *our* similarity. They can't stand that we have, that we want, the

same right to food, to independence, to autonomy, to life. . . . It is our similarity to them that they repress in the most decisive way. All they ask is that we be different. They even do all that they can to see to it that we are paid no wage, or a lesser wage; that we have no food, or less; that we have no right to decision-making, but only to be consulted; and that we love our very chains. They want this "difference"–they love it. They never stop telling us how much it pleases them. They impose it with their actions and their threats, and then with their beatings. (p. 97-98)

But this difference–in rights, food, wages, independence–is never spoken of in this form, its real form. No. It is a "difference," an exquisite internal characteristic with no relation to all those sordid material questions. It is elating, like the bird that sings at dawn or the river that flows; it is the rhythm of the body; it is difference–and that's that. It makes women tender and warm as the soil is fertile; it makes blacks fuck well as the rain falls, etc. . . . Let us be different, let us differ, and then we won't bother anyone. Indeed we won't. Instead of materially analyzing difference in daily social relationships, we slide straight into mysticism.

Women, like blacks and Asians, and also like demonstrators and alcoholics, are thus "different." And, we are told, they are different "in nature." (p. 97-98)

The "difference school" is often viewed as a contemporary creation of United States psychiatrist Jean Baker Miller, developmental psychologist Carol Gilligan and, from a more literary and theatrical perspective, of French writers Luce Irigaray, Helene Cixous, and Julia Kristeva. The establishment applauds those thinkers on both sides of the Atlantic as pioneers heralding in a new era of gender relations. In fact, the "different but equal . . . if not better" analysis of women is far from original. Drawing from Cynthia Eagle Russett's historical study of the Victorian construction of womanhood (1989), we hear the difference arguments articulated 100 years ago from nineteenth-century anti-feminists and feminists alike. Anti-feminists Geddes and Thompson, for example, insisted that each sex is higher in its own way. "Man thinks more, woman feels more," they wrote in 1889 (pp. 90-91). Feminists of the same period, such as Antoinette Brown Blackwell and Eliza Burt Gamble, argued that "The sexes had complementary and strictly equivalent strengths" (p. 98).

Geddes and Thompson attributed sex differences to biological, particularly metabolic, gender specificities. Miller and Gilligan disassociate from such classic explanations, unlike their French counterparts whose perspective is unabashedly anatomical. One might suppose that Miller and Gilligan disassociate from biological arguments because those arguments have historically been used to assert a natural basis for male domination. They are unconvincing, however, as they slip into naturalist language and as they reassure the reader–again and again–that gender differences are not inherent. For example, Miller (1986), whose "Self-in-Relation" theory has come to be identified as *the* psychology of women, writes:

> Here again, it is not a question of innate biological characteristics. It's a question of the kind of psychological structuring that is encompassed differentially by each sex. (pp. 88-89)

Miller recognizes the fact that the characteristics which differentiate women from men have been imposed by male domination. But she does not conclude, as feminist psychologists Oliva Espín and Mary Ann Gawelek (1992) suggest one might, that those characteristics are the "consequence of defense mechanisms developed by [white middle-class] women to deal with oppression" and may be neither healthy nor female (p. 89). To the contrary, Miller celebrates psychic products of domination as if they were women's special rewards for non-resistance. She explains that:

> In the course of projecting into women's domain some of its most troublesome and problematic exigencies, male-led society may also have simultaneously, and unwittingly, delegated to women not humanity's "lowest needs" but its "highest necessities"–that is, the intense, emotionally connected cooperation and creativity necessary for human life and growth. . . . Precisely because they have [performed these necessities] women have developed the foundations of extremely valuable psychological qualities. (p. 25-26).

Examples of those qualities include women's tolerance for feelings of vulnerability, weakness, and helplessness and their highly developed sense of emotionality, all of which prepare them to participate in the development of others (pp. 29-48). According to Miller, women's disturbed functioning arises from their failure to use their strengths in their own behalf. She urges women to do better than in the past with their same "marvelous" qualities and to cultivate their "contributing strengths . . . *however attained*" (pp. 38-39, emphasis mine) not only for the benefit of women but also for the benefit of men and children.

Unlike culturalists and unlike survival theorists, Miller does examine normative psychic responses to the pressures of domination. But rather than develop a framework for interpreting and interrupting psychic compliance with those pressures, she and other difference theorists validate compliance–called cooperation or caring in the case of women. Miller returns repeatedly to the fact that women have been forced by men to develop "valuable qualities," each time commenting that those qualities are positive in themselves as personality traits independent of their historical origins and material functions. Women are thus severed conceptually from their social context while the normative psychic disturbances caused by domination are reformulated for both dominant and oppressed persons as healthy expressions of self.

Carol Gilligan is less ambivalent in her defense of normative patterns than Jean Baker Miller. Gilligan (1982) developed her "different voice" in reaction to Lawrence Kohlberg's "general" cognitive-development theory based solely on boys (1966). In righteous response to Kohlberg's male bias, she declares his theory legitimate for boys only and proceeds to develop a separate complementary developmental scheme for girls. In fact, Gilligan completes Kohlberg's authorization of psychological dimensions of male dominance with an authorization of psychological dimensions of female submission. Next to a normative theory of *general* development for boys she gives us a normative theory of *different* development for girls.

Kohlberg is well aware of male superior power in the world and he does not shy away from analyses of material influences on development.[9] Those analyses do not lead him to question normative development but rather to affirm it. It is important to recognize here that Kohlberg's sexism lies not in his having limited his sample to boys. His sexism lies in his having used the male category as the generic human and having accepted social patterns of male superiority and female inferiority as natural healthy guidelines for development.

Gilligan and her co-researchers elaborate how "problems tend to be recast by girls as a drama of inclusion and exclusion rather than of dominance and subordination" (Gilligan, 1988, p. 148) and how "girls tend to stress their feelings of connection to other people by defining dependence in opposition to isolation rather than to independence or autonomy" (Mendelsohn, 1990, p. 246). Given the absence of historical and material context, one is led here to assume that those tendencies flow from some inherent difference between female and male psyches. Girls may normally do such recasting just as boys may normally cast their reality in terms of dominance and autonomy; the question is whether those tendencies should be taken as measures of healthy development rather than as psychic responses to social imperatives. Gilligan comes up with almost exactly the same female qualities as Kohlberg–nurturance, caring, what Kohlberg calls "niceness"–and then chastises society for not perceiving those qualities as equal to the male quality of justice. I suggest that both female caring and male justice are fraught with psychic defense and rigidity, not to mention social inequity. We do not need to deny differences between women and men nor between other social groups defined by relations of domination. The political–as well as psychodynamic–task is to elaborate such differences as *social categories* created within a system of imbalanced relations which are dynamic, changeable, psychologically problematic, and grossly unacceptable for a democratic society.

## CONCLUSION

I have attempted to demonstrate in this wide-ranging discussion that compliance with oppressive social norms is a psychic disturbance. Those labeled deviant, extreme, or different–whatever their individual abnormalities–share with those not so labeled a foundation of normal psychic rigidity determined by intra-familial and extra-familial enactments of social position. That foundation functions obscurely to reinforce defensive distortions of reality and to perpetuate interlocking systems of domination.

At the onset of this discussion I asserted that psychological theorists have thus far failed to give psychodynamic coherence to historically repetitive relations of domination because of their (unconscious) refusal to recognize normative relations as problematic. More explicitly, I believe that psychic attachment to domination patterns and psychic defense against any disruption in social position work forcefully and oppressively against the development of politically contextualized psychological theory. But even assuming psychic flexibility and political courage, psychological theorists are handicapped by deeply ingrained resistances to material and historical analysis particular to their disciplines. Overcoming those resistances is an epistemological as well as clinical project. The human malaise caused by familial and cultural transmission of institutionalized domination falls rightfully within the domain of psychology.

## NOTES

1. A recently elaborated study by Maria P. P. Root (1992) offers promise with the concept of "insidious trauma," which refers to normative cumulative experiences of abuse linked to subordinate social status. Root postulates no concept for normative cumulative experiences of dominant rigidity since her study is focused exclusively on psychic responses to oppression from the subordinate position.

2. I have deliberately chosen the word Shoah, meaning disaster, and rejected the word Holocaust, meaning sacrifice and connoting a religious act.

3. I am indebted to Liliane Kandel for urging me to include the word "democracy" in this text and to both her and Marion Pheterson for their important questions and reservations about an earlier, less, precise statement of these distinctions.

4. Diverse essays on the mass murder of 14 university women at the Montreal School of Polytechnology in 1989 address these analytical distortions in the Canadian journal *Sociologie et Sociétés*, Vol. XXII, No 1, April, 1990. See Bertrand (1991) for an English translation in *Feminist Issues*.

5. French ethnologist Nicole-Claude Mathieu elaborates the asymmetrical illogical ways in which men are made a general universal social category and women, if mentioned at all, a particularized "physiologico-psychologico-sociological mixture" (1974, p. 355; see also 1978; 1989; 1990; and, for her collected essays in French, 1991). The ideological entrenchment of men as universal and women as particular is elaborated also by linguist Claire Michard (1988; with

Claudine Ribéry, 1986), writer Monique Wittig with special focus on lesbians (1992), sociologist Christine Delphy (1984), and sociologist Colette Guillaumin in relation to both sex and race categories (1981a/b; 1982; 1993; see also 1992 for collected essays in French). Together with Italian ethnologist Paola Tabet (1986; 1987), these scholars are the leading theorists of the French feminist materialist anti-naturalism school. Their work has been the most significant theoretical support for my analysis.

6. The DSM-III-R (*Diagnostic and Statistical Manual of Mental Disorders*, American Psychiatric Association, 1987) category of "Self-Defeating Personality Disorder" is a psychiatric example of attaching abuse to women's individual psyches; see Caplan and Gans (1991) for analysis and critique. Note that postulation of a "Delusional Dominating Personality Disorder" (Caplan, 1991) poses no challenge to the underlying distortion; locating domination in the minds of men is as insidious an erasure of sexist social relations as is locating submission in the minds of women.

7. The relation between danger and material exploitation is particularly cogent in relation to women's reproductive and sexual labor. For classic feminist materialist analyses of reproduction and sexual economic exchange, see Tabet, 1986; 1987. For prostitute testimonies and analyses of the relation between danger from state repression and vulnerability to exploitation and abuse, see Pheterson, 1989.

8. Parallel concepts to this politicized notion of psychic strategies of self-defense have been developed mostly in disciplines other than psychology such as philosophy, ethnology, or sociology and in grass-roots therapy movements. Examples that could perhaps be fruitfully integrated in psychological theory include "impacted misinformation" or "sedimentations of oppression" (Ricky Sherover-Marcuse, 1982; 1986), "dominated consciousness" (Nicole-Claude Mathieu, 1989), "internalized oppression" (Suzanne Lipsky, 1977; Gail Pheterson, 1986), "arrested consciousness" (Herbert Marcuse, 1969), and "pig" (Hogie Wyckoff, 1977). I have deliberately chosen the classic psychodynamic term "defense" because I believe the mechanism functions according to many classical, although historicized and materialized, principles.

9. For example, he notes that children choose their father as "the one who is best in the family" because "he works and makes the money" (1966, p. 102). Or, a three-year-old told his mother: "When you grow up to be a Daddy, you can have a bicycle, too (like his father)" (p. 95). If Kohlberg doesn't specify "girl," "children" means "boys."

# REFERENCES

Adorno, T. W., Frendel-Brunswik, E., Levinson, D. J., & Sanford, N. R. (1950). *The authoritarian personality.* New York: Norton.

American Psychiatric Association (1987). Diagnostic and statistical manual of mental disorders–III–R. Washington, DC: APA.

Arendt, Hannah (1943). We refugees. In *Menorah Journal 31* (pp. 69-77). Reprinted (1978) in *The Jew as pariah* (pp. 56-66). New York: Grove.

Bergmann, M. S., & Jucovy, M. E. (Eds.) (1982). *Generations of the holocaust.* New York: Basic Books.

Bertrand, Marie-Andree (1991). Feminists targeted for murder: Montreal 1989. In *Feminist Issues, 11*(2), 3-25.

Brownmiller, Susan (1975). *Against our will: Men, women and rape.* New York: Simon and Schuster.

Cameron, Barbara (1981). Gee, you don't seem like an indian from the reservation. In Cherríe Moraga & Gloria Anzaldúa (Eds.), *This bridge called my back* (pp. 46-52). Watertown: Persephone.

Caplan, Paula J. (1991). Delusional dominating personality disorder (DDPD). *Feminism and psychology, 1*(1), 171-174.

Caplan, Paula J., & Gans, Maureen (1991). Is there empirical justification for the category of self-defeating personality disorder? *Feminism and psychology, 1*(2), 263-278.

Colao, Flora, & Hunt, Miriam (1983). Therapists coping with sexual assault. In Joan Hamerman Robbins & Rachel Josefowitz Siegel (Eds.), *Women changing therapy* (pp. 205-214). New York: Haworth.

Davis, Angela Y. (1981). *Women, race and class.* New York: Random House.

Delphy, Christine (1984). *Close to home: A materialist analysis of women's oppression.* Amherst: University of Massachusetts Press.

Epstein, Helen (1979). *Children of the holocaust.* New York: Putnam.

Espín, Oliva M., & Gawelek, Mary Ann (1992). Women's diversity: Ethnicity, race, class, and gender in theories of feminist psychology. In Laura S. Brown & Mary Ballou (Eds.), *Personality and psychopathology: Feminist reappraisals* (pp. 88-107). New York: Guilford.

Fernando, Suman (1989). *Race and culture in psychiatry.* New York: Tavistock/Routledge.

Freud, Sigmund (1974). Anxiety and instinctual life. In James Strachey (Ed./Translator), *New introductory lectures on psycho-analysis* (pp. 81-111). London: Hogarth. (Originally published in 1933).

Gilligan, Carol (1982). *In a different voice.* Cambridge, MA: Harvard University Press.

Gilligan, Carol (1988). Exit-voice dilemmas in adolescent development. In Carol Gilligan, J. F. Ward, and J. M. Taylor (Eds.), *Mapping the moral domain* (pp. 141-158). Cambridge, MA: Distributed by Harvard University Press.

Goldenson, Robert M. (Ed.) (1984). *Longman dictionary of psychology and psychiatry.* New York: Longman.

Guillaumin, Colette (1981a). The practice of power and belief in nature. Part I: The appropriation of women. *Feminist issues, 1*(2), 3-28. (Originally published in *Questions Féministes, 2,* 1978.)

_____ (1981b). The practice of power and belief in nature, Part II: The naturalist discourse. *Feminist issues, 1*(3), 87-109. (Originally published in *Questions Féministes, 3,* 1978.)

_____ (1982, Spring). The question of difference. *Feminist issues*, 33-52. (Originally published in *Questions Féministes*, 6, 1979.)

_____ (1991, Fall). Madness and the social norm. *Feminist issues*, *11*(2), 10-15. (Originally published in *Sociologie et sociétés. XXII*(1) April 1990.)

_____ (1992). *Sexe, race et pratique du pouvoir*. Paris: côté-femmes.

_____ (1994). *Racism, sexism, power and ideology*. London: Routledge.

Horney, Karen (1937). *The neurotic personality of our time*. New York: Norton.

Kohlberg, Lawrence (1966). A cognitive-development analysis of children's sex-role concepts and attitudes. In Eleanor E. Maccoby (Ed.), *The development of sex differences*. Stanford: Stanford University Press.

Laplanche, Jean, & Pontalis, J.-B. (1988). *Vocabulaire de la psychoanalyse* (9th ed.). Paris: Presses Universitaires de France.

Lipsky, Suzanne (1977, Winter). Internalized oppression. *Black Re-emergence*, 2, 5-10.

Littlewood, Roland, & Lipsedge, Maurice (1989). *Aliens and alienists: Ethnic minorities and psychiatry* (2nd ed.). Boston: Unwin Hyman.

Lorde, Audre (1984). *Sister outsider*. New York: Crossing.

Marcuse, Herbert (1969). *An essay on liberation*. Boston: Beacon.

Mathieu, Nicole-Claude (1974, Summer). Notes towards a sociological definition of sex categories. *The human context, 6*(2), 345-361. (Originally published in *Epistémologie Sociologique*, 11, 1st semestre 1971.)

_____ (1978). Man-culture and woman-nature. *Women's studies international quarterly, 1*, 55-65. (Originally published in *L'homme, XIII*(3), 1973.)

_____ (1989, Fall). Part I. *Feminist issues, 9*(2), 3-49. (Originally published in *L'Arraisonnement des Femmes: Essais en Anthropologies des Sexes*, edited by N-C Mathieu, Editions de l'École des Hautes Études en Sciences Sociales. Paris, 1985.)

_____ (1990, Spring). When yielding is not consenting: Material and psychic determinants of women's dominated consciousness and some of their interpretations in ethnology. Part II, *Feminist issues, 10*(1), 51-90. (Originally published in French with Part I.)

_____ (1991). *L'anatomie politique*. Paris: côté-femmes.

Mendelsohn, Janet (1990). The view from step number 16: Girls from Emma Willard School talk about themselves and their futures. In Carol Gilligan, N. P. Lyon, and T. J. Hanmer (Eds.), *Making connections* (pp. 233-257). Cambridge, MA: Harvard University Press.

Michard, Claire (1988). Some socio-enunciative characteristics of scientific texts concerning the sexes. In Gill Seidel (Ed.), *The nature of the right* (pp. 27-59). Philadelphia: John Benjamin's Publishing Co.

Michard-Marchal, Claire, & Ribéry, Claudine (1986, Fall). Enunciation and ideological effects: "Women" and "men" as subjects of discourse in ethnology. *Feminist issues, 6*(2), 53-74. (Originally published in *L'Arraisonnement des*

*Femmes: Essais en Anthropologies des Sexes* edited by N-C Mathieu, Editions de l'École des Hautes Études en Sciences Sociales. Paris, 1985.)

Miller, Jean Baker (1986). *Toward a new psychology of women* (2nd ed.). Boston: Beacon.

O'Hare, Janet, & Taylor, Katy (1983). The Reality of Incest. In Joan Hamerman Robbins & Rachel Josefowitz Siegel (Eds.), *Women changing therapy* (pp. 215-229). New York: Haworth.

Pheterson, Gail (Ed.) (1989). *A vindication of the rights of whores.* Seattle: Seal .

_____ (1986). Alliances between women: Overcoming internalized oppression and internalized domination. *Signs: Journal of women in culture and society, 12*(1), 146-160.

Root, Maria P. P. (1992). Reconstructing the impact of trauma on personality. In Laura S. Brown and Mary Ballou (Eds.), *Personality and Psychopathology: Feminist Reappraisal* (pp. 229-265). New York: Guilford.

Russell, Diana E. H. (1973). *The politics of rape.* New York: Free.

_____ (1982). *Rape in marriage.* New York: Macmillan.

_____ (1984). *Sexual exploitation: Rape, child sexual abuse, and sexual harassment.* Beverly Hills, CA: Sage.

Russett, Cynthia Eagle (1989). *Sexual science: The Victorian construction of womanhood.* Cambridge, MA: Harvard University Press.

Sherover-Marcuse, Ricky (1982, February). Unlearning Racism. *Second Opinion.*

_____ (1986). *Emancipation and consciousness.* New York: Basil Blackwell.

Smith, Lillian (1978). *Killers of the dream* (rev. ed.). New York: Norton. (Originally published in 1949.)

Tabet, Paola (1986). Imposed reproduction, maimed sexuality. *Feminist issues, 7*(2), 3-31. (Originally published in *Nuova DWF Donna Woman Femme, 23-24,* 1985.)

_____ (1987, May). Du don au tarif. Les relations sexuelles impliquant une compensation. *Les Temps Modernes, 490,* 1-53.

Wardi, Dina (1992). *Memorial candles: Children of the holocaust.* New York: Routledge.

Wittig, Monique (1992). *The straight mind.* Boston: Beacon.

Wyckoff, Hogie (1977). *Solving women's problems.* New York: Grove.

# PART III:
# GUIDES TO ANTIRACIST PRACTICE

Racism is not merely an ideology; it is a practice. Antiracism is also not just a political position, but requires being put into practice. The title of this section refers not only to feminist therapy practice but also to antiracist practice in all aspects of our lives. Good intentions are only the beginning.

# Cross-Cultural Awareness Development: An Aid to the Creation of Anti-Racist Feminist Therapy

Carole Pigler Christensen

## *INTRODUCTION*

The Civil Rights movement of the 1960s and the feminist movement of the 1970s have both affected therapeutic models. Only recently have there been attempts to marry the two. Those advocating feminist therapy have been faulted for neglecting to incorporate their "sisters of color" as an integral part of their theoretical formulations. The purpose of this paper is to assist those wishing to move toward the integration of an understanding and awareness of the interface between feminist therapy and anti-racist therapy. Using the author's original developmental model, case illustrations indicate how feminist therapists operating at different developmental stages of cross-cultural awareness may integrate anti-racism in their personal and professional lives.

Until quite recently in the history of the helping professions, any discussion of racism (as opposed to race) as it affects therapeutic efforts was as taboo as open discussion of racism in the wider society. However, during the last three decades, minority therapists from the fields of social work, psychology, and counseling have examined the deleterious effects of racist beliefs, expectations, and behaviors on therapeutic processes and outcomes (Katz, 1985; Christensen, 1984).

A presentation of a model to aid anti-racist feminist therapy must begin with a definition of the terms that are often used, but about which little consensus exists. For the purposes of this paper, the definitions below are offered.

Broadly defined, *feminist therapy* is practiced whenever the female perspective is valued and the impact of sexual inequality on women's lives is understood (Russell, 1989).

This author agrees with Green's (1982) definition of *race* as a Euro-American folk concept. Although all peoples have apparently developed methods of classifying those considered dissimilar from themselves, the belief that humankind could be hierarchically divided into distinct white, yellow, red, and black-skinned "races," connoting the genetic inheritance of human qualities (e.g., intelligence, morality, sexuality) was born and nourished in colonial Europe (Kallen, 1982). In the Americas, this belief system was institutionalized by the practice of slavery, and by various forms of discriminatory or preferential treatment of identifiable groups. Despite recently coming into disrepute as lacking any scientific basis, the concept of race remains an integral part of the North American belief system, incorporated into the theories and practices of the helping professions. In therapy, people of color classified by the dominant (i.e., Euro-American) group as being "the same" are often mistakenly believed to share the same culture and behaviors. Based on these conscious or unconscious beliefs, those perceived as racially superior or inferior perceive differential or discriminatory treatment, whether overt or covert.

*Cross-cultural relationships* exist when the client and therapist are from different cultural or ethnic backgrounds. Culture becomes important whenever the unique customs, values, norms, roles, and life-styles populations have developed over time become important. Cultural differences are potential barriers to positive therapeutic relationships and outcomes, whether rooted in foreign traditions or stemming from economic, social, and political realities (Christensen, 1986).

Although presented as peripheral, if at all, in the literature of feminist therapists, the dynamics of culture and race are clearly important. It is well documented that women (and men) from backgrounds other than White, North American, or European-American: seldom seek therapy voluntarily; often do not return after the initial interview; tend to be offered short-term rather than long-term therapy; and often express dissatisfaction with the therapeutic process and outcome (Christensen, 1984).

Black female sex roles can be defined as the constellation of qualities understood to characterize the social roles of black females in North American culture (Linder, 1984). Because of racism, black women's sex roles and color are singularly and uniquely inter-twined (Amott & Matthaei, 1991; Christensen, 1988). For more than a century (Rodgers-Rose, 1985), legalized oppression was per-petuated by white women as well as by white men, both of whom were beneficiaries of the privileges that resulted from black slavery (e.g., white men's access to the bodies of black women to produce slave children; labor and wet nurses provided by black women).

Based on the above, "anti-racist feminist therapy" can be de-fined as actively promoting the re-examination of traditional theo-ries and practices in order to practice in a manner equally free of racism *and* sexism. This may require post-graduate training to un-learn deleterious skills or techniques, or to learn to adapt old skills and theories to make them more relevant and appropriate to mi-nority women; and to help majority group women overcome con-scious and unconscious dominating behaviors.

## Assumptions Underlying this Paper

1. As with most therapists of any orientation, most feminist ther-apists' educational background and training will have omitted serious and in-depth attention to culture, ethnicity, and race as important variables affecting the therapist and the client in therapeutic encounters.
2. As a consequence of colonialism, people living in the Amer-icas are affected by racism, whether they reside in North, Central, or South America.
3. In the North American context, cross-cultural therapeutic en-counters are a common occurrence.
4. Since the therapist must use "the self as instrument" in any relationship, it is the *whole* self, including prejudices, biases, taboos, and values that enters every interaction, whether verbal-ized or not.
5. In the North American context, when clients and therapists perceive themselves to be dissimilar in skin color, race becomes a salient variable in cross-cultural therapeutic encounters.
6. Racism and therapy are antithetical; racist belief systems, be-

haviors, and institutional practices belie the offering of therapeutic conditions to a client.

Although feminist therapists suggest that they help women to
understand societal factors contributing to their problems, they
commonly fail to acknowledge the effects of racial identity, racism,
and the power inherent in the helper's role (Douglas, 1985). Even
when class or poverty is considered in theories, that racism causes
some groups to have disproportionate numbers among the poor is
seldom acknowledged (Heiss, 1984).

## CROSS-CULTURAL AWARENESS DEVELOPMENT: THE CHRISTENSEN MODEL

Cross-cultural awareness development is the process whereby an
individual is enabled to interact with someone of a different racial,
cultural, or ethnic background with authenticity, respect, openness,
and acceptance (Christensen, 1989). I suggest that the stage the
feminist therapist has reached in this developmental process determines the degree of success of therapeutic encounters.

Cross-cultural awareness development is rooted in knowledge
and understanding gained through meaningful, personal experiences with people dissimilar to oneself; it cannot be fully achieved
through theoretical learning. It is the ethical responsibility of therapists to ensure that they seek opportunities for cross-cultural awareness development outside of therapeutic encounters, rather than
hoping, somehow, to learn from their clients.

Personal experiences offer the feminist practitioner an opportunity for meaningful and intense discovery of self in relation to a
woman (or several women) from another background. New
learning occurs about sociocultural factors shaping individual and
group responses. This results in new insights, leading to questioning values, attitudes, and beliefs. Eventually, the feminist therapist reaches new levels of appreciation of commonalities and differences between dissimilar groups. Since this model holds no implicit
expectation that "therapists" are necessarily from the dominant
culture, feminist therapists from any racial or cultural background
should find the model relevant and applicable.

Cross-cultural awareness development proposes a five-stage process in which women from majority and minority group backgrounds have parallel but significantly different experiences. These differences are based on the life experiences of those who: (a) based on skin color, or perceived racial identity, are arbitrarily considered part of the majority group, whether or not they are natives of the country in question, or share the culture of the dominant group; (b) were integrated into another culture where they were part of the majority, before immigrating to their present country of residence; and (c) have known only minority status in their country of birth and residence.

It should be noted that the concepts of majority and minority groups are not defined in terms of numbers. Rather, the majority group is that which exerts the greatest influence, occupies powerful decision-making positions, and determines the life chances of other groups in a given society. The culture of the majority group is sanctioned and transmitted by agents of socialization, including those governing the helping professions. Consequently, the feminist therapist from the majority group may consider herself to be in a "minority" position as a female, but she is part of the majority or dominant culture. Even if she is critical of the patriarchal and racist structure of society, the Euro-American female must acknowledge that both are part of her cultural background.

Each stage in the cross-cultural development model has distinguishable characteristics that may typify the individual for any length of time. For both majority and minority group members, in Stages 1 through 3, transitions to the next stage are marked by one or more identifiable experiences or events, when what happens is disquieting, and does not fit the individual's expectations. This leads to fundamental re-evaluations, altering feelings, behavior and, eventually, one's worldview. "Worldview" refers to how a person perceives his/her relationship to the world (nature, institutions, other people) and encompasses attitudes, values, and concepts affecting how she thinks, defines events, and behaves. The final transition, from Stage 4 to 5, involves continuous confirmation of the altered worldview in daily life, including therapeutic encounters.

Cross-cultural awareness development can begin at any age, whenever opportunities for meaningful learning about other cultural, ethnic, or racial groups occur. It seems unlikely, however, that progression through Stage 5 would occur during childhood, since understanding how complex sociopolitical and economic systems interact to maintain stratified social positions is required. In addition, self-awareness and acceptance is a prerequisite for completing all five stages of the model. Many never develop cross-cultural awareness in an entire lifetime, due to lack of opportunity (e.g., living and dying in a homogeneous area) or interest, social norms, prejudice, or even an aversion to those considered to be outside of one's own group.

Depending on previous life experiences, therapists start at various points. An individual may begin beyond Stage 1, may get stuck at any stage, and may never proceed to Stage 5. Painful or disillusioning experiences may cause a person to regress to an earlier stage. However, therapists may progress so rapidly, due to a chain of meaningful events, that they may seem to skip a stage. Furthermore, when in transition, it is possible to have all of the characteristics of a particular stage and find that some aspects of the next stage also apply.

Table 1 presents an overview of the author's Cross-Cultural Awareness Development Model. Each stage of development will be discussed in terms of how the model can be applied to anti-racist feminist therapy.

## APPLICATION OF THE MODEL
## TO ANTI-RACIST FEMINIST THERAPY

Anti-racist therapy suggests that the therapist acknowledges: (a) growing up in a racist society; (b) racism's effects on herself and on client populations; and (c) that she may not be competent to deal with the effects of the above as part of the therapeutic process, making additional training necessary.

### STAGE 1: Unawareness

Feminist therapists at this stage may have immersed themselves in feminist theory. However, they have never given serious consideration to race or culture as variables affecting therapeutic pro-

## TABLE 1. Stages in the Developmental of Cross-Cultural Awareness*

| Person from Majority Cultural, Ethnic, or Racial Background | Person from Minority Cultural, Ethnic, or Racial Background |
|---|---|

### STAGE 1: Unawareness:

Serious though has never been given to cultural, ethnic, or racial differences, or their meaning and influence for individuals and groups.

| | |
|---|---|
| (a) Glibly accepts idea of equality, multiculturalism; or the superior/inferior positions of own/other groups in society, without speculation. | (a) Believes in equality of all people; or has accepted the position of his/her group in society without speculation. |
| (b) Oblivious to all but the most blatant acts of racism or ethnic discrimination, and often relabels such acts as being due to something else. | (b) Able to deny or negate even glaring forms of racism or ethnic discrimination, relabelling such acts as possibly being due to something else. |

**Transition:** A specific event of strong and undeniable personal import.

### STAGE 2: Beginning Awareness:

Accompanied by uneasiness and/or beginning sense of cognitive dissonance.

| | |
|---|---|
| (a) Begins to be aware of ethnic and racial stereotypes, and to wonder if, and how, these relate to discriminatory acts. | (a) Begins to be aware of covert and overt ethnic and racial prejudice and discrimination, and to wonder if, and how, these impact on minority people's lives. |
| (b) Begins to question assumptions and beliefs previously accepted about social position of various cultural, ethnic, and racial groups. | (b) Begins to question reasons for societal position of own and other cultural, ethnic, and racial groups. |
| (c) Accompanied by attempts to disassociate self from sharing responsibility for suffering and harm of disadvantaged and oppressed minority groups. | (c) Accompanied by beginning sense of shared experience with members of own and other disadvantaged or oppressed minorities, but with ambivalence. |

**Transition:** A meaningful personal relationship, providing intimate and intense opportunities to learn about a dissimilar group.

*© Carole Pigler Christensen. June, 1984

**TABLE 1 (continued)**

### STAGE 3: Conscious Awareness:

Evidence of sometimes conflictual pre-occupation with cultural, ethnic, and racial differences and their possible meanings, in historical and present-day context.

| | |
|---|---|
| (a) Fully aware of cultural, ethnic, and racial differences, but unsure of how to integrate and use emerging knowledge and understanding in daily life. | (a) Fully aware of cultural, ethnic, and racial differences, but unsure of how to integrate and use emerging knowledge and understanding in daily life. |
| (b) The following phases may be experienced: curiosity; denial; guilt; fear; powerlessness; anger. | (b) The following phases may be experienced: excitement; denial; rejection; sadness; powerlessness; anger. |

**Transition:** The working-through of feelings and responses relating to powerful and prolonged soul-searching and learning experiences.

### STAGE 4: Consolidated Awareness:

Characterized by involved commitment to seek positive societal change and promote intergroup understanding. Views human differences as positive and rewarding.

| | |
|---|---|
| (a) Positive acceptance and integration of self-identity, and acceptance of other cultures, ethnic groups and races. | (a) Positive acceptance and integration of own cultural, racial, or ethnic identity, and acceptance of other groups. |
| (b) Accompanied by desire to help other majority or dominant group members to reach this new level of understanding. | (b) Accompanied by desire to help others of own minority group to this new level of understanding. |

**Transition:** Gradual and imperceptible shift in allegiance from own groups to humankind. An affair of the heart.

### STAGE 5: Transcendent Awareness:

Beyond limitations of societal dictates regarding appropriate and/or acceptable manner in which to relate to various cultural, racial, and ethnic groups.

(a) Cross-cultural awareness is a "way of life", and need no longer be consciously sought.

(b) Comfort is experienced in all human environments, with individual responding appropriately, but effortlessly and spontaneously.

(c) Although aware of how others, of majority and minority backgrounds, may view one's actions and responses, this is not a major factor in determining behaviour in cross-cultural situation.

cesses and outcomes. They are unaware of how ethnic, cultural, or racial background impact on the daily lives and life chances of minority populations. Feminism and racism remain compartmentalized in the thinking of these therapists.

## Majority Group Therapists

Even when dealing with clients of other cultural and racial backgrounds, therapists at this stage know minority populations mainly as reflections of stereotypes represented in the media. These therapists look for validation of their beliefs in the real people seen in therapy. Privileges associated with majority group status are taken for granted. At the same time, therapists at this stage have never thought about how minority group therapists may experience feminist theory. They may boast that in therapeutic encounters, they "treat all women exactly the same," since they have a firm belief in equality. Those convinced of the inferiority of some groups, or of their inability to benefit from therapy, may feel quite justified in refusing to treat them, or in offering them limited forms of treatment.

*Example.* S. is a feminist therapist employed in the counseling service of a college in a southern city. About 10 percent of her clientele are black or Hispanic. She noted that most of the women of minority background did not join the group she started to discuss problems with male/female relationships on campus. Those who came did not return after the first session. She told a co-worker that she's not surprised, since these women are "just not psychologically minded" and therefore did not "fit in."

## Minority Group Therapists

The minority therapist at this stage is almost indistinguishable from her majority group counterpart, except by her minority group background. They may be uncomfortable treating clients from their own background and other minorities, although comfortable with white clients. Therapists from the majority group are very comfortable in the presence of such minority therapists. Minority therapists at this stage have accepted and internalized the majority culture's views and attitudes toward minority groups, as expressed in the popular culture and in the therapeutic literature.

*Example*. M. is an African-American feminist social worker who was recently hired in the social service department of a major inner-city hospital. Upon noting that a disproportionate number of her clients were black, she explained to her supervisor that she grew up in an affluent, predominantly white neighborhood, and did not feel comfortable with inner-city African-American culture.

## *Transition*

The transition to the next stage is sparked by a precipitating event or situation of undeniable import to the therapist, jolting her perceptions. Whether perceived as positive or negative at the time, the occurrence can be pinpointed as the first time that issues relating to ethnicity, culture, or race were recognized to play an undeniable role in a therapeutic process or outcome.

## *STAGE 2: Beginning Awareness*

Beginning awareness is characterized by a sense of uneasiness as the feminist therapist begins to question why various groups respond differently to therapy, and whether their life experiences affect the therapeutic process and outcomes.

## *Majority Group Therapists*

The majority group therapist begins to be more aware of how what is recorded in the literature about various minority groups affects therapists' expectations and behaviors during therapy. Research questions, results, and interpretations which were previously accepted uncritically begin to be questioned in terms of who wrote them and from what perspective. Although still unable to draw deliberate similarities between feminist thinking and anti-racist theory, there is a beginning desire to question and explore how she is perceived by minority clients. There is considerable reluctance to recognize racism in oneself.

*Example*. D. is a feminist therapist in private practice. She has often related, rather proudly, that her parents taught her never to feel superior since we are "all God's children." D. was shocked when a

Puerto Rican client telephoned saying, tearfully, that she would not be coming back because she would not tolerate being insulted about her ethnic background at every session. D's efforts to encourage the client to come in, free of charge, to help her to understand what had caused this reaction, were to no avail.

## Minority Group Therapists

There is a growing, albeit uneasy, identification with others of one's own minority group. References to one's group are experienced differently than before, and there is a growing curiosity about the experiences of those with whom one is identified by others. This is accompanied by a sense of loss since one is no longer totally comfortable with the dominant group, whose values, motives, and attitudes are now questioned. Similarly, the positive meaning of feminist therapy for those of minority backgrounds is no longer taken for granted.

*Example.* B., whose parents were born in India, attended an Ivy League university and married a white American several years ago; she considers herself assimilated to United States culture. A psychiatrist in training at a family therapy unit frequented by many immigrants, she recently found herself questioning how best to respond. The chief psychiatrist assigned her to conduct an interview with an Indian immigrant family for Grand Rounds, attended by the entire department and other professionals. He identified a major aspect of her role to be helping these Indian parents to understand that arranged marriage is a "primitive, cruel custom" that will not be tolerated in North America.

## Transition

The transition to Stage 3 is generally marked by an opportunity to learn about a dissimilar group through an intimate, intensely meaningful relationship. Although this may occur in private life or in a therapeutic situation, it usually involves one or two people, rather than a large group. Feminist therapists will generally find this process facilitated when relating to another woman, rather than to a man. The experience allows the individual to move from an intellectual understanding to one involving deeper emotions. As a result, the feminist therapist experiences a greater sense of empathy toward minority populations, although her understanding of these groups may remain somewhat superficial.

## STAGE 3: Conscious Awareness

This stage is characterized by a preoccupation with issues relating to how feminist therapy relates to the experience of racism, discrimination, and prejudice as these affect the lives of client populations. Questions that have previously been ignored or suppressed about how race, culture, and ethnicity affect therapeutic processes and outcomes now rise to the surface of the therapist's mind. The cross-cultural literature is examined avidly and workshops dealing with this subject are actively sought. In particular, there is growth in *self-awareness* as the therapist struggles to discover the role *she* plays in the complex systemic factors that create and sustain stratification based on the ideology of race.

### Majority Group Therapists

The therapist at this stage is consciously, almost constantly, aware of race and culture, searching to understand their impact, both in therapeutic situations and in daily life. There is a diminishing tendency to differentiate between the client in daily life situations and in therapy, and a growing desire to see the total reality lived by the client. The feminist therapist finds herself increasingly able to draw parallels between feminist and anti-racist approaches. At the same time, there is intense soul-searching, resulting in considerable conflict and confusion. Arguments with colleagues often ensue as the therapist often finds herself alone in her thinking about and assessment of the role played by race and culture in clients' problems. Depending on the nature of the therapist's experience and the individual personality, the following states are usually experienced, with the therapist often vacillating between them or getting stuck at a certain state for a time:

*Curiosity* about various groups, reasons for their societal positions, and their experience in and outside of therapeutic relationships.

*Denial* that certain forms of oppression occur; that differential treatment is offered to population groups based on race and cultural background; and that the therapist bears some personal and professional responsibility for the pain and suffering experienced by minorities.

*Guilt* may be overwhelming when the therapist acknowledges oppression and accepts responsibility for perpetuating inequality in subtle or overt ways in her professional and personal life. Such feelings are exacerbated in feminist therapists who understand oppression as a real force in the lives of white women. There may also be a sense of relief that, as one identified as part of the dominant group, the therapist is not subject to the worst forms of racism and discrimination.

*Fear* may result from identification with the victim, and fantasies about what she might do to retaliate were she in the victim's place.

*Powerlessness* comes from the realization that despite her growing awareness, she is limited in the extent to which she can bring about real, immediate, and/or lasting change in the lives of minority clients.

*Anger* is directed mainly at the majority group and the institutions which they control. However, the minority group's apparent inability to mobilize and fight back may arouse anger. This is particularly true for therapists limited in their understanding of the power differential between majority group women and those women (and men) from oppressed minority backgrounds.

*Example.* F. is a feminist counselor working in a storefront center for single mothers. She grew up with people from many backgrounds and chose to work with minority women. Although she obtained a small grant to pay for transportation and refreshments for the African-American and Hispanic women, they have insisted on having self-help groups run by leaders of their choice. F. vacillates between anger at being excluded because of her race, and identifying with the women's need to "own" the group. She is curious about what the women will discuss, but feels guilty as a white female who knows that there are times when women need to exclude men to empower themselves. She fears losing power and control, and denies that there is any reason for their not trusting her.

## Minority Group Therapists

As the minority group therapist begins to get in touch with her roots and becomes aware of the systemic reasons for her group's status, she may discover a conflict between her feminist values and her minority status based on race or culture. Although not yet fully identified with her minority culture, the dominant culture is no longer the primary reference group for determining acceptable norms, values, and beliefs. A sense of alienation from the majority culture, and even from friends and colleagues, may precipitate a personal and professional crisis. There may be a feeling that most of what one learned as a therapist was a denial or misrepresentation of one's minority background and its meaning in daily life. Depending on the life experiences and personality of the individual, vacillation between the following affective states, or getting stuck at a certain state for some time, are common:

*Excitement* stems from a sense of anticipation about opportunities to answer the question, "Who am I," and to try to meet the challenge of integrating feminist practice with minority racial and cultural identity.

*Denial* of the harsh realities of certain forms of racism, prejudice, and discrimination may still lead the minority feminist to disassociate herself from her group, or to deny that she too is affected. She may also deny that her profession, institution, or colleagues are involved in behaviors or setting policies harmful to minorities, including her own.

*Rejection* and alienation from the majority group culture often coexists with rejection of one's own culture. Other cultures with which the therapist may be wrongly identified (e.g., Koreans confused with the Chinese) may also be rejected.

*Sadness*, even depression, may be experienced as the therapist realizes the full weight of the plight of oppressed minorities and that majority group women in power positions participate actively in the oppression of women of color.

*Powerlessness* is sensed as the complexity of the sociopolitical and economic systems that maintain the racially and ethnically stratified status quo is more fully comprehended.

*Anger* may be directed toward majority group women, as well as men, both of whom may at times be viewed as "oppressors." Anger toward minority women who fail to assert themselves, and to act in a unified fashion, may also be felt.

*Example*. D. is a fourth-generation Japanese-Canadian psychologist at an outpatient clinic where most patients and all other psychologists are from Euro-American backgrounds. When the issue of compensating Japanese-Canadians for property confiscated during World War II was discussed in the cafeteria, D. was shocked to hear colleagues she considered fair-minded speaking in a most derogatory fashion about Japanese people. She began to wonder how they really felt about her, and to reassess her true degree of acceptance by whites in personal and professional interactions. Reading about the evacuation experience and seeking out those who remembered it became a preoccupation.

## Transition

The transition from this stage comes only through prolonged and emotionally demanding soul-searching and learning from interactions that serve to increase self-awareness, rather than knowledge alone. Feminist therapists may experience considerable disillusionment and question their allegiance to a movement that generally ignores issues important to women of color.

## STAGE 4: Consolidated Awareness

Feminist therapists at this stage are fully aware of differences in the status, life experience, and treatment of individuals and groups based on ethnicity, culture, and race, and have incorporated this in their analyses and treatment approaches. The role played by historical and current factors is understood. They have achieved a sense of balance based on acceptance of themselves and women from backgrounds other than their own as both female and members of cultural and racial groups. Even when considering them unacceptable, they understand the psychosocial and economic dynamics underlying attitudes and behaviors. Opportunities and methods are sought to express a commitment to societal and institutional change, and to enhance the likelihood of positive treatment outcomes for minority populations generally, rather than only for specific clients or target groups.

## Majority Group Therapists

The role played by the majority group in the oppression of minorities is fully understood; positive self-identity is reinstated while appreciation of other groups is maintained. A person's racial or cultural background is no longer important in choosing intimate social relationships. Professionally, just as she would intervene if sexism were noted, the therapist now risks taking a stand when she sees a client's race or culture used inappropriately to mislabel or to provide an easy explanation of behavior (e.g., resistant, multiproblem client, non-verbal group, unmotivated for treatment, not psychologically minded). Racism is not denied even if well disguised or "subtle."

*Example.* N. was often annoyed when she saw black and Hispanic clients at the women's counseling service offered short-term, crisis-oriented treatment by white feminist therapists, even when there was need for more intensive long-term intervention. She decided to start a group to which colleagues could refer these clients for long-term therapy, and offered screening workshops for staff with an excellent cross-cultural and anti-racist component.

## Minority Group Therapists

The minority therapist is fully and comfortably identified with her cultural and racial group and acknowledges positive and negative aspects of past and present occurrences. She has fully integrated feminist and anti-racist components into private and professional spheres of life. There is an appreciation of how people's life experience may lead to attitudes and behaviors which she personally finds unacceptable.

*Example.* P., an African-American feminist therapist, heads the social service department of a family service agency in a large urban center. She finds herself constantly challenged by those who are uncomfortable with a woman of her background in a position of authority. Nonetheless, she has introduced cross-cultural and anti-racist staff training programs. Under her leadership, the department is moving toward developing more appropriate and relevant services for underserved populations.

## Transition

The transition to the next stage is gradual, even imperceptible, resulting from the experience of learning from, and interacting with, those dissimilar from oneself. Eventually, continuous growth in self-awareness brings a shift in allegiance from one's "own" cultural or racial group to humankind.

## STAGE 5: Transcendent Awareness

A sense of peace with oneself and others characterizes this stage. It is based on a deep understanding and appreciation of real differences and their underlying causes, coupled with the ability to perceive fundamental human qualities as the unifying dimension transcending differences.

### Majority and Minority Group Therapists

The feminist therapist at this stage need no longer consciously *try* to be accepting of those dissimilar to herself in race or cultural background. She is constantly aware of human similarities, whether working with clients or in private life. However, she remains cognizant of the meaning society associates with race, culture, and ethnicity and of the unique life experiences of different client populations. Feminist therapists at this stage are spontaneously able to establish rapport with people of various groups and do not hesitate to become fully involved with clients, whatever their background.

*Example.* T. is a psychiatrist of Hispanic descent who has comfortably integrated feminist and anti-racist approaches. She is perfectly bilingual and uses the surname of her African-American husband. She finds herself equally able to establish rapport with patients of African-American, immigrant Hispanic, and European backgrounds. As a dark-skinned Cuban, she is rather amused by the surprise on the faces of those meeting her for the first time who appear to think that dark skin and psychiatry are antithetical. Her colleagues, whether or not they are feminists, tend to want her to go along with the notion that being female means having the same experience of oppression. When appropriate in diagnostic sessions,

T. does not hesitate to challenge misinterpretations based on psychodynamic explanations which do not fit the reality of some patients.

## SUMMARY AND CONCLUSION

The author proposes that for most feminist therapists to work toward anti-racist practice requires unlearning old modes of thinking and behavior and the learning of new attitudes, values, and activities. The first step in learning to practice anti-racist feminist therapy is to acknowledge that racism exists on individual, institutional, and cultural levels. The second step is to examine how one perpetuates racism in attitudes and behavior in personal and professional life. This can be aided by becoming more aware of how interactions and comfort levels are affected when serving clients different from oneself in cultural or racial background; and by allowing, or creating, opportunities to learn and to grow in this regard. The third step, and perhaps most important, is to recognize that cross-cultural awareness is a developmental process which, not unlike other types of development, requires the practice and integration of new learning and skills. Only when feminist therapists of all races are able to comprehend how their lives converge and are divergent, due to social constructs, will they be fully competent to provide effective therapeutic conditions and positive outcomes. Finally, it is the responsibility of every female therapist claiming to be committed to equality to work consciously and systematically toward becoming an *anti-racist* feminist therapist.

## REFERENCES

Amott, T., & Matthaei, J. (1991). *Race, gender, and work: A multi-cultural economic history of women in the United States*. Montreal: black Rose Books.
Christensen, C. P. (1984). Effects of cross-cultural training on counselor response. *Counselor Education and Supervision, 23*, 311-320.
_____ (1986). Cross-cultural social work: Fallacies, fears, and failings. *Intervention, 74*, 6-15.
_____ (1988). Issues in sex therapy with ethnic and racial minority women. *Women and Therapy, 7 (2/3)*, 187-205.

_____ (1989). Cross-cultural awareness development: A conceptual model. *Counselor Education and Supervision, 28,* 270-287.

Douglas, M. A. (1985). The role of power in feminist therapy: A reformulation. In L. B. Rosewater & L. E. A. Walker (Eds.), *Handbook of feminist psychotherapy* (pp. 241-249). New York: Springer.

Green, J. W. (1982). Chapter one: Ethnicity and social services. In J. W. Green (Ed.), *Cultural awareness in the social services.* Englewood Cliffs, NJ: Prentice-Hall.

Heiss, J. (1984). Women's values regarding marriage and the family. In H. P. McAdoo (Ed.), *Black Families.* Beverly Hills, CA: Sage.

Kallen, E. (1982). *Ethnicity and human rights in Canada.* Toronto: Gage.

Katz, J. H. (1985). The sociopolitical nature of counseling. *The Counseling Psychologist, 13,* 615-624.

Linder, D. M. (1984). black sex role research: Some uses and abuses of data. In B. W. White (Ed.), *Color in a White society.* Los Angeles: National Association of Social Workers.

Rodgers-Rose, L. F. (Ed.) (1985). *The black Woman.* Beverly Hills, CA: Sage.

Russell, M. N. (1989). Feminist social work skills. *Canadian Social Work Review, 6,* 69-81.

# Treatment Considerations When the Therapist Is the Minority in the Patient-Therapist Dyad

Helen L. Jackson

## *INTRODUCTION*

Since the 1960s interest in and research in cross-cultural therapy and the impact of race and ethnicity on the outcome, content, and process of therapy have grown. With demographic changes resulting from recent immigration to the United States by Mexicans, Haitians, Cubans, Vietnamese, Cambodians, and Salvadorans, to mention just a few, and with the impact of the Civil Rights movement of the 1960s as well as the growth of Community Mental Health Clinics which tend to serve minority groups, the study of the treatment of racial and ethnic minority clients has grown.

Most studies of racial and ethnic minority treatment have focused on comparing the service utilization or treatment success of white therapists treating minority clients (e.g., Sue et al., 1974), and on examining whether the white therapist can effectively treat minority clients. Very little attention has been given to the treatment dyad where the therapist is of a minority culture and the patient is from the dominant white American culture.

Though often denied or distorted, racism and prejudice do exist in our American society and necessarily affect therapeutic relationships, especially those that are cross-cultural. Afro-Americans are victims of persistent discrimination that, more than a century since the Civil War, still relegates them to second-class citizenship; the gulf between Afro-Americans and whites cannot be blamed on some idea of a self-perpetuating underclass.

Because racism continues, therapists and supervisors of novice therapists cannot and should not be indifferent to cultural variables or discrimination in therapy situations and settings. One example of such discrimination is the finding, again by Sue et al. (1974), that Afro-American patients, more often than white patients, were assigned by intake workers (and possibly by agency policy as well) to paraprofessionals or to less well-trained or less experienced professional staff, for treatment in mental health clinics. Thus, racial discrimination was seen by Sue et al. (1974) as a possibly important factor with regard to the dropout rate of Afro-American patients. Also, the patient's race was identified as *a* factor which might impede the development of trust and rapport in treatment.[1]

It has been clearly documented that racial and ethnic differences can affect the treatment process. For example, some studies have shown that there is a tendency for patients to prefer therapists of their own race (e.g., Harrison, 1975). Others (e.g., Parloff, Waslow, & Wolfe, 1978) have concluded that there are no definitive results on the effects of racial matching or mismatching. Atkinson (1983) concluded, however, that while Afro-Americans tend to prefer therapists who are similar to them in race, this is not true for other ethnic groups and he found little evidence that ethnically similar therapist/patient dyads had better outcomes.[2]

Most research along these lines has focused on patient or client variables rather than on therapist variables. This has probably happened because of the disproportionately small number of minority therapists in the past. That number is growing, however, and the dyad of minority therapist and white patient needs more attention than it has been given.[3]

While there is certainly the need for white therapists to be sensitive to cultural and racial issues in the treatment of their minority patients we need to be sensitive also to the training needs of the *minority* therapist. We need to look at what it is like for the minority therapist to be treating a white patient in a society where oppression of ethnic minority groups is not only historic but is active currently. Turner and Armstrong (1981) found, in fact, that Afro-American therapists are more likely than white therapists to do cross-racial therapy. This finding supports my assertion that minority therapists need as much cross-cultural training as white therapists need, if not more, and training that is certainly different in particular and relevant ways.

In this chapter I identify some of the issues a minority therapist faces when treating nonminority patients. My recognition of these issues derives both from personal experience as a minority therapist and from my many years of supervising both minority and nonminority trainees in psychology, psychiatry, and social work. One such issue is that graduate and training programs have not given sufficient attention to assisting the professional development of minority mental health professionals; there has been a failure to recognize, understand, and resolve the subtle forms of stereotyping, and of attitudes concerning race and ethnic background, and how these operate in the therapeutic relationship when the patient is from the dominant culture and race. I also believe that too few research articles have been published, even in the past ten years, to inform and guide such training.

I agree with Mayo (1974) who contends that if psychotherapy is a valued and effective technique it should be applicable to minority patients. Though Mayo was referring particularly to Afro-American patients, I am convinced that therapists' tendency to confuse culturally specific phenomena with psychopathology, their lack of proficiency in interpretation of nonverbal nuances, and unwillingness to accept sociocultural variables as therapeutically relevant, all continue to exclude large numbers of minority-race individuals from individual therapy/psychotherapy/treatment.

## MINORITY THERAPIST/WHITE PATIENT

Although Mayo (1974) states that Afro-American therapists have found ways to work therapeutically with nonminority patients, there has been little in the literature documenting how it has been done and what types of experiences and training may be utilized to facilitate it further.

While it might seem easy to resolve problems in cross-cultural therapy if the therapists were to treat only people from their own racial-cultural background, I doubt that this is practical; it certainly should not be a prerequisite for effective treatment. Few minority therapists would want their range of practice to be so limited and constricted, and it would in itself be racist.

Although there is some literature on the Afro-American therapist/white patient dyad, I am aware of very few studies which examine other minority ethnic groups as therapists of white patients. Consequently, in this chapter I will talk mostly about the Afro-American therapists. I believe, however, that similar issues exist for other minority therapists; it is clear that more research needs to be done on various ethnic/racial minority groups as therapists of patients from the dominant white culture.

Gardner (1971) found that an Afro-American therapist might be concerned about acceptance by the white patient and that this might lead that therapist to: ingratiating behavior; gratification of transference wishes; and "acting white." The therapist might exhibit a neurotic need for reassurance and admiration from the patient. The same or another minority therapist might, in reaction to racial conditions in America, act out anger, resentment, and hostility with the patient. In other words, unconscious feelings about one's own race, racial relations in America, racism, and the race of the patient, are all part of the probable countertransference.

Griffith (1977) summarizes some of the issues associated with the minority therapist and nonminority patient dyad. He suggests that *status contradiction* is one of the major issues. He describes this status contradiction as one in which the white patient simultaneously sees the Afro-American therapist as having low or inferior status because of the therapist's membership in the black race and at the same time having high status because of the therapist's professional training and role.

Following are some questions that, for me, illustrate the dilemmas that fall under this rubric of status contradiction:

- Is the white patient able to view the therapist as someone capable of understanding his or her life experience, which is necessarily different–at least in part–from that of the therapist?
- Can the two find some common ground of experience to facilitate the development of a therapeutic alliance?
- Does the white patient believe that the minority therapist is competent to do the job? This is often difficult if the patients'

prior experience with minorities has been with minority people in menial jobs.

- How do white patients feel not being in control or in charge when relating to a minority therapist? Can they allow themselves to feel vulnerable, even helpless?

How, when, and whether these contradictions get resolved by the patient during the treatment process is very important.

Using cognitive consistency theory as a model, Griffith (1977) proposes that being treated by an Afro-American therapist could elicit in patients avoidance responses for the purpose of keeping their original attitudes intact. Avoidance might be manifested by the white patient refusing to be treated by the Afro-American therapist, dropping out of treatment without openly revealing his or her feelings, or resisting the establishing of a therapeutic alliance. Patients may use other means of placing themselves in a position of power in the relationship, such as: inappropriate anger; challenges to the therapist's credentials or interpretations; putting down Afro-Americans generally; or taking a patronizing stance.

Another way white patients may avoid cognitive dissonance is by denial and rationalization (Griffith, 1977). Patients may deny that racial/ethnic differences exist, stating a belief that the Afro-American therapist pretty much holds beliefs and values similar to their own culture/race. The therapist should be aware, however, that at least some white patients may have a strong tendency to identify with Afro-Americans, assuming, for example, that the therapists's views will be synchronous with their own felt opposition to oppression. This may create another difficulty in the therapeutic relationship between an Afro-American therapist and a white patient; if white patients are extremely sensitive to the oppression of Afro-Americans they may tend to be overly solicitous in therapy and reluctant to disclose or explore painful feelings, or feelings perceived as negative or hostile, because of their concern about how the Afro-American therapist has unduly suffered under oppression.

I also want to note that white patients who are excessively concerned about confidentiality may actually prefer a minority therapist as a means of reducing fears that their secret feelings will leak out into their own community.

Gardner (1971) has noted that the color of the therapist alone can elicit in the patient fantasies of a symbolic nature about blackness. He holds that the specific manner in which white patients deal with the race of the therapist follows their usual pattern of coping and defending against painful feelings in other areas of their lives. For example, Gardner describes the oral-dependent patient as idealizing the Afro-American therapist as a maternal object with unlimited supplies of love and oral gratification to give. Patients with issues related to sibling rivalry may want to see themselves as the Afro-American therapist's only or favorite white patient, experiencing intense feelings of jealousy or rage at discovery that this is not the case.

One prominent preoccupation of white patients treated by Afro-American therapists that Gardner (1971) found was the fear that the Afro-American therapist would discover conscious or unconscious racism in them. This led them to avoid disclosure of any fantasy material which might suggest that they had these negative racial attitudes. Gardner found the transference phenomena in white patients treated by Afro-American therapists particularly fascinating and thinks transference occurs even more rapidly in this dyad.

In one of only a few papers that describe the treatment progress of a white patient treated by a minority therapist, Tung (1981) very nicely describes the reactions of a white ten-year-old boy treated by a Chinese therapist. Stages in the boy's treatment included one in which he projected aggression and evil onto "Chinks" and expressed ambivalent feelings about forming an attachment to such a different-looking therapist. Tung also described the therapist's countertransference, particularly around the many play therapy sessions in which the child repeatedly killed "Chinks" in his play.

A major problem which can arise for the minority therapist would be any unresolved feelings about discrimination and racism. Some therapists are better able than others to listen to and address or contain communications by the patient which suggest discriminatory and racist attitudes.

## A CASE EXAMPLE

Working in a children's psychiatric hospital and in private practice, I have had to address racial/ethnic issues in treatment, as a minority therapist working with nonminority patients and their parents. In one case, in an institutional setting, the racial attitudes of the adoptive parents of a hospitalized ten-year-old white girl significantly affected the development of a treatment alliance with the girl. The adoptive mother of the girl had, in her relationships with her own mother, experienced a sense of rejection; as a result she now rejected many traditional American values. Her life-style was similar to that of the hippies in the 1960s. Her need for control and power in the treatment was evident in her attempting to dictate the frequency and length of therapy sessions and to reject my interpretations. She attempted to undermine me by criticizing me to cottage staff, and by trying to get approval from them for things contradictory to the limits I was attempting to set in family therapy. I saw this as a form of splitting.

The adoptive mother articulated concerns of not feeling understood by me because of what she perceived as differences in our social class and values; nevertheless, she experienced significant difficulty exploring the obvious *racial* difference. Her negative feelings during the early stages of therapy interfered as well with the child's formation of a treatment alliance with me, lest she be disloyal to her adoptive mother. The child would express negative feelings towards minorities within the cottage peer groups but for some time would deny such feelings toward me. The issue of racial difference between the family and myself was eventually worked through, but only with much persistence on my part.

## *SUMMARY*

As a young therapist, my own fears of rejection and failure, and my need to prove that I was as competent as a white therapist, contributed to my being overly sensitive to patients who did not connect well with me or who dropped out of treatment prematurely. As a result, I may have been less confrontational than might have been therapeutically appropriate. As my confidence and personal insight grew, this issue decreased significantly. Novice therapists may feel as I did, and need help with such feelings via supervision.

The minority therapist, like therapists from the majority white American culture, needs to be able to deal with racial/ethnic/cultural material in a therapeutic, direct and objective manner, seeing the patient as an individual and avoiding any temptation to over-generalize the patient in a stereotypical manner. Even when there are few signs of conscious racism, I believe that racial stereotypes will inevitably be present in both the patient and therapist on an unconscious level. Minority therapists are no less prone to experiencing and acting out feelings related to racial/ethnic issues with white patients than white therapists are with minority patients. No matter how disturbed the patient, none of us can be completely immune to racial or ethnic transference and countertransference nor should we be; there is always at least a grain of personal meaning for us in our patient's perceptions of us.

## NOTES

1. For a sensitive discussion of this issue see, for example, Braveheart-Jordan and DeBruyn in this volume.

2. Especially when the patient is Afro-American and the therapist is white, other factors may also be present. Another example of research that focuses on the minority patient/white therapist dyad is work by Mayo (1974), who examined utilization of a community mental health center by Afro-Americans and also looked at diagnosis and treatment disposition of the Afro-American patient. She found that Afro-Americans applied for services less frequently than any other ethnic group and perceived the center differently than other patients did. Language, cognitive style, appearance, and behavior of Afro-American patients were found to have been mislabeled as pathological and as deficient. According to Mayo this indicated that to the white therapist the Afro-American patient was not amenable to traditional outpatient individual psychotherapy. An additional finding in this study was that Afro-American males were treated in a biased manner in the mental health clinic, generally seen by white female mental health professionals as hostile, angry, inappropriate, and in need of hospitalization.

3. I have to date seen no research on whether there are significant differences in process or outcome depending on whether the minority therapist is female or male. This is surely an intriguing focus for future research.

## REFERENCES

Atkinson, D. R. (1983). Ethnic similarity in counseling psychology: A review of research. *The Counseling Psychologist, II*(3), 79-92.

Gardner, La Maurice H. (1971). The therapeutic relationship under varying conditions of race. *Psychotherapy: Theory, Research and Practice, 8*(1), 78-87.

Griffith, Marlin S. (1977). The influences of race on the psychotherapeutic relationship. *Psychiatry, 40,* 27-40.

Harrison, Don K. (1975). Race as a counselor-client variable in counseling and psychotherapy: A review of the research. *Counseling Psychologist, 5*(1), 124-133.

Mayo, Julia A. (1974). The significance of socio-cultural variables in the psychiatric treatment of black outpatients. *Comprehensive Psychiatry, 15*(6), 471-482.

Parloff, M. B., Waslow, E. E., & Wolfe, B. E. (1978). Research in therapist variables in relation to process and outcome. In S. L. Garfield & A. E. Bergin (Eds.), *Handbook of psychotherapy and behavior change: An empirical analysis.* New York: John Wiley.

Sue, Stanley, McKinney, Herman, Allen, David, & Hall, Juanita (1974). Delivery of community mental health services to black and white clients. *Journal of Counseling and Clinical Psychology, 42*(6), 794-801.

Tung, May (1981). On being seen as a "Chinese therapist" to a Caucasian child. *American Journal of Orthopsychiatry, 51*(4), 654-661.

Turner, Sylvester, & Armstrong, Stephen (1981). Cross-racial psychotherapy: What the therapists say. *Psychotherapy, Theory, Research, and Practice, 18*(3), 375-378.

# Racism and Violence Against Women

## Lenore E. A. Walker

### *INTRODUCTION*

During the past decade, many feminists struggling to redefine the psychology of women have recognized that to not include the full diversity of women's experiences, and especially to exclude women of color from the task, no matter what the reason, would result in the formulation of another non-generalizable theory of human behavior, albeit from a white woman's perspective (Dutton-Douglas & Walker, 1988; Rosewater, 1990). The study of woman abuse has rarely included empirical analysis of race, culture, or ethnicity. Campbell (1985) reviewed the cross-cultural studies on wife-beating and concluded that there simply are no racial, cultural, or ethnic differences in rates of woman abuse given its overwhelmingly high prevalence in most societies, or that an even more likely explanation is that the abuse of women "is a personal expression of [men's] hostility against women that may be expressed in addition to or instead of, institutionalized aggression toward women in that culture." There is similar agreement among other domestic violence researchers (Greene, 1990; Ho, 1990; Pagelow, 1984; Straus, Gelles, & Steinmetz, 1980) on rape (Koss & Harvey, 1991; Levy, 1991) and other forms of sexual assault including therapist's sexual misconduct with clients (Pope, 1990), incest (Courtois, 1988), sexual harassment (Bravo & Cassedy, 1992; Fitzgerald et al., 1988) and prostitution (Barry, 1991).

The literature on the effects of violence that is perpetrated on women documents the psychological significance of such trauma (Courtois, 1988; Herman, 1992; Kilpatrick et al., 1989; Walker, 1991). As logic would suggest, the data demonstrate that the experience of other oppression in addition to violence does have a greater psychological impact on an individual woman. But, there are still many important questions that remain unanswered concerning the nature of that psychological impact: Is the impact additive or multiplicative? Does it change when a third or fourth form of oppression is added such as a combination of homophobia, racism, classism, and sexism? Is the type of violence committed against women of color the same as the violence committed against white women? Is the experience of the violence and the meaning it is given similar in women of different cultures? Are there different rates of violence if the woman lives in her own culture in her country of origin or if she now lives in the United States either within a cultural enclave or in the mainstream? Does the meaning of the violence differ depending upon what kind of violence is experienced? And are the perceived and actual available resources different for women of different races, ethnic groups, and cultures who experience violence?

This chapter will explore the impact of racism, sexism, classism, and violence in varying combinations; the interactions are often difficult to separate in reality. The combination of prejudice plus power, institutional or individual, whether deliberate or unintentional, will constitute the working definition of racism as the above-mentioned questions are explored.

## DEFINITIONS, INCIDENCE, AND PREVALENCE RATES OF VIOLENCE AGAINST WOMEN

The most common forms of violence against women have many commonalities including the fact that it is mostly (although not exclusively as in the case of some lesbian battering relationships) men who commit the violence. It is also interesting that in each culture where violence against women is reported, there is a myth that it occurs most commonly in the lower-status groups, often women who are darker-skinned and live in poverty. Research has demonstrated that woman abuse occurs across all demographic groups.

### Battered Women

Walker (1979) has defined a *battered woman* as a woman who is physically, sexually, and/or seriously psychologically abused, usually by a man, although sometimes by another woman partner, with whom she is in an intimate relationship, in order for the abuser to get what *he*[1] wants, without regard for the woman's rights. Physical abuse ranges from pushing, shoving, hitting, punching, kicking, hair-pulling, head-banging, choking, and being thrown across the room or into objects, to being threatened or harmed by weapons such as guns, knives, automobiles, and other dangerous objects. Sexual abuse includes being physically forced into sexual acts as well as being intimidated into having sex as a way of preventing further abuse. Psychological abuse is similar to the psychological torture that occurs when someone is taken hostage or held as a prisoner-of-war, such as name-calling and humiliation, isolation from other meaningful relationships, monopolization of the woman's perceptions, inducing debility by sleep deprivation or other physical difficulties, financial control, over-possessiveness, intrusiveness, and attempts at mind control (Walker, 1984).

Walker (1989a) analyzed information concerning the first 100 women whom she evaluated and for whom she was willing to testify as to their use of self-defense when they killed their abusive partner. Although one-third of them were women of color, they accounted for only 25% of those who were found not guilty on grounds that they were justified in believing they needed to defend themselves. Although Afro-American women were 21% of the group studied, only 10% of them were acquitted. She concludes that black women were judged the most harshly and were twice as likely to be convicted and sent to prison as white women or other women of color. Campbell (1985) also analyzed indigent Afro-American families to find out violence rates. Her results indicate that differences in the abuse of women because of race and culture are complex and not as easy to interpret as it might seem.

## Rape and Sexual Assault

*Rape and sexual assault victim/survivors* are women who have been sexually abused by strangers, acquaintances, or family members. Sexual assault laws have been expanded to include fondling, unwanted and inappropriate touching of genital areas, oral, vaginal and/or anal penetration (sodomy), by fingers, mouth, objects, as well as a man's penis. Some other forms of rape and sexual abuse include date rape, sexual harassment, and sex between client and therapist or other trusted professionals. As with woman battering described above, there is no research that would support different types of sexual abuse being used more in any particular racial, ethnic, or cultural group. Like other forms of interpersonal violence, most sexual assaults are committed by perpetrators who are the same race, ethnic, or cultural group as their victims. There is, however, a long history of sexual assaults going unpunished where the woman is of color and the perpetrator is white. Also, there is a tradition of not acknowledging some forms of ritualized women abuse, such as clitoridectomies, excusing the abuse behavior as having "cultural relativity."

## GIVING MEANING TO VIOLENCE BY INTIMATES

Although there are no data to support differences in incidence and prevalence rates and types of violent acts experienced by women of color and white women, there is reason to believe that women in different groups may give different meaning to it (Belle, 1984; Greene, 1990; Ho, 1990; Wyatt, 1985). For example, a woman, of any race, who grew up on urban streets where potential violence is a constant part of reality may be less shocked than more sheltered rural or suburban woman, should each experience the same violence. In either case, the negative effects of the victimization may still cause trauma effects (Herman, 1992; Ryan, 1971; Walker, 1991). The same is true for women who come to this country as undocumented labor, those who have experienced state-sponsored violence in their war-torn countries (Barry, 1991; Batres, 1990; Marcelino, 1990), and those who may never learn to be literate in English, or integrate with the mainstream culture (Loo, 1987).

## HELP-SEEKING AND AVAILABLE RESOURCES

The issue of differences in resources available for women of color who become victims of violence is important in understanding the impact of that violence. To help them heal from the abuses, violence victims need the availability of medical care, good psychotherapy where indicated, social services, and legal care. They also need to know that they are safe from further abuse and they need the support and validation from family, friends, and community members (cf. Bass & Davis, 1988).

Abused women's complaints, that the available resources are not useful for victims, are abundantly documented (Belle, 1984; Brown & Root, 1990; Herman, 1992; Koss & Harvey, 1991; Walker, 1989a, 1989b). In the United States there appears to be bias against women of color in medical settings, especially against indigent Afro-American women according to the former Surgeon General, Everett Koop, who declared domestic violence a public health problem. This bias extends to women in general and women of color specifically in the legal system according to gender bias task force reports filed in many states during the late 1980s (Shafran, 1990). Victim compensation laws have to some extent helped women who report the crime to get financial compensation for medical, psychological, and legal assistance; other new laws supporting victims of rape, assault, and other crimes also try to prevent some of the more egregious and outrageous secondary victimization that previously took place within the system. Nevertheless, the invalidation of women in the criminal justice system, and the system's unwillingness to properly protect women, place all women, but especially women of color, at greater risk for further violence (Goolkasian, 1986; Shafran, 1990; Walker, 1989).

## Criminal Justice System Response

The criminal justice system is still a bastion of male supremacy in this country and elsewhere (Walker & Corriere, 1991). Males run the various segments of the criminal justice system and have the power to define women's realities, particularly the police departments (Edwards, 1989). Men from poor, urban, minority cultures are more likely to be arrested, charged, and convicted of crimes than are white, affluent, rural or suburban men. Thus, women of color face their own dual loyalties if considering whether to call upon the legal system for help. To protect themselves, they will have to collaborate with a legal system that has a history of not being fair to men of color.

Often minority women are invalidated when they report crimes committed against them. Many women of color believe that those within the legal system do not perceive their duty as being to protect them as vigorously as a white "lady" with more status in the community. Women who behave "ladylike" become "good" victims who are more believable and therefore more likely to get an overloaded system to identify with them and work harder on their behalf (Walker, 1989a).

If a battered woman of color kills in self-defense, the more closely she resembles the stereotypical "good" victim, the more likely she will be acquitted of murder. On the other hand, an indigent women of color who appears "tough," or too assertive, or aggressive, is seen as so atypical of what is supposed to be passive victim behavior that she is more likely to be viewed as the abuser or at least as mutually violent; she is less likely to be seen as a battered woman with Post Traumatic Stress Disorder and Battered Woman Syndrome that impacted her state of mind and therefore, not entitled to claim self-defense (Walker, 1989c). This analysis is frequently used against women who use "foul," aggressive language such as men use, even if the woman is scared to death when doing so. Women who appear stereotypically passive, however, even if their culture socializes them into appearing passive in public, may be misdiagnosed as having some kind of personality disorder, and therefore, believed to have somehow provoked their abuse by not taking better care of themselves (Caplan, 1991).

Children who have been sexually abused also have great difficulty being validated within the legal system and mothers who have been abused are rarely given enough credibility to protect them (Walker & Edwall, 1987), although they are often blamed for failure to do so, and for the children's subsequent emotional problems (Goodman & Helgeson, 1988; Walker, 1990; Wyatt, 1985). It is often difficult for a woman of color who is battered to find an advocate to argue her parental skills in court, especially in cases that involve juvenile dependency and neglect actions. The fear of having children removed from their care keeps many women of color from reaching out for help for the abuse.

## Medical Care

Medical care offered to abused women varies from place to place but rarely do poor women of color get adequate medical treatment anywhere. Care in county hospital clinics is impersonal and relationships with mostly white male doctors are mostly non-existent. Although there are protocols available for the medical profession to use with abused women, the protocols are frequently ignored (Klingbeil & Boyd, 1984; Koss, 1992). White women are often overprescribed psychotropic medications; poor, minority-culture women are rarely even given pain medications! Abused women who are not adequately treated often begin to get more anxious and frantic, knowing that should they be seriously injured they will not be given adequate medical care and that could result in permanent injuries or even death. Many appear hysterical to males who are unaware of the impact of abuse (Caplan, 1991). Stress-related illnesses are increasing as minimal care is offered to victims (Koss, 1992).

## Psychological Intervention

Most mental health professionals have had little training in providing assessment, support, and psychotherapy with abuse victims. Studies (Hansen, Harway, & Cervantes, 1991; Koss, 1992; Pope, 1990) have shown that most therapists neither recognize the seriousness of violence against women, especially those few women of color who present for treatment, nor want to provide intervention services specifically to deal with stopping the violence. Knowledge of how cultural issues impact on the victim has become recognized as being such important information that it appears on some state licensing examinations even though it is rarely taught in courses in training programs. Most of the training materials available do not deal directly with issues for women of color.

Criticisms of personality disorder diagnoses in general (Brown, 1992), as well as of the specific ones proposed by a task force that had no empirical data to support them (Caplan, 1991; Walker, 1987), focused both on racist assumptions that all women must match some white, North American, middle-class standard and on sexist assumptions that mental health for women would be based upon well-documented male biases. Brown (1992) suggests that women of color who must deal with small or large oppression on a daily basis will be less likely to have the resilience needed to deal with abuse, should it occur, because they are worn down from the power and control issues that arise out of racism. She names a new disorder, Oppression Artifact Disorder, as a way of calling attention to the negative impact on mental health that results from simply being a person of color living in a racist world.

The differences between special treatment for trauma and treatment for long-standing personality disorders is critically important in understanding how dangerous misdiagnosis can be. With trauma victims, validation and empowerment are essential to the victim's becoming a survivor; in treating those with disordered personalities, a remake of the entire personality system is the more acceptable therapeutic goal. One requires strict boundaries between the therapist and client and the other assumes that with sufficient support and ethical behavior on the part of the therapist, the client can set appropriate boundaries herself. Treatment for trauma victims is focused on working with a women's strengths; treatment with those with disordered personalities focuses on her limitations.

## Safety Issues

Safety issues for abused women of color take on an even greater urgency than for majority-culture women because sometimes safety requires being hidden. It is difficult for a minority woman who can be identified by skin color or facial features to be able to hide in some non-urban areas. While some battered-women shelters have been sensitive to the needs of women of color, most are not. Sometimes there are subtle barriers in the way, such as the location of the shelter in a particularly homogeneous neighborhood, so that the women of color are highly visible, or an all-white staff and no other women of color with whom a particular woman can identify. This is also true for rape crisis centers and women's centers where feminist counseling is provided. Access to community resources will reflect the community norms and sensitivity about racism and sexism as well as other issues such as women with disabilities, lesbian women, those with alcohol and drug addictions, and so on.

## *CONCLUSIONS*

In summary, this chapter has reviewed the data on incidence and prevalence of violence against women of color and found that when compared to the data on violence against white women, there does not appear to be any difference in the rate or type of violence experienced by women of color. However, the impact of the violence is different for women of color because of several factors:

(a) The meanings ascribed to abuse may differ among women of diverse racial, ethnic, cultural, and class backgrounds and the impact of violence may be heightened regardless of race if poverty is a factor. These factors are not necessarily the result of racism.

(b) The services available for women of color are often different from those available to North American white women. Those differences are heightened by factors such as fewer women of color as providers of help; large numbers of women of color who are also indigent and, thus, not able to afford such private services as may be available; white male dominance in the criminal justice, medical, and psychiatric systems that invalidate the experiences of women in general and women of color specifically. These factors have developed in tandem with racism.

(c) Discrimination against all people of color makes women of color more cautious and, perhaps, less likely to take advantage of those limited services that are available.

Obviously, racism is not limited to the community's attitudes towards violence against women, but when found provides an interaction effect that serves to keep both women and people of color oppressed.

### NOTE

1. The pronoun *"he"* will be used to denote the abuser in this chapter to call attention to the more frequent occurrence of male violence against women, the greater power males have in most societies, and the androcentric nature of violence against women even when committed by women against each other. This is not to negate the existence of lesbian battering nor to invalidate some of the research that suggests there may be some uniquely female patterns in lesbian violence. However, the theories expressed in this article must still be tested on non-male perpetrated violence against women while they have demonstrated some degree of reliability and validity in the heterosexual dyad.

# REFERENCES

Barry, Kathleen (1991). Prostitution, sexual violence and victimization: Feminist perspectives on women's rights. In Emilio Viano (Ed.), *Victims' rights and legal reforms: International perspectives. Proceedings of the Sixth International Institute on Victimology* (37-52) Onati, Spain: International Institute on Sociology and the Law.

Bass, Ellen, & Davis, Laura (1988). *The courage to heal: A guide for women survivors of child sexual abuse.* New York: Harper & Row.

Batres, Gioconda (1990, November). *Sexually abused children in Costa Rica.* Presentation to the LII Congreso Medico Nacional, Colegio de Medicos y Cirujanos de Costa Rica, San Jose, Costa Rica.

Belle, Deborah (1984). Inequality and mental health: Low income and minority women. In L. E. A. Walker (Ed.), *Women and mental health policy* (pp. 135-150). Beverly Hills: Sage.

Bravo, Ellen, & Cassedy, Ellen (1992). *The 9 to 5 guide to sexual harassment.* New York: Wiley.

Brown, Laura S. (1992). A feminist critique of personality disorders. In Laura S. Brown & Mary Ballou (Eds.), *Personality and psychopathology.* New York: Guilford.

Brown, Laura S., & Root, Maria P. P. (Eds.) (1990). *Diversity and complexity in feminist therapy.* New York: Haworth.

Campbell, Jacqueline C. (1985). Beating of wives: A cross-cultural perspective. *Victimology: An International Journal, 1-4,* 174-185.

Caplan, Paula (1991). How DO they decide what is normal? The bizarre, but true, tale of the DSM process. *Canadian Psychologist, 32*(2), 162-170.

Courtois, Christine (1988). *Healing the incest wound.* New York: Norton.

Dutton-Douglas, Mary Ann, & Walker, Lenore E. A. (Eds.) (1988). *Feminist psychotherapies: An integration of therapeutic and feminist systems.* Norwood, NJ: Ablex.

Edwards, Susan S. M. (1989). *Policing domestic violence: Women, the law and the state.* London: Sage.

Fitzgerald, Louise F., Shullman, S. L., Bailey, N., Richards, M., Swecker, J., Gold, Y., Ormerod, A. J., & Weitzman, L. M. (1988). The incidence and dimensions of sexual harassment in academia and the workplace. *Journal of Vocational Behavior, 32,* 152-175.

Goodman, Gail S., & Helgeson, Vickie S. (1988). Children as witnesses: What do they remember? In L. E. A. Walker (Ed.), *Handbook on child sexual abuse: Assessment and intervention* (pp.109-136). New York: Springer.

Goodman, Gail S., & Rosenberg, Mindy S. (1987). The child witness to family violence: Clinical and legal considerations. In Daniel J. Sonkin (Ed.), *Domestic violence on trial: Psychological and legal dimensions of family violence,* (pp. 97-126). New York: Springer.

Goolkasian, G. A. (1986). *Confronting domestic violence: A guide for criminal justice agencies.* Washington, DC: U.S. Department of Justice.

Greene, Beverly (1990). What has gone before: The legacy of racism and sexism in the lives of Black mothers and daughters. In Laura S. Brown, & Maria P. P. Root, (Eds.), *Diversity and complexity in feminist therapy* (pp. 207-230). New York: Haworth.

Hansen, Marsali, Harway, Michele, & Cervantes, Nancy (1991). Therapists' perceptions of severity in cases of family violence. *Violence and Victims, 6,* 225-235.

Herman, Judith L. (1992). *Trauma and Recovery.* New York: Basic Books.

Ho, Christine, K. (1990). An analysis of domestic violence in Asian American communities: A multicultural approach to counseling. In Laura S. Brown & Maria P. P. Root (Eds.), *Diversity and complexity in feminist therapy* (pp. 129-150). New York: Haworth.

Kilpatrick, Dean G., Saunders, B. E., Amick-Mullen, A., Best, C. L., Veronen, L. J., & Resick, H. S. (1989). Victim and crime factors associated with the development of crime-related post-traumatic stress disorders. *Behavior Therapy, 20,* 199-214.

Klingbeil, Karil S., & Boyd, Vickie D. (1984). Emergency room intervention: Detection, assessment, and treatment. In Arthur R. Roberts (Ed.), *Battered women and their family intervention strategies and treatment programs* (7-32). New York: Springer.

Koss, Mary P. (1992). Medical consequences of rape. *Violence Update, 3*(1), 1-11.

Koss, Mary P., & Harvey, Mary R. (1991). *The rape victim: Clinical and community interventions* (2nd ed.). Newbury Park, CA: Sage.

Levy, Barrie (Ed.) (1991). *Dating violence: Young women in danger.* Seattle: Seal.

Loo, Chalsa M. (1987). *Chinatown: Most time, hard time.* New York: Praeger.

Marcelino, Elizabeth Protacio (1990). Towards understanding the psychology of the Filipino. In Laura S. Brown and Maria P. P. Root (Eds.), *Diversity and complexity in feminist therapy* (pp. 105-128). New York: Haworth.

Pagelow, Mildred (1984). *Family violence.* New York: Praeger.

Pope, Kenneth S. (1990). Therapist-patient sexual involvement: A review of the research. *Clinical Psychology Review, 10,* 477-490.

Rosewater, Lynne Bravo (1990). Diversifying feminist theory and practice: Broadening the concept of victimization. In Laura S. Brown, & Maria P. P. Root (Eds.), *Diversity and complexity in feminist therapy* (pp. 299-312). New York: Haworth.

Ryan, William (1971). *Blaming the victim.* New York: Pantheon Books.

Shafran, Lynn H. (1990). Overwhelming evidence: Report on gender bias in the courts. *Trial, 26,* 28-35.

Straus, Murray, Gelles, Richard, & Steinmetz, Suzanne (1980). *Behind closed doors: Violence in America.* New York: Doubleday.

Walker, Lenore E. A. (1991). Post-Traumatic Stress Disorder in women: Diagnosis and treatment of Battered Woman Syndrome. *Psychotherapy, 28*(1), 21-29.

_____ (1990). Psychological assessment of sexually abused children for legal evaluation and expert witness testimony. *Professional Psychology: Research and Practice, 21(5),* 344-353.

_____ (1989a). *Terrifying Love: Why battered women kill and how society responds.* New York: Harper & Row.

_____ (1989b). Psychology and violence against women. *American Psychologist, 44,* 695-702.

_____ (1989c). When the battered woman becomes the defendant. In Emilio Viano (Ed.), *Crime and its victims: International research and public policy.* Proceedings of the Fourth International Institute on Victimology, NATO Advanced Research Workshop, Il Ciocco, Tuscany, Italy, (pp. 57-70). New York: Hemisphere Publishing.

_____ (1987). Inadequacies of the Masochistic Personality Disorder diagnosis for women. *Journal of Personality Disorders, 1,* 183-189.

_____ (1984). *The battered woman syndrome.* New York: Springer.

_____ (1979). *The battered woman.* New York: Harper & Row.

Walker, Lenore E. A., & Corriere, Sandra W. (1991). Domestic violence: International perspectives on social change. In E. Viano (Ed.), *Victim's rights and legal reforms: International perspectives. Proceedings of the Sixth International Institute on Victimology* (pp. 135-150). Onati, Spain: International Institute on Sociology and the Law.

Walker, Lenore E. A., & Edwall, Glenace E. (1987). Domestic violence and determination of custody and visitation. In Daniel J. Sonkin (Ed.), *Domestic violence on trial* (pp. 127-152). New York: Springer.

Wyatt, Gail E. (1985). The sexual abuse of Afro-American and white American women in childhood. *Child Abuse and Neglect, 9,* 507-519.

# Psychotherapy with Chicanas at Midlife: Cultural/Clinical Considerations

## Yvette G. Flores-Ortiz

Psychotherapy with Chicanas at midlife requires an understanding of the cultural, social, and political contexts that influence their psychological reality.

Chicanas[1] are triple minorities, women impacted by gender oppression in the form of patriarchal cultural values; by racism and discrimination; and by class segregation (Andrade, 1982; Melville, 1980; Mirande & Enriquez, 1979).

Chicanas are a heterogeneous group, with different political orientations, migration histories, levels of acculturation, and varying degrees of adherence to traditional Mexican cultural values (Flores-Ortiz, 1993b; Mirande & Enríquez, 1979). Chicanas comprise a young and fast-growing population with a mean age of 23 (U.S. Department of the Census, 1990).

While the feminist and Chicano movements theoretically opened doors of education for women, Chicanas still constitute a small fraction of college-educated and professional women (de la Torre & Pesquera, 1993). Most Chicanas remain undereducated, underemployed, and underpaid (Hayes-Bautista, Schink, & Chapa, 1988; U.S. Census, 1990). Chicanas in their forties and fifties comprise the majority of clerical and service workers.

I wish to thank the women who have joined me in the path of mutual discovery, balance, and growth, and thus have taught me a lot of what I know about psychotherapy.

I wish to thank my family, especially my children, for helping me face my interstices.

I wish to thank my colleagues in Aztlan, especially Drs. Adaljiza Sosa-Riddell, Vicky Ruiz, Beatriz Pesquera, and Angie Chabran-Dernesessian, for their *companerismo* and mentorship. I want to thank Gloria Anzaldúa for her inspiration and Dr. Michelle Ritterman for understanding the borderlands.

The impact of gender, race, and class oppression on Chicanas has been best articulated by poets and novelists. Anzaldúa (1987), for example, describes the impact of these forces as a condition of being "on the border." Anzaldúa views Chicanas as women between cultures, on the border of the Anglo/Mexican world, on the border between traditional and contemporary cultural values, on the border between Anglo and Chicana feminism.

> A border is a dividing line, a narrow strip along a steep edge. A borderland is a vague and undetermined place created by the emotional residue of an unnatural boundary. It is a constant state of transition. (Anzaldúa, 1987, p. 3)

The psychological impact of triple oppression often is manifested during developmental transitions. For Chicanas at midlife, the borders of race, class, and gender intersect, forcing a confrontation with the "unnatural boundaries," highlighting cultural value conflicts which may bring about emotional distress.

## CULTURAL/CLINICAL CONSIDERATIONS

Culture is the lens through which people perceive reality. Culture forms the beliefs and values which are transmitted through language, the arts, and behavior; culture contextualizes individual psychology. For Chicanas, cultural paradigms include expectations to fulfill a number of roles: mother, sister, spouse, *companera* (comrade) in the political struggle. Chicanas often feel they *must* comply with *all* these roles. A major psychological task is the balance of these obligations.

Moreover, the psychological context of midlife Chicanas has been influenced by the expectations of white feminism and the legacies of the Chicano Movement. While the Movement provided a vehicle for activism and fostered a sense of personal integrity, many Chicanas experienced sexism from the male leadership. Furthermore, feminist white women, who would appear to be natural allies along gender lines, often were perceived to be racist and classist.

The two decades since the Chicano Movement reached its peak

have seen many promises remain unfulfilled. It is in this context of broken dreams and promises that many Chicanas have reached midlife.

For Chicanas facing the midlife transition, a number of factors come into play. Within the *cultural ideal,* the 40-60 year period is a time when women can reap the benefits of their traditional roles. From a cultural perspective, the woman has now earned the right to relax, be treated well, and expect loyalty and devotion from the children and grandchildren.

This cultural ideal reflects an assumption that all women are heterosexual, will marry young, and will enter the twilight years of maturity after the children are grown; after the productive (i.e., reproductive) life is over.

Economic and political realities may prohibit or limit the fulfill-ment of the cultural ideal. Many Chicanas need to continue working outside the home well into retirement age. Working-class Chicanas often continue to be burdened by economic exploitation in low-paying jobs. Even the relatively few Chicanas in professional or leadership positions are often hesitant to retire, because their num-bers are small and they feel a responsibility to mentor and support younger colleagues. Pressure and efforts to fulfill the Chicano cul-tural ideal, the goals of the Movement, and feminist aspirations lead many women to feel they inhabit parallel worlds. Anzaldua (1987) describes many Chicanas as feeling *alienated* from the mother cul-ture and *alien* in the Anglo world. This dual alienation can result in women feeling caught within *los intersticios,* the spaces between the different worlds they inhabit.

Historically, many Chicanas have dealt with this alienation by attempting to inhabit only one world, through monoculturalism or efforts at assimilation (see Keefe & Padilla, 1987), or by attempting to bridge both Anglo and Chicano worlds, and thereby creating a new hybrid, *mestizo* reality. The psychological impact of these struggles has begun to be documented only recently (see Flores-Ortiz, 1993a,b).

These struggles are depicted in the following cases.[2] These three women were seen in weekly psychotherapy; their stories are used to highlight "life in the border."

### Balancing Roles: "La superchicana"

"Lupe," a 40-year-old single, heterosexual college professor from a working class background, sought psychotherapy because she was experiencing writer's block. Her inability to finish her manuscript threatened a career promotion. Lupe described herself as a feminist and as an independent, fulfilled woman, who had discarded the "shackles of her oppressive Latino culture."

As we explored her writer's block, a number of cultural/gender issues became evident. For her birthday, her cousins had given her a surprise party attended by the extended family. Lupe suddenly realized she was the only woman without any children. She then began to feel different and distant from her cousins and sisters. Even though Lupe was the only college-educated woman in her family, she minimized the reality that her professional status had distanced her socioeconomically and socially from the rest of the women in the family. For Lupe, "belonging" required some denial of differences.

One of the women Lupe interviewed for her book had mentioned in passing how difficult it had been to fulfill the expectations of the Chicano Movement to be culturally loyal and politically active. This woman referred to Lupe as *la superchicana*, the one who had done it all. Lupe realized that she had not done it all. She had neither married nor borne children. This insight had paralyzed Lupe.

In psychotherapy Lupe explored the cultural context of her distress. Through a critical analysis of *cultural ideals* and values, Lupe was able to see that many cultural expectations still shackled her. A turning point for her was the realization that she had internalized the belief that a 40-year-old woman is old and *should* have accomplished the cultural mandate of motherhood. Lupe decided to rewrite her own story; to reframe the next two decades of her life as times of discovery and growth, instead of degeneration and loss. She became more involved in the lives of her nieces and nephews to fulfill her own desires of being "maternal."

Subsequently, she explored the institutional racism and sexism that also blocked her writing. Her department did not support her Chicano scholarship, she had no friends on campus, and she often taught more courses than her male colleagues.

Lupe expressed tremendous anger at white women professors, colleagues, and administrators who either ignored or patronized her. Through our dialogues, Lupe realized she blamed white women entirely for the pain racism had caused her. She had always expected to be mistreated by white men; thus, she tended to focus mostly on the impact of oppression from white women, from whom she had expected support.

Lupe could express her anger at white women and at racism quite freely, yet she felt disloyal if she expressed even resentment towards other Chicanos. In part, she did not feel entitled to be angry towards "her people" because they were the only support she had. After four months of psychotherapy, Lupe resumed work on her book.

### The Myth of Martyrdom: "Una mujer sufrida"

"Mrs. López," a 47-year-old Mexican American married mother of six was brought to psychotherapy by her husband because of her sadness and loss of interest in activities she previously loved. Mrs. López' symptoms began shortly after her last child left home to go to college and the onset of menopause. Her sons were married to Anglos and lived in other cities. She had minimal contact with her grandchildren; unable to care for them she felt unneeded and unloved. Her lifelong job at a cannery gave her little sense of worth.

Our weekly *platicas* (conversations) centered on the frequency of her daughter's calls from college. Over time, Mrs. López was able to talk about her own youthful dreams and aspirations and her sense of betrayal by her children. She had done all that was expected of her; she was a devoted wife, a loyal daughter, and a good mother. Yet, she was not reaping any rewards. She felt old and tired, neglected by her children, and guilty about her disappointments. Eventually Mrs. López talked about the cultural expectations of maternal sacrifice and suffering she had seen her own mother and grandmother epitomize. With encouragement from her husband, Mrs. López began to make some goals for herself. She attended a junior college. After taking a few courses, she became more comfortable with her role as a college student. As she began to understand the academic demands her daughter was experiencing, they grew closer.

After six months of individual therapy, Mrs. López' depression lifted and she became more interested in rebalancing her personal and family life; Mrs. López began to look at menopause not as the end of her life, but as a marker for a new beginning.

After nine months of therapy, Mrs. López terminated treatment. After her college graduation, she began work as a paralegal.

Central to the psychotherapy with Mrs. López was an analysis of the role anger and disappointment played in her feelings of sadness. As a traditional woman, Mrs. López did not feel entitled to ask for anything. Her children and husband *should* know what she needed, just as she had known what her own mother needed. However, the cultural discontinuity created by her sons' marriages and her daughter's move away to college precluded the continuation of culturally expected patterns. In addition, her lack of familiarity with the pressures her children experienced led her to feel neglected by them. The therapy focused on contextualizing both her cultural reality and the children's, thus facilitating mutual respect and understanding.

### Reclaiming Her Birthright: On Being a Lesbiana

"Flor" is a 50-year-old Chicana who requested therapy because of conflict with coworkers and family members who did not know she was a lesbian. Flor felt unhappy with her "double life" and the fact that all her lovers had been white women who never fully accepted her "Mexican-ness." Flor believed that to be with a white woman she had to act white; to be with other Chicanas, she had to act "straight." Within the larger Chicano community where Flor was a longtime activist, she felt she could not be out as a lesbian.

Flor understood intellectually the demands of her culture of origin and she had a clear political analysis of the oppression she faced as a lesbian of color. Her understanding, however, did not reduce her emotional pain. Flor described having lived her life in stages; first she was a daughter and then a wife. At age 25 she joined the Chicano Movement, became a feminist and left her husband. In her thirties she went to college, obtaining a graduate degree; and then she "came to terms with being a lesbian." In her fourties she began to feel aimless, without goals or direction. Thinking about her upcoming fiftieth birthday, she wondered if life was worth living. She began to question the meaning and worth of her involvement in the women's and Chicano movement. She felt alone, unsupported, and betrayed by the promises of her youth.

Flor was seen in weekly psychotherapy for two years. She struggled with suicidality as she explored the roots of her depression, her sense of isolation, and her compartmentalized life. She feared the loss of affection from her family if she came out to them. She feared the loss of support from white lesbians if she confronted them about their racism. Yet she felt she could no longer be silent about her sexuality or her rage. Initially reluctant, Flor eventually joined a support group for Latina lesbians. She gradually began to write and paint, to express the feelings she could not describe in her own voice.

The weekly psychotherapy consisted of a critical analysis of her story; the cultural values that impinged upon her were discussed and contextualized in political and feminist terms. Flor was shocked to realize that she often defined herself in terms of the needs of others. After six months of therapy, Flor had to undergo a hysterectomy. The subsequent therapy focused on her sense of loss. Flor mourned the children she would never have and confronted her belief that a woman without a uterus is not a woman.

The remaining time in therapy focused on self-acceptance; for the first time Flor paid attention to her physical, spiritual, and emotional needs. She began to utilize her friends as a resource and decided to have a coming out party for her fiftieth birthday. She began to look towards the next decade as one of self-definition in which she could integrate her culture, her sexuality, and her love of community and family.

## TOWARD A FEMINIST CHICANA PSYCHOLOGY

A feminist Chicana psychology must include an analysis of Chicanas' triple oppression. An essential aspect of psychotherapy with Chicanas at midlife is an understanding of their subjective experience of being women on the border, women who face the conflictive demands and expectations of two cultures; women whose own voice is rarely heard. Within this context, the role of psychotherapists may be to facilitate a discovery of the bridges across the interstices of the Chicanas' life and reality.

Mrs. López struggled with fulfilling traditional cultural ideals in an Anglo context; this necessitated a rebalancing of roles. Flor and Lupe had attained higher education yet did not "feel" middle class. Both women were actively involved in feminist and Chicano politics, yet felt alienated from white feminism and a male-centered Chicano Movement.

Lupe felt pressured to choose between feminism and familism; Flor felt she had to choose between cultural/ethnic loyalty and self-acceptance. Like other Chicana lesbian activists within the Chicano Movement, Lupe felt silenced and invisible. She sought solace in the feminist movement, yet faced racism and found little support and understanding of her culture (see Trujillo, 1991). Both Flor and Lupe paid the psychological price of feeling disloyal to their intersecting worlds.

In the midlife transition all three women faced the interstices. For each this transition required a reanalysis of gender roles and a redefinition of "their place" relative to their families, the Anglo world, and their culture. This analysis placed them face to face with the classism, racism, and gender oppression they had experienced throughout their lives. It was in the critical analysis of the confluence of racism, sexism, heterosexism, and economic oppression that these women found balance and a renewed sense of Self. The suppressed or hidden rage and pain began to flow freely in the therapy and, over time, was transformed into sources of strength.

Through a therapeutic dialogue, these three women and others have found their own voice. This process could easily exist outside of psychotherapy, in classrooms, through mentoring relationships, in informal gatherings.

Midlife may be a time of reappraisal and self-discovery for women who follow the traditional path of early marriage and motherhood; a time when they can balance the I and the We. For women who postponed traditional roles, it may be a time of conflict and crisis as they face the possibility of not fulfilling some cultural mandates. For lesbians it may be a time to reclaim the culture and demand acceptance.

Midlife may be a time for women to finally feel entitled to be themselves; to dream their own dreams. For Chicanas it may entail a conscious confrontation with patriarchal values, institutional, social, and personal racism, and legacies of colonization. Ultimately, midlife may be the moment where Chicanas re-create themselves and become the new *mestizas* (Anzaldúa, 1987, Flores-Ortiz, 1993b); women who need not inhabit the margins or the interstices, but rather take a central place in the concentric circles they inhabit.

## NOTES

1. The term Chicana is used here to describe Mexican-origin women. This term is preferred by the author and was used by the three women whose stories are told in this paper. The extent to which the impact of racism, classism, and gender oppression affects women from other Latin American countries or socioeconomic levels has not been studied. Generalizations from this paper to other Latinas without a clear analysis of their context is discouraged.

2. The names used are pseudonyms. Facts not central to the clinical understanding of the case have been changed to protect confidentiality. All three women gave written consent to have their stories told.

## REFERENCES

Andrade, Sally (1982). Social science stereotypes of the Mexican American woman: Policy implications for research. *Hispanic Journal of the Behavioral Sciences, 4*(2), 223-244.

Anzaldúa, Gloria (1987). *Borderlands/la frontera*. San Francisco: Spinsters/Aunt Lute.

de la Torre, Adela, & Pesquera, Beatriz (Eds.) (1993). *Building with Our Hands*. Berkeley: U.C. Press.

Flores-Ortiz, Yvette G. (1993a). La mujer y la violencia. In Norma Alarcón et al. (Eds.), *Chicana Critical Issues* (pp. 169-182). Berkeley: Third Woman Press.

_____ (1993b). Depression, acculturation, and marital satisfaction among chicana workers. In Vicky Ruiz (Ed.), *Las obreras: Chicana workers*, (pp. 151-176). U.C.L.A.: Aztlan, Journal of Chicano Studies.

Hayes-Bautista, David E., Schink, Werner O., & Chapa, Jorge (1988). *The burden of support: Young Latinos in an aging society*. Stanford: Stanford University Press.

Keefe, Susan E., & Padilla, Amado M. (1987). *Chicano ethnicity*. Albuquerque: University of New Mexico Press.

Melville, Margarita (Ed.) (1980). *Twice a minority: Mexican American women*. St. Louis: Mosby Press.

Mirande, Alfredo, & Enriques, Evangelina (1979). *La Chicana: The Mexican American woman*. Chicago: The University of Chicago Press.

Trujillo, Carla (Ed.) (1991). *Chicana lesbians: The girls our mothers warned us about*. Berkeley: Third Woman Press.

United States Department of Commerce: Bureau of the Census (1990). Statistical Brief, SB-4-90.

# Karuna Counseling:
# Transitions Within a Collective

Linda F. Weiskoff

"Karuna Counseling for Women and their Friends," located in Atlanta, Georgia, is one of the oldest counseling collectives in the United States, existing since the early 1970s. Karuna's history includes the evolution from an all-white to a bi-racial organization. What follows are the reminiscences of some of the past and present Karuna members who met during the spring of 1991 for a series of discussions and interviews about Karuna's history with respect to racial integration,[1] as well as my own summary and interpretations. This chapter offers the reader an in-depth view of Karuna's process of integration, and shares the knowledge that we have gleaned from this experience.

## EARLY DAYS OF THE COLLECTIVE

The early 1970s in Atlanta was a time of tension and anticipation, both in the general public and in the women's community. The old white power structure running the city was about to give way to a new city government run by African-Americans. White women's bars actually flew the "rebel" flag; African-American women who wanted to patronize them were required to meet higher standards for entry than were expected of other customers.

Racism became increasingly discussed and debated within the white women's community, especially with the advent of consciousness-raising groups. However, activism was focused on self-empowerment. Lesbians began claiming their power in the face of devaluation by established women's advocacy groups (e.g., Georgia chapters of the National Organization for Women and the National Abortion Rights Action League). It was out of the interest in self-empowerment that Karuna was born in 1974, composed of women responding to the community's request to form a feminist mental health structure.

At its inception, the collective was composed of nine white women, one-third of whom were lesbian, two-thirds heterosexual. Some of the group members identified themselves as social activists while others were more strongly identified as mental health professionals. The women were unified in their support of feminist values and the rights of lesbians. Much of the group's energy was devoted to fighting homophobia. During those early years, racial diversity was not addressed.

In 1977, Beverly Jones, an African-American applicant, was turned down for membership with the explanation that, in spite of her experience as a therapist, she did not meet Karuna's criteria because she did not have a degree. To some, this reasoning deflected the racial issue. It also clearly showed the group's inclination toward professionalism, to the discomfort of the social activists.

Beverly's reaction to the rejection was disappointment which then turned to anger. This experience reinforced her misgivings about feminism. "My experience, not just with Karuna, but with other feminist groups, was that feminism was for white women, and if a black woman was to approach that theoretical frame, then it had to be something different from what feminism was. . . . It felt exclusionary."

Marlene Johnson, an African-American woman who later joined Karuna, shared her feelings about the women's movement and feminism in the 1970s by saying, "As a black lesbian, I saw a lot of the movement as being for white women, and I saw it for white straight women who not only didn't accept black women, but weren't terribly accepting of lesbians. So I had two shots against me. . . . Having experience with the black movement, which didn't give women power, and certainly gave nothing to lesbians, and then having watched the feminists, I really didn't have high hopes for Karuna doing something, or really making a change, or for being heard."

## FACTORS CAUSING A SHIFT TOWARD INTEGRATION

Within the next few years, Karuna's composition changed. Racial diversity continued to surface as an issue. Some members believed that rejecting Beverly had been a big ethical mistake. Not until the departure of the women who had been uninterested in racial diversification, however, was there an opportunity for change. Some of the newer members wished to racially integrate the organization.

Judith Horton: "Three of us had been part of the Women's Union, which really dealt with a lot of classist and racist issues. And here we were with other people, maybe forming a different kind of bloc or a different kind of energy [than the old Karuna]. I remember thinking, 'Yes, let's do this. This is important.'"

Another factor in the movement toward racial diversity was the high value Karuna placed on processing feelings and ideas. Personal experiences and differences were respected, and openness was encouraged. All decisions were made through a lengthy process of reaching consensus. Each individual's wisdom and participation were valued by the group. Each woman was encouraged to have her own voice and take responsibility for herself. Karuna had become a place where lesbian and heterosexual women got to know each other intimately. Karuna's history of honoring and processing differences promoted racial diversity.

Several other factors influenced Karuna's ability to make the shift. The collective accomplished some difficult tasks by gaining recognition in the mental health community. In addition, Karuna won a dispute with the federal government, gaining non-profit status.

The collective felt empowered enough to take a look at itself with respect to racism and racial diversity. Phyllis Glass recalled: "When I first came in, soon after Beverly had been rejected, it felt like the ghosts that got talked about were homophobia and the issue of needing a degree. People were concerned with getting accepted into the mental health community and dealing with sexual orientation. . . . Once we got strong enough in those pieces of our identity, we had the energy to look at this part."

Beverly's tenacity was another important factor in Karuna's movement toward integration. Beverly believed Karuna reflected something important in her. While other African-American women in her life talked about being stuck in ways that despaired of change, Karuna represented the experience of meeting with a group of women, getting power, and moving toward change. As a result, after Karuna's initial rejection, she decided not to abandon the issue. She developed a workshop on racism and, in 1980, offered it to Karuna. Members were receptive to the invitation.

Phyllis: "I remember feeling excited, relieved, and scared to death."

Beverly presented her racism workshop with her friend Marlene. The experience heightened the group's sensitivity and helped collective members acknowledge the degree to which racism was institutionalized within the organization. The group invited Beverly to join. Beverly stated that she wouldn't feel safe as the only woman of color in the group, and the invitation was extended to Marlene. Although Marlene had an appropriate degree, she lacked direct clinical experience which had been an important selection criterion. She also refused to call herself "feminist," preferring instead the label "womanist." Her acceptance was a clear statement of social activism, rattling those members whose priority was professionalism.

## BEGINNING THE INTEGRATION

The period that followed was characterized by struggle and suspicion. The collective dealt with conflicts in values and definitions and underlying mistrust on both sides. Marlene, unlike Beverly, was skeptical that the organization could overcome the white elitist attitudes she saw inherent in feminism. Due to her lack of counseling experience, the collective required her to attend a course in feminist therapy developed by one of the long-time collective members. This unique requirement fed into Marlene's distrust and concerns about tokenism in the group.

In part, Marlene's cynicism came from her disappointment with Atlanta's lesbian community. "I had hopes they'd be different from the general community, but they were just as racist. I felt burned by the lesbian community and was cynical about any organization talking about wanting to deal with racism." Marlene decided to join the collective but felt "I was part of a quota system and not seen as myself. Feedback was–I wasn't viewed as a therapist."

Ilene Schroeder: "I think that was partly right, but not so much 'Oh, this will fill our quota.' It was more out of wanting to be politically correct. I think that was a naive way in which we were all feminists in those days. We had a growing edge kind of feminism . . . and also this naive politically correct shit."

Integration was scary. The racism workshop had challenged Karuna members to examine their values and become more deeply introspective. Marlene was even more threatening to the group.

Isabelle Bagshaw: "I was terrified that Marlene didn't call herself a feminist. This was an important part of my identity and I didn't know how much I could loosen up."

The classes in feminist therapy were a requirement for Marlene and also for Eleanor, a new and differently abled white member. Eleanor, like Marlene, lacked the credentials to satisfy Karuna's "professionalism." Both felt resentful and believed that the group did not acknowledge their individual expertise. They questioned whether or not the group considered them truly equal collective members.

In current discussions, their questioning has been validated.

Judith: "This whole question of how to shift from an all-white organization to a bi-racial one–I think we were struggling with that, as well as with education and class. We were scared, so we said, 'Okay, we'll give them some special training, these people who aren't like us.' And it didn't work. Thank god y'all persisted."

Another way in which the new members took issue with the old was around Beverly and Marlene's desire to bring in male therapists to see heterosexual couples with them. Was Karuna going to remain a space where women would not have to deal with a male presence, or were we going to accommodate a different priority?

Ilene: "I remember several meetings in which we argued about whether or not to use male consultants. Were we going to let the expertise of these women affect us? So even though we had invited them to join, we said, 'Too bad; we're not going to listen to you. You've got to do it our way.' The white definition of feminism was running afoul of making a multi-cultural definition."

## DEEPER LEVELS OF INTEGRATION

At this point, several things helped to alleviate tension and increase group cohesiveness. Karuna decided to hold a meeting specifically about racism, in which everyone talked very personally about her experiences with race and integration. This was helpful and hopeful. As Eleanor remembers, "I was scared before it happened and relieved afterwards. It felt like . . . the air had been cleared. Somehow we demonstrated a willingness to listen, be open and talk." Eventually one source of resentment was removed when the person who taught the feminist therapy classes left Karuna and they were discontinued.

In 1984, another African-American woman, Linda Grays, joined the collective. This balanced the racial composition. Beverly felt for the first time that Karuna had a genuine commitment to diversity. Linda G. remembers: "There was an acceptance and a valuing of my blackness–not as a token, and not as, 'Well, let's pretend that it's not really there,' but from the standpoint of, 'This is who you are and we want to get to know you better.' "

In 1985, a small group composed of both African-American and white staff members, went to California to attend a training retreat on the use of the Radical Psychiatry Model.[2] Upon their return, they proposed that Karuna adopt the model to aid in processing feelings and addressing differences. The collective agreed.

We risked and learned from each other and we no longer felt as threatened as we had earlier. The feminists no longer tried to "educate" Marlene, and Marlene and Beverly no longer educated the group about racism. We found a way to be respectfully vocal about our differences. We became more empathic with one another. As we got to know each other more personally, strong friendships were formed. Comfort replaced tension.

Marlene: "Part of what I liked about Karuna was when [the African-American women] stopped being an experience, like going to parties and being the 'black' friend, and started being a part of Karuna. Then it was okay."

As Karuna became bi-racial on a deeper, more intimate level, white members experienced the impact that integration had on themselves and their practices. They became more aware of the narrowness of their upbringings.

Beth-Ann Buitekant: "Being brought up in the dominant culture you're never taught about other cultures. It's almost impossible to know another person's experience [unless you have some interface with the culture]." Nicki Scofield: "With Karuna being bi-racial, we've been able to help each other fill in some of the class, race, and culture gaps which prevent us from knowing our clients more intimately."

Karuna's diversity has helped deepen white members' respect for difference, allowing them to become acquainted with a spectrum of ways to be with clients, and challenging them to give up the notion that there is only one right way. It has allowed the group to do therapy in an atmosphere which encourages addressing prejudice in an open manner. Racial diversification has actualized some members' beliefs.

Isabelle: "It really validated something within me. Some of the good feminist values that I have weren't fully acted on until I was able to be in a place that had racial diversity." Linda Weiskoff: "In a very personal way the experience has helped me to clarify my definition of what a woman is. I bring this with me to every client I see."

## CONTINUING CONCERNS

The increase in African-American staff members was not accompanied by a corresponding increase in African-American clientele. Marlene shares her view of some reasons for this: "This is partly due to the black cultural view that therapy is a white institution, but there is some movement toward [embracing] therapy in the black community. The extended family [the traditional therapy institution for African-American people] is falling away as the community gets more educated and urbanized. As a result, more blacks are seeking therapy. . . . Also, I have a much different relationship with my black clients than I do with white ones. Black clients tend to be shorter-term and more crisis-oriented. They have less discretionary money to spend."

In 1988, Linda G. left Karuna to begin a psychology internship. As a result, the collective was faced with the task of maintaining a bi-racial balance. Although Karuna had consistently attracted white therapists, there was little interest from women of color. We began to strategize about recruitment of African-American staff members.

Linda W. remembers: "During one retreat, [recruiting women of color] was our main agenda item. We discussed it, drafted search letters, made lists of potential recipients and when we came back we dropped the ball." Limited energy plus the group's lack of genuine interest in the tasks involved in launching a full-scale search halted the process.

In June 1990 Marlene left the collective. Having been with Karuna for more than ten years, she was ready to make an occupational change in her life. This was in part due to her dissatisfaction with Karuna's shift away from social activism to professionalism. At the same time, two other long-term members also left the organization. One left for similar reasons and one went on to a psychology internship. This dealt a powerful blow to Karuna, creating major upheaval in the organization. We were faced with replacing half our staff. Once again the issue of racial diversity was in competition with other issues, namely the group's survival. In addition, two of the three outgoing members were lesbian, creating the loss of a significant lesbian presence at Karuna.

Judy Sanderson: "We also didn't have many lesbians on our staff, and we had to address that situation as well." It took less energy to draw from a pool of interested white lesbian applicants than to search for women of color who were not necessarily eager to apply.

Marlene speculates that it was difficult to find African-American women interested in joining Karuna because they "have either bought into the mainstream and into its power base, and stay in state jobs for security, or their interest is in contributing to their own grass roots."

As the group stabilized, discussions about recruiting women of color began anew. In mid-1992, the group began an active search for African-American staff members which was met with interest by several women of color. We are hopeful that Karuna is becoming an organization that is attractive to women of color.

## CONCLUSION

Several themes emerge from Karuna's experience which are important considerations for women interested in developing multi-racial feminist organizations. As the examination of Karuna's process illustrates, simply taking steps to include women of color in an organization does not address the complexity and depth of the integration process. Developing into a bi-racial collective has been quite difficult for Karuna. In making the choice to become bi-racial, an all-white organization went through a painful process of introspection.

Ilene: "You can start off as aware as you can be of your own biases, and you discover you hold ones you didn't know you had–lo and behold you're trapped in your own prejudices. It's a difficult process figuring it out and learning to remediate it." The group continues to examine differences and individual prejudices today.

A bi-racial organization has a fragile existence, in need of consistent attention in two areas: maintaining intimacy and open communication within the collective, and maintaining public relations in order to facilitate recruitment of women of color both as staff and as clients. Our attention to this is always in competition with other issues, demanding our time and energy. It's easy to get distracted. Every woman in a group wishing to become racially diverse must be willing to make this a very personal priority.

Adopting the Radical Psychiatry model made a difference in the clarity and depth of the group's interactions. An outside structure can be very helpful to a group wishing to improve communication. However, a group's commitment to its use is essential to success. Although the Radical Psychiatry model was a helpful guide, ultimately the responsibility for its use, and for clarifying and deepening Karuna's communication, is ours.

In spite of the help Karuna has received and the members' interest, Karuna's goal of maintaining a racially balanced staff has yet to be realized. We have done quite well on a personal level, developing communication and intimate relationships. However, on an organizational level, in recruiting both staff and clients, we have been less than successful.

In light of Karuna's experience, women interested in developing multi-racial organizations in the 1990s might consider bringing together women of different races at an organization's inception. This would not circumvent the struggle to achieve true integration. However, it would provide a positive context for dialogue and would allow for greater diversity in a group's approach to issues, problems, and solutions.

Several considerations stand out as important in the formation and maintenance of multi-racial organizations. The group must have racial diversity as an important value. Members must be open to and nurturing of a group identity that is broader and more inclusive than their personal identities. Finally, there is a need for consistent attention to the process and willingness to actively strive for intimacy within the group.

## NOTES

1. Of the 29 women who have been members of Karuna, 15 participated in the discussions and interviews. They are:

| | |
|---|---|
| Susan Barrett 1974-79 | Judy Sanderson 1981-93 |
| Ilene Schroeder 1975-81 | Eleanor Smith 1982-86 |
| Phyllis Glass 1977-84 | Jesse Harris-Bathrick 1982-84 |
| Sharon Saunders 1977-87 | Linda Grays 1984-88 |
| Isabelle Bagshaw 1978-90 | Linda Weiskoff 1988-94 |
| Judith Horton 1979-90 | Nicki Scofield 1990-1 |
| Beverly Jones 1980 | Beth-Ann Buitekant 1990-1 |
| Marlene Johnson 1980-90 | |

It should be noted that since the conclusion of the discussions on which this chapter has been based, new members have joined the collective, and additional new members ar expected in the near future.

2. The Radical Psychiatry Model provides a structure for direct communication. This model values and teaches personal honesty and openness, taking responsibility for one's own reactions and feelings, checking on one's intuitions, and negotiating needs. It places a priority on egalitarianism.

# The Full-Figured Black Woman: Issues of Racism and Sizeism

Jan Faulkner

## INTRODUCTION

Body size and race are often treated (by some therapists) as separate problems that oppress full-figured black women. An assumption that "if you look better, you will feel better and people will treat you better" is considered acceptance. Sizeism is seen as the dominant oppression of full-figured black women. This fails to take into consideration the conscious and emotional impact of the woman's race regardless of her body size and/or personal appearance. What then is the impact of body size and race combined, on the lives of full-figured black women, and how can it best be addressed in therapy?

This paper focuses on group work with nine full-figured black women. The purpose of the group was to utilize a feminist perspective of self- and mutual empowerment to help them deal with the race and size oppression experienced in their day-to-day contacts in the workplace. I recognized the need for such a group through my therapeutic work with individuals experiencing the dual oppressions.

I am a black full-figured female, a Clinical Social Worker with more than 20 years of experience working with oppressed women in individual and group therapy. I described the group as a supportive educational, ego-enhancing experience for full-figured black women.

Originally planned to run for six months, the group continued for two-and-a-half years. Its longevity was due to two main factors. First, there was a commonality and recognition of each other that helped create working bonds. Second, I found that the processes described in this paper required considerable time for participants to internalize. Years of accommodative responses to oppression do not change swiftly into successful and relatively safe resistance to such oppressions as racism and sizeism.

We met for two hours once a week in a large, well-lighted, open-windowed bodywork classroom, chosen because it provided room for light physical exercises, large mats and chairs for relaxed lounging, and ventilation for cooling down after exercises as we prepared to move into the discussion time.

All the members were full-figured black women I had interviewed and screened for the following criteria: ages between 25 and 50; actively engaged in or recently terminated from individual psychotherapy; employed for the past five or more years (and currently); ability to participate in ongoing light physical exercises, swimming, and other activities; self-identified as well as identified in the workplace and the general community, as African American; and, importantly, currently experiencing stress over issues of body-size and race in the workplace.

## THE GROUP AND ITS DEVELOPMENT

The women in general functioned at a highly insightful and emotionally productive level in the group. They were all at a management level in their work settings, although with marked racial imbalance between black and non-black staff. Their economic comfort freed them to make use of the group experience by investing themselves fully in inner as well as interpersonal work.

My approach to the group was primarily experiential. I focused on general group dynamics to facilitate supportive and educational group learning experiences, and emphasized the positive aspects of self-love. Each woman was encouraged to get physically and emotionally in touch with her body as a love object belonging solely to her, to touch, tend, and clothe in a manner that pleased her. Once a woman was able to "capture" the pleasure of her body, she learned the power one can experience as the owner of a large, much-loved body, a power that projects an aura of self-respect and self-love.

Members were expected to assume responsibility for insight work and behavioral changes resulting from the collective experience.

Each session began with about half an hour of light physical stretches and relaxation exercises, designed to create a safe environment to lighten our load. (By *load* I mean the tendency to physically constrain oneself by holding and/or carrying one's weight.) Many women told of the discomfort associated with holding their stomachs in all day at work. One described how she literally ran to her car and collapsed at the end of each work day. Others described feeling faint due to the limited breathing possible when one holds in the stomach for extended periods of time. Several considered sizeism the main oppression, because they experienced rejections by black friends and relatives as well as at work.

When weather permitted, we would go next door to an elementary school and walk laps around the track. The physical exercise periods concluded with quiet, cooling-down sessions spent mentally stroking various body parts. We then gradually moved to begin the discussion part of the meeting. Any woman could begin the meeting by indicating a need for time to talk about some specific concerns regarding events occurring during the past week. Early on, I discouraged talk about their children and partners; my goal was to keep them totally self-focused.

By the end of the fourth group session the women had moved to an increased self-disclosure of early life experiences around body size, which I saw as progress. I channeled the group's workability and shared content into an ongoing series (approximately 20 sessions) of guided imagery exercises. The purpose of the exercises was to take the women back to early visual image of themselves. Each woman was asked to describe her body size, skin color, and hair texture (physical features prized by many black people), to project a complete childhood picture. These exercises gradually moved each woman from childhood to young adult images.

In general, the women had fond body-image memories until about age seven or eight. Several winced, recalling the negative responses at that age from most of the adults and children in their lives. They had moved from being fat babies to being fat little girls. One woman used humor to describe the pain of being told repeatedly, "you are too big to sit here, too big to act like that, too big to

climb there. I was ten years old before I realized my last name was
not *too big*, the first and second being *you are*."

As the women became more comfortable with self-disclosure,
they were encouraged to identify the first person to respond to their
"fat little girl" image in a loving, esteeming manner that gave
positive support to the self-image. For most, this experience had
occurred between the ages of nine and fifteen. Such recall initially
provoked a lot of laughter and joking as they focused on an identified person. The person identified by one woman was a "white
woman whose daughter owned the building we lived in," who
picked her up on the woman's way home from a Senior Center.
"She provided a surprise snack each day and never told me I was
too fat. We would play school until my mother came home from
work."

These sessions also produced an outpouring of sad feelings, loss
issues, and sometimes shame-ridden accounts about some of the
persons who first esteemed them: teachers, relatives, family friends,
and strangers; only two of the people named as acceptant and nurturing were primary care providers. Several women were surprised
when they realized the supportive persons were of a different race.
Up to this point cross-cultural differences had not been mentioned
or recognized as sources of affirmation. Reports varied from positive ego-enhancing learning experiences with loving, caring
teachers, scout leaders and older girls, to fondling encounters with
male relatives, family friends, and strangers. All the women had
thought of those as caring gestures at the time of occurrence. Recalling the experience as adults, sad feelings of anger and abandonment were evoked.

Several women recalled how "lost" they felt when the person
identified was no longer an important part of their day-to-day existence. "I thought I'd die when our next-door neighbors, who were
childless, moved away. I was 14. She used to clean me up and
they'd both take me shopping at the Mall, and to lunch at McDonald's every Saturday. We'd pretend I was their daughter and they
would buy me panties and socks. My folks never asked me where
we went or what we did. God, they haven't cared about me for a
long time."

Another woman offered, "Well I used to go off with this old man who hung around our school. All the other girls were afraid of him. I pretended I was afraid too, then I'd slip off with him. He'd take me to this rib place on the other side of town, buy me all I could eat, and then sit in his car kissing and feeling me up. When he finished he'd give me 20 dollars. I used the money to buy lipsticks and other stuff."

Recalling such experiences now aroused feelings that had not been conscious since the encounters or the time they had felt abandoned. Analyzing the total experience also provided the women with some insights into how wounded they felt when the relationships were terminated. Several spoke of having "felt ugly," of "going undercover," which was later defined as "really piling on the clothes." They assessed this behavior as a defensive move, not consciously planned to hide their hurt. It was also important that most of those experiences were not with their primary caretakers.

In another exercise the group was encouraged to mentally remove the piled-on clothing and explore what they were hiding. Each woman was asked to stand and name three physical features she liked about herself, and why. Initially they responded to this in shy ways. Some blushed, giggled, closed their eyes, covered their faces. The rest of the group usually responded with appreciative catcalls and whistles, but in a positive and approving manner that encouraged freer and more playful efforts by others when it was their turn. They agreed that this was behavior they had abandoned in their teens.

The new-found freedom to present their bodies in a playful situation supported the second part of the exercise, which required that each woman name three physical features she liked about another in the group, and state why. The fact that the women had two major commonalities, body size and race, provided safety and contributed to this being an empowering experience, especially when a woman spoke of *why* she liked certain features in another, and the group supported her observations.

The women became quite prideful about what they themselves liked and what others liked about them. Their pride was manifest in their posture, dress, and general self-presentation. I interpreted these changes as their internalizing the positive group experience, especially when they reported using the good feelings outside the group setting. For example, one woman reported buying a bright pink dress to wear to a baptism. When her mother saw the dress she said, "That is a bright pink." The member responded, "You should see what it does for my skin tone." The woman later reported a positive response to the dress by most of the family members attending the event. She concluded that she had laid the groundwork for that positive response by identifying what she liked about herself and what she liked about the dress.

Still, most were so defended around body size that they either felt totally vulnerable to racism at work or denied the presence of any racist attitudes among their non-black co-workers. When I reintroduced some of their earlier shared concerns about dealing with racism in the workplace, one woman expressed a loss of the positive group experience. I then asked each woman to verbalize three reasons she is proud to be black, a request that resulted in prolonged silence. I therefore encouraged them into a new round of the earlier mirroring exercises.

Eventually I asked each woman what she liked about the "blackness" of what had been presented. I defined "blackness" as *both one's visible physical appearance and the mental concept of the physical self.* Most responded in a descriptive manner only: skin color, hair texture, anatomical structure; lip, nose, and eye size, unable to experience "blackness" except in physical appearance. This exercise was more difficult than any they had done before. It required deep reflection and observation of both self and others.

At this point I gave them copies of various readings to support their efforts.[1] This helped them to develop thoughtful responses. After each statement, I called on the group to describe ways in which the woman could use her cited reasons to protect herself from racism. For example one woman said she liked having deep dark skin because, "I'm so visible and I get attention others [black and non-black] don't get." She described an experience common in designer boutiques: the owner would dismiss a clerk and say, "We only carry junior sizes." The group member said she experienced the exchange as special attention. Some others considered the owner's actions as implying that the woman did not belong there, that her presence required handling by a person in charge.

The group questioned whether the rejection was due to body size or race. Most thought it was size. One significant observation was that some women's need to protect themselves against body-size vulnerability is so pressing that it impairs their ability to even consider certain behaviors as racist.

Next we focused on behavior designed to teach a positive projection of one's physical appearance as a powerful, self-caring, antiracist and anti-sizeist statement. For example, the women were taught, when entering a room where everyone stops what they are doing and stares, to shift to their most prideful, purposeful stride, then to cross the room, turn slowly, smile, and proceed about their business. I call this exercise "seizing the power of presence," the power that creates a hush in a noisy room when a full-figured black woman enters, or evacuates an entire section of a swimming pool when a full-figured black woman jumps in.

To contrast the above with experiences in the workplace, I asked questions like: Who is the one person at work who is always good for a hug or a squeeze? Who is the one person at work whom staff rely on to plan and organize all food-focused activities? Who is the office confidante? Who is always looked to for a good laugh?

The women readily equated the above questions with the roles they often assumed or were assigned by their co-workers. Their initial responses varied from prideful ("I like to cook") to defensive ("They ask me to do things; I don't ask them"). When I encouraged them to explore their associations with such roles, they recalled fond associations of loving, caring times with full-figured black female authority. However, when I asked them to indicate non-black, societal associations with the same roles they became angry, recalling such epithets as "Aunt Jemima," "Mammy," and "the cleaning woman."

One woman shared how the director of the Center would telephone her and jokingly say, "I need an hour today, so I'll swing by with lunch and we'll meet in your office." They considered his ease in sharing personal problems with her as an issue of credibility. They asked whether it was easy for him to "tell her everything" because she lacked status and power. She realized that the group experience would help her to become more self-observing in her interactions with the director.

One woman spoke of a white female boss who often asked her

for hugs and back rubs. Others described how they were often made to feel sexless because of the intrusive way many of their co-workers and bosses would touch their bodies. In general they expressed anger about being expected to be always in a jovial mood, open to dirty stories, and available for compassion on demand. One director rarely referred to his black female manager by her professional title. He might introduce her by saying, "This is where you come when you need to know things," though another time he referred to her as the "chief cook and bottle washer," while introducing her white assistant as "the one who knows everything."

Some of the group complained about being called on to assist with heavy physical jobs at work, such as helping to move large objects, changing the water cooler bottle, or resolving disputes between disruptive clients or customers. They began to recognize the unspoken message: Your racial background and body size make you the one to be called on. These comments illustrated their increasingly insightful assessment of the work settings as places where they were simultaneously penalized for both body size and race.

The most obvious and common sizeist rejection was exclusion from social events outside the workplace. Some events were reportedly kept secret or had invitations extended only to thinner females of color, although physically large black males might be included. The women experienced such rejection as trickling down from the top administration to the bottom work force. Another sizeist obstacle was evident in promotion selection. Thinner women of color were often the competition, or, in their absence, white women regardless of body size. If a full-figured black woman was promoted, she was rarely called on to represent the agency outside the work setting. She was denied professional visibility even among the varied departments, limiting her opportunities to become more widely recognized. One woman stated that her employer frequently passed over her to send others to conventions and conferences saying, "We need you here to take care of the place." The group agreed that such treatment does little to promote or support creative growth and intellectual stimulation.

## SUMMARY

The full-figured black woman's needs are unique; special ego-enhancing interventions and learning experiences are required to promote intra- and interpersonal growth around body size and racial identity. This series of ongoing group exercises heightened the women's consciousness and their ability to deal productively with rejection whether within or outside the workplace. The concepts of "blackness" and "seizing the power of presence" were introduced as techniques of empowerment to be used against the almost consistently negative verbal and non-verbal messages from society.

Sharing experiences from outside the group setting proved to be collectively empowering. The effectiveness of the exercises was impressively clear as the women began to realize that what is internalized remains within them to be used at will.

## NOTES

1. The assigned readings were:

Boyd-Franklin, Nancy (1991). Recurrent themes in the treatment of African American women in group psychotherapy. *Women and Therapy: A Feminist Quarterly, 11*(2), 25-40.

Clance, P. R., & Imes, S. (1978, Fall). The impostor phenomenon in high achieving women: Dynamics and therapeutic intervention. *Psychotherapy Research and Practice, 15*(3), 241-247.

hooks, bell (1988, September). Straightening our hair. *Z Magazine*, 33-37.

hooks, bell (1989, January). Giving ourselves words: Dissident Black women's speech. *Z Magazine*, 39-42.

Shapiro, S. (1988, November). Bubble identity. *Ms. Magazine*, 30-34.

Black and female: What is reality? (1987, February). *Vital Signs* 4(1). (entire issue).

# Understanding the Training Experiences of Asian American Women

Donna K. Nagata

An important step in developing effective psychotherapy for women of color includes increasing the number of women therapists who are themselves from underrepresented groups. Unfortunately, there are many barriers to attaining this goal and women therapists of color are inadequately represented in psychology. Asian American women are no exception. For example, despite the fact that Asian Americans represent the fastest growing ethnic minority group today (O'Hare & Felt, 1991), there are currently few Asian American women therapists. Expansion of the numbers of Asian American women in this role requires that we take an in-depth examination of the overt and covert racist assumptions which impact their recruitment and training experiences. These assumptions can be reflected in insensitive and/or ignorant behaviors on the part of supervisors and faculty, many of whom may have little awareness of the discrepancies between their perceptions of the graduate training experience and those of their Asian American trainees.

The cost of unresponsive training is high. Failure to examine insensitive or racist assumptions will severely limit our training programs from adequately addressing the training needs of Asian American women. (Hopefully, the material presented in this chapter will illustrate these points.)

It is obviously impossible, and indeed inappropriate, to document training experiences which apply to all Asian American women. There are critical differences among Asian American ethnic groups and, as noted by Mazumdar (1989), gender impacts Asian American women differently even within the same class and ethnic group. Emphasis here is placed upon case examples drawn from the training experiences of Chinese American and Japanese American women and the reader must be cautious in making broad generalizations from the material presented. At the same time, there are commonalities of experience shared by many Asian American women. Chan (1988) describes these as follows:

> Asian American women are, paradoxically, seen both as invisible, and as sexually attractive because of our race and gender. We are perceived as being quiet, submissive, willing to please, and even safe to pursue because we would not likely be rejecting. And, because of cultural values that we as Asian American women are brought up with and cherish, we *are* frequently agreeable, gentle, willing to please others before ourselves. (p. 36)

Hence, while the range of individual and group differences is recognized, important connections may also be drawn between the descriptions in this chapter and the experiences of other Asian American women.

The case examples presented here were based upon the graduate experiences of Asian American women trainees. (Note: All identifying information has been altered to maintain confidentiality.) Each illustrates the need for greater sensitivity to the dilemmas faced by this group. For each case incident described, there is a discussion of: (a) the details of the incident, (b) the impact of the incident upon the trainee's personal and social behaviors, and (c) suggestions for alternative ways in which the incident could have been avoided or handled in a more culturally sensitive manner. The presentation of this material should provide the reader with insights into the training experiences of the Asian American women portrayed. Hopefully, these insights will then serve as a catalyst for promoting greater sensitivity within clinical graduate programs.

## *PRE-TRAINING ENTRY ISSUES*

One problem with current training models is their presumption that the responsibility for mentoring and training women of color begins when a trainee *enters* a clinical graduate program. In reality, the forces of culture and racism have critical developmental impacts on Asian American women *prior* to their entry into these programs. Such forces may decrease the likelihood that these women will even begin training and therefore warrant closer examination. There are two major interacting levels of impact which affect the entry of Asian American women into therapist training programs. These include: (a) impacts related to racism and discrimination, and (b) impacts related to Asian American cultural values.

Impacts related to racism include the societal stereotypes of Asian American women as "Lotus Blossom Babies," "China Dolls," exotic, and subservient (Tajima, 1989). Asian American women exposed to these stereotypes are unlikely to be encouraged to pursue professional careers. Racism also affects Asian American women at a broader level. More than a century of anti-Asian sentiment, characterized by social and legal discrimination in this country, has left many Asian Americans with a sense of disenfranchisement. For many Asian American women, the social stereotypes of docility combined with a legacy of societal oppression work to diminish the chance that they will seek a clinical graduate training program.

There are also critical impacts related to Asian American cultural values. These include: the importance of the nuclear family; the press to stay close to home and family; the emphasis upon male rather than female achievement (value of sons over daughters); and the emphasis upon choosing careers in fields other than psychology or social work (e.g., medicine). Each of these cultural values may also discourage Asian American women from entering therapy training programs. Not all cultural values will have equal relevance for a given Asian American woman. Although the valuing of male children over female children is present to some extent in most Asian cultures, the importance of this value to American-born Asian women would be different than for an immigrant Asian woman (Mazumdar, 1989). Nonetheless, many cultural values continue to shape the career decisions of Asian American women, regardless of generational status in the United States.

Cultural values may also affect the likelihood that an Asian American woman will enter a clinical graduate training in less direct ways. Asian Americans underutilize mental health services (Sue & McKinney, 1975). Psychotherapy may be viewed with distrust; feelings of stigma or shame may be attached to seeking help.

Such views of psychotherapy are likely to lead family members or friends to discourage an Asian American woman from pursuing a career as a therapist.

The impact of cultural values and the broader effects of racism also interact with each other. For example, a Japanese American woman may be discouraged by her family from attending a clinical psychology program because it is far from home and because it is not seen as a "practical" career. The term "practical," however, often translates into "secure" and issues of security for many Japanese Americans are tied to their past experiences of racism, particularly during the World War II internment. The importance of examining cross-generational impacts of racial discrimination are evident in my own research on the third-generation (Sansei) adult children of former Japanese American internees. Data from this study revealed that Sansei who had parents interned often perceived their mothers and fathers as expressing a heightened level of concern about career security for their children (Nagata, 1993). Here, the factors discouraging a Japanese American woman from pursuing a career as a therapist have roots both culturally and in historical racism.

Each of the points raised thus far illustrate potential barriers faced by Asian American women before beginning training programs and suggest the need for graduate schools to more actively recruit Asian American women. More expansive outreach efforts implemented early in the college career are needed to encourage more Asian American women to enter clinical programs. Recruitment visits by those Asian American women who have completed their training would be especially valuable in this regard. The barriers described, however, may lead to continued conflicts for these women after they have entered their training program. Illustrations of the potential dilemmas faced by Asian American women during training are addressed in the following section.

## ISSUES RELATED TO THE RETENTION AND DEVELOPMENT OF ASIAN AMERICAN WOMEN IN TRAINING

Once an Asian American woman does enter a graduate program, she may encounter additional barriers which make it difficult to complete her training. In this section, illustrative case incidents are used to exemplify how racial and ethnic insensitivities toward Asian American women can be manifested overtly and covertly in a training program and how such incidents may affect the experiences of these trainees. Each case is presented briefly, followed by a description of the ways in which the trainee responded to the insensitivities she experienced. Alternative methods for avoiding/responding to these incidents are also presented. Occurrences such as those described here are important to examine since they can affect the likelihood of an Asian American woman completing her training program. In addition, even if an Asian American woman completes her training in the face of such incidents, the impact of insensitive training can produce long-lasting effects which continue beyond the training years.

## CASE EXAMPLE 1:
## THE INVISIBLE MINORITY

### Description

A first-year Chinese American graduate student arrived at a large university program. She felt isolated and missed family contacts, which had been frequent prior to moving to graduate school. There were no other Asian American students in the program. Although there was a Black Graduate Student Organization in her department, there was no comparable group for her to join. When she broached these feelings of isolation with a male Caucasian American faculty advisor and commented on her disappointment that membership in the Black Graduate Student Organization was limited to African Americans, the advisor's response was "Oh come on, you're doing just fine. You don't really need that kind of group."

### Personal and Social Impact

The trainee felt not only "unheard," but felt the message from the advisor was that she was not as "needy" as the African American students. (The perception of the African American students as somehow needy was in itself prejudiced, and made the Chinese

American woman uncomfortable.) The advisor also implied that Asian Americans are "not like the other minority groups." Related to this was a message that the trainee did not feel the effects of racism–that as a member of the "model minority" she was doing just fine. In fact, the trainee had recently been confronted in a shopping mall by a young white male who called her a "gook." In addition, the trainee wondered whether her problems were belittled because she was a woman or because she did not express herself forcefully enough. However, since she had been raised not to complain or challenge authority, she decided not to confront the advisor further. The advisor's disregard for this trainee's sense of isolation resulted in her withdrawal from further contacts with faculty, putting additional burden upon her to handle the situation and further increasing her sense of isolation from the program.

### Recommendations

Increasing the numbers of Asian Americans, or more specifically Asian American women, in training programs could create a "critical mass" of Asian American graduate students and perhaps provide the trainee with a potential support group. However, the burden of correcting the dilemma described here also rests with the faculty. Faculty must become aware of stereotypes such as the model minority myth which they may hold implicitly. Such stereotypes may not be apparent to the faculty when asked to directly assess their feelings toward Asian Americans. In the present case, the stereotypic viewpoint emerged only when the trainee's status as an Asian American was compared to that of other ethnic minority group trainees (i.e., as a Chinese American woman contrasted with African American students).

It is also important to recognize that the advisor regarded the trainee's mentioning of her discomfort as a seemingly minor issue. In contrast, the trainee regarded her comments as requiring a good deal of assertion on her part to overcome her tendency to avoid confrontation. Advisors and supervisors, then, must be aware that their own ethnocentric definitions of assertive behavior may differ from those of Asian American women trainees. In a more sensitive response, the advisor might have taken the time to explore the trainee's comments further, encouraging her to elaborate on her sense of isolation. Such an effort would, if done sincerely, allow the trainee to express her concern more fully.

## CASE EXAMPLE 2:
## THE QUIET ASIAN FEMALE

### Description

In this incident, a Japanese American trainee was enrolled in year-long class on psychotherapy. Class discussion took place frequently in an unstructured manner. During the first semester, the trainee maintained a low profile, speaking only on occasion. She found it difficult to "jump into" the ongoing discussions and felt more comfortable staying out of these interactions. This behavior was culturally consonant in that she had been raised not to express her opinions openly or to engage in debate. Her mid-year evaluations were mediocre, citing her lack of oral participation as a weakness in her classroom performance. Dedicated to doing well, the student made a direct effort to talk more during the second half of the course. Classmates spontaneously commented how much they noticed and enjoyed her contributions that semester. However, when the end-of-year evaluations were distributed, the student's marks remained mediocre. Dismayed, she went to see one of her evaluators for the class and asked for an explanation. The faculty member, a Caucasian American female, stated that the trainee received the low evaluations because she (the instructor) simply could not remember the trainee "ever" saying anything in the class. The trainee suggested the possibility that the instructor's perception had been affected by a stereotype of her being a quiet Asian female. In response to this suggestion, the instructor proceeded to talk about a Japanese gardener who had worked for her, describing in glowing terms how wonderful the gardener was and how much she liked him.

### Personal and Social Impact

The student acknowledged she had been quiet the first semester, but felt that the faculty member's racial stereotype of her being a quiet, docile, Asian female overrode her actual behaviors the second semester. This, as might be expected, was both angering and discouraging, for it indicated that her evaluations were not linked to her performance, but rather to a persisting stereotype. At the same time, because the faculty member was in a position of power and experience, the student began to doubt her own sense of reality and competence. The feelings of disenfranchisement from her own graduate training were so strong that she began looking into the possibility of transferring to alternative graduate programs and avoided further contacts with the instructor.

### Recommendations

This case example reflects the more overt ways in which racism can enter the training process. The faculty member never entertained the possibility that her own biases might have affected her evaluation. Instead, she responded to the trainee's challenge by making another racially insensitive remark regarding her gardener, as if that might build a bridge of understanding between them. In a more sensitive response to the situation, the faculty member could take the time to explore the trainee's perceptions of her class participation. She also would avoid attempts to link the trainee with other Japanese Americans (i.e., the gardener), since this devalues the individuality of the trainee.

The incident raises an additional issue regarding the role of silence in the classroom. The trainee in the described vignette received a low evaluation because she did not speak in class. Her lack of verbalization was taken to mean that she did not understand the material for the course. In contrast, many Asian and Asian American cultures value silence and may discourage women from speaking out or challenging others publicly. The attribution of ignorance to the trainee's silence was erroneous. Therefore, when possible, training faculty should also be encouraged to explore the variety of meanings silence might have outside of their own cultural experience.

### CASE EXAMPLE 3: THE INSCRUTABLE ASIAN

### Description

A Japanese American trainee was engaged in marital therapy, working with a couple in which the wife was Japanese and the husband Caucasian American. A male supervisor, also Caucasian American, listened to audiotapes of the therapy sessions and commented that he felt the trainee was "holding back" too much in her work. He noted that he found it hard to "decipher" her style of intervention. At the same time, the supervisor asked the trainee to explain aspects of Japanese culture, presuming that the trainee would know how these values were related to the experiences of the Japanese wife, whom he referred to as "Madame Butterfly."

## Personal and Social Impact

This incident raised several important reactions in the trainee. First, the wife in this particular case was from Japan, while the trainee was a third-generation Japanese American who had never been to Japan and could neither speak nor understand the Japanese language. It is understandable that the supervisor might wonder whether the trainee had personal knowledge about Japanese culture, particularly if he were unaware of her background. However, the presumption of expertise about Japan was insensitive. When put into the role of the "expert" on Japan, the trainee felt both embarrassed at being unable to provide the information the supervisor requested and angry at being placed in a position of feeling apologetic about something which was not her responsibility. At the same time, the supervisor's presumptions left little room for the trainee to explore her feelings as a therapist working with a Japanese client.

The supervisor also expressed concern about the trainee's therapy style, which was perceived by the supervisor to be "held back." From the trainee's perspective, the supervisor saw her as an "inscrutable Asian," whose behaviors shrouded some deeper agenda. Finally, the supervisor's demeaning reference to the client as "Madame Butterfly" was seen by the trainee as a demeaning, racist, and sexist insult to both the client and the trainee.

The combination of the supervisor's insensitivity and ignorance left the trainee feeling frustrated and unsure of her confidence in his supervision. However, out of respect for his authority, she did not openly challenge him.

### Recommendations

This case strongly illustrates the need for trainers and supervisors to learn about the cultural background, history, and generational issues of Asian American women from particular groups. The supervisor presumed the trainee's level of ethnic identification without taking generational status into account. Clearly, it is important that supervisors/trainers recognize the need to understand an Asian American woman's generational background. This has important implications not only in terms of the degree to which she has knowledge of her ancestral culture and language, but also in terms of how she views gender and role relationships. For example, the supervisor in the present incident seems to assume that the trainee has some "shared experiences" in common with the wife in this marital case since they are both of Japanese heritage. In reality, the trainee has little in common with the client in this regard. Finally, supervisors should examine whether they hold stereotypes such as that of a "Madame Butterfly" which affect their perceptions of all Asian American women.

The fact that the supervisor himself was a Caucasian American male also raises the possibility that important countertransference issues were present in his perceptions of this case. Yet, such issues were never discussed. Similarly, it would have been helpful if the supervisor had provided a forum for the trainee to explore her reactions to working with the couple. Questions related to the trainee's views on interracial marriage, Japanese women, and Caucasian American men could also be discussed as potential countertransference issues from her perspective.

## SUMMARY AND CONCLUSIONS

The situations described in the previous cases illustrate the variety of ways in which an Asian American woman may encounter racial, cultural, and gender insensitivities. Some incidents are more blatant than others, but all affected the training experiences of the women involved, leaving them with the emotional burden of feeling unheard, mislabeled and/or misunderstood by the individuals who had the greatest responsibility for their clinical training.

Looking back at the cases as a whole, I was struck by the frustrations experienced by the trainees. Graduate training is stressful in itself. The additional barriers cited here only exacerbate the level of stress. Such seemingly isolated cases can accrue over time throughout the course of a trainee's experiences and combine with incidents of racism and prejudice outside of the training program to negatively impact her development as a therapist.

Unfortunately, the power differential between faculty/supervisors and the Asian American women trainees described, as well as the presence of Asian American cultural values discouraging the challenging of authority, typically prevented the trainees from more actively challenging the behaviors they encountered. And, in the case where the Japanese American trainee challenged the instructor's perceptions of her level of class participation, the trainee's concerns were dismissed. Ironically, Asian American women may find that even their *assertive* behaviors are invisible to those who have stereotyped them. This creates yet another barrier to their sense of inclusion in the training process.

Research has noted that the issue of power in the supervisory setting has real consequences for women trainees in general. Nelson and Holloway (1990), for example, reported that both female and male supervisors tend to assume the role of "expert" and are especially unlikely to encourage or support female trainees in assuming power within supervisory sessions. Of particular relevance here is the possibility that Asian American female trainees may be even less likely to receive such support if a supervisor holds ethnic and racial stereotypes about Asian American women in addition to preconceptions about women more generally.

Also of note is the fact that the cases described demonstrate a striking lack of attention to the strengths of the Chinese American and Japanese American women trainees. For example, stoicism and a respect for authority were culturally consonant and positive qualities from the perspective of the trainees. Yet these same qualities tended to be viewed by their supervisors and faculty as negative passivity, a lack of knowledge, or a "held-back" therapy style. A greater sensitivity to recognizing the role of these strengths in the training process is needed.

What can be done to improve the training experiences of Asian

American women? Hiring of more Asian American women faculty in graduate programs would have important benefits on many levels, potentially providing increased sensitivity to the experiences of Asian American women trainees and nurturing "their sense of belonging to the profession" (Paludi et al., 1991). However, as noted earlier, only a limited number of women are in these positions. Clearly non-Asian American faculty and supervisors must learn to recognize how their own insensitivities affect their day-to-day interactions with Asian American women. While we now emphasize teaching clinicians to be culturally sensitive to the life experiences a client may bring to therapy, little emphasis has been placed upon gaining a sensitivity to the ethnic and cultural experiences graduate students of color bring to their training programs. Recognition of diversity must occur at the level of training as well as at the level of clinical intervention.

Steps can also be taken to increase the numbers of Asian American women trainees within a given program. Beginning with early outreach efforts, programs should try to enhance the enrollment levels of Asian American women. This increase in numbers would serve two important functions. First, the greater number of Asian American women is an important way to increase the presence of women from a variety of Asian ethnic groups. This greater range of diversity might then reduce the likelihood of gross stereotyping across all Asian American women. Second, greater numbers of Asian American women in a particular program could enhance the likelihood that trainees would find a support group for themselves. Chow (1989) has noted the importance of networking and coalition-building in empowering Asian American women. Interactions with other Asian American women in their training program would provide trainees with opportunities to make such connections. With the support of a peer group, these women might also prefer expressing concerns about their training experience collectively, rather than as individuals. It should be remembered, however, that the burden of responding to ineffective training experiences should not rest with the trainees.

In summary, increased responsiveness to the training experiences of Asian American women will require many levels of intervention. Of key importance is the need to recognize the insensitivities reflected in current training interactions. Only then can we foster an environment which emphasizes the full development of Asian American women therapists.

## REFERENCES

Chan, Connie S. (1988). Asian American women: Psychological responses to sexual exploitation and cultural stereotypes. *Women and Therapy, 6*, 33-38.

Chow, Esther Ngan-Ling (1989). The feminist movement: Where are all the Asian American women? In Asian Women United of California (Ed.), *Making waves: An anthology of writings by and about Asian American women* (pp. 362-377). Boston: Beacon.

Mazumdar, Sucheta (1989). General introduction: A woman centered perspective on Asian American history. In Asian Women United of California (Ed.), *Making waves: An anthology of writings by and about Asian American women* (pp. 1-22). Boston: Beacon.

Nagata, Donna K. (1993). *The legacy of injustice: Exploring the cross-generational impact of the Japanese American internment.* New York: Plenum.

Nelson, Mary Lee, & Holloway, Elizabeth L. (1990). Relation of gender to power and involvement in supervision. *Journal of Counseling Psychology, 37,* 473-481.

O'Hare, William P., & Felt, Judith C. (1991). *Asian Americans: America's fastest growing minority group.* Number 19. Washington DC: Population Reference Bureau.

Paludi, Michele A., DeFour, Darlene C., Brathwaite, Jacqueline, Chan, Betty, Garvey, Colleen, Kramer, Nina, Lawrence, Debra, & Haring-Hidore, Marilyn (1991). Academic mentoring for women: Issues of sex, power and politics. *Focus: Notes from the Society for the Psychological Study of Ethnic Minority Issues, 5,* 7-8.

Sue, Stanley, & McKinney, H. (1975). Asian-Americans in the community mental health care system. *American Journal of Orthopsychiatry, 45,* 111-118.

Tajima, Renee E. (1989). Lotus blossoms don't bleed: Images of Asian women. In Asian Women United of California (Ed.), *Making waves: An anthology of writings by and about Asian American women* (pp. 308-317). Boston: Beacon.

# Overcoming Bias Through Awareness, Mutual Encouragement, and Commitment

### Rachel Josefowitz Siegel

Beverly Greene, Ellyn Kaschak, and I began our three-way conversations in 1989. We three wanted to prepare for a panel discussion on racism and anti-Semitism by listening to each other and exploring our own oppressions as well as our own biases. Our monthly conference calls turned into deeply meaningful consciousness-raising sessions. In this section, we each share some of the reflections that emerged out of these conversations. We begin by telling our stories.

I am a Jewish immigrant, a refugee from Hitler Europe. I was 14 when we landed in New York in the spring of 1939. My childhood memories are filled with incidents in which the fate of my family rested on the decision of a particular border guard or bureaucrat, and in which my fear of this non-Jewish person of power was matched by my fear of endangering the whole family if I said or did the wrong thing. In these memories the enemy was always white, whiter than the members of my family and me.

Now I am a well-aged Jewish feminist who has lived the past 50 years with full citizenship rights and in relative safety. My perceptions and decisions are grounded in a feminist awareness of the interrelatedness of all women's oppressions, and filtered through memories of early, life-threatening anti-Semitic experiences. I speak up about anti-Semitism and racism within feminist organizations and about racism, sexism, and homophobia within Jewish groups, sometimes running the risk of being perceived as overly sensitive, crazy, paranoid, or a traitor to my own people. All of this is pertinent to the roots of my responses to racism and anti-Semitism.

Interwoven with our personal histories, our three-way conversations focused on the themes of visibility, invisibility, and overvisibility that Evelyn Torton Beck (1982) explores more fully, on our relationship to privilege, and on the unnamed and seemingly mysterious hurdles that appear when feminist women work on forming coalitions. These themes are all related and somehow bound together by a fear so profound that it was almost impossible to articulate.

## *FEAR*

We talked a lot about fear.

The *fear of being less than perfect* is one of the biggest stumbling blocks in any effort to understand the self or the other, and in any effort to overcome individual biases or to build coalitions. Of course each person's biases and imperfections are going to show! How else could she correct them? Her racist and anti-Semitic assumptions and behaviors will show repeatedly, and when they do she has to remain open to correction without retreating into paralyzed avoidance of the other person, without dropping the task at hand. Easier said than done.

*Xenophobia, the fear of strangers*, is a fear that warns individuals not to get too close, not to let down their guard, and not to give up their defenses. It is a learned and exaggerated response to the realities of living in a dangerous world, a world more dangerous for those who are oppressed.

Underlying all other fears, the *fear of annihilation and genocide* is least accessible to consciousness or discussion. Based on historical events, which some have experienced within their own or their parents' lifetimes, women of color and Jewish women carry the knowledge of unspeakable evil perpetrated against their own people. They know that the unthinkable has happened and can happen again. Xenophobia and the fear of being perceived as less than perfect are grounded in this reality and serve to protect or overprotect us against the potential of reoccurrence.

These fears are real and legitimate, and can easily become generalized or exaggerated. In each situation, our task is to learn to distinguish between levels of impending danger, between friend and enemy, between innocent insensitivity of those who are *other* and potentially malevolent force or power. If women are to trust each other and form coalitions, they must begin at this level of self-awareness. In any given situation, however, some of this fear is generalized and counterproductive. Fear is woven into the very fabric of all oppressive biases and oppressively hierarchical practices and institutions. Fear is part of the glue that maintains existing biases. When people are categorized as *we* or *they*, fear becomes part of the process of projecting onto those whom *we* see as unlike ourselves all of the attributes that *we* would like to deny within ourselves. *We* are the good self. *They* are the bad self. All players must be maintained in that position and must deny that this is going on. Socially unacceptable traits can thus remain invisible to the self, while *we* stereotype those whom we call *they* or *other* and imbue *them* with negative traits. Women of color and Jewish women are easy targets for such stereotyping and scapegoating, even among feminists, and one way to escape being the target is to make someone else the target. I am not implying that Jewish women and women of color are more prejudiced and biased than anyone else, but neither are they less so.

Even feminists who consider themselves anti-racist and opposed to anti-Semitism are never completely free of bias or fear. They may have made a personal or group commitment to overcome biased attitudes but still be far from reaching that goal within themselves or their institutions. In order to get closer to that goal, each person must reach deep within herself to examine and unlearn the very roots of her fears and false assumptions, and reach far across and toward the other to believe, understand, and unlearn the behaviors that are oppressive to the other. Therapists cannot begin to help clients work on these issues until they are well-versed in the process of examining and overcoming their own fears and biases.

## THE EFFECTS OF RACISM AND ANTI-SEMITISM ARE NOT THE SAME

While the roots of racism and anti-Semitism grow in similar soil, the experiences of racism and anti-Semitism cannot and must not be equated. These two evils are related and do interact, to the benefit of the established power structure. Their effects on the individual cannot be compared, yet the differences in their manifestations must be noted.

Women who have been oppressed by racism or anti-Semitism can learn from each other's experiences, can feel with each other, and can be allies in combating each other's oppression. Women can do all this and do it better when all begin to understand the differences and complexities of each situation.

Pain is not hierarchical; one pain is not more legitimate than another, nor can anyone assume that she truly understands or feels another's pain. Family memories of slavery, lynchings, internment, or mass migrations are not alike for various women of color, nor do they match the memories of pogroms[1] and gas chambers. While racism and anti-Semitism may take very similar forms, their manifestations and their effects on the individual are never the same. In the United States today, everyday racism is much more overt, vicious, widespread, and institutionalized while anti-Semitism is generally more subtle, more easily denied.

In the United States and Canada, women of color, no matter how well-educated or how wealthy, have limited access to positions of power and privilege. They are seen as members of an oppressed minority even when they are in the majority. The color of their skin usually leaves them no choice about their visibility, even when it would be safer or less painful to "pass" as white.

Most Jewish women, however, have the privilege of whitish skin, and can choose not to draw attention to their Jewish identity. This strategy does not insure against discrimination, especially if they "look Jewish," or if their names or mannerisms convey their Jewishness. While they can attempt to "pass" or to assimilate, it can be at some cost to their self-esteem, and they can be deeply troubled about when or where to make their Jewishness visible. Jewish women are often not recognized as a legitimate minority or not perceived or self-perceived as an oppressed group.

Discrimination in the workplace and specifically in academia is another area in which racism and anti-Semitism are not the same, even when they take similar forms and overlap with sexism and homophobia. Racism is frequently more overt. Anti-Semitic and some forms of racist discrimination are easily hidden or denied when they are disguised as the rejection of people with "unsuitable" traits.

Women of color and Jewish women both exist in an environment that is predominantly white-centered, and overtly or covertly more oppressive to us than it is to non-Jewish white women. Jewish women also find themselves invisible in a Christian-centered world.

Jewish women and women of color are often pitted against each other when token gestures are made to recognize their presence or their needs. In many organizations, Jewish women can belong in large numbers without having their needs recognized while women of color are not even present.

While all women would benefit from forming alliances against patriarchal oppression, women of color and Jewish women cannot carry the full responsibility for doing this work, or for fighting racism and anti-Semitism.

## *LEARNING TO WORK TOGETHER*

How can feminists put their good intentions into meaningful action and not give up on the job because it gets too hard? It will be hard because all of us, as individuals, groups, and institutions, will have to overcome some fears, give up some privileges, and let go of some grudges. When *we* no longer means *we* versus *they*, we will begin to be open to our own and each other's pain. We have to change behaviors, and it won't be enough to do it as individuals, we have to do it within the therapy hour and on an institutional level. That means working with women who have different levels of self-awareness on these issues, different levels of openness to self-correction, and different levels of sensitivity to the pain inflicted by each other's mistakes.

We have access to some strategies that have worked for us in other situations: we will need to be more honest with ourselves and with each other as well as more tolerant of our own and each other's imperfections (Bulkin, Pratt, & Smith, 1984; Conlon, daSilva, & Wilson, 1985). We need to learn to correct ourselves and each other without trashing or attacking.

We need to openly remind ourselves that while our pain and our histories of oppressions are different, they are nevertheless equally legitimate and equally worth attending to (Siegel, 1990).

We need to become more literate about each other's issues, listen more carefully to each other, and attend each other's presentations.

We need to support each other's causes and advocate for each other.

We also have to learn to take turns. We are not superwomen, though it is often expected of us. We cannot do all things at the same time. There will be times when we need to be fully united in making a special effort against racism and there will be times when we need to be fully united in making a special effort against anti-Semitism.

We cannot expect women of color to be more diligent against anti-Semitism than other feminists, though some women of color have done that, nor can we expect Jewish women to be more diligent against racism, though some Jewish women have been.

We can and should expect a commitment to some reciprocity, to trustworthiness, and to trusting each other's motives in combating all forms of women's oppression.

## PERSONAL OBSERVATIONS

The three of us, Beverly, Ellyn, and I, have learned from working together on this paper that the process itself has opened each of us to further and ongoing self-scrutiny. We found that it took personal courage to begin to talk about these issues with each other across ethnic and racial boundaries, as well as within our own ethnic group. We found that the work is painful and includes a tendency to procrastinate or to avoid. It was encouraging and empowering to work together rather than in isolation. The scheduling of monthly conference calls kept us on track and provided a supportive outlet for talking through some of the internal and external pressures that interfered with the work. We often felt that we were breaking ancient taboos and needed the mutual reinforcement of our collective commitment to go on with confronting the inevitable pain.

While we offer our own thoughts and observations on racism and anti-Semitism in an effort toward better understanding and cooperation between women of diverse backgrounds, we cannot offer a model or a formula that can easily be applied in therapy or generalized to other groups.

One of our observations is that the work needs to be done on a very intense and personal level as well as on an institutional level, and that it must be uniquely specific to each woman and to each situation.

We found that every attempt to make generalizations about ethnic or racial groups of women led to an awareness of diversities within each group.

It seemed to us that while we wish to be known, recognized, and respected as members of one or more specific ethnic groups, we also need to recognize the differences within each group and the diverse ways of wanting to address the issues of our interactions with each other.

## NOTE

1. "Pogrom" is a Russian word denoting attacks by one population against another; it has come into common usage referring specifically to massacres of Jews by Russians in licensed outbursts of mass violence that included the killing, raping, looting, and destruction of Jewish communities in Russia between 1881 and 1921.

## REFERENCES

Beck, Evelyn Torton (1984). Between invisibility and overvisibility: The politics of anti-Semitism in the women's movement and beyond. Working Paper In *Women's Studies, 11,* 209 N. Brooks St., Madison, WI, 53713, Women's Studies Research Center.

Bulkin, Elly, Pratt, Minnie Bruce, & Smith, Barbara (1984). *Yours in struggle: Three feminist perspectives on anti-Semitism and racism.* Brooklyn, NY: Long Haul Press.

Conlon, Faith, daSilva, Rachel, & Wilson, Barbara (1985). *The things that divide us: Stories by women.* Seattle, WA: Seal Press.

Siegel, Rachel Josefowitz (1990). Turning the things that divide us into strengths that unite us. In Laura S. Brown & Maria P. P. Root (Eds.). *Diversity and Complexity in Feminist Therapy* (pp. 327-336). New York: Haworth Press.

# An African American Perspective on Racism and Anti-Semitism within Feminist Organizations

## Beverly Greene

It is easy enough to agree that racism and anti-Semitism constitute attitudes that are inconsistent with the philosophy of feminism, just as they are inconsistent with the basic spiritual core of Christianity, Judaism, and other major religious beliefs. However, many persons who would consider themselves faithful to these beliefs harbor both racist and anti-Semitic attitudes.

My understanding of these issues has its origins in my experience as an African American woman with Native American admixture, born and raised in the urban Northeast, in the shadows of the multi-ethnicity of New York City. My parents are "survivors" of an American "holocaust," the Mississippi and Georgia of the late 1920s through the late 1940s. For those unfamiliar with the racism of the rural South, my father's walk to school would include passing a tree whose branches held "strange fruit." "Strange fruit" (Allen, 1939) was the term made famous by the Billie Holiday classic of the same name, calling up the macabre images of the work of Southern lynch mobs. Strange fruit were the dead bodies of black men hanging by the neck, often castrated and visibly disfigured. This was done as a means of reminding those who would forget their subservient place that "talking back" to white men or being accused of looking at a white woman for too long could signal the swift end of your life or that of a loved one. Such was the atmosphere of my parents' lives from childhood to early adulthood. My grandparents were the children of slaves and the descendants of

Cherokees who fled into the Carolina and Tennessee hills rather than face the Cherokee nation's western exile. Some 4,000 Native Americans died in what our government referred to as the "removal" in 1838. It would be remembered by others as "the Trail of Tears" (Ehle, 1988). Generations later, the accurate portrayal of America's history would be carefully adjusted to conceal such deeds by depicting the victims as the "savage" aggressors.

My childhood memories are replete with the visible and absolute signposts of racism observed on visits to my parents' birthplaces. This was in contrast to the superficially civilized, covert, insidious racism of the Northeast, where signs were not required to tell us where and when we were unwelcome. Those childhood visits to the South afforded me precious time with my maternal great-grand-mother, our family's then oldest living member and tangible link to the history of both our family and our people. Mary Eliza Roberson did not come to America via the portals of Ellis Island. Rather, she came through America's back door, on a ship filled with slaves, shortly after the eruption of the Civil War. In her early years she would find herself far from her birthplace, a forgotten island in the British West Indies. Never again to see the other members of her family, deliberately left at different ports, or left behind, she found herself the property of a Southern white family by her twelfth birthday. At war's end, "emancipation" would free her to marry Will Roberson and become the mother of eight children. She would watch as her sons, grandsons, and great-grandsons left these shores to defend a country which on their return, relegated them to the routine horrors and degradations of racial segregation and discrimination. One hundred years after coming to America, in the middle of the 1960s, amid the social explosions of Northern and Southern cities, civil rights marches, firebombings of churches, beatings and murders of black men, women, children, and their white allies, she died. In over 112 years of life she would witness the continuation of a slowly moving struggle which had presumably ended with her emancipation. The simple unabridged right to vote and the desegregation of public facilities would for too many years remain too much for black Americans to ask without risking life and limb. In over a century of life, she would not see America keep its promise of "freedom and justice for all." What is more, her children would not live to see it. Her grandchildren would not see it. Both her great- and great-great-grandchildren remain challenged by the require- ment to manage the dominant culture's prejudices and barriers amid the continuing admonition that "changing these things takes time." The question that remains for black people is how many generations of our time are or should be required to demonstrate our right to the same opportunities granted white Americans at birth.

This undermines my faith in American institutions to protect me or mine unless it conceals an exploitive purpose. It is this frame of reference which is brought to bear on my understanding of femi- nism as a philosophy, as opposed to its practice, and of both the possibilities in black and white alliances and the barriers to them.

## THE WOMEN'S RIGHTS MOVEMENT: BLACK WOMEN NEED NOT APPLY

The nineteenth-century women's rights movement has some of its origins in the struggles for the abolition of slavery. While the abolitionist movement included many notable white women's rights activists, their advocacy for the end of slavery did not include advocacy for a change in racial hierarchies. Involvement in the abolitionist and women's rights movements did not provide its white supporters with a "spiritual transformation" on the matter of racial equality (hooks, 1981). Rather, the racism which permeated American society in the nineteenth century and continues to the present was reflected in a women's rights movement in which Southern and Northern white women vigorously supported racial segregation across class lines (Davis, 1981; Giddings, 1984; hooks, 1981). Many, including Elizabeth Cady Stanton, expressed indigna- tion that "inferior niggers would be granted the right to vote while superior white women remained disenfranchised" (Harley & Ter- borg-Penn, 1978).

Susan B. Anthony asked veteran feminist supporter Frederick Douglass not to attend the National American Woman Suffrage Association convention in Atlanta in the early 1890s so as not to jeopardize the wooing of Southern white women, who most vehe- mently opposed having black women join them as members in women's clubs (Giddings, 1984; Harley & Terborg-Penn, 1978; hooks, 1981; Hull, Bell-Scott, & Smith, 1982).

White feminists as a group have continued the American traditions of their foremothers in presenting a slowly changing but still frequently arrogant and unexamined white, middle-class perspective on what issues are important to all women. Cole (1986) refers to this as a "homogenizing of women's diverse cultures . . . in the interest of paying homage to a mythical uniformity called sisterhood." This perspective fails to incorporate many unique and important aspects of and concerns in black women's lives. Among those issues pertinent to this discussion are considerations of visibility and invisibility, and the concept of privilege.

For black women there is a ubiquitous factor of the visibility of skin color. When one's racial minority status is disparaged and visible it means that you have no choice about being the target of racism, nor can you conceal your status when it is dangerous. As a result, black women must respond to that racism, consciously or unconsciously, in ways that may be collectively similar as well as unique to the individual, reflecting the diversity among black women as a group. In addition to the issue of skin color privilege, institutional racism has created hierarchies of privilege associated with skin color variations. Social and physical desirability associated with lighter skin left black women with the issue of skin color privilege, and the jealousies, resentments, and shame which accompany social meanings attached to skin color. The fact that black women cannot generally conceal their racial identity does not mean that Jewish women should reveal their ethnicity when confronted with threats to their safety. "Passing" was a survival technique employed by black persons with light skin color and straighter hair textures. While this survival technique may become a liability when used on a long-term basis, it was often effective in helping its users escape imminent disaster or to obtain material goods, services, or jobs which would not be rendered to a black person. In essence, a black person "passed" when they allowed an observer or observers to assume that they were white, consciously concealing the true nature of their ethnic identity.

Individuals have the right to make distinctions between appropriate assertiveness and taking unnecessary physical or psychological risks of harm. For black women however there is no question about whether or not they will have to overtly manage the dominant culture's projections and distortions about who they are in conjunction with the license given to individuals, by the institutions of the dominant culture, to behave as if the distortions they have created are true. The only real question is how one will address them at any given time.

The phenomena associated with racism are ubiquitous, insidious, and subtle. For most black persons, they constitute a daily, continuous barrage of what Maya Angelou depicts as "the little murders and petty humiliations." For many others, racism takes on the proportions of "the grand executions" which are by definition life threatening (Angelou, 1989). They consist of the looks, gestures, insulting remarks, double standards for the same phenomena, and exclusion from many avenues of opportunity. Whether they require a direct or indirect response, they always take their toll and must be managed in addition to all other life stresses.

Despite our physical visibility, our needs, perspectives, and contributions to this society are neither considered nor integrated. We are expected to cheerfully serve when required and, like the stereotype of the mammy, fade invisibly into the woodwork when others' agendas have been addressed. In popular movies and television, there is frequently a mammy figure who cheerfully takes care of the white family that employs her. Her own family and her personal needs are usually invisible. These depictions reinforce the notion that her existence focuses on serving whites and that she is delighted to do so. Derivatives of this historically unidimensional view of black women are still with us in contemporary environments.

For black people, there is a consistent issue of safety. It is not safe to be black in America. Black males have never been allowed by white males to protect black females. Black families are limited in the ways that they can protect their children. All mothers fear the impact of the criminal elements of our society, and the dangers they pose to their children's development and their lives. Black men and women, however, are disproportionately the victims of violent crimes and are often the victims of the very institutions charged with our protection. For a black mother, police brutality as a danger to her children, particularly but not exclusively to her young male children, is a significant and realistic concern.

This history and present context of double standards for the same phenomena suggest that the concepts of work and privilege must be reexamined. Work outside the home is often presented as the key to white women's liberation (Cole, 1986; hooks, 1981). This fails to take into account the experience of black women who were brought into this country as unpaid, and later cheap, labor and were sexually exploited in the same process. We must acknowledge the difference between having the opportunity to work and having to work. Our history has never included being idealized, even with its pitfalls, as wife and mother; rather we were blamed for the family ills attributable to institutional racism. Work for black women is usually seen as an inescapable, burdensome necessity about which we have little choice and for which we will be paid less than our white counterparts. It was often our white counterparts who were our employers. In their work in many white women's homes, black women did not find themselves treated as "sisters" and did not find white women behaving as allies in a struggle against a mutual oppressor. For many of us, being liberated from the expectation of a life of work within and outside the home, often for lower wages, would be truly liberating.

Money, status, and education, often perceived as privileges which enhance one's life chances, do not do so for black women in the ways that they may for white women. While black women may have different levels of advantage relative to one another, they do not have the same range of choices and options as their white counterparts. They are still required to demonstrate both their humanity and credibility, despite any credentials they may possess. Acceptance and often entry into many levels of mainstream American life, be it jobs, housing, or social status remains a privilege accorded those with white skin regardless of their ethnicity, and continues to overtly and covertly exclude all but a few black persons. Similarly, while many Jewish women have economic privilege, high levels of education, and political influence born in part of white skin privilege, those privileges do not necessarily compensate for oppression in the spheres of ethnicity and gender (Smith, 1992). Both Jewish women and middle-class or affluent black women are often treated by members of both groups as if their class standing renders them immune to serious forms of race and gender oppression, because the form that oppression assumes is often less visible. Furthermore, the oppression and exclusion of black people by white people, and the image of white women, regardless of ethnicity, as "pampered," makes it difficult for many black women to see any white person as oppressed (Smith, 1992).

## AFRICAN AMERICAN AND JEWISH WOMEN: TENSIONS AND ALLIANCES

This leads to a consideration of alliances between black and Jewish women and contemporary tensions between black and white women. The history of black men and women in America is one of being unwilling participants in our immigration. We have been abused, used, and legally objectified in all spheres. Paradoxically, this occurs in a land which formally professes to value cultural diversity and democracy. The personal biases and bigotries of white persons are interwoven in the fabric of and legitimized by America's most basic institutions. The personal bigotries of black people, and the problems associated with internalized racism, which must be acknowledged and are certainly troublesome, are not legitimized as a part of America's institutions. This may intensify our experience of racism. White persons may perceive racial discrimination as isolated and personal, whereas black persons may experience such incidents as having more than person-to-person implications. We are, as black persons, used to being outsiders and observing white persons and their lives closely. We do this as America's domestics and servants, as well as members of a marginal group, forced to understand the workings of the dominant culture in ways that its members are never required to understand us.

This history may predispose black women to be wary of alliances with white women, regardless of their ethnicity. In the eyes of black women, Jewish women accrue and use the privileges accorded to people with white skin just as much as white women of other ethnic groups. This does not imply that Jewish women are responsible for erecting the system of American white skin privilege, rather, that they benefit from it to some extent. Smith (1992), however, warns that while Jewish women benefit from white skin privilege, they may not do so equally when compared to other white women. It is acknowledged that many Jewish women may accrue those privileges only if they covertly agree to conceal and in some way relinquish their Jewish identity. This form of assimilation, however, carries the danger of internalizing the dominant culture's racism and its anti-semitism as well. While ethnic invisibility conceals Jewish women from those who would be dangerous, it unfortunately renders them invisible as well to those who might be seen as potential allies.

Similarities in the struggles of African American and Jewish persons may make it difficult to understand racial tensions or gaps in understanding between them; however, the realistic magnitude of those tensions may be overstated. There is no substantive evidence of any more or less tension between African American and Jewish women than between African American and white women in general. Jewish women may harbor the unfounded expectation that racial tension should not exist between black and Jewish women at all; if they believe they understand and support our struggles they will be perplexed and may feel betrayed by evidence of these tensions.

We are often presented to one another as if we are competitors pitted against one another. Perhaps if one hears this enough one may begin to behave as if it were true. What is important however is that we do not accept this presumption too readily, but rather inquire as to what purpose might be served by having us believe it, and who would be best served by it. Rarely do African Americans or Jewish people truly benefit in the long run when such divisive tactics are successful.

We need to question the need for such concepts as "black anti-Semitism" and "Jewish racism." Do these phenomena substantively differ from anti-Semitism and racism? Why is special language necessary to articulate them? Do they not indicate a notion that both black and Jewish people are to be held to a higher standard of ethical behavior toward each other than white persons?

This does not mean that our respective heritages are, or are experienced, as the same. Black women have a legacy of not being heard in America. The experiences of white persons have been institutionalized as the normative experience, and their views of black persons are presumed to represent the realities of who and what we are. One result of this practice is that some white women's experiences and needs have been accepted by white people as the standard for all women. These views are often based on what the dominant culture's needs are at any given time, rather than on a realistic and respectful assessment of who *we* are. Furthermore, those assessments often reflect rationales intended to justify our exploitation.

As an African American woman I suggest that we need our perspectives to be heard before we can believe or be assured that they are understood. This can only be accomplished if we are present in significant numbers in all levels of decision making in organizations that purport to represent our interests, and if we are speaking for ourselves and not having others presume to speak for us.

The comparison of our oppression as black people to that of other immigrant groups as "the same" can be demeaning and insulting to black women, as it has traditionally been used to minimize our experience, deny aspects of the uniqueness of that experience, and deny our access to opportunities accorded to white persons. The minimization of our experience of oppression stands in stark contrast to the appropriate importance accorded to remembering the Holocaust, exploring the losses associated with it and the meaning of those losses to its survivors and their descendants. Discussions of slavery and its connection to the contemporary experiences and perceptions of African Americans is usually met with the notion that this historical episode ended with emancipation and has little bearing on the current status of African Americans or their view of themselves as Americans. The importance of assessing the impact of this historical period on African Americans is underscored by Toni Morrison who notes that slavery for black people was like having World War II for 200 years.[1] In this context of resentment, anger, and confusion, Smith (1992) warns that responding to the natural temptation to react to racism from Jewish persons by "throwing anti-Semitism back at them," while understandable, has the ultimate effect of "lining us up with our enemies in an intricate system of oppression that, by definition, we oppose if we are feminist."

We share with Jewish persons a history of genocide, oppression, and a loss of millions of our people's lives and talents in some of humanity's most shameful and loathsome tributes to greed, cruelty, entitlement, and fear. We share experiences of being targeted as the reason for the inadequacies, insecurities, envy, and disappointments of others. We cannot however assume that to understand one's own oppression is to understand another's, or that it precludes oppressive behavior toward others. Perhaps the contrary should be expected. We know that persons who are abused as children often go on to repeat this legacy with their own children, unless they are helped to understand what they have been taught about themselves and others.

We must move to the level of acknowledging different levels and kinds of exploitation, as well as privilege, without seeing them dichotomously as either the same or in direct competition with one another, but perhaps as simply different. Smith (1992) accurately notes that anti-Semitism, like racism, has assumed many different forms and that neither is invalid simply because it is not identical to the other. Furthermore, she asserts that there is much diversity among white women as a group, just as this diversity is reflected among black women as a group. We must therefore be wary of reductionistic explanations of these complex phenomena and their equally complicated sequelae. Feminist organizations, like other well-intentioned groups, often come together under the naive halo of sisterhood and unity without any meaningful exploration of the diversity within or between groups of women or of what forms it may assume. Inevitably, if such organizations grow, they encounter the difficult, often unexpected and frequently painful, struggle of incorporating those differences into the group's agenda. The struggle to do this is often perceived as a threat to a presupposed "unity."

Women who consider themselves feminists are not free of the many troublesome attitudes and struggles that all other human beings face. Aspiring to the ideals of feminism and making a commitment to the struggle this inevitably entails, however, makes as good a starting point in this undertaking as any. Perhaps that is a good place to begin.

# NOTE

1. Toni Morrison made this comment during a television interview with Bill Moyers sometime in 1991 or 1990, but I have been unable to locate the precise reference.

# REFERENCES

Allen, Lewis (1939, April). *Strange fruit.* Original Recording by Billie Holiday, 20 April 1939, New York. Edwin B. Marks Music Corp. BMI.

Angelou, Maya (1989). [Interview with Maya Angelou and Alice Walker]. The Oprah Winfrey Show [televised broadcast]. 6 June. Chicago, IL: American Broadcasting Company.

Cole, Johnetta (1986). *All American women: Lines that divide, ties that bind.* New York: Free Press.

Davis, Angela (1981). *Women, race and class.* New York: Vintage Books.

Ehle, John (1988). *Trail of tears: The rise and fall of the Cherokee nation.* New York: Anchor Doubleday.

Giddings, Paula (1984). *When and where I enter: The impact of black women on race and sex in America.* New York: Morrow.

Harley, Sharon, & Terborg-Penn, Rosalyn (Eds.) (1978). *The Afro-American woman: Struggles and images.* Port Washington, NY: Kennikat Press.

hooks, bell (1981). *black women and feminism.* Boston: South End Press.

Hull, Gloria T., Bell-Scott, Patricia, & Smith, Barbara (Eds.) (1982). *All the women are white, all the blacks are men, but some of us are brave: black women's studies.* Old Westbury, NY: Feminist Press.

Smith, Barbara (1992). Between a rock and a hard place: Relationships between black and Jewish women. In J. Salzman (Ed.), *Bridges and boundaries: African Americans and American Jews* (pp. 136-140). New York: George Braziller in association with the Jewish Museum of New York.

# In the Beginning–Again

Ellyn Kaschak

It is Sunday morning at 11 a.m., California time. My telephone rings, but I already know that it is the operator placing a three-way conference call. I am ready with a pen, paper, and a steaming cup of coffee. It is the hour that Beverly, Rachel, and I have set aside to continue our ongoing discussions of racism and anti-Semitism as we have experienced them in our lives and especially in our years in the feminist movement. We will discover in these conversations differences in our individual experiences, as well as commonalities in our perceptions, fears, and hopes. We will discover a tentativeness, an uncertainty with ourselves and each other about how much truth we can stand, a kind of danger even in the relative safety of our shared commitment to living our feminist beliefs. These discoveries will be implemented not by a group facilitator, but by telephones, modems, and FAX machines–the consciousness-raising paraphernalia of professional women in the 1990s.

While Rachel and Beverly are both speaking from their homes in New York State, I find myself three time zones away from my original home, also in New York; three times zones further into the diaspora. On these designated Sundays, we try awkwardly and painstakingly (taking the pain) to find just the right words to begin a trialogue. And first there are the questions. I ask myself how I got involved in this discussion with these particular women and more unexpectedly with myself. We are of different generations with different experiences. Rachel's and my skin are the color that society names white while naming Beverly's black, although, significantly enough, neither of the colors that we name black or white would be so named anywhere but on the human flesh, by virtue of which society and history conspire to divide us.

I demand of myself and of these other two women as much courage and honesty as each of us can bring to these discussions. I demand of myself that I go back to my beginnings yet another time. I believe that fully engaged anti-racism activism has to start with the act of reclamation and the insistence on the fullness of my own experience. So we begin the excavation, the reclamation project, as carefully as if a tangible structure is going to stand upon the foundation we are helping to create. In reality something of much greater consequence is in the making.

And just where is the beginning for me? Perhaps with a family that kept its past a secret. There were no stories to pass through the generations, neither example nor admonition. The silence itself was the loudest admonition of all. There would be no memories, no demons from which to run, no holocaust, and even further—no pogroms, no rapes, no murders and terrors just for sport, just for the fun of it, just a drunken night out, just for being Jews. After all we were Americans. Yet, in many ways, I have spent my life fleeing from memories of things I never experienced or was even told about. Until recently I would not have said that I was fleeing, but rather traveling, sightseeing in other people's lives as a psychologist and psychotherapist; a guide on other people's journeys, a visitor from another psyche.

The words that the three of us speak on these Sundays begin to matter, to alter the foundation of these ancient fears. These conversations are to become for me a pivotal part of remembering a home I never had, of a nostalgia for a future that may be possible. They are conversations that actually began generations ago. The three of us continue them, trying to move ourselves closer to understanding, to changing, to finding ourselves, and even to finding our way to each other.

Perhaps there is another place for me to begin. Some years ago, I joined a feminist organization already several years in existence. Soon after joining, and on two completely separate occasions, I was taken aside by two Jewish women members, who firmly cautioned me with almost identical words. "We are working on diversity in this group and we don't mean issues of Jewish women. There are already too many of us." This was said to me in a conspiratorial tone with an assurance that I would know exactly what they meant. And what amazed me most is that I did. As insiders, we were outsiders. By virtue of being too visible, we—or at least an important aspect of each of us—must be kept invisible. Somehow to be invisible is to be safe from harm.

What was the nature of the unchallenged and almost invisible anti-Semitism in this feminist organization? Was it a more general influence in other women's organizations and in the feminist movement itself? If so, how was it being internalized, or at least not questioned, by Jewish women? Apparently I could be visible among my feminist colleagues, but my Jewishness could not. This was not so difficult for me as it might seem, as my Jewishness was scarcely visible to me at the time. I could just leave it that way. I had little idea what it meant to me to be a Jew, but I knew that, if I wasn't supposed to think about it, then I had better start doing so right away. My interest was captured.

Viscerally at least, I understood that Jews were too visible and were somehow both in danger and to blame, but, upon reflection, I realized that I didn't understand at all. Exactly what were we to blame for? Exactly what and from whom were we hiding and why? Who were "we" anyway?

So I considered some possible answers.

1. Jewish women are too powerful and too pushy, let alone feminist Jewish women.
2. We are competing for limited resources and should not infringe upon the gains of women of color.
3. Jewish women are just regular (generic) white women and must move over and make room for women of color. Jewish women of color do not exist.
4. Jewish women are among the most privileged and, therefore, culpable of white women and, as such, are conspicuous.
5. In keeping with the principles of neo-femininity currently in vogue, we should be aware that women are relational and are more comfortable (and should be) working for the needs of others than for ourselves. The latter would be selfish, if not

downright masculine. Thus, Jewish women should not express concern about the issues of Jewish women.

As I thought about these possibilities, I felt a welling fear of being seen if these were the ways I would be seen. Both invisibility and visibility were dangerous. Or perhaps what passed for visibility was closer to transparency in its presumptuousness.

Certainly I had grown up on the borders, as an outsider in many ways as a Jewish woman, a position that was implicated in my stance on many other issues. Yet none of the stories that I had heard told by other Jewish women were mine. Was I even united with other Jewish feminists and, if so, in what ways? Jewish was not the first or even the second or third adjective that I would have used to describe myself.

The life-changing strength of feminism has been its grounding in and insistence upon knowing women's real experience. Once again I had to think about who I am and how it informs my attitudes with respect to resisting and combating racism and anti-Semitism. Although not identical kinds of oppression, neither are they separate. Irena Klepfisz (1990) writes:

> These two facts are permanently etched on my consciousness. (1) The oppressed group divided against itself, incapacitated, paralyzed, unable to pull together while the enemy grows stronger and more efficient. (2) Two oppressed groups facing a common enemy unable to overcome ancient hatreds, struggling separately. . . . And I think about these two facts whenever I hear about a completely Jewish demonstration against the American Nazi Party in the Midwest and then hear about a completely Black demonstration against the same American Nazi Party, this time on the East Coast. (p. 57)

Feminist politics are not an abstraction, but a lived practice. While many feminists invoke the principles of diversity and anti-racism work, practicing them is not an easy thing. I certainly do not mean to oversimplify the reasons for the difficulties, which are complex and have a long history, but I do believe that to do this work genuinely and effectively, we have to begin again with ourselves, not with abstract, external, and "objective," or even altruistic, principles. Even invoking good and correct principles like justice, who is, after all, blind, leads us only further away from ourselves, for our task is to see, not to be blinded. My task was to understand how I live my own ethnicity and how it informs my other personal and political values and actions. That is, as the personal is political, so must the political be personal.

As the three of us continued to talk, we told each other many, but not all, of our stories. Every person has a rich inner diversity or, better said, this dichotomy between inner and outer is a false one and until each of us can appreciate her own diversities, we cannot be true allies to each other in the shared struggle against racism and anti-Semitism.

As I began to think about my own history, I did not set out to decide which was my real story, but which, at the time, mattered to me more than others. As the three of us talked together, a few common themes emerged, which seemed to matter deeply and viscerally to all of us, themes of invisibility and the concomitant fear of visibility and of being outside.

For many African-Americans, Jews, and other members of identifiable and identified groups, who we are and are not is persistently defined by others. In this way, we come to know ourselves in opposition to the presumptuousness of others. This results in an experience of fragmentation rather than an appreciation of diversity, a sense of transparency rather than of visibility. My stories begin there, but also say "No" to being defined in opposition either by a Christian or Jewish audience, a black or a white audience. They are not even stories yet, but images, the beginning pieces of a complex puzzle.

## ACT I:
## THE AUTHOR AS A YOUNG JEWISH GIRL

### Scene 1

A comment made by Cynthia Ozick (1983) strikes a chord with me. "My own synagogue is the only place in the world where I am not named Jew" (p. 125). My family was neither self-consciously religious nor opposed to it, but made it clear that religious participation and education, such as it was, was for boys, popularly known as the boys-should-be-bar-mitzvahed school of thought. Otherwise religion was something old-fashioned that our grandparents practiced. This was an interesting intervention and my first experience with a paradoxical injunction utilizing the resistance. That is, in order to rebel, I had to become interested in a Jewish education and, true to form, I did. In the synagogue, I sat in the back and observed. This phase soon passed. It turned out that my parents were right. Religion was for boys. I was an outsider, allowed entrance only in carefully circumscribed ways.

## Scene 2

As a child, I passed most Saturday afternoons at the local matinee with my friends. There we all sat together in the dark offering up hours of childhood to the flickering altar of black and white images before us. On the way home, we would follow the route that took us past the neighborhood Catholic church, where my friends would stop in for confession, while I sat waiting for them on the church steps. At the movies, I was an insider, a best friend, a co-conspirator in mischief. There were no steps outside the theater. Outside the church, I was a Jew. Sorrowfully, I was more a Jew on the church steps than I was in my father's and grandfather's synagogue.

## Scene 3

The Passover Seder, a time to celebrate the release from slavery and from exile. A bittersweet time, a time to remember. Yet the family ritual involves only the youngest and oldest males. Only they seem to have something to remember. My grandfather reads seemingly endless words in a Hebrew that only he understands. As always, there are the questions, but only the youngest boy present is permitted to ask them. I have many questions of my own, but I am silent. "Why is this night the same as all other nights? Why are all the women in the kitchen cooking and preparing the food? Why are only male voices heard? Why don't I belong in either room? Why don't I get to ask any questions?"

## ACT II:
## THE AUTHOR AS AN ADULT AND A FEMINIST

### Scene 1

In my university class on gender and ethnicity, the students un-self-consciously discuss how the churches that they attend or attended as children compare with an African-American congregation in which one student participates. It occurs to none of them that not everyone attends church. In another class, a Jewish student, upon learning that I also am a Jew, says a few words to me in Yiddish that I do not understand. It is an assumption, an attempt at connection which leaves me feeling even more separate. A friend, hearing that I am preparing this article, asks why I do not use a "more Jewish form" than acts and scenes. Why not something from the midrash? I do not know what the midrash is and again the presumed connection sets me apart.

### Scene 2

In my therapy office, I sit in my comfortable leather chair listening intently to the feelings, thoughts, and struggles of those who sit opposite me. We are not always, but are often, separated by more than the yards of oriental carpet that lie between us. What will I say when I hear someone say that she is told by her friends that she must have been Jewish in a previous life because she has such an affinity for Jews. One aspect of that affinity, I later learn, is her propensity to indulge herself "like a Jewish American Princess." Often I hear from patients struggling to convey to me just how difficult their mothers are that they are Jewish mothers even when they are not Jewish. Jewish mothers, they tell me, come in all ethnicities. My heart quickens. Do I respond? What do I say? Why am I more easily and openly indignant when I hear racist comments? Whom am I protecting?

### Scene 3

I attend a feminist Seder unlike those of my childhood, unlike one that could even have been imagined in the years of my childhood. Women cook and clean, but also pray and read and sing and testify. I do not understand most of the Hebrew and do not feel the connection to Judaism that most of them do. The faces around the table are all what society calls white and somehow less interesting to me in their sameness. I miss the familiar sounds of the Spanish language which has become my second language as an adult. How have I come to be fluent in Spanish and ignorant of Yiddish or Hebrew? Yet the language of the Seder is the language of liberation and release from exile and that part matters to me. That it is all said in women's voices matters most of all, for women's voices are my own.

Finally Beverly, Rachel, and I realize regretfully that it is time to bring our discussions to a conclusion. Each of us has come to know herself better. We have moved toward each other, learned about some of our differences, as well as about the ways that we share histories of destruction and betrayal. While we are respectful of and interested in each other's experiences, we have begun to be less polite with each other. We feel a little safer together than we did separately. What reason is there for us to trust each other? Yet we begin to.

I have developed a new appreciation for being an outsider/insider, for how it allows, no, demands cultivation of a multiple perspective, of an ability to maintain the complexity of individual and group membership, of my own and others' experiences. In a very real sense, women are the new immigrants of the American Dream. Yet we must take care neither to assimilate nor to melt, but to respect and maintain our own diversities and differences from each other. The more of myself, neither transparent nor opaque, that I can bring to the struggle, the more self-knowledge and insistence upon the complexity of the questions and of the answers, the more of an ally I can be to other women.

For me, the commitment to these discussions had its source in my experience in a feminist organization. In the inevitable interplay of the inner and the outer, the private and the public, we three present this work at a conference of the very organization whose Jewish members stimulated me to ask these questions. Additionally, several of us join together to found a Jewish Women's Caucus in the same organization. In this way, we create a form within which the voices and lived experiences of Jewish women can be made known to themselves and to others. And as we begin to understand the shape of all our lives as Jews, as women, and as feminists, we can begin to build an alliance with African-American women that rests more firmly on a foundation of self-knowledge, self-acceptance, and the understanding of the forces that both oppress and bind us together in the shared work of liberation.

Act III begins.

## REFERENCES

Klepfisz, Irena (1990). Dreams of an insomniac. *Jewish Feminist Essays, Speeches and Diatribes* (p. 57). Portland, OR: The Eighth Mountain Press. p. 57.

Ozick, Cynthia (1983). Notes toward finding the right question. In Susannah Heschel (Ed.), *On Being A Jewish Feminist*, p. 125 (New York: Schocken Books.

# Rethinking the Role of Guilt and Shame in White Women's Antiracism Work

Clare Holzman

In antiracism workshops I have taken part in and in my reading about antiracism training, the subject of guilt keeps coming up (Katz, 1978, p. 137; Landerman and McAtee, 1982, p. 24; Northwestern University Women's Center Campus Climate Project, 1989; Pheterson, 1986, p. 152; Pinderhughes, 1989, pp. 99-100). There is widespread agreement that guilt is an immediate, powerful response of white women[1] learning about racism, and I seem to be no exception. There is almost equally widespread agreement that my guilt is unproductive and that I should cut it out; but for some reason I continue to feel guilty.[2] This paper is the result of my efforts to understand what is going on inside me that I have been calling guilt, and how I can learn to work through it so that it will be less of an obstacle to my progress toward antiracism.

I have come to three conclusions. First, not all guilt is unproductive. In moderate doses, guilt motivates me to keep trying to change. Second, much of what I and others have been calling guilt may often be shame, which can also be productive if it isn't excessive. Third, when I am trying to explore and modify my racism, whether in an antiracism training situation or in therapy, I am the most open to learning when I am treated in a way that does not itself generate irrational and overwhelming guilt and shame. Furthermore, there are times when what is most useful to me is help in formulating concepts and strategies for coping with my guilt and shame instead of being immobilized by them. If the needs of the group call for a different kind of process, it is my responsibility to seek out other opportunities to work through my guilt and shame issues.

A previous version of this paper was presented at the Advanced Feminist Therapy Institute, Woodstock, Illinois, May 19, 1990.

Guilt and shame have been defined in many contradictory ways (Ausubel, 1955; Banman, 1988; Kaufman, 1985; Klein, 1975a, Lewis, 1971). The following definitions are my composite of the ideas that I have found most helpful in my own self-exploration:

*Guilt is the discomfort I feel when I have done something that harms another person or violates a moral prohibition. Guilt, like anxiety, is a signal that something is amiss and needs to be corrected. Anxiety tells me that I am in danger and need to make myself safer. Guilt tells me that I have done something wrong and need to correct it or make reparation. Irrational guilt is either guilt over something I am not actually responsible for, or guilt whose intensity is disproportionate to the offense.*

*Shame is what I feel when I fail to live up to my ideals for myself. Shame, like guilt, is a signal that prompts me to change my behavior. The focus is not on the harm done to others, but on the defect in myself. Shame involves feelings of exposure and an impulse to hide. In fact, the Indo-European root of the word "shame" also means "to hide." Irrational shame is a feeling of having been exposed as a fundamentally and irremediably defective human being.*

As a white woman living in a racially oppressive society, I have much to feel realistically guilty about. I benefit daily from racial oppression without even having to be aware of it (McIntosh, 1988). To the extent that I passively accept the fruits of my white privilege, I am guilty of colluding with racism to harm its targets for my own benefit. Furthermore, because I have internalized the racist attitudes and beliefs of my society, I often speak and act in racist ways that directly or indirectly harm people of color. When I become aware of a specific way in which I have been passively or actively racist, I feel guilty. This guilt is constructive to the extent that it motivates me to change my attitudes and behavior and to work toward changing racist institutions. I can never be free of this guilt until I live in a society that is no longer racist and until I have overcome my own racism.

My guilt is unproductive when it is misdirected, or when it is so intense that it immobilizes me instead of motivating me. One way this can happen is that my rational guilt can trigger irrational guilt based on early childhood fantasies (Klein, 1975a) or on actual childhood experiences. Another is that I may fail to make a clear distinction between what I am personally responsible for and what I have no control over. Thus, I am responsible for my own actions or failures to act, but I am not responsible for the actions of my ancestors or for the existence of the entire structure of institutionalized racism.[3] Preoccupation with guilt over things beyond my control is often an avoidance of facing the things I can control; making reparation often involves giving something up or doing something difficult or frightening.

The remedy for excessive guilt is to clarify what is real and what is fantasy, what is my responsibility and what is not, and then to turn my attention to what I can do about it in the real world. According to Klein, one of the fringe benefits of making reparation at a reality level is that it reduces the intensity of unconscious guilt as well, freeing me for greater creativity and productive work (1975a, pp. 335-336).

I will have difficulty moving past guilt to constructive work if I am using my guilt to persuade myself that I am a good person (Lewis, p. 44), or to elicit sympathy, or to ward off anticipated attack by others. All of these shift the focus from examining racism to taking care of me. They are especially damaging in group settings where there are women of color present and I turn to them to comfort me and relieve me of my guilt by forgiving me (Pheterson, 1986; Root, 1989). Although comforting words and expressions of forgiveness may be temporarily soothing, the only lasting way to be free of rational guilt is to make reparation.

I said earlier that much of what gets labeled as guilt in antiracism work is in fact shame. Guilt and shame often occur together or sequentially, so it is easy to confuse them (Banman, 1988, p. 85; Lewis, 1971, pp. 27-28). When I feel guilty, I am focused on the harm I have done to the other person or the rule I have broken, and I want to make reparation. When I feel ashamed, I am focused on feelings of exposure, acute self-consciousness, and worthlessness, and I want to hide. Guilt can induce shame, because I may believe that my transgression was caused by my deficiency and reveals it to others. Banman describes a shame/guilt cycle in which "the humiliated fury often experienced in shame leads to an aggressive fantasy or impulse. This impulse usually triggers guilt and inhibition, but since inhibition is perceived as passivity and failure, shame follows" (p. 85). Guilt can also be a defense against shame, and vice versa (Banman, 1988, p. 85; Lewis, 1971, p. 27).

Because I hold the ideal of being nonracist, I will experience shame whenever I am confronted with the persistence of my racism. Since I have been raised in a shame-bound family within a shame-bound culture, healthy shame quickly triggers irrational shame in me. For the moment, I feel that I have exposed myself as a hopeless case, someone who is inherently racist and always will be, or someone who is too stupid, selfish, lazy, or heartless to do the work required to overcome it. At that moment I feel numb and paralyzed. The reactivation of developmentally early shaming experiences throws me back to a time when I had few resources to draw on in coping with my shame (Alonso and Rutan, 1988). I feel helpless, impotent, and vulnerable. When I feel intense shame, I am unable to think clearly or act effectively. I just want the ground to open and swallow me up. Obviously this is not a productive emotional state in which to try to learn what to do about racism.

Becoming aware that I am feeling shame, especially if I am being observed by others, is itself a shaming experience (Kaufman, 1985, p. 29; Lewis, 1971, p. 27). I feel that if I am experiencing shame, I must have something to be ashamed of, and now everyone else will know it too. For this reason, and because shame has its origins in preverbal experiences, I rarely talk about my shame, so I have few opportunities to resolve it (Alonso and Rutan, 1988, p. 6). Instead, I carry within me an enormous reservoir of old shame that is waiting to be reactivated by any new shaming experience.

One way in which I can prepare myself to confront my racism is to arrange for supportive environments in which to work through old shame so that the total burden that is waiting to sandbag me will be reduced. Then when I work on unlearning my racism, I can give myself permission to experience rational shame without fearing that it will trigger a catastrophic reaction.

When I feel either guilt or shame, I often become angry at the person I perceive as the cause of my distressing feelings (Banman, 1988, p. 85;). I also project my own "badness" onto the other person (Klein, 1975b). Both of these mechanisms prompt me to attack the other person by counterblaming (Zuk and Zuk, 1987,

p. 224). This diverts attention from my faults to those of someone else. It allows me to feel powerful instead of helpless, and creates distance between me and the other person so that I feel less vulnerable. In order to identify and work on my racism, I must learn to recognize and restrain my impulse to counterblame and keep the focus on examining myself.

Guilt and shame are appropriate emotional responses to becoming aware of one's racism, and can be major sources of motivation for change. However, in order for these emotions to be productive rather than immobilizing, many white women will need a training or therapy experience that provides a structure, a conceptual framework, and concrete strategies for dealing with guilt and shame constructively and keeping them at or returning them to the rational level. In antiracism training settings, this experience may be one component of a larger program, or may be offered as a specialized workshop focusing on this particular topic. In therapy, it will be helpful for the therapist to keep in mind that whenever the issue of racism comes up, whether it is raised by the client as something she wants to work on or by the therapist in response to racism expressed by the client, issues of guilt and shame are likely to be present.

In order for a woman to risk the extreme vulnerability associated with guilt and shame, it is important that the trainer or therapist be scrupulously and explicitly respectful of her boundaries, dignity, and fundamental worth. Shaming techniques such as belittling, sarcasm, or expressions of disgust, contempt, or condemnation are counterproductive. They reproduce childhood shaming experiences and are likely to trigger irrational shame (Kaufman, 1985, pp. 18-22). In a group setting, the trainers must not only maintain these standards themselves, they also have the task of guiding the participants in maintaining them in relation to one another. For many white women, an important step in unlearning racism has been an attempt to become aware of all the racist ideas we have been harboring and suppressing and to express them out loud in order to get help in exploring them thoroughly (Adams and Schlesinger, 1988, pp. 208-210; Pinderhughes, 1989, pp. 224-225). This is a process that is never completed, and it is difficult for it to happen at all unless there is some assurance of safety from attack. In the absence of such safety, there is a tendency to parrot what is believed to be acceptable to the group, and for the learning process to be drastically inhibited. (Careful thought must be given to the impact of this process on any women of color who may be present. They should have the option of absenting themselves from the training at this point.)

An analysis of racism as a system that is imposed on individuals, both oppressors and oppressed, helps to alleviate irrational guilt and shame. The analysis developed by Ricky Sherover-Marcuse is a good example of this. It stresses that no one is born a racist or chooses to become a racist, that we all resisted and were damaged by our induction into the system, and that what we have learned can be unlearned.

A discussion of the normality, inevitability, and usefulness of guilt and shame in the process of unlearning racism will help a woman not to feel guilty and ashamed about feeling guilty and ashamed. She will benefit from encouragement to talk about these feelings when they arise, help in distinguishing rational from irrational guilt or shame, and support in exploring how to move from feelings to constructive action.

People differ in the extent to which guilt and shame are central to their experience, and in their readiness to explore them. It is counterproductive to try to impose these concepts on a woman who does not perceive them as relevant to herself. In group settings, different women will be at different points in their resolution of guilt and shame issues, and the needs and goals of the group as a whole may call for a different focus. It is important, however, that these issues not be dismissed without providing some validation that they are legitimate causes for concern and that they can be worked through successfully.

To summarize, guilt and shame are powerful emotions that are frequently evoked when white women attempt to explore and modify their racism. Although intense, irrational guilt and shame can be immobilizing, moderate levels of these emotions can serve as useful signals that a woman is not living up to her standards for herself and as productive motivators for change. Therapists and trainers can help a woman to work through guilt and shame issues by providing a supportive environment in which to explore them, a conceptual framework for understanding them, and strategies for coping with them. The payoff is increased freedom to think clearly and act effectively in resisting racism.

## NOTES

1. The concept of race and the racial categories used are inventions of the human mind and have political consequences. There are valid objections to all of the terms currently in use to designate race, and yet we have to use some set of terms in order to communicate. In this paper "white women" means women who benefit from the privilege accorded to those who are so designated; "women of color" means women who experience racist oppression.

2. Katz (1978), Landerman and McAtee (1982), and Pinderhughes (1989) discuss the need to work through guilt feelings in the group. Although Landerman and McAtee describe guilt as a natural and inevitable part of the process for white women confronting racism, I have found no reference that considers it constructive. Katz talks about the need to transform guilt into a motivating force, and supports feelings of internal conflict and responsibility, but characterizes guilt per se as "self-indulgence" that "benefits no one."

3. This concept may be specific to contemporary Anglo-American culture, with its emphasis on individualism. In some cultures, guilt and shame because of the actions of one's ancestors, family members, or others with whom one is closely connected may be an integral part of the culture. These cultures may also have institutionalized ways of coping with guilt and shame based on the behavior of others. I am grateful to Gloria Enguídanos for bringing this to my attention.

## REFERENCES

Adams, Anne Currin, & Schlesinger, Elfriede G. (1988). Group approach to training ethnic-sensitive practitioners. In Carolyn Jacobs & Dorcas D. Bowles (Eds.), *Ethnicity and race: Critical concepts in social work* (pp. 204-216). Silver Spring, MD: NASW.

Alonso, Anne, & Rutan, J. Scott. (1988). The experience of shame and the restoration of self-respect in group therapy. *International Journal of Group Psychotherapy, 38,* 3-14.

Ausubel, David P. (1955). Relationships between shame and guilt in the socializing process. *Psychological Review, 62,* 378-390.

Banman, John (1988). Guilt and shame: Theories and therapeutic possibilities. *International Journal for the Advancement of Counseling, 11,* 79-91.

Katz, Judy H. (1978). *White awareness.* Norman, OK: University of Oklahoma Press.

Kaufman, Gershen (1985). *Shame: The power of caring* (rev. ed.). Rochester, VT: Schenkman Books.

Klein, Melanie (1975a). *Love, Guilt, and Reparation.* New York: Delacorte Press/ Seymour Lawrence, 306-343.

_____ (1975b). *Envy and Gratitude.* New York: Delacorte Press/Seymour Lawrence, 1-24.

Landerman, Donna, & McAtee, Mary (1982). Breaking the racism barrier. *Aegis, 33,* 16-26.

Lewis, Helen Block (1971). *Shame and guilt in neurosis.* New York: International Universities Press.

McIntosh, Peggy (1988). *White privilege and male privilege: A personal account of coming to see correspondences through work in women's studies.* Working Paper No. 189. Wellesley, MA: Center for Research on Women, Wellesley College.

Northwestern University Women's Center Campus Climate Project. CCP Workshops. Unpublished manuscript, 1989, p. 1.

Pheterson, Gail (1986). Alliances between women: Overcoming internalized oppression and internalized domination. *Signs, 12,* 146-160. Reprinted in Lisa A. Albrecht & Rose M. Brewer (Eds.) 1990. *Bridges of Power.* Santa Cruz, CA: New Society Publishers.

Pinderhughes, Elaine (1989). *Understanding race, ethnicity, and power.* New York: Free Press.

Root, Maria P. P. (1989). An open letter of resignation. *FTI Interchange, 7*(3), 4.

Zuk, Gerald H., & Zuk, Carmen V. (1987). Parental blaming and the acquisition of guilt: A developmental task of childhood. *Contemporary Family Therapy, 9,* 221-228.

# On Becoming One's Own Theorist: A Puerto Rican Journey Toward Antiracist and Antisexist Family Therapy

### Gloria M. Enguídanos

Sex roles are very well-defined in Puerto Rican culture. Either by necessity or by choice, these roles change as a woman–either alone or within a family–moves to the United States mainland and confronts the demands of acculturation. The development of increased independence is unavoidable, especially if she is employed outside of the home. These changes may affect more than a woman's psychological integrity; the cohesion of the family may also be threatened.

However strong their need to feel liberated, Puerto Rican women have not followed the Anglo version of the feminist movement, whether as a result of the different agenda each group has or as a consequence of the racism felt by Hispanic[1] women. Confronting the mainland's racism and oppression of Puerto Ricans is devastating not only because they suffer wounding of their self-esteem, but because they find this kind of prejudice incomprehensible. Having been raised in a country where a mixture of races peacefully coexist, they find it impossible to understand that their worth in the U.S. is measured by their skin color or by their accent when they speak English. This devaluation is experienced by both women and men. As one woman told me, "I have more in common with Puerto Rican men, since we are both victims of racism, than with Anglo women, who see their struggle as separate from men. These women have not known racism as we have. They really do not understand."

## FAMILIES IN TRANSITION

The process of acculturation can be defined as development of the ability to adopt from the larger Anglo society the cultural skills

*333*

necessary to function in an Anglo country, without sacrificing the person's original identity and integrity. In contrast, assimilation occurs when individuals relinquish personal identity in an effort to *imitate* cultural patterns in order to integrate themselves into the larger society.

The acculturative process seems to me to be more difficult and to take longer for *puertorriqueños* than for any other Hispanic group. This may be because of the functional proximity of the island, primarily for those who settle in the New York area and tend to take advantage of low air fares and convenient flight schedules to travel back and forth frequently. Another factor is their relationships with family still in Puerto Rico. Losing the Puerto Rican identity due to assimilation into Anglo culture could bring rejection from those family members remaining on the island, a price too high to pay in a society where family contact and approval are of prime importance.

Regardless of the rate and level of adaptation, when Puerto Rican women come in contact with the majority culture, they may go through psychological changes that will affect not only their sense of self but also their interaction with family members. Intergenerational conflicts occur when children learn the new language faster than their parents and acquire values, attitudes and sex roles that differ from those of their parents (Ramírez, 1969).

Ho (1987) summarizes beautifully the five primary values that Puerto Ricans adhere to, the first of which is *familismo*, or the need to place the family ahead of their personal needs. This is part of a matriarchal tradition of extended family responsibilities and inviolable ties. It can appear overwhelming and is often misunderstood by Anglos as an unhealthy dependency system.

*Personalismo* is an inner dignity and an expectation of respect for that dignity. If I show respect for you, I will demand from you that same respect for myself. This indicates a personal sense of worth which has implications in therapeutic work with Puerto Ricans.

*Espiritualismo* (which is different from *espiritismo*) is the acknowledgment that unless we have the assistance of a higher power we have difficulty finding meaning and fulfillment in life. Some of us also believe that we can contact that higher power directly.

*Espiritismo*, which many Puerto Ricans profess, is the belief that there is an invisible world surrounding the one that is visible to all of us. A mixture of African, European, and Indian religious traditions forms the historical foundation for *espiritismo*. Spirits, who exist in the invisible world, have the power to either harm or protect us, and we are better off being aware of them.

Finally, they cultivate a sense of *fatalismo* and destiny. They hold a reverence for both the spirit and the soul, which engenders a sense of fate. This belief, that whatever happens in a person's life is part of that individual's fate which is determined from birth, may explain why Puerto Ricans underutilize mental health services. The sense of *fatalismo* leads us to accept tragic events at the same time that it helps prevent despair. The belief persists that nothing can be done to change the course, dynamics, or nature of any person's life experiences. Both the tragic political fate of the island and the frequent tropical hurricanes have contributed to and reinforced Puerto Rican *fatalismo*.

## ISSUES CONCERNING THERAPY

Ho (1987) found several techniques to be useful and relevant when working with ethnic minorities. For example, he believes that system communication and family structure theories can be helpful in explaining the new interactions of recent immigrants when they are confronted with the larger Anglo society. He also maintains that ecological, systemic, and emic[2] approaches can be helpful in dealing with the problem of being poor and part of a minority in this country. He feels, however, that more work is needed to make those theories culturally and ethnically specific.

According to certain early family therapists (e.g., Minuchin, 1974; Haley, 1973, 1976; Ackerman, 1958; Whitaker, 1975), a person's sense of autonomy is conditioned by his or her participation in the family subsystem, a subsystem which is based on the superiority of the father as head of the household. If this is so, and I believe it is too often the case, then such family therapy promotes the dominance of men over women (Bograd, 1990; Hare-Mustin 1989; Goldner, 1989; Walters, 1990). Kaschak (1992) also believes that "the basic power inequity of gender differences and the influence of larger social systems, such as gender arrangements, have been deemed irrelevant and thus steadfastly ignored by mainstream family system theorists" (p. 17).

Some authors are attempting to develop more relevant techniques. One example is the recent book *Metaframeworks* (Breunlin, Schwartz, & MacKune-Karrer, 1992). In their words, these authors intend to "transcend individual models of therapy" by taking "disparate models and linking them together" (p. 7). This position assumes that one can, depending on the circumstances, move easily from one theory or technique to another when involved with helping individuals as well as families. Since I believe that a good therapist is her or his own theorist, this concept is appealing to me. If one considers that family therapists frequently have difficulty looking at the individual apart from the family, and that practitioners of individual therapy seldom consider the family system, the ability to move from one theory or technique to another seems valuable. No single theory of either individual or family therapy can conceptualize the complexity of human experience and how specific groups process those experiences. The authors of *Metaframeworks* suggest that "placing theories within particular domains essentially classifies them and allows us to search for underlying patterns among the ideas represented by the theories" (pp. 23-24).

## MY OWN STORY AS A CASE STUDY

Both sides of my family moved from Spain to Puerto Rico around the middle-to-late 1800s. My mother's father was a medical doctor who also composed music for the clavichord. My father's family, who came to Puerto Rico as political figures, were also landowners. My father continued in his father's trade; he owned the coffee and sugar cane plantation where I spent a crucial part of my developmental years.

My mother instilled in her children the *familismo* which had been conveyed to her. She was a kind, generous, abnegated mother who dedicated her life to us and to those grandchildren who later lived with her. She had many artistic skills that she passed on to me, and I to my children. From our father we acquired a sense of pride and dignity as well as intellectual curiosity. Since both parents are now deceased, I can only wonder if they knew how successful they were in transferring their legacy to us, especially their daughters. My sister and I, as well as my daughter and those nieces I know best, are all independent, high achievers, opinionated, and well-educated.

Both my sister and I promised our father before we married that we would not abandon the completion of our college education. I married a University of Puerto Rico professor who was ten years my senior. He had fled Spain in an attempt to escape the dictatorship of Francisco Franco. Many Spanish intellectuals were forced to leave their country for fear of government reprisal and were lured to Puerto Rico because it was both a Spanish-speaking country and a United States territory offering the "advantage" of U.S. citizenship.

I was dazzled by the celebrity of these Spanish intellectuals who were often guests in our home. Eventually, the self-centeredness of some of them and the inequality of my relationship with them, which mirrored my relationship with my husband, became a burden to our marriage. Under these and other disproportional stresses our relationship started to crumble. In an attempt to rescue the marriage, we came to the United States seeking an experimental change of life-style for one year. My husband got a teaching position with the University of Texas. We arrived in Texas with our Puerto Rican-born daughter, and a baby on the way. I not only suffered under the difficulties of a pregnancy, but I did not know enough English to carry on an intelligent conversation. I felt very lonely for my family back in Puerto Rico and for my culture, and had a very difficult time adjusting to life in this country. I was also feeling very dependent, a role difficult for me to accept.

Instead of a year, however, we remained in the United States and held the crumbling marriage together for 24 years. My three sons were born in Texas, but after nine years of life there I became obsessed with Texas racism and by the complexity of a Texan character that seemed to me to promote an incomprehensible kind of nationalism. The assassination of President Kennedy in Dallas in 1963 reinforced my intention to leave a state that I considered a threat to my children's well-being. We moved to Indiana, a state not necessarily free of racism, but we were in Bloomington, an oasis that felt like a good place for raising my four children. Bloomington still has a place in my heart, primarily because it was there that I buried one of my sons, and also because it was there that I got my confidence back.

In an attempt to repair our marriage, we went to see a family therapist, male, who tried to convince me that the future of the marriage depended on my accepting the subordinate role from which I was trying to free myself. To help me with my "depression," he referred me to a psychiatrist who prescribed a medication that accelerated both my heartbeat and my "depression," as well as my uncertainty. One day, after I found myself dangerously speeding in my car, at risk of killing myself, I threw the pills down the toilet, told the three men what I thought of them, and left all of them never to return.

After my divorce I worked several years for the State of Indiana developing programs for seasonal and migrant farmworkers and directing a Multiservice Center that provided a diversity of services to families, including family therapy. Later, in California, I worked for nine years in the Mission District of San Francisco, primarily with Latino families. Presently I work with college students of diverse ethnic background. This current work has given me a helpful perspective on how family issues affect the learning processes of students.

## TOWARD AN ANTIRACIST, FEMINIST FAMILY THERAPY

The following suggestions for working with Hispanic/Latino/Chicano families can fairly readily be applied to work with other ethnic minorities, if one is willing to become her/his own theorist. They are the outcome of my experiences working with different minority groups, as well as formal study of the work of others. They are also based on my personal experiences as a Latina living and working in the United States who has been, more often than I care to recall, a target of racism. The format of the suggestions is intended for clarity and quick reference. It is not intended as an exhaustive list or as a cookbook approach to therapy with Puerto Ricans or any other minority group.

1. Be aware of your own values and careful not to impose them on your clients, whatever your background.
2. Understand that each person within the family unit has developmental needs that should be given equal chances for fulfillment.

3. When the family's needs differ, help *all* the members acquire the tolerance and understanding needed for the process to continue. This may mean making drastic changes in the family's usual interaction patterns.
4. Power issues inevitably influence the outcome of therapy. It is important not to identify power in rigid male terms, but rather in terms of power shared fluidly for the fluctuating needs of all.
5. A lesbian or gay man may be a victim of silent tolerance within her or his family. This means that their sexuality, while tolerated, may never be acknowledged by them.
6. If you have read that Hispanic society is a "macho" society, do not assume that every male is, wants to, or should be macho, or that every female has accepted a subservient role.
7. Do not assume that if a woman considers herself liberated, it means she has a struggle going on with the men in her life.
8. Help the Hispanic male in his own struggles. His sense of manhood may be dependent on having a dominant role that may need to change now for the sake of his family. While this role is changing, his self-esteem may suffer greatly, and he will need help finding other sources for his sense of manhood.
9. Help couples assume parenting roles together. Any mother, but especially an immigrant, may have lost her female support system and the family may need her husband to be an active partner in raising the children.
10. Do not assume that if the women or men in the family are married it means they are heterosexual. One or the other may be living a double life, known to *or* secret from the rest of the family.
11. Help the family redefine roles and expectations that may not be useful anymore.
12. Be an advocate, especially for single mothers. Help them understand the larger societal system in which they live, and empower them by teaching the skills necessary to tackle bureaucracies.
13. Encourage family members to explore feelings of being targets of racism. If you belong to the majority or privileged group, become aware of your own biases and what it means

for you to have that advantage. (See Carole P. Christensen, this book.)

14. Be aware of different stages of acculturation and the levels your client family may be reflecting at a given time.

15. Understand that if one member of the family does not know the English language this may influence the acculturation process of everyone in the family.

16. Do not assume that a person who speaks accented English is ignorant.

17. Understand the politics of being poor in this country. Carmen Vázquez, in this book, speaks eloquently to this point.

18. For a mother to have a close relationship with her adult children, even permitting them to live in the same house with her, does not *necessarily* mean they are "enmeshed"; its meaning depends on the interpretation *they* make of their culture, and/or on their power relations.

19. Help empower the Hispanic/Chicano/Latino lesbian or gay man to make changes that she or he sees as desirable or necessary, no matter what the individual's present role or position may be, while keeping in mind the importance of the immediate as well as the extended family for most Hispanic women.

20. Puerto Ricans and other Latinos may also be black. If the individual or the family is perceived as African American, or Afro-Caribbean be aware that they may be doubly discriminated against on the mainland, as black *and* Latino. Understanding both types of discrimination can be useful in helping the family through their struggles in the United States, whether they are immigrants or have been here for generations.


# A MI HERMANA EMMA[3]

Quiero dedicarle este artículo a mi hermana Emma Muñoz-Sleator. Ella también vino a vivir a los Estados Unidos pero por diferentes razones a las mías. Vino como joven recién casada con un norteamericano que conoció en Puerto Rico. Aunque la historia de Emma es muy diferente a la mía, ella también ha tenido dificultades en su proceso de adaptación a este país. El haberse casado con un buen hombre que siempre le ha dado su apoyo probablemente le ayudó en ese proceso. Consideo a Emma, no solo mi hermana biologica, pero también mi hermana espiritual.

También quiero dedicarlo a mi esposo Bill Clark, un norteamericano el cual es también un amigo querido.

## NOTES

1. "Hispanic" is a generic label for a diverse group of Spanish speaking and/or Spanish surnamed people in the United States who reflect varied histories and a wide range of ethnic values. The term is a controversial one. Many Hispanics prefer the term Latino(a). Hispanics/Latinos may be divided into a considerable number of subgroups according to geographical area of origin, language patterns, and locations in which they ultimately settle. Within the subgroups there are differences in educational levels, socioeconomic statuses, reasons for migration to this country, length of residency here, and in whether or not individuals within these groups are foreign born. Among Hispanic/Latino people there is a preference to be referred to by their country of origin. This reflects the fact that each Hispanic country has a unique history that helped shape its people's character.

Chicanas/os are people of Mexican ancestry who are United States citizens by birth rights.

2. "Emic" is a term not widely known or utilized by family therapists. It derives from the notion of a "dual perspective" proposed by Norton (1983). According to Norton, every ethnic minority is rooted simultaneously in two systems, the larger society and the society the group identifies with. The nurturing environment of the immediate society defines the various elements of each particular culture and determines the person's need and sense of identity.

3. *To my sister Emma.* I want to dedicate this article to my sister Emma Muñoz-Sleator. She too came to live in the United States, though for different reasons. She married an Anglo man whom she met in Puerto Rico. Although her story is different from mine, Emma, who has a very supportive husband, has also had a difficult time adjusting to this country. She is both my biological and my spiritual sister.

I would also like to dedicate this article to my husband Bill Clark, an Anglo man who is also a dear friend.

## REFERENCES

Ackerman, Nathan (1958). *The psychodynamics of family life.* New York: Basic Books.

Bograd, Michele (1990). Scapegoating mothers: Conceptual errors in systems formulations. In Marsha Mirkin Pravder (Ed.), *The social and political contexts of family therapy*, 69-87. Massachusetts: Allyn and Bacon.

Breunlin, Douglas C., Schwartz, Richard C., & MacKune-Karrer, Betty (1992). *Metaframeworks: Transcending the models of family therapy.* San Francisco: Jossey-Bass.

Goldner, Virginia (1989). Generation and gender: Normative and covert hierarchies. In Monica McGoldrick, Carol Anderson, & Froma Walsh (Eds.), *Women in families: A framework for family therapy,* 42-60. New York: Norton.

Haley, Jay (1973). *Uncommon therapy: The psychiatric techniques of Milton H. Erickson, M.D.* New York: Norton.

_____ (1976). *Problem solving therapy.* San Francisco: Jossey-Bass.

Hare-Mustin, Rachel T. (1989). The problem with gender in family therapy theory. In Monica McGoldrick, Carol Anderson, & Froma Walsh (Eds.) *Women in families. A framework for family therapy,* 61-77. New York: Norton.

Ho, Man Keung (1987). *Family therapy with ethnic minorities.* California: Sage Publications.

Kaschak, Ellyn (1992). *Engendered lives: A new psychology of women's experience.* New York: Basic Books.

Minuchin, Salvador (1974). *Families and family therapy.* Cambridge, MA: Harvard University Press.

Norton, Dolores G. (1983). Black family life patterns. The development of self and cognitive development of black children. In Gloria Johnson Powell (Ed.), *The psychosocial development of minority group children.* New York: Brunner-Mazel.

Ramírez, Manuel (1969). Identification with Mexican American values and psychological adjustment in Mexican American adolescents. *International Journal of Social Psychiatry, 15,* 151-156.

Walters, Marianne (1990). A feminist perspective in family therapy. In Marsha Mirkin Pravder (Ed.), *The social and political contexts of family therapy,* 51-67. Boston: Allyn and Bacon.

Whitaker, Carl (1975). Psychotherapy of the absurd. *Family Process, 14,* 1-16.

# PART IV.
## TESTIMONY, THEORY, AND PRACTICE

We can think of no finer conclusion to this book than the following work, which embodies and synthesizes testimony, theory, and practice.

*–The Editors*

# So She May Walk in Balance: Integrating the Impact of Historical Trauma in the Treatment of Native American Indian Women

Maria Braveheart-Jordan
Lemyra DeBruyn

The impact of traumatic historical events on the indigenous peoples of the Americas by European cultures has powerful implications for clinical interventions with Native peoples of today. This paper will introduce the general concept of "historical trauma," outlining the specific history of the Lakota/Dakota (Sioux) of the Northern Plains as it relates to the theory of historical trauma and unresolved grief (Braveheart-Jordan & DeBruyn, 1994; Braveheart-Jordan, dissertation in progress). It is our contention that all tribal histories include traumatic events that could be similarly analyzed. We have chosen these tribes because they reflect a common theme throughout American Indian histories, they are tribes with which we have worked and, for one of us, reflect our ethnic background.

## TRADITIONAL CULTURAL PERSPECTIVES

Available literature on the role of American Indian women reveals that women were powerful figures in Indian cultures and were instrumental in the creation of the Lakota and many other tribes (Albers & Medicine, 1983; Allen, 1986; Deloria, 1944; Neithammer, 1977; Powers, 1986). The most sacred object of the Lakota, the pipe, and the Seven Sacred Rites, were brought to the people by the *Ptehincala San Win* (White Buffalo Calf Woman) (Black Elk & Brown, 1953). The creation of the Lakota people is intimately involved with the feminine, since it is believed that the Lakota came from under-ground as did the Buffalo Nation to whom White Buffalo Calf Woman was related. In her work on Oglala (Lakota) women, Powers asserts that the Lakota "are a people born of woman," and that the Buffalo Nation is a metaphor for the Lakota once living in a subterranean world (1986, p. 38). In ritual the buffalo is referred to by *pte,* a buffalo cow, rather than *tatanka,* a buffalo bull. Powers relates accounts of *Ptehincala San Win* appearing to two male warriors and her instructions to "help the women in raising the children" and to "share the women's sorrow" because of women's grief over deceased relatives and their responsibility to care for the family (1986, p. 47; Densmore, 1918, p. 65).

Not only were women an integral part of Lakota rituals, they were also considered to be so powerful during their menses that they isolated themselves during menstruation to avoid interfering with the power of medicine men (as well as to rest and be attended by other women). The onset of a young woman's first menstruation was also a time of celebration and ceremony which involved the entire community. According to Powers (1986), the *isnati awicalowanpi,* held about ten days after the menses, was also known as the Buffalo Ceremony:

> Because it was performed to invoke the spirit of the buffalo and thereby secure for the initiate the virtues most desired by Oglala [Lakota] women–chastity, fecundity, industry, and hospitality–as well as to announce to the people that the girl was a woman now. (p. 67)

The Lakota and the buffalo are mythically part of the same people, the Buffalo Nation. From a Lakota perspective, association with *pte* is sacred and an honor, which further emphasizes the respected traditional role of women as spiritually powerful. The Buffalo ceremony ended with a "giveaway," where prized family possessions were given to friends and community members in the pubescent girl's honor.

Complementarity and dyadic social structure in Native American culture is identified in numerous sources (e.g., Medicine, 1983;

Powers, 1986). There were clearly defined gender roles, often viewed ethnocentrically by anthropologists and ethnographers from European male-dominated worldview backgrounds. Erroneous assumptions were made about division of labor among men and women, devaluing the traditional role of Indian women (Medicine, 1983). According to Luther Standing Bear (1933), when Lakota men were home and not hunting, they assisted women with child-rearing and meal preparation. Both sexes could seek divorce by "throwing away" their spouse (*wicasaihpeyapi* for a woman divorcing her husband and *wiihpeya* for the male-initiated divorce) (Powers, 1986, pp. 88-89). Since women owned the tipi and its contents, the man would get only his sacred objects, hunting equipment, and clothes. Polygamy was not the norm; more than 90 percent of Oglala Lakota marriages were monogamous (Powers, 1986, p. 16). When a man would take a *teya* or co-wife, it was usually the wife's sister. He first had the consent of the primary wife.

Traditional Lakota society included women as singers for men's sacred societies. Women also had their own medicine societies and sodalities for interests related to their roles. Bea Medicine (1983), a Sihasapa Lakota anthropologist, outlines alternative gender roles for males the *winkte* (a transvestite and sometimes homosexual), and for females, the "warrior woman," among several plains tribes. These alternative roles were spiritually determined through specific dreams and their recipients were endowed with specific powers (Allen, 1986). Although Dr. Medicine notes that she never discovered any Lakota term for lesbian women (Medicine, 1990), Paula Gunn Allen (Laguna/Lakota) asserts that lesbians were called *koskalaka* among the Lakota. There is some controversy in the literature regarding both the extent and acceptability of homosexuality, despite the supernatural origins of such (see Allen, 1986; Hassrick, 1964: DeMaille, 1983;[1] Medicine, 1983, 1990: Powers, 1986).

The role of mother was highly valued by both Lakota women and men. Unlike in European cultures, women and children were not viewed as property. The Lakota word for children is *wakanheja,* a derivative of the word *wakan,* meaning "sacred." The responsibility of caring for children was certainly an elevated position. Clearly, the power of Indian women prior to European contact was far more equal to that of men than could be realized through the hierarchical worldview of the European invaders. Luther Standing Bear (1933) poignantly notes the value of women in the dedication of his book, *Land of the Spotted Eagle*: "For it is the mothers, not the warriors, who create a people and guide their destiny." Lakota women have continued to value their traditional roles despite the devaluation and negative stereotypes imposed by the dominant society in the United States.

## THE HISTORICAL LEGACY

Legters (1988) asserts that American Indians are indeed victims of genocide, as defined by the United Nations Convention on Genocide in 1948. Genocide, as defined by the Convention, is:

> any of the following acts committed with intent to destroy, in whole or in part, a national, ethnical, racial, or religious group, and includes five types of criminal actions: killing members of the group; causing serious bodily or mental harm to members of the group; deliberately inflicting on the group conditions of life calculated to bring about its physical destruction in whole or in part; imposing measures intended to prevent births within the group; and forcibly transferring children of the group to another group. (p. 769)

Although there is not sufficient space in this paper to describe all the significant historical events in American Indian history which support Legters' assertion, we outline the meaning of historical trauma for the Lakota, in particular, and for Native Americans in general. Citations which document genocidal federal actions and policies include Brown, 1970; Deloria, 1969; Joe, 1986; Kehoe, 1989; Mattes, 1960; McDermott, 1990; and Stannard, 1992.

By and large, it is only recently that Native history has been understood as one of massive trauma, unresolved grief, and a legacy of genocide (McDonald, 1990; Braveheart-Jordan & DeBruyn, 1994; Braveheart-Jordan, dissertation in progress; Thornton, 1987). Non-Native historians and anthropologists have rarely interpreted the same history with such a perspective (see, for example, Washburn, 1988).

For the Lakota, the introduction of alcohol, the federal practice of negotiating treaties with Indian men alone, and the imposition of the reservation system combined to undermine the status of Indian women. Albers (1983) traces the impact of the reservation economy and federal Indian boarding schools on Dakota women in one North Dakota community. Much of what she describes is generalizable to other Lakota/Dakota reservations and to many other Indian tribes. The practice of establishing "paper chiefs" whom the government could manipulate into signing treaties undermined the power of traditional leaders and the power of women.

Wood alcohol and grain alcohol were purposely traded to tribes and introduced at treaty negotiations in an effort to intoxicate leaders to facilitate the signing of treaties (DeRosier, 1970). Smallpox-infested blankets were traded to tribes in a deliberate attempt to further decimate the population. The words of General Sheridan in 1868 echoed the sentiment behind the Indian policy of the United States: "The only good Indians I ever saw were dead" (Brown, 1970).

*Maka Ina,* Lakota for "mother earth," was losing her power as the European concept of land ownership became imposed upon the Lakota. The Black Hills were illegally confiscated by the United States government, and the Great Sioux Nation was divided into separate reservations in violation of the 1868 Treaty of Fort Laramie. Under the Dawes Allotment Act of 1887, four-fifths of Indian land was lost as the United States government parceled individual allotments to Indian men and opened the "surplus" to white settlement, national parks, and other government interests.

The psychological consequences of this action must be understood in terms of the Lakota relationship to the land, a relationship which is similar among all Indian tribes. The land is the origin of the People, who came out of the earth, and is the interdependent and spiritual link to the near-extinct buffalo relatives. For Lakota women, the devastation can further be understood in the context of the attack on the female symbols of *Maka Ina* (mother earth) and *pte* (female buffalo).

The federal policy of forced assimilation was enacted as the second phase of solutions to "the Indian problem," following the initial policies of colonialism, colonization, and annihilation. The Bureau of Indian Affairs (BIA), initially established in 1824 under the War Department, became responsible for the provision of educational and social services to Native Americans.

The legacy of the hostile origin of the BIA has continued beyond the transfer of the agency to the Department of the Interior in 1849. In fact, throughout the remainder of the 1800s, Congress debated reversing the transfer and placing the BIA back under the control of the War Department.

Land was held "in trust" for Indians by the federal government. Early Bureau superintendents were military men. Many current BIA agency offices, where Indians must come to apply for social services today, are located at forts which have retained the names of earlier times. For example, some of the Bureau agencies in the Dakotas are Fort Yates, Fort Thompson, Fort Berthold, and Fort Totten. Districts, towns, and settlements on many reservations are named for white military leaders. One example is McLaughlin, South Dakota, on the Standing Rock Sioux Reservation, named after Major James McLaughlin, the BIA Superintendent who was responsible for the attempted arrest and subsequent murder of Sitting Bull, the famous Hunkpapa spiritual and traditional leader of the Lakota people. Thus, Lakotas live with a daily reminder of a tragic past controlled by hostile aggressive forces, even within the confines of our own reservations.

In 1879 the first Indian boarding school was established in Carlisle, Pennsylvania, founded by a retired Army officer, R. H. Pratt. The school housed students year-round, reflecting the fear that Indian pupils would lapse into traditional ways if given the opportunity to visit their parents and communities over the summer (McDonald, 1990). During the late 1800s, Congress asked the Army to relinquish abandoned forts to the Bureau of Indian Affairs for conversion into boarding schools based on the Carlisle model. The style of education at these schools was as military as the setting, complete with haircuts, uniforms, marching drills, work details, and punishment for speaking Native languages. Not surprisingly, many students ran away from these facilities, and numbers of Indian parents refused to surrender their children to school and government authorities.

In 1893, lawmakers authorized the Secretary of the Interior to use whatever means necessary to induce attendance, including withholding rations, clothing, and other supplies from parents whose children were not in school (McDonald, 1990). This assault on the *wakanheja* (children) distressed and grieved the Lakota women, robbing them of their honored, traditional role as mothers.

The Lakota *wicasa*, or man, was robbed of his traditional role as hunter, protector (warrior), and provider. He lost status and honor. This negatively impacted his relationship with Lakota women and children. A further assault on the Lakota and all Indian peoples was the prohibition against indigenous spiritual practices in 1883. This law directly opposed culturally syntonic coping behaviors expressed through rituals, and interfered with the Lakotas' ability to carry out the Seven Sacred Rites brought by the *Ptehincala San Win*. In 1890, with buffalo scarce because of widespread purposeful slaughter by settlers and traders, hunting was confined within reservation boundaries. The Lakota way of life deteriorated from one of a complementary, interdependent, and independent nation into that of impoverished communities dependent on inadequate government rations.

The situation was desperate. People were starving because of reduced rations. Men were prohibited from hunting outside reservation boundaries for food (McDermott, 1990). The Lakota responded with the introduction of the Ghost Dance, originating among the Paiute, which promised the return of the buffalo, reunion with deceased relatives, and the disappearance of the white man (according to the Lakota interpretation). Threatened by the Ghost Dance, the military reacted by arresting and disarming Big Foot's band, as well as other Ghost Dancers, near Wounded Knee in December 1890. The "campaign" ended with the massacre of approximately 300 primarily unarmed men, women, and children. As predicted by *Ptehincala San Win* when she first appeared to the people, Lakota women grieved: for deceased relatives, Lakota men and children, and for the loss of the Lakota way of life, where women had been recognized as having status and power.

## MODERN FEDERAL INDIAN POLICY AND THE CURRENT STATUS OF WOMEN

In 1934, Congress passed the Indian Reorganization Act, which "incorporated" many tribes under constitutions and forms of gov-

ernment modeled after that of the United States. This policy further
eroded the power of Lakota *wicasa* leaders, but did not exclude
Lakota *winyan* (women) from participating in the tribal governmental process. *All* Lakota power was undermined. Major decisions
had to be approved by the Bureau of Indian Affairs Superintendent,
representing the Secretary of the Interior of the United States.

Continual shifting in power for Dakota/Lakota men and women
came with the reservation economy, as women began to secure
more permanent employment in BIA clerical jobs, domestic work
off reservations, and other such menial employment, while men
were hired in temporary manual labor positions (Albers, 1983).
Although Indian women had lost status and power, they regained
more of their traditional role functions, such as caretakers of the
children as reservation day schools were being developed.

The Relocation Program of the BIA in the 1950s furthered the
assimilation effort of the government. The program encouraged
Indian men to move to urban centers for work. However, social
services and family support were inadequate. The Relocation Policy
coincided with Congress's efforts to terminate tribes and abrogate
treaties within the same time period. Not only did these policies
continue the old federal pattern of attempting to wrest more land
from Indian people but, like the boarding school policy, they further
undermined and separated Indian families and *tiospayes,* i.e., the
extended families.

Modern social problems now plague Native American Indian
men, women, and children. The national suicide rate for Native
Americans is 1.2 times the national average. Alcoholism, domestic
violence, and child abuse, as in the rest of the nation, remain overwhelming problems. For South Dakota, the Indian suicide rate has
been reported to be 3.2 times the Caucasian rate in the state. Unem-
ployment is 60 to 90 percent for most Lakota reservations, not an
unusual statistic for Indian reservations throughout the country
(BIA Labor Force Report, 1989; Indian Health Service, 1990;
South Dakota State Health Department, 1985).

The role of modern Native women illustrates the shift from role
complementarity in the past to a hierarchical relationship with Indian men in the present. For example, in her book, *Lakota Woman,*

Mary Ellen Crow Dog describes the dilemma of many modern Indian women in terms of relationships with Indian men:

> There is a curious contradiction in Sioux Society. The men pay lip service to the status women hold in the tribe. Their rhetoric on the subject is beautiful. They are still traditional enough to want no menstruating women around. But the big honoring feast at a girl's first period they dispense with. For they are too modern. . . . They did not comfort me, or give away horses in my honor. . . . The whole subject was distasteful to them. The feast is gone. (Crow Dog and Erodes, 1990, pp. 65-67)

The implications of these words are that many Indian women now experience oppression from Indian men. Once-complementary relationships are now fraught with tension and ambivalence. Gender roles are no longer enacted in ways that help people feel powerful and honored. Alternative roles like the *winkte* are losing acceptance as a spiritually sanctioned and tolerated option. Male-dominated and female-subservient social systems have infiltrated and become a part of reservation communities as individuals are forced to adopt an alien model of government.

The United States federal policy of forced assimilation has been successful in that tribes have become "socialized" into a system that oppresses the disenfranchised and less powerful, that is, women and children. However, just as the policy has failed to completely abrogate treaties and blend Native Americans into the mass of other people of color in the United States, it has also not succeeded in completely destroying the fabric of all Native families, cultures, and languages.

## AMERICAN INDIAN WOMEN AND THE FEMINIST MOVEMENT

Given the current state of affairs for American Indian women, we now examine feminist principles in light of the relationship of American Indian women to the feminist movement. Until very recently, Native American Indian women have been conspicuously absent from the feminist movement in the United States. The ethnocentricity of the American feminist movement toward white middle-class women has largely negated its relevance to women of color (Abramovitz, 1988). Further, some radical feminism directly conflicts with traditional values for Indian women, as it ties subordination of women to the biological capacity to bear children. As outlined earlier, this capacity has been esteemed by Indian women and Native American cultures as the origin of women's spiritual and social power. Radical feminism's tendency to "universalize the female experience" (Abramovitz, 1988, p. 23) may rightly be viewed as oppressive by American Indian women as a reenactment of racist distortions and federal imposition of European cultural values.

Native American women repeatedly feel disenfranchised from feminist movement efforts, and often find the predominantly white leadership of the movement insensitive to the unique experience of indigenous women. Most Indian women object to the radical feminist promotion of "female superiority" and separatism, viewing such perspectives as betrayal of Indian men who are also oppressed, of the traditional values of women as caretakers, and of the indigenous system of complementarity with men.

Liberal feminists are also viewed with suspicion as they represent the views of the federal government that has betrayed and abused Native people. Within the Battered Woman's Movement, for example, Indian women have experienced conflicts with advocacy groups due to cultural insensitivity among many whites and to basic philosophical differences which have their origins in the historical experience of Native American women. Many Indian women have dropped out of the advocacy groups they found to be oppressive. This situation has further served to isolate and limit the political power of Indian women.

## RECLAIMING POWER:
## INCORPORATING TRADITIONAL CULTURE
## AND THE HISTORICAL LEGACY IN THE TREATMENT
## OF NATIVE AMERICAN WOMEN

In order to provide treatment and healing experiences that are meaningful for Native American women, there are a number of areas to explore. In this section we: argue the need for therapists to develop "cultural competence" in all treatment modalities; discuss cultural sensitivity in diagnostic assessments; outline the therapeutic content regarding historical trauma that a culturally competent therapist must explore with the client; address transference and countertransference issues surrounding historical trauma; and describe community healing utilizing self-help groups, peer counseling, and community rituals that incorporate traditional and modern approaches.

## Developing Cultural Competence

James W. Green (1982), in *Cultural Awareness in the Human Services*, advocates for the development of "ethnic competence," which he defines as the ability to "conduct one's professional work in a way that is congruent with the behavior and expectations that members of a distinctive culture recognize as appropriate among themselves" (p. 52). This approach includes creating awareness of one's own cultural limitations (p. 54), and, we would add, an appreciation for one's own culture. Green adds that ethnic (or cultural) competence involves an openness to cultural differences, acknowledging "cultural integrity" (the validity of culture as having value and meaning), and the ability to utilize cultural resources (pp. 55-58). What he calls "ethnic competence" is congruent with what we prefer to call *cultural competence*. The term cultural competence expands to allow for and incorporate cultural differences within the same ethnic group in the therapeutic setting, in this instance American Indians.

Developing cultural competence goes beyond "cultural sensitivity," by which we mean having an awareness of the behaviors, norms, and values of the culture of the client with whom one is working. Cultural competence encompasses flexibility in adapting and modifying one's behavior to achieve congruence with a client's behavior. Examples include averting one's own eyes regularly when a client does not utilize eye contact, or using metaphors as a therapeutic intervention when a client uses an indirect communication style.

We have a number of suggestions that include Green's recommendations regarding ethnic competence and take them a step further. We concur with Green's suggestion that a therapist become a participant observer, that is, participating in community activities where one has a chance to observe interactions among different age groups, across sexes, among the same sex, and in different contexts. Native dances that are open to the public are excellent places to observe and, in many instances, help cement relationships between the therapist and the community by the therapist showing such an interest.

Issues of cultural competence apply not only to the non-Native therapist, but to the Native therapist as well. Such is particularly true when a Native therapist is working in a community other than his or her own, especially if the client's tribe had a historically adversarial relationship with one's own tribe. This situation could potentially interfere with the development of the therapeutic relationship. For example, in our experience clients have at times requested to change therapists based on such historical tribal relations. In the majority of cases, the culturally competent Native therapist can overcome this obstacle by: first, acknowledging the adversarial historical relationship; second, suggesting a trial time frame to work together; third, facilitating the client's expression of his/her negative feelings while not becoming defensive; and fourth, developing the culturally congruent style of communication–through observation of the client and participant observation as noted previously–with which the client is most comfortable.

For the non-Native therapist, it is important for her to raise the issue of European conquest/domination, to give the client an opening to discuss her feelings about that history. Timing is important, and these issues should probably be raised when there are cues from the client for which the therapist must be watching. Examples of such clues include: comments about not trusting Caucasian people, bad experiences with Caucasian therapists or service providers in the past, or resistance, such as canceling appointments or not showing up at all.

However, the therapist must not assume that being Caucasian or non-Native will necessarily be consciously considered negative, for the client may not be comfortable with her own identity. In these instances, the client might be offended by the therapist pointing out the color differences too early in the therapeutic process.

In order to become culturally competent regarding specific aspects of historical trauma and sensitized to the local Indian community (whether reservation or urban), it is imperative for therapists first to read the tribal and community history(ies)[2] of their American Indian clients and consult with traditional leaders (where such behavior is considered appropriate), community members, and local Indian personnel. Second, they should participate in community events to the extent appropriate.

These efforts are important for two reasons: first, to gain awareness of the specific cultural backgrounds of clients and, second, to integrate the specific historical traumatic events for the clients' respective tribes into the therapeutic context.

A third and equally necessary task for the therapist is, through observation and gentle experimentation in the therapeutic context, to "learn how to ask" questions of the client in a way that is most effective and nonthreatening. Learning about the context of sociolinguistic settings, communication styles of client and therapist, and the significance of different types of communicative events (Briggs, 1986) will aid in this process.

## Cultural Sensitivity in Diagnostic Assessments

An important factor in diagnostic assessment is the cultural context of the client, and whether the "symptom" may be a manifestation of culturally normative behavior. An example of the danger of erroneous assessment is described in the following case vignette:

> A Lakota Indian mother, a recovering alcoholic with four years of sobriety, was attempting to regain custody of her daughter. She and her daughter were referred for therapy by the non-Indian state social services worker. The social worker had assessed the mother as not having bonded with the child, and described the mother as "cold and unfeeling," noting that the mother displayed no physical affection for the child. In contrast, the culturally competent Lakota therapist who next assessed the mother and child, observed evidence of bonding and affection for the child. The therapist was able to report her findings to the social services department, explaining that there is a traditional value of reserve which often prohibits

expression of affection and any strong affect in front of outsiders. The child was returned to the mother.

Many Native Americans have been misdiagnosed as "avoidant"
or "schizoid personalities" because of a culturally incompetent
therapist's misinterpretation of similar culturally determined behavior patterns. Avoidance of eye contact among traditionally oriented Indians in many tribes is considered a sign of respect rather
than avoidant behavior. Another source of diagnostic error occurs
when an Indian woman discloses spiritual beliefs and experiences
which are often viewed by culturally incompetent therapists as hal-
lucinations and delusions. Rather than viewing such experiences as
supernatural manifestations and culturally syntonic beliefs, these
therapists often diagnose the Native woman as exhibiting "magical
thinking," and label her as "borderline personality disorder" or
even "psychotic."

Identifying the presenting problem and understanding precipitating factors are challenges when working with Indian women,
who may be reticent in directly communicating the real reason for
seeking help. This behavior may be due to a sense of shame about
the problem, or a function of a cultural style of indirect communication where directly asking for help could be viewed as impolite or
too aggressive. Further, through directly asking for help, the client
may feel that the therapist would be in an awkward position if he or
she could not help the client and had to say "no." This concern is
an outgrowth of a value of respect, noninterference, and not being
presumptuous in asking directly for help. In one case, a Lakota
client seen by a culturally competent Lakota therapist did not reveal
the full reason for seeking treatment until the fourth session. The
therapist had the feeling the client was withholding information, but
waited until the fourth session to share this observation. This sense
of timing on the part of the therapist allowed the client an opportunity to develop more trust, and to avoid embarrassment by being
asked directly too soon what the matter was.

### Therapeutic Content Related to Historical Trauma

Many Indian women neglect to share painful memories about
boarding school placement and traumatic separation from home.

Although this behavior is sometimes a function of repression, often Native clients will not mention such experiences, assuming that a culturally different therapist would not understand.

Therapists must begin to explore the existence and quality of historical trauma with their Native clients, not only in the clients' generation, but in generations past. Native people are very much tied to the extended family system and to ancestors. Among the Lakota, for example, prayers and ceremonies include an expression which means "all my relations," reinforcing the connection with current living relatives in the *tiospaye,* or extended family network and ancestors, as well as the plant and animal world.

The multigenerational family treatment as conceived by Murray Bowen (1978) and the family-centered ecological treatment perspective of Ann Hartman and Joan Laird (1983) are applicable in the treatment of Indian families within the context we advocate. The legacy of historical trauma and subsequent grief must be addressed through an exploration of traumatic "cut-offs" due to death, boarding school placement, alcoholism, and displacement and separation of the extended family network. In the case of the Lakota, specific examples would be: separation of the *tiospaye* during the flight of some of the Hunkpapa band following Sitting Bull's murder in 1890, the massacre of many Lakota relatives at Wounded Knee in 1890, and the division of the Great Sioux Nation into separate reservations in 1889. Other losses may include traditional structures, such as warrior societies, women's societies, and some rituals. In many tribes such losses include language and traditional homeland.

Nancy Brown Miller (1982) offers suggestions for clinical assessment of American Indians from her experience in an urban setting. She advocates recognizing Indians as individuals first, and not making assumptions that ethnic identity informs one about a person's cultural values or patterns of behavior (p. 182). Miller adds that "some aspects of a client's cultural history, values, and lifestyle are relevant to your work with the client" (p. 182). We contend, however, that the latter view minimizes the impact of historical trauma on all Native people. Conversely, we therefore contend that all aspects of a client's cultural history, values, and lifestyle are relevant in assessment and treatment.

Part of the problem with Miller's analysis is that her findings regarding the relevance of cultural factors are based on a study of non-Indian professionals rating the amount of culture and history referenced in their treatment of Native Americans in Los Angeles. We suggest that these areas were not adequately explored by the non-Indian professionals who were probably not what we would call culturally competent to conduct such an assessment.

Without the exploration into aspects of historical trauma and culture we are suggesting, most Indian clients will not share their issues of culture and history. Our own experience contrasts with that of Miller's: we often hear Indian clients say that they can never discuss spirituality or negative feelings about historical trauma with culturally incompetent therapists (most often Caucasian) because "they wouldn't understand" or "they'd think I was crazy." The exception is made when a Caucasian therapist has demonstrated cultural competence that has become evident to the Indian client. An example of historical trauma in the clinical setting is demonstrated in the following vignette:

> A 30-year-old Lakota woman had repressed all memory from the time she had been taken to boarding school at age seven until attending a public high school at the age of 16. Well into treatment, she recounted the following: "I remember some Bureau of Indian Affairs employee coming to take me to school. My mother had packed my bag but didn't tell me what was going to happen. I thought maybe I was going on a trip. I think my mother didn't know how to tell me and that she was probably dumped off herself at boarding school." In a following session, she said: "They should give back the Black Hills. The old people say that it is why we have so much alcoholism and so many problems. We can't take care of the land the way we're supposed to, so the people are suffering."

As outlined previously, an additional burden for Native American women is the loss of status and power traditionally relegated to Native women. The following combines comments from two Native women's support groups. The women focused on relationships with Indian men, the conflicts in fulfilling their traditional role expectations in a modern world, their sense of powerlessness, and their grief in the losses of honored positions as Indian women.

These women felt they were not only grieving the loss of relatives through death, but a deeper and more pervasive communal loss, resulting from genocide, massive human trauma over generations, loss of land to which they were spiritually and emotionally tied, and the impairment of the egalitarian relationships with Indian men. They felt pain about the emasculation of Indian men by the dominant society, and the subsequent negative consequences for themselves now as victims in the pecking order. They expressed guilt about the economic advantages they had as women over Indian men, because they were more employable in clerical and domestic positions. They expressed concern that, if they "sounded too feminist," they would be betraying Indian men.

The women described early losses which for some included separation from family in childhood as a result of boarding school placement. Grief was expressed over the loss of the historical right of Indian women to raise children because of the imposed federal policy of removing children to boarding schools.

In addition to their grief, these women had insecurities about their own parenting skills, since a number of them had been completely raised in a boarding school setting without the benefit of culturally normative parenting role models. Some of the women described grief over the inability to protect their own children who had also been sent to boarding school.

Other major concerns for fully half the women in each group were childhood histories of physical and sexual abuse, rape as adults, and current domestic violence. In almost all cases, the abuses were multigenerational and, in many instances, were directly associated with their boarding school experiences.

### Understanding and Managing Transference and Countertransference

In this section we argue that manifestations of transference reactions must be viewed within a cultural and historical context. Transference is defined as the feelings, attitudes, and behavior a client develops toward the therapist which are based on the client's early childhood experiences with primary caretakers. Conversely, countertransference is defined as the therapist's reactions to the above, as manifested through the therapist's behaviors and affective expression in the therapeutic relationship.

The therapist must be careful not to assume from a Native client's appearance that she is either "assimilated" or "traditional." Although his article was written in 1951, psychoanalyst and anthropologist George Devereaux offers a relevant case example of a Plains Indian female patient. Although she was a professional who appeared to be assimilated, the patient was nevertheless behaving in the transference like a typical "Indian maiden who hides mutely under her buffalo robe and lets her suitor do all the talking." When Devereaux made this cultural transference interpretation after having exhausted all other usual psychoanalytic interpretations, the patient responded by speaking freely and rationally once again.

We agree with Devereaux (1951), who asserts, "Since transference phenomena are frequently patterned upon early familial relationships, the correct interpretation of a Plains Indian transference behavior presupposes an understanding of the typical Plains Indian familial roles and social interaction patterns" (p. 412). In essence, Devereaux advocates for cultural competence in order to properly conduct treatment with Indian patients.

We assert that, just as therapists must be sensitive to indirect transference communications with all patients, the therapist must be especially aware of negative feelings on the part of a Native American client towards the dominant culture, the government, and governmental agencies which may impact negatively upon the development of transference. The indirect communication style of many Indian persons across tribes presents an additional challenge, as therapists must listen with a "fourth ear" for clues to the true feeling of the client. Indian clients may also be intimidated by the authority of Caucasian therapists, or view them as being so unlike significant objects from the past that it may take a longer time for transference to develop.

Indian therapists may be viewed in a different context, one that might facilitate an idealizing transference, unless tribal or familial differences are historically negative. Some Indian therapists might be viewed by clients as possessing traditional spiritual healing powers; some may—other may not. Managing this kind of transference is challenging, because disappointment might be more extreme than in the usual shift from an idealizing to a more negative transference.

If an Indian therapist is from a tribe that has a historically negative relationship with the client's tribe, it can be an obstacle to developing a working alliance in treatment. This situation may also be true for Indian therapists from the same tribe as the client, if they are from a family with some history of conflict with the client's extended family.

Countertransference feelings may also become quite intense. Caucasian therapists may experience negative prejudicial feelings or confusion if they have not developed cultural competence. Guilt feelings about the association with the oppressing group can also intensify countertransference feelings. The danger in this instance is being either too withholding or, in contrast, overgratifying with Indian clients when motivated by these more intense countertransference feelings.

Indian therapists must be aware of overidentification and overindulgence with Indian clients and/or withholding as a defense against acting out of one's countertransference reaction. Indian therapists are not immune to experiencing intense tribal and familial loyalties which could impact negatively on countertransference in cases of interfamilial or intertribal conflicts.

The intense grief that must be experienced and worked through in any therapy that addresses historical trauma is emotionally difficult for both the Caucasian and Indian therapist to manage; intense guilt feelings for Caucasian therapists, and intense survivor guilt for Indian therapists, will be deep from either perspective. Both must learn to work through their feelings in their own right and to tolerate those feelings during a session so that the Indian client does not move away from expressing pain because she perceives the therapist's own discomfort.

### *Community Healing: Traditional and Modern Approaches*

Self-help groups and peer counseling efforts that include traditional values to facilitate improved coping skills and self-determination for Native American women are having success in numerous Native communities (DeBruyn, Wilkins, & Artichoker, 1990). An example of a successful grassroots Indian-operated peer-counseling and prevention program is the Winyan Wasaka Project ("Strong Women" in Lakota) at Denver Indian Health and Family Services. In the spirit of complementarity, a man's project, Ikce Wicasa ("Common Man" in Lakota), was later developed, adapting the Winyan Wasaka curriculum to be appropriate for men. These projects are vehicles for cathartic sharing of trauma and ties to the historical past because they sponsor groups for participants that address such feelings and coping skills. They also sponsor community activities.

Traditional ceremonies include such examples as the Releasing of the Spirits, the Wiping of the Tears memorial ceremonies that were conducted in December 1990, 100 years after the murder of Sitting Bull and the Wounded Knee Massacre. On August 25, 1991, members of the Sisseton-Wahpeton Sioux tribe held a traditional burial for 31 ancestors whose remains from 125 years ago were returned by the Smithsonian under the Native American Graves Protection Act (Haase, 1991). These actions are consistent with the therapeutic value of grief rituals and community memorialization as noted by numerous therapists (Doka, 1989; Fogelman, 1988a, 1988b; Pine, 1989).

## CONCLUSION

In this paper we have focused on the importance of integrating the concept of historical trauma and traditional cultural perspectives into the therapeutic content of clinical interventions with Native American Indian women. We have addressed issues of transference and countertransference as well as what it means to become a culturally competent therapist. We have cautioned against utilizing feminist theory without consideration of cultural and historical factors relevant to Indian women clients. We have discussed the effectiveness of psychoeducational groups that are semistructured, based on an empowerment model of providing coping skills and other skills development for Native American Indian women. In fact, these groups incorporate traditional values and attitudes where many modern Indian women are, sometimes unknowingly, recreating "women's societies," while discussing politics, men, and professional job opportunities and dilemmas.

We conclude that healing Native American Indian women must involve the incorporation and reclaiming of the communal traditional spiritual, social, and cultural power of Indian women, regardless of, and with all respect for, different individual Indian women's beliefs and religious affiliations of modern times. The healing efforts we propose and which already exist are those of empowerment inspired by traditional sociocultural and spiritual power which utilize indigenous models.

The healing of Native American Indian women will never be complete without the identification of traditional and modern ways for Indian men to renew their power and complementary roles. Hence, we also call for and strongly acknowledge the need for restoring complementary relationships with Indian men who need to reclaim their traditional power as well.

While this challenge is an overwhelming task for a colonized, disenfranchised people who are victims of genocide and colonial paternalism, Native American Indian women have already been involved in efforts to implement these healing and empowerment efforts. Indian women have formed organizations and advocacy groups such as the Sacred Shawl Society and the White Buffalo Calf Woman Society to address issues of domestic violence. They have developed support groups and peer-counseling organizations like Winyan Wasaka and Tewa Women United, much like precolonial women's sodalities and societies. Many of these women have received male-dominated tribal council support of their efforts.

By no means is the research on or understanding of the impact of historical trauma on Native American Indian populations complete (Braveheart-Jordan, dissertation in progress). Rather, it has just begun. We call for additional American Indian-specific research on grieving the losses resulting from massive human trauma, similar to the literature on Jewish holocaust survivors. We underline the need for tribal programs, Indian Health Service, and Bureau of Indian Affairs human services personnel to receive training on historical trauma and its clinical manifestations.

We strongly believe that only by looking at and grieving the losses of the past, reclaiming the complementarity and mutual respect of traditional male and female roles, and reclaiming personal and community power, can Native American Indian women truly heal. In closing, we quote Paula Gunn Allen (1991, p. 9), who says:

> As one becomes familiar with . . . ways of the People [Native American Indian], one learns how to "walk in a sacred manner" as the Lakota put it, "walk in beauty" as the Diné [Navajo] say, or "walk in balance" as the Keres [Pueblo] term it.

## NOTES

1. Although DeMaille makes important contributions to the understanding of sex roles in traditional Lakota culture, his work implies an assumption of male domination and subservience of Lakota women despite conflicting ethnographic and Indian sources.

2. We add a word of caution regarding the literature available on histories of American Indians in North America. Much of the literature has paternalistic overtones that distort actual historical events.

## REFERENCES

Abramovitz, M. (1988). *Regulating the Lives of Women*. Boston: South End Press.

Albers, Paula (1983). Sioux women in transition: A study of their changing status in domestic and capitalist sectors of production. In P. Albers & B. Medicine (Eds.), *The Hidden Half: Studies of Plains Indian Women*. Latham, MD: University Press of America.

Albers, Paula, & Medicine, Beatrice (Eds.) (1983). *The Hidden Half: Studies of Plains Indian Women*. Latham, MD: University Press of America.

Allen, Paula Gunn (1986). *The Sacred Hoop*. Boston: Beacon Press.

Allen, Paula Gunn (1991). *Grandmothers of the Light: A Medicine Woman's Sourcebook*. Boston: Beacon Press.

Black Elk, & Brown, Joseph Epes (1953). *The Sacred Pipe*. New York: Penguin Books.

Bowen, Murray (1978). *Family Therapy in Clinical Practice*. New York: Jason Aronson.

Braveheart-Jordan, Maria, & DeBruyn, Lemyra (1994). *The American Indian holocaust: Healing historical unresolved grief*. Unpublished manuscript.

Braveheart-Jordan, Maria (in progress). The Return to the Sacred Path: Healing from Historical Unresolved Grief Among the Lakota and Dakota. Doctoral Dissertation in progress. Smith College School for Social Work.

Briggs, Charles L. (1986). *Learning how to ask: A sociolinguistic appraisal of the role of the interview in social science research*. Cambridge: Cambridge University Press.

Brown, Dee (1970). *Bury my heart at Wounded Knee*. New York: Henry Holt.

Bureau of Indian Affairs Labor Force Report (1989). U.S. Department of the Interior, Washington, DC.

Crow Dog, Mary Ellen, & Erodes, Richard (1990). *Lakota woman*. New York: Grove Weldenfeld.

DeBruyn, Lemyra, Wilkins, Beverly, & Artichoker, Karen (1990, November). *It's not cultural: Violence against Native American women*. Paper presented at the 89th American Anthropological Association Meeting.

Deloria, Ella (1944). *Speaking of Indians*. New York: Friendship Press.

Deloria, Vine (1969). *Custer died for your sins*. New York: Avon.

DeMaille, Raymond J. (1983). Male and female in traditional Lakota culture. In P. Albers & B. Medicine (Eds.), *The hidden half: Studies of Plains Indian women* (pp. 237-265). Latham, MD: University Press of America.

Densmore, Frances (1918). Teton Sioux music. *Bureau of American Ethnology Bulletin, 61*, Washington, DC.

DeRosier, Arthur (1970). *The Removal of the Choctaw Nation*. Knoxville: University of Tennessee Press.

Devereaux, George (1951). Three technical problems in the psychotherapy of Plains Indian patients. *American Journal of Psychotherapy, 5*, 411-423.

Doka, Kenneth J. (1989). *Disenfranchised grief: Recognizing hidden sorrow*. Lexington, MA: D.C. Heath.

Fogelman, Eva (1988a). Intergenerational group therapy: Child survivors of the Holocaust and offspring of survivors. *The Psychoanalytic Review, 75*(4), 619-640.

_____ (1988b). Therapeutic alternatives of survivors. In R. L. Braham (Ed.), *The Psychological Perspectives of the Holocaust and of Its Aftermath* (pp. 79-108). New York: Columbia University Press.

Green, James W. (1982). Cross-cultural social work. *Cultural Awareness in the Human Services* (pp. 49-66). Englewood Cliffs, NJ: Prentice-Hall.

Haase, E. (1991). Repatriation: The first return. *Lakota Times, 11*(10), 9/4/91.

Hartman, L. Ann, & Laird, Joan (1983). *Family-centered social work practice*. New York: Free Press.

Hassrick, Royal B. (1964). *The Sioux: Life and customs of a Warrior Society*. Norman, OK: University of Oklahoma Press.

Indian Health Service (1990). *Trends in Indian Health*. U.S. Department of Health and Human Services, Washington, DC.

Joe, Jennie (Ed.) (1986). *American Indian policy and cultural values: Conflict and accommodation*. Los Angeles: University of California.

Kehoe, Alice Beck (1989). *The ghost dance: Ethnohistory and revitalization*. Orlando: Holt Rinehart.

Legters, Lyman (1988). The American genocide. *Policy Studies Journal, 16*(4), 768-777.

Mattes, Merrill (1960). The enigma of Wounded Knee. *Plains Anthropologist, 5*(9), 1-11.

McDermott, John D. (1990). Wounded Knee: Centennial voices. *South Dakota State History, 20*(4), 245-298.

McDonald, D. (1990, November/December). An historical overview of Indian education. *Children's Advocate*, 4-5.

Medicine, Beatrice (1983). "Warrior Women": Sex role alternatives for Plains Indian women. In Paula Albers & Beatrice Medicine (Eds.), *The Hidden Half: Studies of Plains Indian Women* (pp. 267-279). Latham, MD: University Press of America.

_____ (1990). The feminine role in Lakota war. *Wounded Knee, A Century Past: Remembering Lakota History.* Symposium. Bismarck, ND, December 16, 1990.

Miller, Nancy Brown (1982). Social work services to urban Indians. In J. Green. *Cultural Awareness in Human Services* (pp. 157-183). Englewood Cliffs, NJ: Prentice-Hall.

Neithammer, Carolyn (1977). *Daughters of the earth.* New York: Macmillan.

Pine, Vanderlyn R. (1989). Death, loss, and disenfranchised grief. In K. J. Doka (Ed.), *Disenfranchised Grief* (pp. 13-23). Lexington MA: D.C. Heath.

Powers, Marla N. (1986). *Oglala women.* Chicago: University of Chicago Press.

South Dakota State Health Department (1985). Pierre, South Dakota. Information provided by phone to first author.

_____ (1933). *The land of the spotted eagle.* Boston: Houghton Mifflin.

Stannard, David E. (1992). *American holocaust: Columbus and the conquest of the new world.* New York: Oxford University Press.

Thornton, Russell (1987). *American Indian holocaust and survival: A population history since 1492.* Norman, OK: University of Oklahoma.

Washburn, Wilcomb E. (1988). History of Indian-White relations. *Handbook of North American Indian relations. 4.* Washington, DC: Smithsonian Institution.

# Index

**DATE DUE**